D0975447

Ben McCulloch

and the Frontier Military Tradition

CIVIL WAR AMERICA

Gary W. Gallagher, editor

THOMAS W. CUTRER

Ben McCulloch

and the Frontier Military Tradition

The University of North Carolina Press Chapel Hill & London

Manufactured in the United States of America

The paper in this book meets the guidelines for permanence and durability of the Committee on Production Guidelines for Book Longevity of the Council on Library Resources.

Frontispiece: Ben McCulloch (author's collection)

Library of Congress Cataloging-in-Publication Data
Cutrer, Thomas W.
Ben McCulloch and the frontier military tradition / by Thomas W. Cutrer.
p. cm.
Includes bibliographical references and index.
ISBN 0-8078-2076-8 (alk. paper)
1. McCulloch, Ben, 1811–1862. 2. Soldiers—Texas—Biography. 3. Texas—History, Military. 4. United States. Army—Officers—Training of—History—19th century. I. Title.
F391.M128C87 1993
976.4′06′092—dc20
[B] 92-50812
CIP

97 96 95 94 93 5 4 3 2 1

FOR EMILY, KATE, & WILL

Contents

Maps

Illustrations

Acknowledgments

For their close reading and invaluable commentary on my manuscript—and especially for their cordial encouragement and wonderful comradeship—I am indebted to Norman D. Brown, Gary W. Gallagher, Peter Knupfer, and T. Michael Parrish. As Zachary Taylor said of the Texas Rangers at the conclusion of the Monterrey campaign, "Hereafter they and we are brothers, and we can desire no better guarantee of success than by their association."

Ralph Elder and the staff of the University of Texas Barker Texas History Center and Donlay E. Brice and his colleagues at the Texas State Archives lavished their considerable knowledge of Texas lore on me, for which I am deeply grateful, and two talented amateur historians and indefatigable researchers from San Antonio, Kevin R. Young and Milo Mims, were more than generous in sharing many obscure but important documents that I surely would have missed otherwise. Robert Martin and Fay Philips of the Louisiana and Lower Mississippi Valley Collections of the Louisiana State University Libraries and Wilbur E. Meneray of the Rare Books, Manuscripts, and University Archives of Tulane University's Howard-Tilton Library were also accommodating and congenial beyond the call of duty.

I would also like to express my admiration and gratitude to Matthew Hodgson, who for twenty-two years directed the University of North Carolina Press. With his retirement in 1992 he has left a void in American publishing that will be difficult to fill, but he has also left a multitude of friends and beneficiaries who have profited from his wisdom, patience, and generosity. I am fortunate to be among them.

Ben McCulloch

and the Frontier Military Tradition

SONG.

BEN M'CULLOUGH.

AIR—"Someting new comes every day."

Oh have you heard of the brave old fellow,
He goes by the name of Ben McCullough,
He fills his foes with consternation,
He's the pride of all the Southern nation,
Oh dear, oh 'tis truth what I tell,
'Mid fire and powder he loves to dwell.

He's the man above all the rest, sirs,
That scatters all the Lincoln nests, sirs,
That makes them fly at the smell of powder,
That uses them up like old fish chowder.
Oh dear, &c.

The Kentucky boys he's got to back him,
The Iowa boys will fail to crack him,
The Illinois crew he'll beat all hollow,
Be quick Indiana, if him you want to follow.
Oh dear, &c,

He comes upon his foes like red hot brick bats,
He takes off their scalps like so many wild cats,
Anthony Wayne is no circumstance to him,
Though many of his foes do strive to undo him.
Oh dear, &c.

Huzza for McCullough the brave rifle ranger,
The friend of truth—to vice a stranger,
He's a hard old knot of the hickory tree, sir,
He'll work night and day to set the South free sir.
Oh dear, &c.

Broadside containing lyrics to song
"Ben M'Cullough," printed in Baltimore in 1861
(courtesy T. Michael Parrish)

PROLOGUE

A Knight of the Most Superior Class

From the earliest days of the republic, America's military leadership had been provided by volunteer officers, chosen in time of crisis by their fellow citizens for the qualities they had displayed in everyday life: charisma, courage, and common sense. From their collective military experience, Americans in general and frontiersmen in particular had come to believe the citizens of the republic were capable of defending themselves without assistance from the Federal government. John Sevier, hero of Kings Mountain in 1780, and Daniel Morgan, victor at The Cowpens in 1781, were American fountainheads of this faith, a creed borne out by Andrew Jackson at Horseshoe Bend and New Orleans and by Sam Houston at San Jacinto. Zachary Taylor, "Old Rough and Ready," led Americans to a string of astonishing victories in Texas and northern Mexico despite being what Daniel Webster scornfully referred to as an "illiterate frontier colonel."

Their followers were frontiersmen and democrats, accustomed to fighting their own battles, whether against Indians, the British, or the Mexicans, and to maintaining a fierce independence from the central government at Washington. They had little use for class distinctions, whether hereditary, conferred by a national government, or even by virtue of a superior formal education, and were as intensely suspicious of a military caste, especially an officer corps trained and maintained at government expense, as had been their English and colonial forebears. Indeed, those ancestors had fought two revolutions at least partially in reaction to the imposition upon them of a standing army.

Early in the nineteenth century, the image of the citizen soldier was strengthened by the hostility that flared against the institution that seemed to embody all the negative elements of a professional military force: the United States Military Academy at West Point. In an era of mass democracy and egalitarian aspirations, West Point became a symbol of aristocratic privilege. It was regarded as a potential threat to popular rule, producing "snobbish officers" who monopolized the officer corps. Further, Jacksonian Democrats believed, the caste system created by a professional officer corps would inevitably degrade the enlisted men. Critic David Crockett spoke for the majority on the frontier when he declared that "this academy did not suit the people of our country, and they were against it." The officers it trained and commissioned, he maintained, "are too nice to work; they are first educated there for nothing, and then they must have salaries to support them after they leave there—this does not suit the notions of working people, of men who had to get their bread by labor." Sam Houston, addressing the United States Senate in 1858, declared that "a political influence" was "growing upon the country in connection with the Army," and "its inception is at the Military Academy." Its "inmates," he charged, were "the bantlings of the public" and were "nursed, fostered, and cherished by the government." Upon their graduation, the army must be annually enlarged as places must be found for the newly commissioned officers. "The danger," Houston warned, "is that as they multiply and increase, such will be the political influence disseminated through society that it will become a general infection, ruinous to the liberties of the country."[1]

As Crockett's and Houston's outspoken opposition would suggest, nowhere was the military academy more reviled, or the notion of the natural leader more revered, than in the western Tennessee frontier. When the area was yet raw and largely unsettled, this frontier was producing a remarkable number of soldier-statesmen whose names would dominate American political and military history until the Civil War and whose notions of democracy and national expansion are among the most important concepts in the American experience. Foremost among them is, of course, Andrew Jackson, whose fame as an untutored military genius and a popularizer of a frontier brand of democracy propelled him into the White House in 1829. Hardly less remarkable as soldiers and political leaders were a score or more of his Tennessee neighbors and friends who helped to shape national policy and character in the three decades leading to the Civil War, many of whom found in Texas the perfect stage on which to build their dreams of American empire and to act out their larger-than-life adventures. Second among these only to Jackson in the national mythology and in his impact on the American empire is Sam Houston. A close friend and political protégé of Jackson's, Houston was also a product of the frontier, a great believer in the permanence and manifest destiny of the American Union, and an untrained but highly successful military leader. He, too, was to become the president of an American republic. Another product of western Tennessee's frontier culture, an ardent believer in American democracy as well as an erstwhile friend and protégé of Jackson's, later to become his bitter political foe, was David Crockett. Although never to rise so high as either Jackson or Houston in military rank or political office, Crockett holds a place in the inner circle of those men and women who helped to define the national character and whose lives continue to be looked to as examples by every generation of Americans.

Different in the degree of their achievement and their impression on the popular mind of America, but nevertheless highly influential in the founding and shaping of Anglo-American Texas, were scores of other Tennesseans of the Jacksonian mold. Among these were San Jacinto veteran and Confederate cavalry general Tom Green, Texas Ranger colonel John Coffee (Jack) Hays, and two extraordinary brothers—Ben and Henry McCulloch—who, between them, served the republic and the state of Texas in virtually every military engagement from 1836 to 1865 and who held political offices ranging from county tax collector to state legislator and Federal marshal.

Ben McCulloch displayed prodigious military talent in the Texas Revolution, in Texas's continuing border wars with Mexico, and in the republic's Indian wars. He gained a national reputation as a Texas Ranger and as Zachary Taylor's chief of scouts in the Mexican War. After spending three years in California as a forty-niner and sheriff of Sacramento, he became Franklin Pierce's appointment as Federal marshal for eastern Texas and was

James Buchanan's personal envoy to Brigham Young when, in 1859, the United States was on the verge of using military force to suppress Mormon dissatisfaction with Federal control. Yet despite McCulloch's great popularity, his avid study of military history, and the strong partisanship of Sam Houston and a number of other powerful Texas political leaders, his dream of commanding so much as a regiment of regular cavalry was continually blocked by his want of even a rudimentary formal education. Of the 328 men appointed to the rank of brigadier general in the Provisional Army of the Confederate States, in fact, not even his fellow Tennessean Nathan Bedford Forrest had spent less time in school.

The Jacksonian man, according to historian Richard Hofstader, "was an expectant capitalist, a hardworking ambitious person for whom enterprise was a kind of religion." He was "the master mechanic who aspired to open his own shop, the planter or farmer who speculated in land, the lawyer who hoped to be a judge, the local politician who wanted to go to congress, the grocer who would be a merchant," or, it might be added, the militia captain who dreamed of commanding a regiment of regulars. Heir apparent to the mantle of military leadership passed from Jackson to Houston, Ben McCulloch rose from volunteer gunner on the field of San Jacinto to become the first general appointed from civilian life to the Confederate States Army. Although best suited by temperament, experience, and self-training as a military man, McCulloch also "sought the main chance" as a politician, a Federal appointee, an entrepreneur in a wide variety of business ventures, a land speculator, and even a prospector during the California gold rush.

Like many other Texas Rangers, McCulloch was "a man of rather delicate frame," about five feet, ten inches tall, with light brown hair and beard and a fair complexion. His features, according to one of his men, were "regular and pleasing, though, from long exposure on the frontier, they have a weather-beaten cast." A stranger to the army, one of his sergeants observed, "would little have supposed him to be the famed and dreaded Ben McCulloch." This noncommissioned officer regarded his general as a man with whom there could be "no compromise, no guessing." The strongest of McCulloch's character traits was his self-assurance. As he was to demonstrate time and again during the campaigns in Arkansas and Missouri in 1861 and 1862, "If the world should decide against him, or all the officers in the division, I believe his own conscientiousness would prompt him to say, as would Jackson, 'I'll take the responsibility!'" Despite these thoroughly soldierly virtues, throughout his career McCulloch was frustrated by a growing dominance of professionally trained officers in the nation's military establishment. Yet to the soldiers of the Confederate Army of the West, Ben McCulloch was "a bold, graceful rider, a desperate fighter, a reckless charger, a border man, and an Indian fighter of the highest type. Had he lived in the days of chivalry, he would have been a knight of the most superior class."[2]

ONE

Good Soldiers in the Service of Their Country

Ben McCulloch was at once the son of the eastern aristocratic establishment and a child of the ever-shifting western frontier. He was a self-contradictory blend of the Victorian gentleman who drank sparingly, never indulged in the use of tobacco, treated ladies with utmost respect, and settled his personal quarrels by the rules of the *code duello*, and the southwestern brawler capable of smashing a chair over the head of an antagonist in the dining room of a Washington hotel. A man with no formal education, he was considered one of the country's foremost authorities on arms and military affairs. A frontier Indian fighter, he was the intimate of presidents and senators. Never a member of the plantation elite, he was nevertheless an outspoken partisan of slavery and a radical advocate of secession when he perceived his region's rights and honor threatened.

According to family tradition, the McCullochs descended from one of the oldest families in the Galloway district of southwestern Scotland, and one of the most warlike. Sir Cullo O'Niel, the first laird of Myrton and the first to bear the name that would become McCulloch, is said to have served as captain of horse, standard bearer, and, later, secretary of state to the legendary warrior-king of Ireland, Edward the Bruce. Following O'Niel's death in 1358 the family seat of Ardwall passed through a succession of distinguished descendants to one Henry Eustace McCulloh, a barrister at law and an officer in the royal military service. In recognition of his heroism during the British storming of Cartagena in 1706 during the War of the Spanish Succession, he was granted a royal pension of £600 per year.

After crossing the Atlantic in the mid-eighteenth century, the McCullohs were highly influential in the development of North Carolina. James McCulloh of Grogan had a son named Henry by each of his two wives. The second Henry, a London merchant, was the first of the family to immigrate to the New World, settling in North Carolina in 1741 as a special representative of the Crown. Described as "a typical adventurer in the realm of colonial politics and economics," he speculated in land on an enormous scale, acquiring empresarial grants of over a million acres, making him the second largest landholder in the history of North Carolina. His son, Henry Eustace McCulloh, also a Londoner, joined him in America in about 1761 and took over the management of the North Carolina estates. Despite the family's protests of loyalty to the Patriot cause, however, North Carolina revoked their royal land grants at the end of the American Revolution.[1]

Alexander McCulloch, a son of the Henry McCulloch born of James McCulloh's first marriage, left Scotland for North Carolina as early as 1745 and established Elk Marsh Plantation in Halifax County. He served as an officer in the Orange County militia and in 1760 was appointed colonel of the Edgecombe County militia. In addition, he served as clerk of court in Bute County in 1772, represented Halifax County in the lower house of assembly in 1760, and served in the royal council between 1762 and 1775. Apparently of divided sentiments during the Revolutionary War, he sat out the conflict at Elk Marsh. He prospered in the New World, owning at his death seventy slaves and plantations in Halifax and Warren counties. His marriage to Sarah Hill produced three children, Benjamin, Elizabeth, and Mary McCulloch.

Alexander's son, Benjamin, was born in Halifax in 1737. Benjamin McCulloch married Sarah Stokes and named their first son after his father, Alexander. This Alexander McCulloch was born in Lanesburg County, Virginia, on 16 April 1777 but was raised primarily in North Carolina and was educated at Yale College. Characterized as "one of the stern men of his day, with great decision of character and energy in whatever he undertook," Alexander McCulloch was also very much the country squire. This heir to a $100,000 legacy "was not an economist, and loved to spend money on his friends." His sons later lamented that his generosity was so abused by some of these friends, who defaulted on large security bonds McCulloch signed on their behalf, that "his estate was so much wasted" that he was unable to educate his younger children, "a misfortune fully appreciated by him, as no one better knew the value of an education."[2]

In Nashville, Tennessee, in 1799, Alexander married Frances F. LeNoir, the daughter of a prominent Virginia planter. Frances McCulloch was "proverbial for her kindness to the sick and for being a peacemaker in her neighborhood" but was equally capable of managing the family's plantation "to great advantage" during her husband's many absences. Typical of the westering American, Alexander McCulloch moved his family from Virginia to Tennessee "about the same time as Sam Houston," 1807, and according to family legend, at one time owned the land on which Houston taught in a log schoolhouse. Two of the McCullochs' sons were students under Houston between May and November of 1812. The marriage of Alexander McCulloch and Frances LeNoir was blessed by the births of six daughters and seven sons, the fourth of whom was born in Rutherford County, Tennessee, on 11 November 1811 and was named Ben after his uncle and grandfather. The fifth, Henry Eustace, was born on 6 December 1816 in the same frontier community. Both were to achieve great fame as Indian fighters, Texas Rangers, United States marshals, and generals in the army of the Confederate States of America.[3]

Although the McCulloch tradition of military and community service dated back to the Middle Ages, Ben and Henry's mother was perhaps as great an influence upon her sons' early development and their subsequent careers. As she wrote to Henry in 1851, "Nothing on earth gives me more satisfaction than to hear that my sons and gransons [*sic*] are honest honorable industrious men and good soldiers in the service of their country," and Ben would always "rejoice in the knowledge of the fact that no one can boast of such a mother as your sons. This, if nothing else, must make them never falter in the discharge of their duties to their country."[4]

In response to the Creek attack on Fort Mims, Alabama, in the summer of 1813, Andrew Jackson summoned twenty-five thousand volunteers. "In the vigor of his age," wrote a friend and neighbor, Alexander McCulloch "took up arms in his country's cause, and marched to the tented field with Gen. Jackson, as one of the officers of his staff, sharing with that great man the toils and perils of war." McCulloch served as a volunteer aide to Brig. Gen. John Coffee at the battle of Horseshoe Bend, 27 March 1813, where the military power of the Creek nation expired in a hundred acres of gullied terrain along the Tallapoosa River and where Ens. Sam Houston sustained a severe wound, a barbed arrow deep in the thigh.[5]

Throughout the summer of 1817, following the opening of Alabama to white settlement after the Creek War, Alexander McCulloch surveyed the area west of Black Warrior Creek and speculated in former Indian lands. The following summer he was again in Alabama, this time exploring the banks of the Tennessee River for "such a place as will please me" as a new homesite for the ever-expanding McCulloch family. After no little difficulty, Alexander located a place to his liking near Florence, where he relocated his family in 1819.[6]

In common with many other families on the American frontier, however, that of Alexander McCulloch was ever ready to move west, and by 1830, in an apparent attempt to mend their broken fortune, the family was back in Tennessee, this time within three miles of the village of Dyersburg in the frontier county of Dyer. The McCullochs' new home was ten miles from the Mississippi River and only thirty from one of their nearest neighbors, David Crockett. By the time the McCulloch family arrived in western Tennessee, Ben was assuming the duties of the "man of the house." His formal education had probably ended by the time he was fourteen, although his father's library provided the young man, whom his family remembered as "a diligent and retentive reader," with a good supply of books. His father's frequent absences, however, required that he take over responsibility for the farm and the family. In effect, he would become "both father and brother" to young Henry, who remembered that Ben instructed him in "how to stack the newly made shingles and boards so as to prevent them from being warped by the sun" and taught him to plow and to "lay fence worm," in addition to encouraging and aiding him in acquiring an education, which Henry did "wholly without the aid of a teacher, in the usual acceptation of that term." To Ben, Henry confessed, "I owe all that I am or have been."[7]

As did most of the rural youth in Tennessee during that period, young Ben McCulloch spent almost all of his time in the operation of the farm. He also served, however, in the local militia company and found his principal diversion in hunting. By all accounts, Ben's greatest natural talent, and greatest love, lay in woodsmanship. His mentor was no less than "Old Davy Crockett," whose sons were his daily companions. Ben was a natural outdoorsman, and under Crockett's tutelage he became one of the finest woodsmen in western Tennessee. At an early age he became an expert hunter, raftsman, and flatboatman, acquiring skills that proved highly useful in his later military career. Before he was twenty-one, young McCulloch frequently killed as many as eighty bears during a season and "never fewer than twenty in the course of a winter."[8]

Even as a boy, Ben was known as "a perfect magnetic needle," and not infrequently he was called upon by older hunters to lead the way home. Years later he recollected a hunting trip with his father and another gentleman. Having crossed a river, the hunters hauled their boat into the woods for safekeeping. The day was cloudy, so at the end of their hunt, to locate where they had left the boat, the third hunter took out his compass and pointed the way back. The party followed the course for some time but failed to find not only the boat but the river as well. Beyond a doubt they were lost, and Ben's father soon tired of following the compass. "Well, it is strange," said the gentleman. "The compass can't be wrong." "Damn the compass," said Ben's father, "my boy Ben is worth all the compasses I ever saw." Turning to his son, he said, "If you don't take us right straight to that boat, Ben, you shall never go on another hunt." Loath to lose his favorite pastime, the young McCulloch "took a straight shot, just by guessing the way the woods ran, and brought them to that boat sure enough!"[9]

The skills of the woodsman were not all the young McCulloch learned from Crockett. As a congressman from the McCulloch's district, Crockett made only one speech of any substance, but its import was reflected in the life and career of his young protégé. The speech was in opposition to the United States Military Academy at West Point. Touching prophetically the issue that would become the nemesis of Ben McCullochs' life, Congressman Crockett objected that only the sons of the wealthy could gain admission to the academy, while the sons of the poor either remained in ignorance or, if educated at private expense, were "superseded in the service by cadets educated at the West Point academy." The young men educated at West Point, Crockett and his frontier constituency believed, were "too nice to work" or "too delicate, and could not rough it in the army like men differently raised." Remembering his own role in "the little struggle we had a few years ago," when he had served under Jackson in the Creek War, Crockett told his fellow congressmen that he had seen "thousands of poor men who had also gone out to fight their country's battles, but none of them had ever been at West Point." He concluded that a military academy education was not only unnecessary for commanding troops in battle, but a positive impediment. "Jackson never went to West Point school," he observed, "nor [Jacob] Brown—no nor Governor [William] Carroll; nor did Colonel [Newton] Cannon," under whom Crockett had served, "and a faithful and good officer he was."[10]

Not only did the plain folk of the new American West resent paying taxes so that the children of the elite might be educated at public expense; they seethed as well at the realization that places must be made for these sons of the wealthy in the army, where "they had good salaries, which the poor people . . . had to pay." Such an arrangement, Crockett argued, did "not suit the notions of working people, of men who had to get their bread by labor." Certainly it did not suit the notion of Ben McCulloch, whose lifelong dream was to command a regiment of United States cavalry and whose ambition was to be checked time and again by the want of that essential credential, a commission earned at West Point.[11]

From the age of twenty Ben spent his winters managing a wood yard on the Mississippi River where steamboats called to refuel. In the spring of 1832 he set out for Independence, Missouri, in hopes of signing on with trapper and fur trader Charles Bent to spend a year or two trapping and hunting on the upper Arkansas River or venturing down the trail to Santa Fe. To his great disappointment, however, he arrived in Independence too late, found that Bent and his party had already departed, and so drifted up to the Galena lead mines for a time before returning to Dyersburg in the fall. There he cut a raft of cypress logs, built a flatboat and loaded it with cypress pickets, and floated down the Obion and Mississippi rivers to market at Natchez and New Orleans, an enterprise that he and Henry repeated twice a year until 1835.

Returning from New Orleans in September 1835, McCulloch called upon Davy Crockett, who was organizing an expedition to Texas. Only one month earlier Crockett had been defeated in the congressional election. Severely piqued, he gave a grand barbecue for his friends and former constituents, thanking those who had stood by him despite the efforts of "the government" to turn them against him. To those who had supported the Jackson candidate, said Crockett, "They may go to Hell, and I'll go to Texas," and by early November he was on his way. Ben and Henry McCulloch were avid to go with their idol but could not leave without first making some provisions for their family. Crockett and the McCulloch brothers agreed, therefore, to meet in Nacogdoches on 25 December, when, as "Old Davy" said, "They were to make their Christmas dinner off the hump of a buffalo!"[12]

David Crockett; painting by Henry Huddle
(Archives Division, Texas State Library)

Texas, in 1835, was the new American El Dorado. While the states east of the Mississippi were beginning to fill, filibusters in the 1810s and empresarios in the 1820s spread the word of rich soil and hospitable climate in the sparsely settled Mexican province. The virgin bottomlands of the Brazos and Colorado rivers, the farthest western extent of the southern coastal plains, were perfectly suited to the plantation economy. Rain was plentiful, and access to the Gulf of Mexico was easy. Stephen F. Austin described the country as the best in the world, "as good in every respect as a man could wish for, land first rate, plenty of timber, fine water—beautifully rolling." Land was cheap there, with the Mexican government offering each head of household 177 acres of arable land for farming and 4,428 acres for stock raising at only twelve and a half cents per acre. Cattle were free for the taking. With public land prices in the old states beyond the reach of the ordinary citizen at a minimum of $1.25 per acre, and credit increasingly difficult to obtain, the rich valleys and broad prairies of Texas were more and more inviting.

Perhaps more important, however, was the "westering," the great American tendency to view life beyond the next river or mountain as superior to that in any present place and the ardent desire to be a part of the nation's "manifest destiny" to possess the North American continent from sea to sea. Texas, in 1835, was the focal point of Anglo-American expansionism, and events there were portentous of a cataclysmic confrontation between North American and Mexican forces for control of the route to the Pacific. On 2 October 1835 a tiny band of American settlers at Gonzales had defied the demand of the Mexican commandant for the return of a diminutive cannon and, in a fight that has come to be characterized as "the Lexington of Texas," drove a column of Mexican cavalry back into San Antonio. A war for independence was now inevitable, and men such as Crockett saw an opportunity for land speculation, political advantage, and martial glory. The combination was irresistible.[13]

McCulloch's motivation for going to Texas was even more simple. Ben was twenty-four years old in 1835 and was reputedly "as strong as an Indian." Dyersburg, Ben McCulloch once wrote to his mother, "is a slow country, and slow people live in it." Avid for a life of adventure away from his father's farm, he was only too happy to follow Crockett to Texas.[14]

Ben and Henry left Tennessee in the fall of 1835, crossing the Mississippi at Memphis, passing through Little Rock, and fording the Red River at Campti, Louisiana. They entered Texas in January 1836 at Gaines's Ferry and passed through San Augustine in pursuit of Crockett's party, having missed their planned Christmas rendezvous. Upon reaching Nacogdoches, however, Ben, concerned for the safety of his younger brother, persuaded Henry that his duty was to return to Tennessee to spend another year or two with their aging parents. With great reluctance Henry agreed, and the next morning the two brothers set out, Ben to the west and Henry to the east. In an effort to overtake Crockett, Ben hastened from Nacogdoches down the old San Antonio trail—the Camino Real—crossed the Trinity River at Robbin's Ferry, and intersected the Brazos River at Nashville. Here, however, he was struck with a severe case of measles and had to be nursed back to health by Dorothy Benton from Dyer County, "an angel in a log hut," while his former neighbors found immortality at the Alamo.[15]

Upon recovering, McCulloch descended the Brazos in a canoe, barely in time to join the Texas army under another former Tennessee neighbor and his father's old Creek War comrade, Sam Houston. Following the twin disasters of the Alamo and Goliad, Houston had withdrawn his tiny army from its exposed position at Gonzales and had begun a painful retreat deeper into the settled portions of Anglo-American Texas and toward the friendly border with the United States—a nation of which his friend Andrew Jackson was president. On 31 March, Houston halted his army at Leonard Groce's plantation, where it remained until 13 April, drilling and forming new companies from recruits arriving from the Texas settlements and the United States. There, on 8 April, McCulloch joined Capt. William H. Patton's Fourth Company, the so-called Columbia Company, of Col. Sidney Sherman's Second Volunteer Infantry regiment. As welcome as the new recruits was a pair of six-pounder cannon, renowned in Texas legend as the "Twin Sisters," that arrived at Groce's Retreat on 13 April. Perhaps because of his old acquaintance with the McCulloch family in Tennessee, on the day that the "Sisters" arrived in camp, Houston assigned Ben McCulloch, who had never before sighted or fired a cannon, to the number one gun in the Texas battery, a position of great honor and responsibility.[16]

Also on the morning of 13 April, Houston received word that Mexican general Antonio López de Santa Anna had crossed the Brazos several miles below at Fort Bend, thus flanking Houston out of his position. The objective of Santa Anna's end run was Harrisburg, the seat of the government of the infant republic. Realizing the danger of allowing the Mexican army to gain his rear, Houston raced Santa Anna for the town. The spring of 1836 was the wettest season on record. The prairie had been turned into a swamp by unprecedented rainfall, and the dismounted fieldpieces became

Sam Houston at the battle of San Jacinto;
painting by Stephen Seymour Thomas
(San Jacinto Museum of History Association)

an additional burden as the soldiers carried or rolled them through the swollen creeks and muddy roads of eastern Texas.[17]

Despite the army's desperate run, it finished second in its race with Santa Anna. On the eighteenth, Houston reached the smoking ruins of Harrisburg, where he left some 250 sick and inefficient volunteers before pressing on. The enemy had been reported marching up from New Wash-

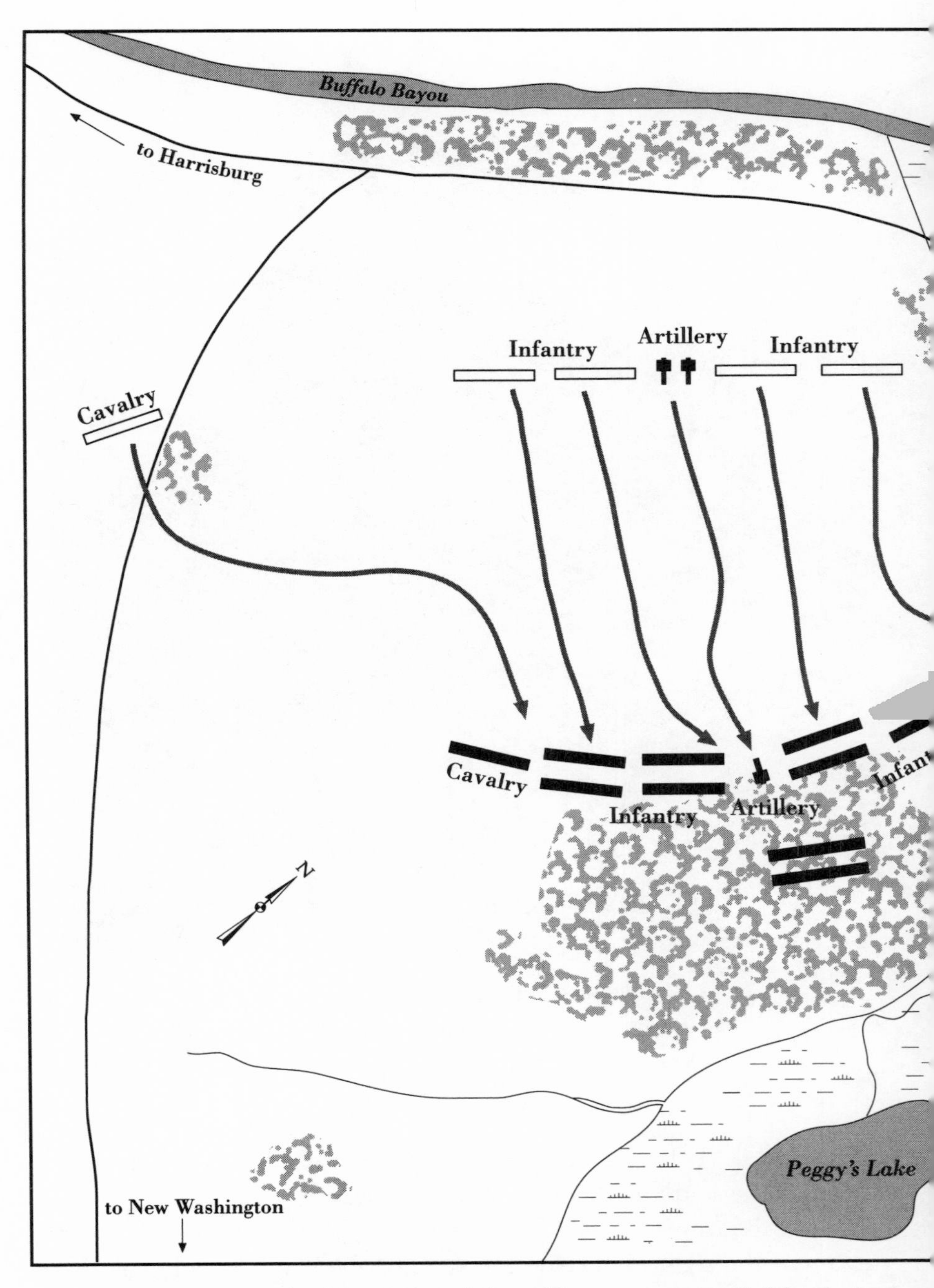

MAP 1. *Battle of San Jacinto (adapted from a map compiled for the San Jacinto Museum of History by W. T. Kendall and Ronna Hurd)*

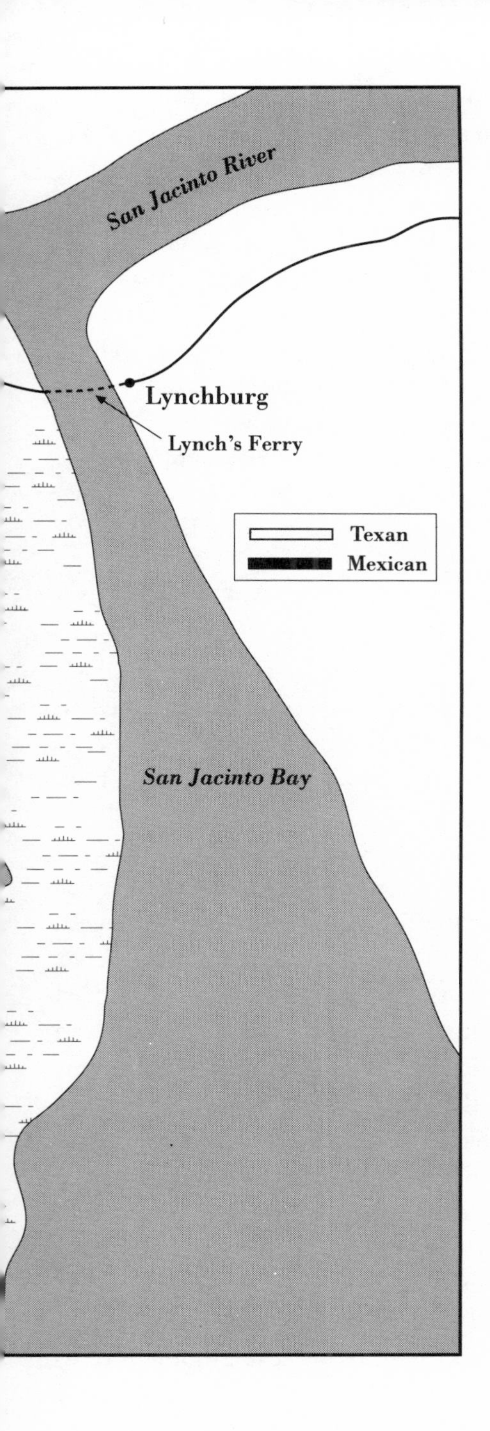

San Jacinto River
Lynchburg
Lynch's Ferry
Texan
Mexican
San Jacinto Bay

ington to cross the San Jacinto River. If it were to do so, Santa Anna's army would impose itself between Houston and the United States border. There it would be able to deal with the Texas army almost at will while carrying desolation to the Sabine River. Houston ordered his troops to march for the crossing of the San Jacinto at Lynchburg. If Santa Anna crossed the river first, all of eastern Texas would be in his hands, as every man in the army was well aware.

With renewed vigor, Houston's men hastened toward the San Jacinto, and this time it was they, not the Mexicans, who won the race. Both armies arrived in the vicinity of Lynch's Ferry on the morning of 20 April. By 10:00 A.M. units were deployed on both sides, and the Twin Sisters opened the engagement, exchanging an intermittent fire with the single Mexican brass twelve-pounder throughout most of the day. Toward evening the Mexican artillery, supported by cavalry, took a position in front and a little to the right of the Texan camp. The Twin Sisters were sent to oppose them, and the Texas cavalry rode out to meet the anticipated attack. The horsemen of the two opposing forces clashed in a brief but hot engagement in which two Texans were wounded. The Mexican infantry column, intended to support the Mexican artillery piece, was driven back by a well-directed fire of grapeshot and canister from Houston's two six-pounders and took shelter in a motte of timber.[18]

Not until the afternoon of the next day was the Texas army formed for battle, with the artillery under Lt. Col. George Washington Hockley holding the center. At Houston's command, the Texan line moved forward, with the Twin Sisters drawn by horses, until the teams became unmanageable, and then pulled forward by their gunners. At a point about two hundred yards from the Mexican line they halted on a gentle rise of ground and opened a murderous fire on the Mexican twelve-pounder. The enemy returned the Texans' fire with both artillery and musketry. Robert Hancock Hunter, one of Houston's soldiers detached to guard the army's baggage at Harrisburg, could hear the Texan artillery as it "popt like popcorn in a oven" more than thirteen miles away. Only when within seventy yards of the Mexican line was the Texan infantry ordered to halt and fire and then to charge the enemy. The artillery fell silent as the infantry rushed forward, and McCulloch abandoned his gun to join the melee.

The Mexican artillery was "loaded to the muzzle" at the moment of its capture, and the Texans turned it upon the Guerrera Battalion, the only Mexican unit on the field still making a show of resistance. The survivors fell by bayonet and sword, and until the routed Mexicans reached the bayou, "it was nothing but slaughter."[19]

McCulloch's account of the battle of San Jacinto is characteristically brief and modest: "We commenced firing at two hundred and ten paces from the enemy's breastwork, and kept in advance of our line until we were less than one hundred paces from the enemy, when they gave way and were pursued by us two hundred and fifty paces beyond the breastwork; but we were prevented firing by our own men who had outstripped us in the race."[20]

From the plain of San Jacinto the army moved to a camp on Spring Creek, a tributary of the Lavaca River in present Victoria County. There a three-thousand-man force of Texans and United States volunteers under Thomas Jefferson Rusk was poised to parry an anticipated thrust into Texas by Mexican general José de Urrea. The incursion failed to materialize, however, and although he was elected first lieutenant of the artillery company on 6 May and transferred to the more exciting cavalry company of Maj. William H. Smith on 5 June, McCulloch found the idleness of camp life not to his liking. On 18 July, therefore, he resigned from the army to explore the valleys of the Lavaca and Guadalupe rivers.

As the Texans in the army dispersed and began planting corn, their places were filled with new volunteers from the United States. To this influx McCulloch contributed a company of thirty Tennesseans, raised on a trip back to his home state in the fall of 1836. Under the recruiting system authorized by Texas law, McCulloch was entitled to command the company with the rank of first lieutenant, but he declined the commission, deferring instead to his friend Robert Crockett, the son of his old mentor. Instead, McCulloch operated a sawmill in Houston, and in the spring of 1837 he returned once again to Tennessee, this time to learn surveying from his father. What Ben McCulloch gained on his first trip to Texas, however, proved inexpressibly valuable: the enduring partisanship of Sam Houston, characterized over the next twenty-five years by frequent attempts to gain advancement for his young protégé. McCulloch repaid his mentor with skill, courage, and steadfast loyalty.[21]

Ben returned to Texas in February 1838, settling in Gonzales, where he set up his office as a surveyor. Located where navigation of the Guadalupe River—a beautiful, winding stream flowing from the Texas hill country—began, and situated on the main road linking eastern Texas with the Rio Grande, Gonzales was the last outpost of Anglo-American civilization. Beyond was only the isolated town of San Antonio—still predominantly

"Day of San Jacinto" by Henry McArdle. McCulloch is depicted at the extreme left of the painting, rifle in hand and wearing a white shirt, just below the cannon.
(Archives Division, Texas State Library)

"Surrender of Santa Anna" by Henry Huddle. McCulloch is standing, hat in hand, just above the wounded Sam Houston.
(Archives Division, Texas State Library)

Mexican in population and culture—in what was otherwise the wilderness domain of the warlike Comanches and Kiowas. Although "some handsome improvements" had graced Gonzales before the Texas Revolution, in March of 1836 Sam Houston's army had reduced the village to ashes on its retreat before Santa Anna. Following the Texan victory at San Jacinto the community's former citizens began to return, but for the next several years the "resources of the place," as German naturalist Ferdinand von Roemer assessed them, remained "in keeping with its cheerless aspect." Von Roemer found that "no sugar, coffee or other necessities could be bought in the entire place—nothing but bad whiskey."[22]

Although working out of Gonzales, for the next two years McCulloch had no permanent home and, beyond surveying, had no regular means of support. According to his close friend John Henry Brown, "His home was in every homestead." With Henry, who had immigrated to Texas in 1837, and other young men of the community he sometimes kept a "bachelors' hall" and occasionally made a crop of corn. Henry later remarked that "no two brothers ever lived, perhaps, that were more endeared to each other, or who dwelt together in more perfect harmony." Their partnership included joint ownership of all of their lands, goods, cattle, and horses, even after Henry's marriage in 1840 and until Ben's death. In their early years in Texas, however, their assets were few. In 1840 Ben's estate consisted of one saddle horse and 960 acres of bounty lands under survey but without final General Land Office title.[23]

TWO

Look at Ben McCulloch! He Is Running a Whole Gang of Them!

About the beginning of the eighteenth century the Comanche Indians left their country along the upper Yellowstone and Platte rivers and came to the South Plains, driving the Apache and other tribes before them. Having acquired and adapted themselves to the horse, they became dependent upon the vast herds of buffalo that roamed the South Plains, at the same time acquiring formidable skills as mounted warriors. As raiders they were unexcelled, often penetrating deep into Mexico and occasionally as far south as the Yucatan. By the early nineteenth century, Comancharia stretched from central Kansas to the vicinity of present-day Austin, Texas. For 175 years the Comanches and their Kiowa allies dominated the other Indian tribes of the region and provided an effective barrier to the northern expansion of the Spanish empire. Their wars with the Anglo-Americans in Texas began almost simultaneously with the Texas Revolution in 1836 and lasted until their final defeat at the battle of Palo Duro Canyon in 1874. Comanche raids almost invariably cost the Anglo-American settlers many horses and at least a few lives, and so numerous were these forays into Guadalupe—which most of the early settlers pronounced "Warloop"—and adjoining counties by 1837 that the Texas congress authorized several community leaders, including the McCulloch brothers, to raise companies of rangers to intercept them.[1]

Typical of the warfare between these two expanding empires was the October 1838 Comanche raid on the Guadalupe River settlements. Warriors struck across the river from the present site of Cuero and kidnapped thirteen-year-old Matilda Lockhart from Andrew Lockhart's family and two more children from the home of Mitchell Putnam, carrying them into the Guadalupe Mountains. Word was sent up the river as far as Gonzales, and the McCullochs, with veteran Indian fighter Capt. Mathew (Old Paint) Caldwell, raised volunteers to pursue the raiders and free their captives. The settlers struck the Comanches' trail and followed it to a point near Cibolo Creek, where it turned north. The McCullochs and their companions followed the trail until they were struck on the fourth day by a "blue norther." In a short time sleet was falling and the ground was covered with ice. By night the trail could no longer be followed, and the men, shivering in their summer clothes, were at the point of freezing. After a miserable night, they reluctantly returned to the settlement, the Indians' tracks hopelessly obscured.[2]

Little daunted, twenty-eight-year-old Ben McCulloch recruited a second party late in February for an expedition to the headwaters of the Guadalupe to cooperate with a larger column led up the Colorado by Col. John Henry Moore. Certain friendly Indians, most notably the Lipans and the Tonkawas, frequently camped near Gonzales and from time to time joined the white settlers in operations against their mutual enemies, the Comanches. On this occasion, Capt. Jim Kerr, a "well known and wily old chief" of the Tonkawa tribe, agreed to lead a group of his warriors in support of the small party of Anglo-Americans Ben could muster. In recompense for their services, McCulloch agreed to furnish the Tonkawas with salt and one hundred rounds of ammunition for the ten or twelve rifles the tribe possessed. The remaining warriors, some thirty or more, were armed with lances and bows and arrows.[3]

About the first of March the mixed task force left the Tonkawa village for the headwaters of the Guadalupe. After only two days' march, however, McCulloch's men happened upon the fresh trail of a band of Waco and Comanche Indians on Peach Creek, a tributary of the Guadalupe. As this trail was bearing directly for Gonzales, McCulloch's party followed it rapidly for three or four hours. Knowing the Comanches and Wacos could be but a short distance ahead, McCulloch persuaded Captain Jim to send two of his swiftest runners up the trail in pursuit, and Ben, who was said to be "as fleet on foot as they and possessed of as much endurance," accompanied them. He had correctly judged that the raiders would conceal themselves once they were aware that they were being followed; when McCulloch came in sight of them, the thirteen Comanches and Wacos entered an almost impenetrable thicket bordering the stream. Thus hidden, the raiders had every advantage, and any attempt to close with them exposed McCulloch's men to the arrows of the unseen enemy. From the first, Captain Jim refused to enter or to allow his men to enter the thicket, saying that the danger was too great and "Tonkawas too scarce" to run such hazards.

Finally, with night approaching, Ben and Henry, with two of the three other Texans, determined to crawl into the thicket and root out the enemy. Captain Jim agreed to place his men around the lower end of the thicket to kill any Comanche or Waco who might attempt to escape. With great caution the white men entered the brush and moved slowly to where they supposed the Indians to be concealed. Each of the four pursuers managed to kill one man and to wound several others. "In thickets," the McCullochs' friend and noted Texas journalist John Henry Brown observed, "nothing is so effective as the rifle ball." Finally, the nine survivors of the war party broke from the brush and made for the branch at the lower end of the thicket. Much to the disgust of the Texans, Captain Jim's Tonkawas allowed them to go unmolested, and by the time the McCullochs and their neighbors cleared the thicket, the hostile Indians were beyond reach. Considered with their neighbors the Karankawas to be "the only Indians known to be cannibals, on the North American continent," the Tonkawas scalped the four dead Comanches and fleeced off portions of their flesh for a ritual feast.[4]

"Impelled by a patriotic sense of duty to hasten home and celebrate their victory," Captain Jim's warriors deserted the field, and, bilked of their opportunity to seek the Lockhart and Putman children, McCulloch and his party returned to Gonzales. While Henry confessed that he was "more than glad" of their allies' defection, Ben was furious with what he considered the cowardice of the Tonkawas.[5]

With the coming of spring the brothers attempted to return to a more settled and peaceful lifestyle. They built a flatboat, loaded it with pecans,

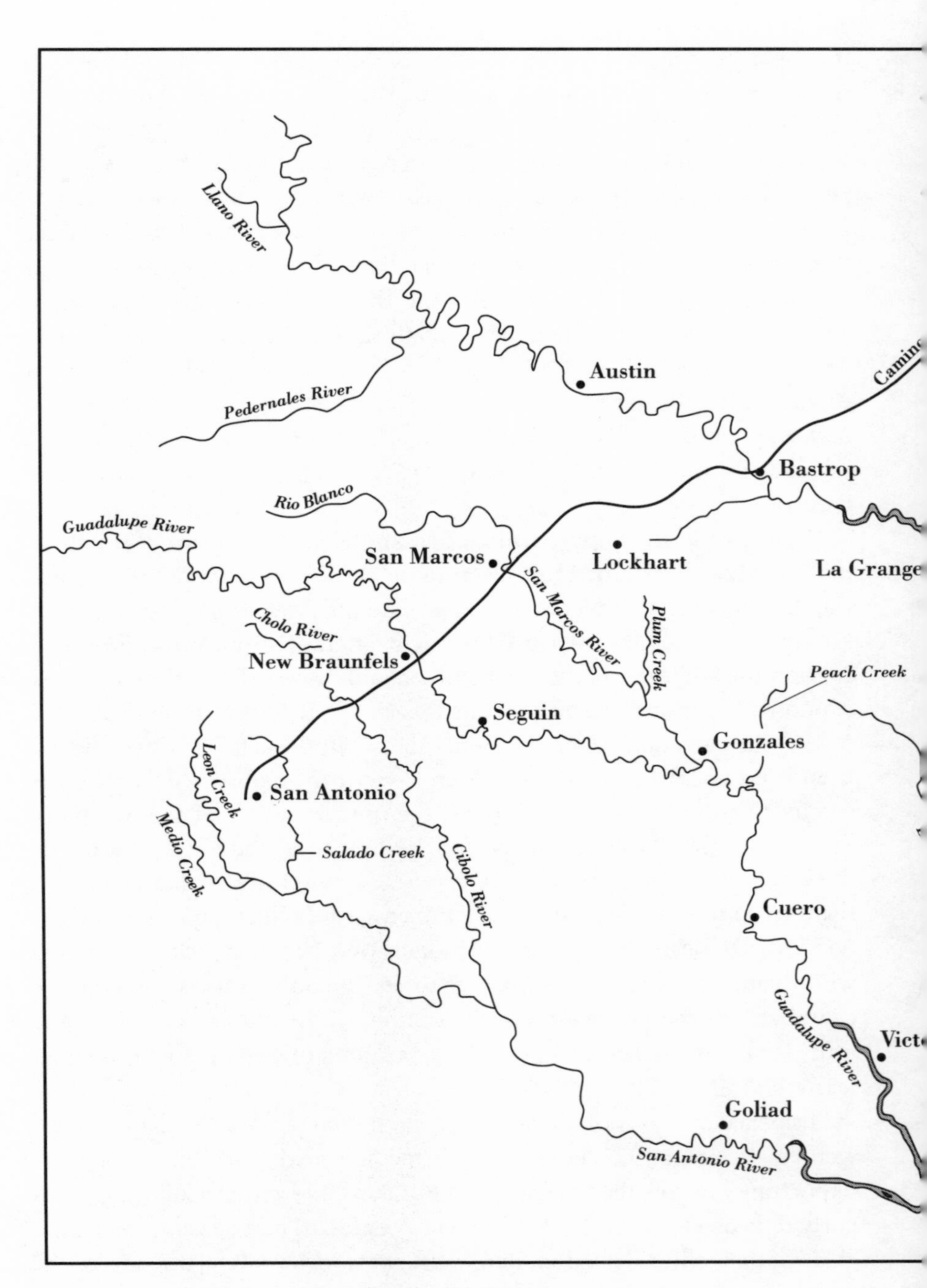

MAP 2. *East Texas*

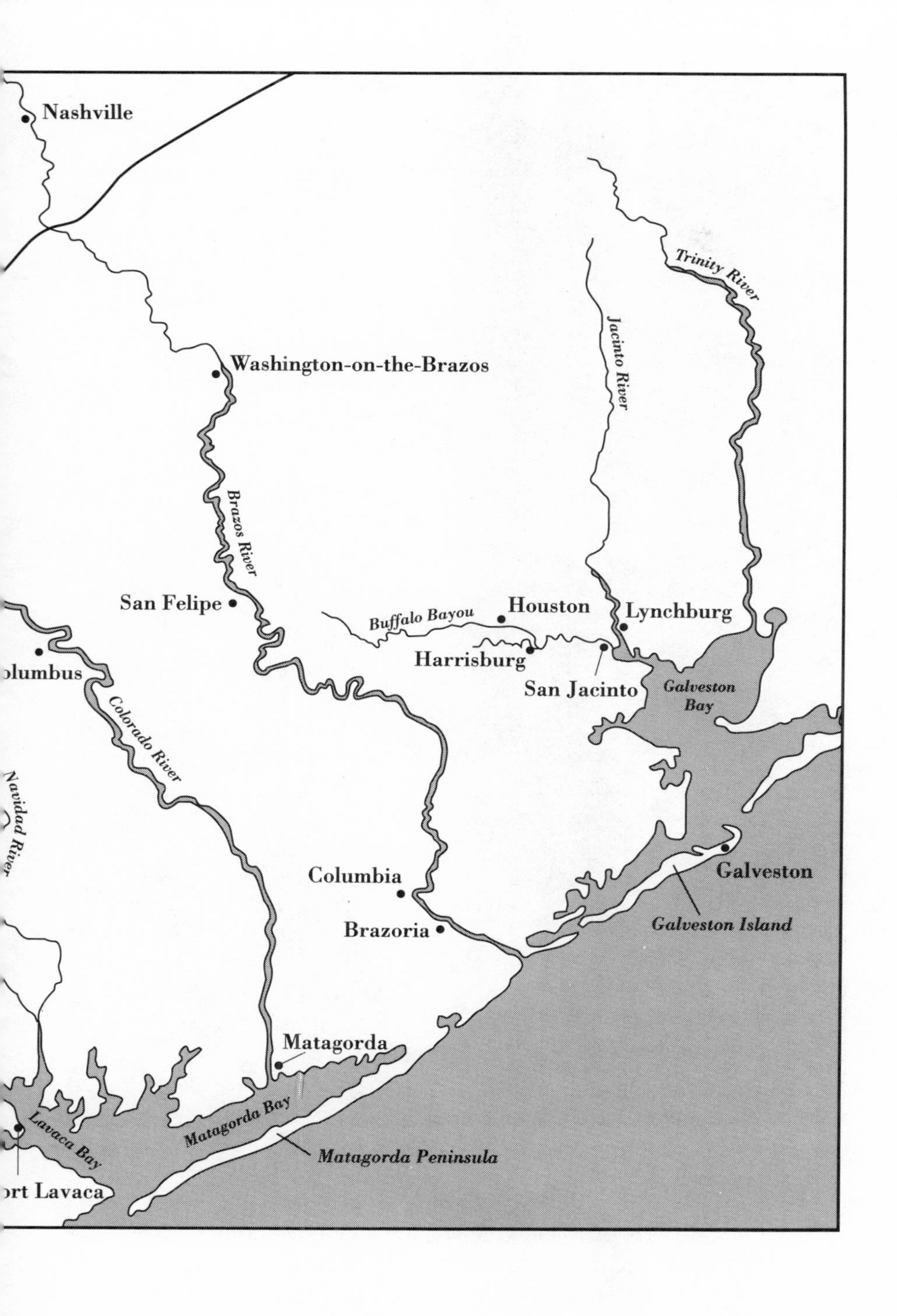

Nashville
Trinity River
Jacinto River
Washington-on-the-Brazos
Brazos River
San Felipe
Houston
Lynchburg
Buffalo Bayou
Harrisburg
San Jacinto
Galveston Bay
Colorado River
Navidad River
Columbia
Brazoria
Galveston
Galveston Island
Matagorda
Matagorda Bay
Lavaca Bay
Matagorda Peninsula

Henry McCulloch. He "had always been among the foremost to meet the enemy," wrote Z. N. Morrell, "as cool and daring as our captain, and greatly endeared to the men by his uniform kindness and social qualities. He was not easily roused, but when stirred was powerfully wrought upon, and had not the fear of mortal man before his eyes."
(author's collection)

and navigated down the Guadalupe to the Gulf of Mexico, where they sold the pecans to a New Orleans–bound merchant and returned overland to Gonzales. Yet scarcely had they resumed their surveying, having established a camp at the present site of Lockhart, when Mathew Caldwell, who had been authorized to raise a six-month company of rangers, offered Ben a commission as first lieutenant. Ben deferred to Henry but, leaving surveying for a while, helped to raise the "Gonzales Rangers" and agreed to serve as a private in the ranks. During the fall and winter of 1839 Ben went after Indians with Caldwell "two, three, or four times," as best Henry could recall in later years. According to Victor Marion Rose, McCulloch's friend and early biographer, the rangers did "a great deal of active, efficient service . . . and several parties of Indians [were] routed."[6]

In November and December 1838 Ben and Henry surveyed the eastern half of a league near the site of the ranger camp at Walnut Springs, laying out one-acre, five-acre, and twelve-acre lots. Like Gonzales, Walnut Springs had been a prosperous frontier settlement prior to the Texas Revolution but had broken up in 1835, its inhabitants falling back on the more densely settled portion of Texas. After 1836, however, the McCullochs, with Mathew Caldwell and a few other frontier families, resettled the location on the banks of the Guadalupe, thirty-six miles upstream from Gonzales and thirty-six miles north of San Antonio. Soon after the town was refounded, the council renamed it Seguin in honor of Col. Juan N. Seguín, a Tejano (a Texan of Mexican ancestry) who was at that time a fast friend of the Anglo-Texans and who had commanded a small company of his countrymen at the battle of San Jacinto.[7]

"The first families," wrote the son of one of their number, Andrew Jackson Sowell, "were few in number, and drawn closer together by their isolation. They were sociable, free-hearted, and respected, and were ever ready to aid and assist those who needed it. They depended on each other in time of danger." In this environment, Henry could write to his mother, "I have friends, sincere devoted friends, whose purse strings are ever loose to me, and whose lives are even at my command, who respect me for what I am, not for any claims I have by birth, by family, or by friends." As its developers had hoped, the rich bottomlands quickly attracted other settlers—an estimated twenty-five heads of family by 1838—and Seguin prospered, becoming the seat of Guadalupe County and allowing the McCulloch brothers their first measure of financial success. Neither brother joined the planter elite, however, and neither ever acquired great wealth. The Guadalupe valley remained a transitional area between the cotton and the cattle kingdoms, and the wealthiest of its inhabitants were small-scale slaveholders and ranchers. In a yeoman society, especially on the frontier, the most effective warriors often laid claim to positions of leadership, and such was the McCullochs' claim to authority in antebellum Texas.[8]

Although the Anglo-Texan victory at San Jacinto and the subsequent Treaty of Velasco had supposedly ended the conflict between Mexico and its breakaway province, President Santa Anna felt that he was neither legally nor morally bound to honor the terms of the treaty, since he had signed it under extreme duress—the threat to his life from Sam Houston and his vengeful army. Internal disorder in the Mexican republic and chronic outbreaks of yellow fever along the Gulf Coast, however, kept border hostilities at a minimum for the first six years of the Republic of Texas. Soon after Seguin was repopulated by the McCullochs and their friends, however, Vincent Cordova, former Mexican alcalde of Nacogdoches and primary judge of the district during the first two years of the republic, affected a plot to overthrow the new government. Compacting with the disaffected Cherokees of Chief Bowles, Cordova sought to foment revolt in Texas and to open a path for reconquest by the Mexican army. With a combined force of some one hundred Mexicans and three hundred Indians, Cordova launched his campaign on 7 August 1838 from an island in the Angelina River. Texas secretary of war Thomas Jefferson Rusk called out the eastern Texas militia in response, and among those reporting to Mathew Caldwell's company "were Ben McCulloch and others of approved gallantry," who harried Cordova past San Antonio and to the Rio Grande but could not overtake him for a showdown battle.[9]

Caldwell returned his company to Seguin, where it disbanded on 15 May. Soon after, however, he and the McCulloch brothers were together again on a different service. In the summer of 1839 Ben and Henry surveyed the first wagon road from Gonzales to Austin, the newly established seat of government of the republic, and Caldwell's ranger company provided an escort. Mirabeau B. Lamar, as president of Texas, foresaw a time of rapid expansion for the new nation and placed its capital far beyond the frontier, drawing Texans both physically and symbolically to the west. By 1839, however, "only a few houses built of logs, clapboards, [and] whipsawed lumber" graced the clearing on the Colorado River that Lamar visualized as "the seat of a great empire." The future city was accessible only by way of the old Spanish Camino Real connecting San Antonio and Nacogdoches.

At that time Indians remained numerous and aggressive in the unexplored and uninhabited area between Austin and the frontier, and John

Henry Brown remembered the route from Gonzales to Austin as "the longest road for its measured length" he ever traveled. McCulloch's party was not beset by Indians, however, and greatly enjoyed the trip despite the dangers and arduous labor of chopping a road through virgin wilderness. Within ten miles of Gonzales the surveying party killed a large buffalo and, taking "such parts of the animal as suited [their] choice," found water a few miles farther up the trail and camped there for the night. The men sharpened sticks and soon had their buffalo roasting over the coals of a campfire. "We had plenty of salt, pepper, and coffee," one of the group recalled, "but only a few of us had any bread." Up the line, however, the surveyors found a rich bee tree. They quickly robbed the bees and, in the words of one, "felt that we were living high."[10]

In addition to his service as an Indian fighter and surveyor, in 1839 Ben McCulloch ran for a seat in the house of representatives of the Republic of Texas against Alonzo B. Swietzer. An Ohio-born physician and sometime writer, Swietzer had arrived in Texas after San Jacinto but was commissioned as a captain in the Texas army on 15 May 1836, soon rising to the rank of lieutenant colonel. He served briefly as an agent to the Comanches and then represented Gonzales County in the third congress from 6 November 1838 to 24 January 1839. McCulloch, however, defeated him by a great majority, and Swietzer was left considerably embittered, accusing McCulloch of "moral cowardice" for refusing to debate him during the election campaign.

Three weeks after the election Gonzales County was again raided by Indians. Caldwell called out the rangers in pursuit and dispatched McCulloch and Swietzer to pick up the marauders' trail. Both men claimed credit for discovering the route by which the Indians had left the county, and a bitter personal dispute arose between them. With what Victor Rose characterized as "a base and slanderous charge," Swietzer challenged McCulloch to a duel, but McCulloch declined, stating that personal quarrels while on campaign must be put aside in the face of community crises.[11]

A great vogue in dueling reached its peak in the Republic of Texas in 1837 and 1838 and, although strictly forbidden by regulations, was most popular among the officers of the army. Even Albert Sidney Johnston, as commanding general of the Texas army, was a principal in a duel on 5 February 1837 when he and Brig. Gen. Felix Huston, a swashbuckling Mississippi planter, slave trader, and soldier of fortune, met on the Lavaca River. After three exchanges of fire Johnston was seriously wounded by a ball passing through his hips. Although he lingered near death for several days and recovered only after months of suffering, Johnston never resented Huston's challenge or the wound, feeling that their meeting was "a public duty" and that he could never have commanded the respect of the army if he had "shown the least hesitation in meeting General Huston's challenge." "We would opine," wrote the editor of the Austin *Texas Sentinel* in the wake of one duel between army officers, "that there was fighting enough to be had on our frontier without resorting to private combats." Nevertheless, the custom was enthusiastically followed, and the journalist, in common with most Texans of his day, decided "not . . . to sermonize on the subject."[12]

McCulloch's unwillingness to fight Swietzer while on campaign was a result of neither enlightened humanitarianism nor cowardice. Whether he had read the document or not, McCulloch was abiding by the *code duello* as set down in 1838 by former governor John Lyde Wilson of South Carolina. According to Wilson's rules, a gentleman, when insulted in public, must "never resent it there" so as not to "offer an indignity to the company." He must, however, "let the time of demand" upon his adversary after the insult be as short as possible. When French Smith, a member of the ranger party from Seguin, overheard McCulloch's demurrer, he remarked on his "cowardly course." Henry, springing to his brother's defense, reportedly retorted, "Ben's attention is called to another, but I stand ready, gun in hand, to show you or any other meddler that there is no cowardice in the blood, and if you doubt it, show yourself a man and make ready." Smith, according to Rose, quietly returned to his campfire, replying, "I seek no difficulty with you."[13]

The issue between Swietzer and McCulloch was dropped as the rangers continued their pursuit of the raiders. The Indians outdistanced their pursuers, however, and the party turned back toward the settlements. Only then did Henry ask Ben how he intended to resolve Swietzer's slur upon his honor. "The matter has rested until some of my friends begin to think I am a coward," Ben replied, observing that even Henry might be "growing impatient." He reminded his brother that "there is a proper time for all things," and he urged Henry to defer his vengeance and his judgment until Ben thought the time best fit "to defend my honor and our name." He added that Henry, too, might have a role to play in the coming fight. Henry, although forbidden by the *code duello* from acting as his brother's second, indicated that he was willing to follow Ben's lead.[14]

As the company lay camped some nights later on the eastern bank of the Blanco River, the McCullochs approached Caldwell's campfire. "Captain," Ben asked, "has your pursuit of the Indians ceased, and if so, do you have any reasonable expectation of a fight between this place and Gonzales?" When Caldwell replied that the expedition was at an end, Ben declared that the time had come to settle his grievance with Swietzer and, rifle in hand, called upon him to stand and fight. Swietzer rose, leaving his rifle and pistols on the ground, claiming that he was not prepared to defend himself.

McCulloch pointed out to Swietzer that his arms were within reach and promised him ample time to pick them up and use them. When Swietzer declined the offer, McCulloch declared him "too base and cowardly to fight," except when drunk. In accordance with the *code duello*, since Swietzer would not fight as a gentleman and since McCulloch could not afford to shoot him "like a dog," Ben contented himself by pronouncing his antagonist "a black-hearted, cowardly, villain, in every respect beneath the notice of a gentleman." Ben then reminded French Smith that on the morning Caldwell's party had left Gonzales, he had seen proper "to put in your jaw" and now demanded an apology or a fight. Smith protested that he had no quarrel with either Ben or Henry. Smith's insulting comments, Ben then surmised, had been the consequence of overindulgence in "Swietzer's mean whisky." Although, according to Governor Wilson's rules, "insults at a wine table . . . must be answered for," general laughter followed Ben's sally, and the tension was broken, at least for the time.[15]

Soon after the company returned to Gonzales, however, Ruben Ross, "a gallant but rash man," delivered a formal challenge to McCulloch from Swietzer. McCulloch refused to recognize Ross's principal as a gentleman, he being, in Governor Wilson's terms, "one that has been publicly disgraced without resenting it," and therefore declined to meet him. Ross, a native of Virginia and a veteran of the battle of San Jacinto, was a man McCulloch respected, however, and as Swietzer's second he was bound by the code of honor to tender himself in his friend's stead. "The true reason of substitution," according to Wilson, "is the supposed insult of imputing the like inequality" charged upon a second's principal, and "when the contrary is declared, there should be no fight," for individuals were free to differ in their estimate of another individual's character and standing in society. Ben freely stated that he believed Ross a gentleman and his social equal. Nevertheless, on the following day, formal notes were exchanged between Ross and McCulloch through the agency of James P. Kinkennon, said to be "of a turbulent and malicious turn of mind," and a meeting was arranged.[16]

On 6 October 1839 they faced each other with rifles at forty paces in a field north of Gonzales. Ross, a trained duelist, fired at the word. His ball struck the under portion of McCulloch's right arm, passing from wrist to elbow and causing him inadvertently to fire. McCulloch, it was said, could drive a nail with a rifle ball at forty paces, and thus Ross's life was probably spared. Although McCulloch was severely wounded—some believed mortally—both men declared their honor satisfied, and Ross sent his personal surgeon to attend to McCulloch's wound. Ross told McCulloch that he regretted the circumstances that compelled him to "meet so brave a man in a private encounter" and expressed the hope that his wound was not serious, as he claimed to have never been McCulloch's enemy. "I assure you," Rose recounted Ross saying, "that it would afford me great pleasure to henceforth claim you for a friend." The two recent antagonists shook hands, and Henry, who but a minute before had been eager to take up his wounded brother's quarrel, told Ross, "I am with my brother in all that he does. His settlement of this affair is perfectly satisfactory to me."

The law felt otherwise, however, and in November Ben was indicted for "contriving and intending to break the peace of this Republic, setting at naught the quiet and good morals of this community" by "wickedly, willfully, and maliciously" accepting Ross's challenge. He was duly arrested on 13 March 1840 and was brought to trial on 6 April. The district attorney chose not to prosecute, however, and the case was discharged.

Ben, with his arm in a sling, took his place in congress and, according to John Henry Brown, "sat quietly but observingly" through the 1839–40 session. Absent from the opening session on 11 November due to his still fresh wound, McCulloch was not named to any of the standing committees of the legislature, but after presenting his credentials on 15 November voted in lockstep with Sam Houston, who was serving as representative from San Augustine County.[17]

Ross and Swietzer, who had left Gonzales after the McCulloch affray to serve as mercenaries in the Mexican revolutionary army, returned in December to find the community polarized into a "McCulloch Party" and a "Ross Party" by the duel, and tensions still running high. Thus matters stood on Christmas 1839, when several young ladies and gentlemen had passed a night under the hospitable roof of Isham J. Good on Peach Creek, ten miles west of Gonzales. During the day they agreed to go into Gonzales for a dance at the home of a friend, which consisted of one large log room with a log kitchen some twenty yards behind. Most of the youth of Gonzales were invited to attend, and the party was well under way when Ross and Swietzer appeared in the room, "both somewhat intoxicated." Although the festivities were marred by the uninvited presence of these two, the party progressed until Ross's conduct became so obnoxious that Henry and his friends suggested that the young ladies retire to the kitchen, where they would be safe from "further insult." The young men posted themselves at the kitchen door and defied Ross to enter. Henry, according to Rose, informed Ross that "the ladies have come here for refuge; you cannot come in." "Very well, gentlemen," said Ross, "if bullying is your game, I am ready," and he drew a brace of pistols. Henry responded with the only shot he had from a single-barreled pistol. The ball struck Ross in the chest, and he dropped across the kitchen door.[18]

A posse of Ross's friends quickly arrested Henry and, as he later claimed, "with force and arms made an assault" upon him and "beat, bruised, wounded and ill treated" him without warrant. Only after he was "obliged to lay out and expend a large sum of money" was he turned over to proper authorities. At that time he was indicted for murder by a grand jury. In Austin the supreme court determined that McCulloch's case was beyond its jurisdiction and remanded it back to the district court. Henry gave bond for his appearance at the April term of the Gonzales district court and was subsequently tried there. According to the bill of indictment, Henry E. McCulloch, "not having the fear of God before his eye—but being moved and instigated by the Devil," had murdered Ross "willfully, unlawfully, and of his malice aforethought." Henry pleaded not guilty, and the jury, whose foreman was Mathew Caldwell, promptly returned the same verdict. According to Brown, "Henry McCulloch stood forth a free man, commanding the respect of every respectable man in the land."[19]

Nevertheless, the unhappy memory of "that fatal night" hung heavily upon him. Although, he wrote to his mother, he had "been driven to acts of desperation," he had "not only law, but . . . justice" on his side, for "the people say I did justice, and my conscience in the sight of Heaven says Amen." Hoping that she would leave Tennessee to make her home in Texas with him, Henry wrote that he and Ben could welcome her "without the least fear of detracting anything from your respectability or standing," for "I am proud to say your sons in Texas have never yet done anything that will not bear strict investigation."[20]

Soon after the shootings at Gonzales and Seguin, and following five years of intermittent warfare between the Anglo-American settlers and the Comanches and their Kiowa allies, a council was arranged between the representatives of the Texan government and of various Comanche bands, the two delegations to meet in San Antonio on 19 March 1840. Approximately seventy-five Indian men, women, and children were in or around the courthouse at the time of the consultation, led by Muguara, chief of a comparatively small band disposed to be friendly to the whites. The Texan delegation was headed by Hugh McLeod, adjutant general and inspector general of the Army of the Republic of Texas, and William G. Cooke, quartermaster general of the republic. Also in town were three companies of Texas regulars and rangers under Lt. Col. William S. Fisher, formerly secretary of war of the Texas republic.

The principal objective of the Texan delegates was to secure the release of the many white captives held by the Comanches, and when the Indians produced but one, Matilda Lockhart, after supposedly promising many others as well, the soldiers were outraged. With their usual haughty demeanor, the Comanches claimed that they had no more captives in their camps and that the white men would have to await their pleasure if more were to be returned. Matilda Lockhart, however, told another tale. The Comanches had other prisoners nearby, she said, whom they planned to bring in one at a time for high ransom. More eloquent than words, moreover, was the girl's face. She had been the object of brutal torture at the hands of the Comanches, and her nose had been burned off by the women who had charge of her. This account infuriated the Texans, who seized the Indian delegates and informed them that they themselves would be hostages until all of their captives were returned. The Comanches responded by producing arms from under their blankets and resisting capture to the death. In a matter of minutes, eight whites and thirty-five Indians lay dead. Additionally, eight Indians were wounded and twenty-seven others were captured.

A Comanche woman was sent to tell her people of the white men's terms. So enraged were the Indians by the events at the council house that rather than liberating any, they immediately put to death thirteen of their captives. The Council House Fight was perhaps the greatest blunder in the history of Texas-Indian relations. Not only did it cost the lives of the Comanches' captives, it also destroyed any confidence the Indians might have had in the Texas government and made future, orderly contact with the Comanches almost impossible. Worst of all, it revived and prolonged the war on Texas's frontier and spurred the Indians to a yet more bloody vengeance.[21]

In retaliation for what they viewed as the white men's treachery, some five or six hundred Comanches entered the sparsely settled country along the northern boundary of Gonzales County and swept down the valley of the Guadalupe in the summer of 1840, killing settlers, stealing horses, plundering, and burning settlements. In their largest and bloodiest raid ever against Anglo-Texas, the Indians penetrated all the way to the Gulf of Mexico, where they sacked and burned the town of Linnville, making prisoners of the Texas women who were unable to escape by boat. The prevailing attitude of the Anglo-Texan community was expressed by John Wesley Wilbarger in his classic account, *Indian Depredations in Texas*: Ben McCulloch "was not one . . . to permit the wily savages to swoop down upon our people with the tomahawk and scalping knife, and then stand by and see them quietly retreat to their mountain homes without giving them battle." When, therefore, the mail carrier from Austin arrived at Gonzales on 6 August and reported a large and fresh Indian trail crossing the road in the vicinity of Plum Creek, a tributary of the San Marcos River, McCulloch organized a company of twenty-four settlers to resist the invasion.[22]

Leaving Gonzales that afternoon, McCulloch's company found the Indian trail above the town and followed it eastward. The following day McCulloch's party fell in with thirty-six men from the upper Lavaca and sixty-five more from Victoria and Cuero. This group was commanded by Capt. John J. Tumlinson, a Tennessee-born San Jacinto veteran, who assumed the leadership of the combined force and continued the pursuit.

The rangers arrived at Victoria at sunset, learning there of the destruction of Linnville, and continued their march until midnight. Proceeding down Casa Blanca Creek the next morning, they discovered the enemy just before noon, twelve miles east of Victoria. On a level and treeless prairie the volunteers confronted the Indians with their immense booty. Tumlinson, however, committed the tactical error of dismounting his men, only to have them encircled by the matchless Comanche horsemen, who diverted attention with their daredevil feints at the Texan line while their women and old men drove the stolen herds to safety. McCulloch insisted on mounting and attacking at once, but Tumlinson, seeing hesitancy in his own ranks, demurred, and the enemy were allowed to continue northward with their plunder, retracing the trail they had descended.[23]

Mounted on worn horses while those of the Indians were fresh, the Texans pursued but did not again bring the raiders to bay. Finding that the command—in truth simply a hastily armed band of citizens—was not likely to engage the raiders again, McCulloch sent word to veteran Indian fighter Edward Burleson that the Comanches had sacked and burned Linnville and had carried off several prisoners. "We made a draw fight with them at Casa Blanca," he wrote, but "could not stop them. We want to fight them before they get to the mountains." McCulloch then left Tumlinson's command and deflected to the west, whipping around the enemy. Riding hard day and night, he reached Seguin.[24]

There he sent out the call for volunteers, instructing all who would join him to rendezvous at Isham Good's ranch on the Gonzales to Austin road, directly in the path of the returning Comanches. Citizens from Gonzales and Seguin rode to the aid of their friends, arriving at Good's at midnight of 11 August. About the same time, Maj. Gen. Felix Huston, the senior officer of the Army of the Republic of Texas, arrived from Austin. The Texans then held a council of war and elected Huston to command the volunteers. McCulloch arrived from Lockhart just after Huston's election and was assigned to the command of the volunteers from the Guadalupe valley. At 1:00 A.M. Caldwell brought in his force of fifty-nine men, and Henry, about two hours before day, came in from Gonzales with a small unit, bringing the Texas force to approximately one hundred men. Tumlinson's group, having followed the raiders to Gonzales, stopped to refresh their exhausted horses and played no further role in the action.[25]

Although he had once been relieved of command of the army for what Sam Houston perceived as a too-aggressive attitude toward Mexico, Felix Huston hung back on the morning of the twelfth, seemingly content to watch the Comanches disappear beyond Plum Creek. McCulloch was anxious to attack while the Indians were still disorganized in the creek bottom and were preoccupied with crossing their noncombatants and plundered stock to safety. If he were "to live 100 years" he told Huston, he never expected to get another such opportunity "to kill and take Indians." In the prairie beyond the creek, McCulloch counseled, the Comanches would be able to form a line of battle and merely skirmish with the Texans while screening the escape of their women, captives, and horses into the hills beyond. Once out of the bottom, he feared, they could not be forced into a showdown and would escape as they had from Tumlinson after the indecisive fighting on the Casa Blanca three days before. Huston, however, inexperienced as an Indian fighter, wanted to wait for Edward Burleson and would not precipitate a general engagement until the veteran Indian fighter and his reinforcements arrived.

The Comanches were thus able to cross Plum Creek unmolested, but the Texan volunteers followed and overtook them about six or eight miles beyond on the prairie near a skirt of post oak timber. The Indians formed a line of battle and prepared for a fight when, "to the astonishment of every Indian fighter present," within 150 yards of the enemy, Huston again called a halt and ordered his men to dismount and form a hollow square.

McCulloch's men anchored one flank near the timber, and Burleson's force guarded the other. There the Texans remained for some thirty or forty minutes while the Comanche women and old men pushed their captives and horses toward the headwaters of the Blanco and San Marcos rivers. Employing their most favored tactic, the Comanche warriors again seized the initiative, riding around their erstwhile pursuers, individually charging and falling back, and keeping the dismounted Texans off balance and fearful of a full-scale attack. One of the most daring warriors rode a fine horse with a red ribbon eight or ten feet long tied to its tail. The Comanche himself was dressed in elegant style from goods plundered at Linnville. He wore a high-top silk hat, a fine pair of boots, leather gloves, and a broadcloth coat, hind part before, with brass buttons shining brightly up and down his back. When he first made his appearance, he carried a large umbrella. He and his comrades repeatedly charged the Texans, launched volleys of arrows, and quickly fell back beyond effective rifle range.

Henry McCulloch, hoping, as he said afterward, "to git a fair pop at one of those fine dressed gentlemen," moved "about half way the space" between the Texans' line and the Comanches, wrote James Wilson Nichols, to "near whare [*sic*] those chiefs ware performing such feats of horsemanship." Nichols directed Ben's attention to Henry, who was standing behind a small mesquite tree from which bullets had completely scaled the bark, and observed that "Henry [was] in a dangerous place." As Ben galloped toward his brother, an Indian started toward him. Nichols raised his gun and "had a good bead on him" when a ball struck him in the hand, causing him to pull the trigger inadvertently. "She fired," said Nichols, "and at the crack of my gun the chief with the buffalo cap was seen to fall, his horse falling at the same time."[26]

Worse, however, than the swarming, darting horsemen on their front were the warriors who slipped into the timber and opened an enfilading fire on McCulloch's company of Guadalupe men. Seeing his neighbors become subject to heavy sniper fire, Ben galloped to Huston's side and demanded, "In the name of God, General Huston, order a charge through the timber and front rank! The Indians are shooting my men!" A second witness to the scene between McCulloch and Huston reported their conversation slightly differently. "General Huston," John Henry Brown recalled Ben saying, "this is no way to fight Indians; they are fooling with us. They are running off with their captives and plunder—order a charge and we can kill hundreds and rescue the women and children." "All right, Ben, a charge it is then! Mount and charge!" Huston reportedly replied. All order was quickly lost as the Indians sought to break up into small units better to elude pursuit, and the battle degenerated into a series of melees between groups of mounted Texans and retiring Comanches. Pack animals and loose horses were abandoned, each Indian "taking care of his own scalp."[27]

During the disjointed and chaotic fighting that followed the impetuous Texas charge, Andrew Sowell observed a band of about fifteen Indians running a quarter of a mile away, and close behind them, "going under whip," was a man who, from his horse and hat, he took to be McCulloch. "Look at Ben McCulloch," shouted one of Sowell's companions, "he is running a whole gang of them! Hurrah for Ben!" As the man closed up on the heels of the flying Indians, however, he did not slack his pace but mixed with them and then took the lead. It was an Indian riding a horse the color of Ben's and wearing a broad-brimmed hat to which he had helped himself at the sacking of Linnville. The real Ben was, at the same time, indeed "running a whole gang of them." With his right arm still in a sling and firing his pistols with his left hand, he, with Henry and two other companions, pursued five Indians, overtaking and killing them at a boggy branch and fighting with what Henry characterized as "his usual coolness and determination." In the running fight of fifteen miles, some eighty Indians were killed; Juliet Constance Watts, one of the two women taken captive at Linnville, was freed; and hundreds of horses and mules were recaptured. Most important, the power of the Comanches in central Texas was broken forever.[28]

Following this signal victory, an expedition under Maj. George T. Howard of the Army of the Republic of Texas left San Antonio on 20 September, pursuing the beaten Comanches to the headwaters of the Nueces River. On 9 September Ben called upon the people of Gonzales County and the nearby towns of Victoria and Texana to join him at Gonzales on 19 September for a rendezvous with Howard on the upper Guadalupe. "The first to go will surely get a fight," he promised his neighbors. After raising twenty-five or thirty men from Gonzales County, McCulloch joined Howard on 29 September.[29]

Major Howard's scouts informed him that the local Indians, who had been raiding the frontier independently of the Comanches who sacked Linnville, had been "alarmed" by the stunning defeat at Plum Creek and were moving westward. Accordingly, Howard's 180-man task force moved northwestward in hopes of overtaking and punishing the recent marauders. Upon reaching the headwaters of the Nueces, Howard's scouts reported fresh signs of a major Indian encampment. "From timidity or some other cause," Howard reported, the scouts "failed to do their duty" to locate and engage the hostiles, so, on the afternoon of 12 October, Howard determined to lighten his command of its baggage and to force march toward the assumed location of the Indian village. A night march, however, was constrained to halt when the scouts lost the trail. At daybreak of the thirteenth Howard called upon McCulloch and Mathew Caldwell to find it again. When the two reported that they had established contact with the Indians, Howard mounted his command and gave chase. After a hard ride of ten miles the Texans burst upon the main Indian encampment at the head of Las Moras Creek, a tributary of the Nueces River. McCulloch estimated that sixty warriors were in the band. Forewarned and prepared, they had abandoned camp with their best horses. Not pausing in the village, the Texans pursued the fleeing Indians for five miles, but overtook and killed only two to four warriors. Only when their horses were exhausted did Howard's men return to the abandoned camp, where they took charge of 125 horses and mules plundered from Texas and northern Mexico and liberated one captive, a twelve-year-old girl stolen from a ranch in Mexico. In addition, a quantity of arms and provisions were taken and destroyed, but McCulloch judged "the whole community very poor."[30]

From the Las Moras, Howard led his four companies to the Frio River, about seventy-five miles from San Antonio, near the Uvalde Canyon. Here McCulloch left the expedition and returned to Gonzales while Howard's remaining men marched to the headwaters of the Guadalupe and the Llano. They encountered no more Indians, however, and so marched for San Antonio, arriving there on 13 October. Henry did not join Ben on this campaign. Instead he had returned from Plum Creek "in safety to the bosom of [his] intended if not with honor without disgrace," and was married to Jane Isabella Ashby four nights later on 20 August.[31]

THREE

To Mier and Back

"All is peace here now," Henry wrote his friend Matthew P. Woodhouse on 27 February 1841, and the Gonzales community was beginning to grow and prosper. Ben and Henry McCulloch worked to bring civilization to Gonzales County in more ways than by defending its settlers. On 30 January 1841, for example, Ben helped to found Guadalupe College and, as a charter member of its board of trustees, was in part responsible for prescribing the school's course of studies. Remarkably, considering the emotional and political tensions between Mexico and the Republic of Texas, the board decreed that "the Spanish language shall be considered and treated as only second in importance and utility to the English" in the new school's curriculum. Equally liberal for the time and place were the decisions to run the college as a "purely literary and scientific" academy, in which "students of all religious denominations whatsoever shall enjoy equal advantages." The board's sole concession to locality was a patriotic one. The "descendants of the defenders of the Alamo," read the charter, "may attend, tuition free, for 100 years."[1]

Additional signs of the passing of the frontier in Gonzales County were seen in religion and politics. "Preaching or prayer meeting [occurs] every Sunday now" in Gonzales, Henry observed to a friend. "The people are so religious that they would hardly pull their neighbor's ass out of the mire, much less go hunting on Sunday." Perhaps a surer sign of the coming of civilization to the frontier was the rise of the Whig party as a challenger to the party of Andrew Jackson. Largely because the Whigs opposed the annexation of Texas, most Texans remained Democrats. In 1841, however, Henry believed that "the Tories have the ascendancy," the Democrats having "been beaten in two elections" for the house of representatives and for county sheriff.[2]

Reflecting the changes in his surroundings as well as his recent marriage, Henry's life became more settled and civilized; but his brother's did not. Ben McCulloch remained single all of his life and never became a member of any church, although he did join the Masonic fraternity and was said to have been "a firm believer in the Bible and an ardent friend of the Protestant Religion." Ben spent most of 1841 surveying and Indian fighting.

Due essentially to economic considerations, the regular army of the Republic of Texas was only a skeleton, and the militia was almost purely a paper organization. On 6 December 1836, during Sam Houston's first presidential term, congress had passed legislation establishing the essential militia structure. The organization, on paper, was formidable. The Texas congress, however, refused to appropriate necessary funds, and the militia law was not implemented. Late in 1837 the second congress made another unsuccessful attempt to vitalize the militia. Through the greatest part of the life of the Republic of Texas, therefore, the real army consisted of only 250 men—the Texas Rangers.

Although every Texan was ultimately his own soldier and police force, the most militant were impelled irresistibly into the Texas Rangers. The term *ranger* was first applied to Texas fighting men as early as 1823 when Stephen F. Austin commissioned ten officers to enforce the laws of the colony. For the next twenty years the force grew in size and responsibilities. Especially in the early years when the infant republic could not afford to maintain a regular army, the rangers provided an inexpensive and efficient frontier defense force. Most effective in small, well-mounted squads, they were prepared to ride great distances at short notice to repel or destroy Indian raiding parties.[3]

In response to Comanche depredations along the frontier, in 1840 the Lamar administration had appointed John Coffee (Jack) Hays—namesake of Alexander McCulloch's Creek War commander and, like the McCullochs, a Tennessean—captain of the Texas Rangers and had authorized him to patrol beyond the line of settlement for marauding Indians. Finding that he could not give up soldiering, Ben McCulloch campaigned with Hays through most of 1840 and, on 26 April 1841, was elected first lieutenant of Hays's "Ranger Spy Company." "The object of the expedition is (I think) to get a fight, if possible, out of the Indians," wrote Henry of one of Ben's forays, "and if not, plunder or anything that comes to hand in the mountains. Ben's principle object is to locate and survey some lands, the remains of his claims." After leading an expedition to the headwaters of the Llano River, where in May 1840 he attacked and destroyed the village of a band of Comanches that had recently raided Gonzales, McCulloch's fame as an Indian fighter was secure. As a result, according to Rose, President Mirabeau B. Lamar invited him to accept a position in the Texan Santa Fe expedition, an ill-fated politico-military-commercial venture planned to divert some of the rich New Mexico trade from the Santa Fe Trail across Texas to Austin and Houston. McCulloch wisely declined the offer, however, "as he had no confidence in the wisdom of the enterprise," and the command devolved upon Col. Hugh McLeod. McCulloch's misgivings were well founded, for on 17 September 1841, after suffering many hardships, the men of the expedition surrendered to Mexican authorities in New Mexico and were marched to Mexico City as prisoners.[4]

Ben chose not to run for reelection to the house of representatives in 1841, although his brother reported that he "could have beaten any man in the county" for any office he chose. Rather, he remained a sometime surveyor and part-time warrior until the last days of the Lone Star Republic, serving as Hays's lieutenant in the fight against the Comanches at Bandera Pass in 1841 and at Paint Rock in 1842.[5]

Eighteen forty-two, however, brought a worsening of relations with Mexico and a renewal of the hostilities that had smoldered since San Jacinto. Although, according to Francis Moore, Jr., editor of the Houston *Telegraph and Texas Register*, "the Texas Rangers, under the gallant Hays and McCulloch, have for years held undisputed sway" over the territory between San Antonio and the Rio Grande, most Texans hoped that the rangers would be ordered to take possession of Laredo, arguing "that the people of that place desire that it may be occupied by our troops" and were "anxious to acknowledge the authority of the Texian government." In

John Coffee Hays. Z. N. Morrell described Hays, whom he called "our intrepid leader," as "five feet ten inches high, weighing one hundred and sixty pounds, his black eyes flashing decision of character, from beneath a full forehead, and crowned with beautiful jet black hair."
(Eugene C. Barker Texas History Center, University of Texas at Austin)

February the Mexican government launched a preemptive raid against Texas, seeking, perhaps, to gain a more secure hold on the Rio Grande valley and to deter further Texan incursions into the area below San Antonio. The invading column had no intention of attempting to reconquer Mexico's former province or even to hold part of its territory for long, but the sudden appearance at San Antonio of a formidable column of Mexican cavalry led by Brig. Gen. Rafael Vásquez touched off a panic such as Texas had not experienced since the dark days following the fall of the Alamo.[6]

The Vásquez raid, in fact, precipitated "the second Runaway Scrape," an exodus of civilians comparable to that caused by Santa Anna's invasion in 1836. Word of the Mexican incursion quickly spread to the outlying settlements, and at Gonzales, McCulloch raised a company and joined Hays's rangers at Bexar. Mary Maverick, wife of the famous Samuel Maverick and one of the runaways, recalled Ben McCulloch's calming presence during those uncertain hours. Fleeing San Antonio, Mary Maverick's party traveled eighteen miles to Cibolo Creek and camped on 2 March. There McCulloch and his Gonzalians met and camped with them. "They had armed in haste," she remembered, "and were going out to San Antonio to 'meet the enemy.' They were as witty and lively as could be, and we all sat late around the camp fire enjoying their jokes and 'yarns.'" Despite the good humor of the party, McCulloch posted guards all night, and in the morning, as the two groups parted, Maverick learned from McCulloch that "Indians had been seen lurking in the neighborhood, which was the reason that [the rangers] had given us their protecting presence during the night."[7]

Jack Hays, who had hastily collected the raw and few volunteers at hand, "one hundred and seven men and boys," to resist Vásquez, was in the dark as to the enemy's size, location, or intentions, "having received no report from any of [his] spies." Texan authorities could not immediately determine whether this was merely a pinprick raid or a serious attempt to reconquer Texas. When the Gonzales company arrived, therefore, Hays dispatched McCulloch to discover the strength and purpose of the enemy. Ben set out toward the Hondo River, where he concealed himself in the chaparral and counted Vásquez's men as they marched north. Finding the Mexican force of five hundred to seven hundred men to be all cavalry, McCulloch feared that it was perhaps only the vanguard of a full-scale invasion force of mixed arms, and so he pushed on eighty miles farther south to the Nueces River. McCulloch's failure to return when he was expected had a severely demoralizing effect on the volunteers at San

Antonio, for the Texans had great confidence in him, and Hays was sure that he was "either cut off or behind the enemy."[8]

When some of Hays's scouts arrived on the morning of the fifth to report Vásquez's force "within six miles of town, covering about one hundred acres of ground, and [to] have 150 camp fires," the Texans immediately determined to evacuate San Antonio. Little time was available to remove valuables, and according to the Baptist missionary-warrior Z. N. Morrell, "All was chaos and confusion." Orders were issued for all ammunition to be destroyed, and kegs of powder were thrown into the river. Liquor and cigars, however, "were plentiful and very soon many of the soldiers were dead drunk, while nearly all were in a mild state of intoxication." John Twohig blew up his store while McCulloch's Gonzales volunteers withdrew the garrison's one tiny fieldpiece, "passing out at the northeast corner of the place as the enemy entered on the opposite side." On 5 March 1842 Vásquez entered San Antonio, raised the Mexican flag, and proclaimed Mexican law.[9]

Satisfying himself at last that no infantry or artillery was supporting the enemy cavalry, McCulloch returned to San Antonio to find the Mexican flag floating over the dome of San Fernando Cathedral. He watched the city until Vásquez began his withdrawal toward Mexico and then reported to Hays on the sixth at Seguin. Hays was much relieved not only to see McCulloch alive but to learn that Vásquez's entire force numbered only "from 500 to 700 men and about 30 Caddo Indians." Further, McCulloch informed Hays, Vásquez had remained in San Antonio only one night and was now retreating toward the Rio Grande. With this welcome intelligence, the Texans returned to San Antonio.[10]

Ben and his Gonzales company remained with the volunteer army, now three hundred strong, hoping to follow Vásquez and strike his retreating column a blow before it crossed the Rio Grande. Although the republic had no regular army in 1842, volunteers were soon pouring into San Antonio by the hundreds. The men were eager to march at once against the Mexicans, but President Houston forbade their doing so, insisting that an effective campaign could not be launched before midsummer. When Hays's scouts reported that Vásquez would cross the Rio Grande at least one or two days before the volunteers could reach them, the little army began to lose what discipline and cohesion it had.[11]

In response to the Vásquez raid, war fever broke out in Texas in epidemic proportions. On 30 March the Austin *City Gazette* demanded an immediate invasion of the northern Mexican provinces. "The Rio Grande should be the theater of every battle," it proclaimed, "and on the enemy should our men subsist until we have our rights and independence acknowledged." In response to the popular outcry—especially loud in western Texas—to assemble an army, President Houston appointed Brig. Gen. Alexander Somervell, who had served as secretary of war in the David G. Burnet administration and who was now commander of the First Militia Brigade, to assume full command of the volunteer troops arriving at San Antonio and to take charge of any military action against Mexico. Somervell arrived at army headquarters on 17 March only to find one faction of the army favoring the appointment of Albert Sidney Johnston to the command and a much larger faction in favor of Vice-President Edward Burleson. Angered by the turn of events that placed Burleson at the head of the army, a move that he regarded as a gambit by Burleson in his campaign for the presidency, and fearful of the consequences of allowing what had degenerated into an armed mob to roam the streets of San Antonio, Houston announced that the troops could not be made ready to invade Mexico in less than four months because of insufficient supplies of arms and ammunition as well as inadequate transport. In the meantime, he would stand for no unauthorized venture. With the rest of the army inactive, two companies of fifty-six men each were ordered on a scout from San Antonio to Corpus Christi and westward. McCulloch's company, one of the two, was sent "through the lower coast country of Texas" in a fruitless attempt to establish contact with the enemy, returning to San Antonio on 16 March.[12]

While Somervell and Burleson disputed command, other volunteers poured into San Antonio. Soon more than twenty-five hundred armed and restless men milled about town, undisciplined and leaderless. As Houston had feared, the army began to exhibit intentions of setting out for Mexico with or without government authorization. Houston, therefore, withdrew official sanction from the army and on 2 April disbanded the militia companies, offering them the option of returning to their homes or of reenlisting under Somervell's command.[13]

When congress passed a bill authorizing an offensive war against Mexico, Houston responded on 22 July with a veto, commending congress for its patriotism but stressing the lack of financial resources in the republic to carry on a war. Rather than finance a potentially ruinous offensive war against Mexico, Houston offered the alternative of a limited strike, a retaliatory raid into Mexico that would, he believed, gain a measure of revenge for the Santa Fe and San Antonio fiascoes "or at least to give protection to our Southwestern frontier." His plan involved the use of the militia and the raising of volunteer companies, "mounted, equipped, and prepared at their own expense." He would rely, he said, on the "chivalry and patriotism of [his] Countrymen."[14]

In accordance with Houston's plan, a small-scale punitive expedition was planned and was authorized to extend Texas's military authority to Laredo and beyond, if necessary, in order to neutralize the Mexican threat to the republic's southern frontier. On 18 June, Houston instructed Ben McCulloch to raise and command a company of cavalry, unattached to any regiment, to serve as scouts. Each of his fifty-six to sixty-six men was to provide himself "a first rate horse and the arms and equipment requisite and appropriate for the service contemplated. Let the preparation for active and arduous duty be perfect," Houston admonished. "Every defect may, in the field, be productive of disaster." Finally, the old general concluded, "do not permit yourself to be diverted from the line of prudence by friendship or personal attachment to any individual who may wish to join your corps ill provided."

Taking, as always, not only a professional but a personal interest in McCulloch's career, Houston instructed his young protégé to "take care also that you have none who are not in all things ready and willing to follow you wherever you are ordered to lead. You will want no man with you who has not made up his mind to follow orders." Remembering, no doubt, the disasters and near disasters caused by an excess of democracy in the Texas revolutionary army, Houston counseled that "it will neither be agreeable to you nor advantageous to the country to canvass your instructions and submit the question of their propriety or inexpediency to the vote of your men" in front of the enemy. Recalling bitterly the events that had led to the republic's humiliating inability to retaliate against the Mexicans after the raid on San Antonio the previous March, Houston reminded McCulloch of "the fruits of insubordination; and rather than you incorporate its elements and materials in your command, I would prefer that it should never be formed." Had it not been for what Houston considered the willful self-indulgence of the volunteer army at San Antonio the previous March, "at this very day and hour we should have been in possession of the Valley of the Rio Grande." In an obvious reference to his political rival, Edward Burleson, Houston reflected that he had been greatly saddened by "the phrenzy of disobedience and the machinations of selfish demagogues, who would rather 'reign in hell than serve in heaven.' "

Finally, Houston advised his young cavalry officer to insure that his command was not "disgraced by that most dangerous and odious of all vices—the lust of plunder. See that you have gentlemen, and not robbers as your associates. I should be pained by any act of yours in the future which would cast a shadow or a stain upon the lustre of your past conduct as a soldier of Texas." Although Mexico was expected to bear the cost of the war, "even the enemy must be treated as the honor of our race and our national name will demand," and plunder was not to be tolerated.[15]

On 21 July, George Washington Hockley, who had been McCulloch's commanding officer at the battle of San Jacinto and who was now serving as secretary of war and marine, confirmed McCulloch's commission and ordered him into the field. Col. John H. Moore, Hockley informed McCulloch, had been authorized to raise a regiment "for the purpose of securing the country upon this side of the Rio Grande, and, if necessary, operating upon the enemy's country." McCulloch was to report with his company to Colonel Moore at the crossing of the Medina River between San Antonio and Laredo on 15 August, "well mounted and equipped and provided with 100 rounds of ammunition and eight days' provisions." News of the expedition was to be kept as quiet "as the nature of the case will admit," and the strictest discipline was enjoined. The length of the campaign was kept open-ended, to be determined "by its success and the situation in which the enemy may be found."[16]

Moore was a well-respected veteran of many of the republic's battles, and, the *Civilian and Galveston Gazette* observed, "never has he been known to discharge a body of men until they have fought a battle." Surely Mexico would now be properly chastised, thought the people of the Texas frontier, and scores of men fought for a place in the expeditionary force. Within two weeks of the time set for the rendezvous, however, news reached Texas that Mexico had freed the Santa Fe prisoners and was even then repatriating them in an apparent gesture of goodwill. On 20 August, Joseph Eve, the United States chargé d'affaires in Texas, received word from his government advising the Houston administration "to suspend any offensive military operations which may be in contemplation against Mexico" until the results of the United States' negotiating efforts on Texas's behalf were known. On the following day Col. Hugh McLeod and 182 Santa Fe prisoners were landed at Galveston by a Mexican warship. Thus Moore's and McCulloch's expedition to the Rio Grande was checked before it began, and the troops that they had gathered returned to their homes gravely disappointed.[17]

The diplomats' vision of peace, however, was shattered within a month when the Mexican army struck again, carrying out a larger-scale version of the Vásquez raid of the previous March. Brig. Gen. Adrian Woll, a French soldier of fortune serving in the Mexican army, crossed the Rio Grande with one thousand regular infantry, five hundred irregular cavalry, and two pieces of artillery and marched toward San Antonio. McCulloch was visiting friends on the upper Colorado River when the Mexicans attacked, and although he hastened to Bexar, he arrived too late to participate in the battle of the Salado, the initial fighting between Woll's men and a hastily assembled army of Texan volunteers under Mathew Caldwell. He arrived at Hays's headquarters on the Salado Creek late on 18 September, however, and was sent to reconnoiter the Mexican position in San Antonio. After a scout to the walls of the Alamo, he advised that an attack on the Mexican position be postponed until the morning of the nineteenth. Unfortunately for the Texan cause, a hard rain fell all of the next day, and consequently no advance was made. About midnight several Texans entered the Mexicans' camp "to engage in a little 'sport' " and found that Woll had evacuated the city under cover of darkness. On learning that the Mexicans had begun their retreat, the Texans followed immediately but were halted for the night by the flooded crossing of the Medina River below San Antonio.[18]

Despite his head start, Woll had traveled only slightly farther than the Texans. McCulloch and Hays, scouting in advance of the ranger company, discovered the Mexican camp on the Medina on the night of 20 September. Seeing an opportunity not only to gather information about the condition and strength of the enemy but also to indulge in some youthful bravado, the two daredevils dismounted, picketed their horses, threw their serapes around their shoulders, and, with their hats drawn well down, boldly entered the Mexican encampment. There, for what must have seemed an eternity, they strolled about, watching soldiers sleeping, playing cards, or smoking and talking in small groups. A dog, more suspicious than its masters, followed them. Satisfied at last of the numbers of the enemy and the proof, perhaps, of their own courage, Hays and McCulloch made their way back toward their horses but were not so fortunate in exiting the enemy's picket line as they had been on entering the camp. Only yards from where their mounts were tied, a sentry shouted, "*¿Quién vive?*" "Texians, damn you!" was Hays's defiant reply; and while McCulloch covered the soldier with his rifle, Hays disarmed him and took him prisoner. The two rangers, with their captive, left the camp without creating a further disturbance and rode for Caldwell's line.

McCulloch and Hays had learned that the Mexican cavalry horses were corralled a short distance from the camp, and McCulloch strongly urged that the Texans attempt to capture or at least stampede them to prevent Woll's army from moving on the morning of the twenty-first. Hays, however, vetoed this suggestion, and when the two rangers returned to the Mexican camp in the morning, they found the bird had once again flown before the trap could be sprung.[19]

No further contact was made with the retreating Mexicans until about 3:00 P.M., when Hays's company, riding half a mile in advance of Caldwell's main column, overtook Woll at the crossing of the Hondo River. Pressing rapidly forward, the rangers approached Woll's rear guard, strongly positioned and supported by a cannon commanding the road from the north. With no knowledge of the fieldpiece, Hays charged the Mexican rear guard, driving it back upon Woll's main force and overrunning the gun before the enemy fired half a dozen rounds. The boldness of the charge took the Mexican army by surprise, no doubt saving Hays's command many casualties. Hays's horse was shot from under him, but only two of his men were wounded. Woll, discovering that the rangers were supported by neither infantry nor artillery, rallied and recaptured the cannon. Severely outnumbered, the Texans fell back three or four hundred yards into a dry creek bed, where Caldwell's main body joined them and began to fortify the position in anticipation of a Mexican attack.[20]

Among the Texan officers a heated difference of opinion arose as to the practicability of attacking the enemy. Unmindful of Houston's advice about canvassing popular opinion, the usually aggressive Caldwell held a council of war, and more time was lost in discussing the situation. McCulloch came to the front and called for volunteers to advance, and Judge John Hemphill urged "with tearful earnestness" the importance of an immediate attack. According to John Holland Jenkins, however, "A lethargy had fallen upon the command that effectively retarded further progress." As night approached on the twenty-second, the Texans stood in their ranks, "suffering for water and tantalized almost to madness by the delay and want of harmony among [their] leaders."[21]

At 3:00 the next morning, Woll hustled his troops across the Hondo and force-marched them toward the Rio Grande. At this point the Texans abandoned their pursuit, but McCulloch and many of his comrades believed that had the command held together, continued its harassment of the retreating Mexicans, and awaited the arrival of the squads and companies of volunteers already on their way to the army, Woll's invasion force could have been absolutely destroyed before it reached Mexican soil. As it was, Caldwell's volunteers returned from the Hondo "greatly exasperated" at being deprived of their showdown with Woll's command. Only a few miles up the road toward San Antonio they met their "old favorite leader," Edward Burleson, arriving with reinforcements. Thomas Jefferson Green spoke for the army—and delivered a rebuke to Sam Houston—when he observed that "General Burleson may not be considered a tactician in the strict sense of the term, but he never failed to observe one rule in winning battles more important than all the minutiae of the drill: that rule is, to fight."[22]

As Caldwell marched north, returning to San Antonio, he encountered unit after unit of reinforcements, all avid to avenge this second blot on their national honor in five months. "Young men are always ready to volunteer on 'wild goose' expeditions," observed ranger William W. (Big Foot) Wallace, and on reaching San Antonio the army of volunteers agreed to make a raid into Mexico as early as possible, with or without government sanction. Ben and Henry McCulloch remained in San Antonio, hoping that an offensive campaign might soon be mounted, and on 3 October Sam Houston again gave command of the volunteers to Alexander Somervell and instructed him to lead them into Mexico if their numbers and discipline indicated a reasonable hope of success. Thus, the president hoped, the popular demand for an invasion of Mexico might be appeased. Even if the adventure failed, the people of the frontier would be shown the futility of hastily organized offensive action against Mexico. The Houston administration, however, was willing to give no further assistance or sanction to the madcap punitive expedition. Nevertheless, an army of seven hundred assembled on the Medina on 25 November 1842 and, "without a wagon, tent, or breadstuff," marched for Mexico, driving before them the beef upon which they subsisted.[23]

Well represented among the old Texas patriots were "broken down politicians from the 'old States,' that somehow had gotten on the wrong side of the fence, and been left out in the cold; renegades and refugees from justice, that had 'left their country for their country's good,' and adventurers of all sorts, ready for anything or any enterprise that afforded a reasonable prospect of excitement and plunder. Dare-devils they were all," wrote John C. Duval, "and afraid of nothing under the sun, (except a due-bill or a bailiff)." The only body of regularly enrolled Texas troops involved in the so-called Somervell Expedition was Jack Hays's company of rangers, of which Henry McCulloch was first lieutenant and which Ben served as a volunteer.[24]

By 2 December Hays's company, the vanguard of Somervell's command,

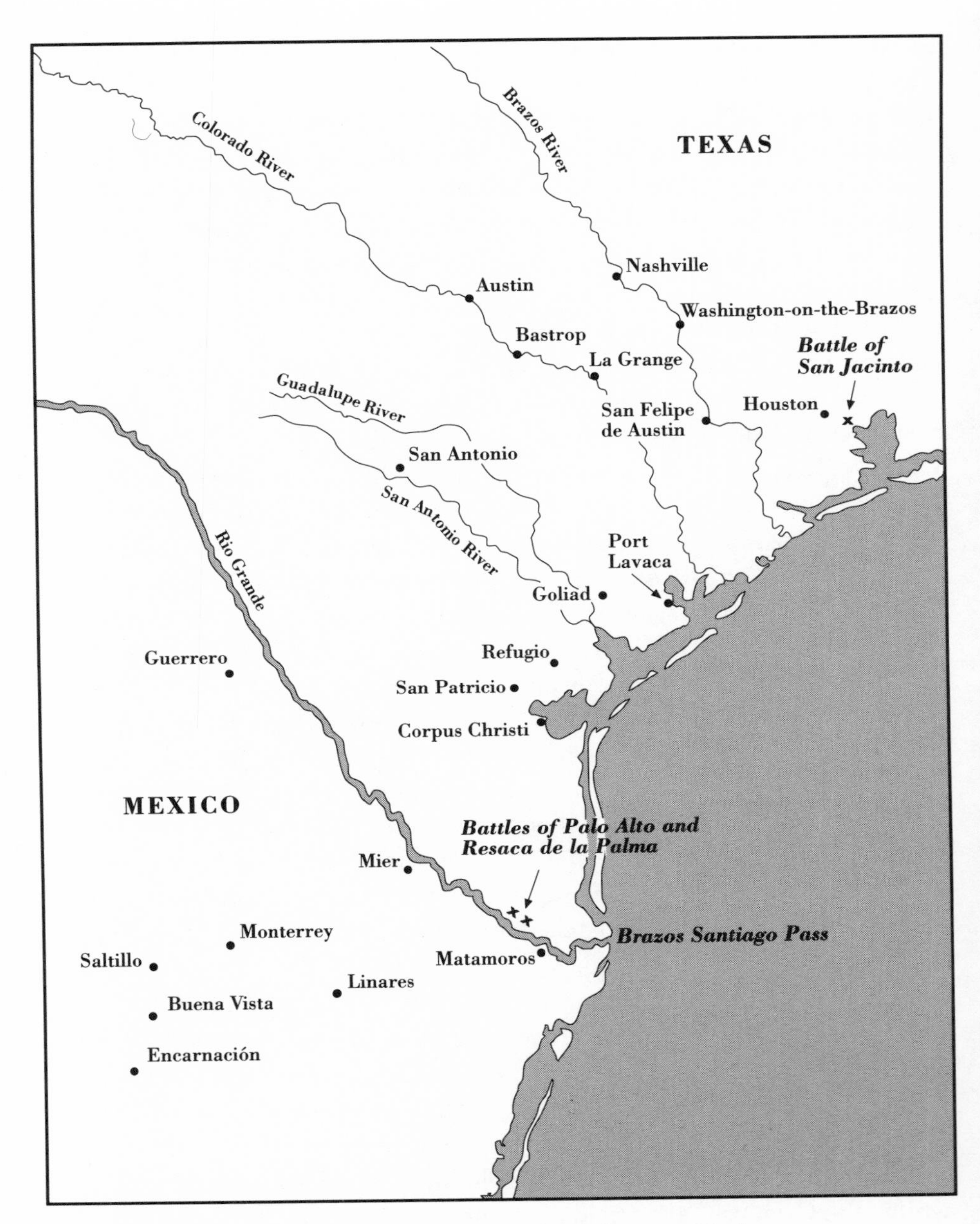

MAP 3. *Southern Texas and Northeastern Mexico*

reached the western bank of the Nueces, deep in the brush country of southern Texas. Somervell dispatched Hays; Ben McCulloch; Flacco, the colorful chief of the Texans' Lipan-Apache allies; and two other men to Laredo to ascertain the disposition of Mexican forces in the area and to determine whether the village could be taken and held. The following day, after a terrific horse race, the scouting party ran down and captured two irregular Mexican cavalrymen, "rancheros," as they were known, from whom they learned that no Mexican force of any consequence was at Laredo.[25]

During the night of 6 December, while the Texans awaited the arrival of the main column under Somervell, one of the prisoners escaped, a breach of security that was to cost the Texas expedition dearly in the days to come. The rangers made a determined effort to recapture the man. McCulloch and Hays pursued him to the outskirts of Laredo only to learn from their resident spies that he had already arrived and had alerted the eighty-man garrison across the river at Nuevo Laredo. Nevertheless, at sunset on 7 December, Somervell resumed his march, reaching Laredo at daylight on the following morning.[26]

During the night Hays and McCulloch swam the Rio Grande in search of boats suitable to ferry Somervell's army into Mexico but were able to locate only a single small pirogue, and the current was too swift and the riverbed too rocky to manage without fear of losing their arms or even drowning. All hope of surprise was now lost, but later that day Somervell's "motley, mixed-up crowd" took formal possession of Laredo, the deepest penetration into southern Texas ever achieved by so sizable an Anglo-Texan force.[27]

Checked by the waters of the Rio Grande, the Texans camped on the northern side of the river while an attempt was made to gather boats to take them into Mexico. Finally, on 15 December, three small boats were procured, and Somervell's command, now reduced by desertion to only five hundred men, began its passage down the Rio Grande toward the Mexican town of Guerrero, sixty miles below Laredo. Scouts reported signs of a sizable concentration of Mexican troops in the vicinity of Guerrero, and McCulloch was dispatched with ten rangers to reconnoiter the route and the town. The rangers took two prisoners, an old man and his son who were herding sheep and goats, and these two agreed to show McCulloch a point along the river where the army might cross. "Owing to the ignorance of his guide," however, McCulloch did not reach the ford until after the Texan flotilla had arrived there and the greater part of the army had crossed.[28]

Even while the Mexicans rallied their forces along the border, Texan discipline, never the best, began to unravel. McCulloch was given command of the camp guard, and on the night of 9 December one of his pickets came very near firing on a drunken Texan who had visited Laredo without a pass and had returned ignorant of the countersign. The following day, Col. Joseph L. Bennet led his 185-man battalion back to San Antonio in disgust. Somervell took Guerrero without opposition, but by 19 December he realized that his small force, so deep in enemy territory and with discipline in rags, could not hope to sustain itself for long in the face of a Mexican counteroffensive. Accordingly, he ordered his troops to disband and to return to Texas. Somervell's order to abandon the expedition was so unexpected and was regarded as so unnecessary that only 189 officers and men obeyed his command. Jack Hays, who held a regular ranger commission from Sam Houston, accompanied Somervell back to Texas, but 308 volunteers refused to return and tendered to Ben McCulloch, then to Thomas Jefferson Green, and then to Henry E. McCulloch, the command of the rump of the army that remained. Each appointee had served under Hays, however, and because they had left Somervell's command with his permission, none felt free to accept. At last Col. William S. Fisher, who had led a company at San Jacinto, had served Houston briefly as secretary of war, and had commanded the two companies of Texas regulars at the Council House Fight, was chosen to take charge of the men who remained at Guerrero and to lead them deeper into Mexico. Mier, a village on the Río Atcantro a few miles below the Rio Grande, was chosen as their objective. Ben McCulloch acceded to the leadership of the thirteen rangers who remained with the truncated invasion force but declined to connect his command with Fisher's except as unofficial scouts.[29]

Setting out on 20 December, the Texan vanguard—led by the McCulloch brothers—ranged down the southern bank of the Rio Grande for three days. It encountered no formidable force of Mexicans but observed numerous small scouting parties. When the Texan army arrived opposite Mier, McCulloch reported his sightings of Mexican scouts to Fisher, who declared his intention to cross his troops that night and attack Mier at daylight the next morning, 23 December.[30]

Rather than see Fisher make a reckless attack on the town with no knowledge of what might be there, McCulloch proposed that Fisher allow him to make a reconnaissance into Mier that night with twenty-five "choice spies" supported by fifty to one hundred men holding the crossing on the western side of the river. Fisher agreed, and McCulloch marched at once. Finding no troops in town, he rode into the main plaza and received the surrender of the place from the alcalde. An American named Janison whom he found there and an old Mexican friend of the Texans from San Antonio informed McCulloch that Brig. Gen. Pedro Ampudia, a veteran of both the Alamo and San Jacinto, with fifteen hundred infantry, was expected from Matamoros that night. After remaining an hour in the town, McCulloch returned to Fisher's camp across the Atcantro. As he reached the top of the hill that commanded the town, he could see the troops of Brig. Gen. Antonio Canales, commandant of the Mier garrison, marching to meet Ampudia.[31]

McCulloch reported his findings to Fisher and advised him to abandon his plan and return to Texas. Fisher, however, remained resolved to cross the river, even in the face of overwhelming Mexican force. McCulloch is reported to have responded, "You have had a trap laid for you which I do not propose to fall into, but will leave you in the morning, and you will find Ampudia where you expect to find your supplies." Thereupon the McCulloch brothers left the Mier expedition and began to make their way back to Gonzales.[32]

Ben and Henry; Tom Green, who had served the Twin Sisters beside McCulloch at San Jacinto; Robert A. Gillespie, one of Hays's most formidable rangers; Dr. Edmund J. Felder; and a man named Katy left Mier together, striking through roadless country and subsisting primarily on wild horses. They crossed the Nueces about ten miles above San Patricio and the San Antonio—"swimming" with recent flood waters—on a raft of logs and doors that had drifted down from the deserted town of Goliad. There McCulloch's party was joined by George Bernard Erath and three others of the camp guard who had escaped capture at Mier.[33]

While broiling a fat mustang over their campfire, McCulloch told Erath of how he had come to the conclusion that there had been "very little prospect for our success without more rule and discipline among us." McCulloch knew that when he "could not make any of the leading men believe in the danger" and when "Fisher himself declared that he had no control of us," the time had come to leave the expedition "before disaster should overtake us." "The finale," wrote Erath, was exactly as the McCullochs, "with their not inconsiderable military experience, had foreseen."

Although outnumbered almost ten to one, Fisher entered Mier on Christmas afternoon and fought the Mexicans for twenty-four hours. According to Canales the Texans killed 40 and wounded more than 60 of his men; but Fisher believed that he had inflicted 500 to 700 casualties on the enemy, and other estimates represent Mexican losses as high as 1,000. The Texans sustained a loss of 16 killed and 17 severely wounded. With food, water, and ammunition exhausted, however, Fisher surrendered, and his men were marched toward Mexico City. At the Coahuilan village of Salado they executed an escape plan, but only three reached the Nueces, the rest being recaptured by Mexican cavalry. Santa Anna ordered their execution, but the governor of Coahuila refused to comply. As a compromise, one in ten of the Mier men—those who drew black beans by lot—were shot by firing squad. The remainder of the prisoners, who had drawn white beans, were sentenced to hard labor in Mexico City and were later removed to the notorious Perote prison. Some escaped, but many more died of disease and privation. At last, on 16 September 1844, the remaining Perote prisoners were repatriated. Thomas Jefferson Green, captured at Mier and incarcerated at Perote prison, wrote in later years that had the army that left San Antonio for the Rio Grande been "managed with skill and judgment," it undoubtedly would have done all that was expected of it. But "dissension, that bane of raw troops, which has so often brought to grief expeditions of this kind, prevailed among our leaders," making the name of the Mier expedition synonymous with disaster in the history of the Republic of Texas.[34]

Ben and Henry at last made their way back to Gonzales, discouraged but still ready to serve Texas and to have one more round with the Mexicans when fate presented the opportunity.[35]

FOUR

The War Is Renewed

Singled out for praise by Inspector General and Adjutant General Memucan Hunt for his services to the Mier expedition as "one of the most useful and efficient officers in the Republic," Ben McCulloch kept an eye toward Mexico, and when the *Neptune* arrived at Galveston on 12 March with news that Fisher and his men had overpowered their guards at Salado and were attempting to make their way back to Texas, he raised a company of horsemen at Gonzales to go to their aid. Described by the Houston *Telegraph and Texas Register* as "well armed and ready to make a foray to the Rio Grande," McCulloch's party was prepared to "dash forward to Laredo as speedily as possible, as he may thus be enabled to cover their retreat and escort them with safety into the settlements." The Mier prisoners had made good their escape only to be recaptured in the desert of central Mexico, however, and McCulloch's rescue mission was never launched. Thereafter, the luckless Snivley Expedition of 1843—designed to interdict the highly profitable St. Louis–Santa Fe trade but doomed to tragicomic failure—only exacerbated relations with Mexico during the next four years, and the Comanches once again became the principal threat to the communities of western Texas.[1]

"Our Government is still unsettled," Henry wrote to his mother, "and no man knows how soon he may have to gear up his wagon and team and leave the western part of the country." Ben was again elected first lieutenant in Jack Hays's ranger company, serving until Texas was annexed to the United States. With his objectivity no doubt obscured by his affection for his brother, Henry maintained that although only second in command of the company, Ben was "first in the feelings and confidence of the people, but Major Hays is the pet" of the government and "must consequently be put over him."[2]

Since winning their independence in 1836, most Texans had wished for annexation to the United States, but New England antislavery sentiment and fear of a war with Mexico had for a decade constituted insuperable obstacles. Only after James K. Polk was elected to the presidency in 1844 on a pro-annexation platform did John Tyler, as one of the last acts of his administration, offer statehood to the Lone Star Republic. As early as 20 February 1844, President Sam Houston, statehood's strongest advocate, had written to Texas's chief negotiator in the annexation talks, J. Pinckney Henderson, instructing him to "urge upon the government the justice" of offering Ben McCulloch a commission in the United States Army if annexation were consummated. He "would make a fine officer for cavalry or dragoons," Houston insisted. A special session of the Texas congress and a convention of special delegates called by President Anson Jones accepted the United States' proposal on the Fourth of July 1845 and in October adopted a state constitution. The United States Congress accepted the constitution on 29 December, and on 16 February 1846 the Stars and Stripes replaced the Lone Star above the Texas capitol. With Texas's annexation to the Union in 1845, Federal troops were expected to take over the duties of the rangers as protectors of the Anglo-American frontier. Although Texas was far from satisfied with the new arrangement and ardently desired to have its own frontier defense force back, on 14 March 1846 the senate of the first legislature unanimously passed a resolution commending the "chivalry and many gallant and daring deeds of Maj. John C. Hays[,] Capt. Benj. McCullough and R. A. Gillespie." This "gallant band," said the senate, "are entitled to the gratitude of the people of Texas and the admiration of the world." For Ben McCulloch, however, no commission was forthcoming. Yet the time was approaching when the United States would call upon Texas for soldiers, and McCulloch would be among the first to respond.[3]

On 18 October 1845 the Houston *Telegraph and Texas Register* reported that President Houston had promoted Hays to the rank of major and that two companies of rangers, under captains McCulloch and John T. Price, had been organized for service on the frontier. By 5 November Hays and McCulloch were on an expedition to the Rio Grande with the intention of reasserting the republic's lost sovereignty there.[4]

In December 1845 Ben was elected to represent Gonzales County in the house of representatives in the first legislature of the state of Texas, and when the congress was organized on 16 February 1846, he was appointed one of its three tellers and was named to the committee on the militia. His first votes were cast for his friends Sam Houston and Thomas Jefferson Rusk to the United States Senate. With two influential friends in high places, Henry speculated, Ben had "fair prospects of obtaining almost any appointment under the U.S. government which would suit him." Although his friend John Henry Brown characterized his contribution as that of "a silent, working member," McCulloch's principal concern while in the legislature was military reform, and he spent most of his time "attending to the getting a bill through congress for the protection of our frontier." Should the law pass, Henry surmised, Ben would probably remain in the Texas Rangers for at least another year.

The government, during the last years of the republic, had allowed the militia to dwindle and lapse until, on 21 April 1846, the legislature passed "an act to organize the Militia of the State of Texas," bringing the new state into conformity with national law. The militia act of 1846 divided Texas into five militia divisions, each commanded by a major general. Ben McCulloch was elected major general of the Fifth Division, the district west of the Colorado River, making him the fourth ranking officer in state service. Despite the new legislation and the threat of war, however, little was done to organize the militia beyond the election of officers.[5]

With annexation, the United States' relations with Mexico quickly deteriorated. Especially disputed was ownership of southern Texas between the Nueces River and the Rio Grande. To support the American claim, President Polk sent four thousand soldiers under Maj. Gen. Zachary Taylor to Corpus Christi in May 1845. After waiting seven months at Corpus Christi while American and Mexican diplomats negotiated unsuccessfully, Taylor moved his army south to the Rio Grande. Near the mouth of the river, opposite the city of Matamoros, the Americans constructed Fort Texas, soon to be renamed Fort Brown. Taylor's move was countered by a concentration of eight thousand Mexican troops at Matamoros under Brig. Gen. Mariano Arista. On the morning of 25 April 1846, Arista dispatched a force of cavalry across the Rio Grande that surrounded and captured a squadron of United States dragoons under Capt. Seth Barton Thornton. Several of Thornton's men were killed in the action, and Zachary Taylor reported to Washington that "hostilities may now be considered as commenced."

One of Taylor's most obvious needs as he moved beyond the Nueces River was for a unit of horsemen to serve as scouts. In ordering Taylor to advance on 12 January 1846, Secretary of War William L. Marcy had authorized him to call upon the Texans, "by whom legs were valued chiefly as a means of sticking to a horse," for "such auxiliary forces as he might require," and despite his well-known animosity toward militia units, Taylor soon called into Federal service three hundred Texas Rangers. On 26 April Hays received orders from Taylor to prepare his companies to join the United States Army on the Rio Grande. By 6 May the Houston *Telegraph and Texas Register* reported that "all the ranging companies on our western frontier . . . are on the march for the American camps." Hays's rangers, with the "company of volunteers from Gonzales under the command of Captain Ben McCulloch," will, the paper calculated, "probably amount to 500 efficient troops. The rangers are all well mounted and have long been wishing for a brush with the Mexicans."[6]

To Texans, the war between the United States and Mexico was but a new phase of the war for independence, leading the *Telegraph and Texas Register* to announce at the outbreak of hostilities that "the war is renewed." Texans' faith in the fighting ability of the state's citizen soldiery had not abated in the least in the ten years since the battle of San Jacinto. "We believe," wrote one editor, that "McCulloch with 200 rangers could cut through [the Mexicans'] ranks as easily as he would dash through a herd of deer."[7]

In common with frontier people everywhere, these rangers had little respect for formal authority. As one Mexican War veteran commented, "There was no discipline among them, and they wouldn't pay attention to any order or anything." "A more reckless, devil-may-care looking set, it would be impossible to find this side of the Infernal Regions," observed a dragoon of the regular United States army. "Take them altogether, with their uncouth costumes, bearded faces, lean and brawny forms, fierce wild eyes and swaggering manners, they were fit representatives of the outlaws which made up the population of the Lone Star State."[8]

Most professional military men were thoroughly perplexed by the rangers and had a difficult time finding a suitable place for them. "Them Texas troops are the damndest troops in the world," Zachary Taylor was quoted as saying; "we can't do without them in a fight, and we can't do anything with them out of a fight." The rangers, according to Col. Albert G. Brackett, a leading mid-nineteenth-century authority on the mounted army, "were good troops for reconnaissances and for scouting, but were not the best class for anything like regular movements." The case for, and against, the rangers was perhaps best summed up by Maj. Roswell S. Ripley of the Second United States Artillery. Writing of the volunteer cavalry regiments from the other states, he commented, "Variously equipped and mounted as they are upon entering the service, the experiment of making a respectable dragoon out of a volunteer must always necessarily fail." With regard to the Texas Rangers, however, he wrote, "One species of mounted force, peculiar to the western frontier of the United States is . . . efficient. The inhabitants of that frontier, from their vicinity to hostile Indians, are well practiced in partisan warfare, and although they will not easily submit to discipline, yet take the field in rough, uncouth habiliments, and, following some leader chosen for his talent and bravery, perform partisan duties in a manner hardly to be surpassed."[9]

Although lacking the formal discipline and regulation uniform of the regular soldiers, the rangers did not lack the essential needs of a frontier soldiery, namely excellent leadership, first-rate arms and equipment, and courage. The rangers were led by men who possessed a higher degree of the qualities they admired in others and found necessary in themselves: bravery, endurance, and a canny if untutored tactical sense in border warfare. Lt. Ethan Allen Hitchcock observed in his Mexico journal that all of the rangers were "well mounted and doubly well armed: each man has one or two Colt's revolvers besides ordinary pistols, a sword, and every man a rifle." George Wilkins Kendall noted that "every man had a horse under him that could 'run for your life,' and save it."[10]

McCulloch raised his company—considered the finest in Hays's regiment—in a mere thirty-six hours after the call for volunteers reached the Guadalupe valley, and he had it ready to ride by 11 May. Although the officers and men of McCulloch's command behaved in an orderly and well-mannered fashion, their appearance belied their stations in life and their levels of education. Upon first seeing his new comrades-in-arms, Samuel C. Reid, Jr., wondered at these men "with long beards and moustaches, dressed in every variety of garment . . . and a belt of pistols around their waists. . . . A rougher looking set of men we never saw." Despite their "ferocious and outlaw look," the company boasted two future generals besides the commander, three to five doctors, at least two lawyers, and one newspaper editor.[11]

Although nominally Company A of Hays's First Texas Mounted Riflemen, McCulloch's command for the most part operated independently of Hays under the direct control of the commanding general. It was assigned the important and hazardous post of spy company, and McCulloch was named Taylor's chief of scouts, a position for which his "intimate acquaintance with the Mexican character and language admirably qualified him," according to a contemporary newspaper account.

Accustomed to only "light marching order," McCulloch's rangers quickly proceeded toward the rendezvous with Taylor's army on the Rio Grande. Unencumbered by wagon train or other baggage, they rode from Gonzales to Corpus Christi in only two days. A tale of how the incredulous rangers marveled as talk around the evening campfire turned to the amount of ammunition expended in the Napoleonic Wars—an estimated one hundred rounds for each casualty—illustrates their ability to march light and live off the land. One of McCulloch's rangers declared that he had only twenty bullets in his pouch, "and if I don't kill or cripple just twenty greasers, it will be because they are licked before I have had time to load and fire twenty times, or else because I have been 'sent under' early. I can't afford to pack lead, and tire down my horse, like they do in the old world."[12]

McCulloch's company reached San Patricio on 13 May and pushed on to Corpus Christi. From there it rode 130 miles down Padre Island, fording the five-mile-wide Laguna Madre on horseback and arriving at Point Isabel on 19 May. Passing over to the mainland and continuing toward Matamoros, the company camped near the battlefield of Palo Alto and at noon the next day passed that of Resaca de la Palma. Disappointed by their failure to arrive in time to take part in the first fighting of the war on 8 and 9 May, McCulloch's men were nevertheless gratified that Samuel H. Walker's company of rangers had acquitted itself well and had contributed materially to the twin American victories. The company arrived at Matamoros on 22 May to find most of Hays's regiment already there.[13]

There, too, the company was joined by the two men who were most responsible for making McCulloch's name a household word in the United States. The first person was America's first war correspondent, George Wilkins Kendall. One of the founders of the New Orleans *Daily Picayune*, Kendall had been a member of the ill-fated Texas expedition to Santa Fe in

1842, had been captured and imprisoned in Mexico, but had been released because he was a United States citizen. His account of the affair, *Narrative of the Texan Santa Fe Expedition*, became the standard history of that misadventure and one of the important books of the 1840s in arousing American interest in Texas. When the war began, Kendall rushed to the Rio Grande. Quickly learning that the only soldiers who had any chance for immediate action were the companies of rangers who rode frequently into the region below the Rio Grande on reconnaissance patrols, Kendall joined McCulloch's company as a self-proclaimed "high private." "Better mounted men or better armed men, or more resolute men than these Texan volunteers," he informed the country, "it would be hard to drum up, and they will give a good account of themselves."

The Mexican War was the first American conflict to arouse the interest of the general population and the first to which people were exposed on an almost daily basis. The nation's newspapers sparked and kept aflame this interest by bringing the campaigns in Mexico directly into thousands of American homes with unprecedented speed and detail, making United States army officers national heroes and in 1848 propelling Zachary Taylor into the White House. Because of the relative ease of communication between the seat of the war and New Orleans, that city became the focus of a huge news-gathering operation. The *Daily Picayune*, New Orleans's premier newspaper, became the nation's most widely syndicated, and Kendall became the most often quoted reporter in America. His dispatches to the *Picayune* made his name and that of Ben McCulloch nationally famous.[14]

The second person responsible for McCulloch's fame was Samuel C. Reid, Jr., the son of an American naval officer credited with regularizing the design of the flag of the United States. After brief careers as a seaman and a surveyor, the younger Reid was admitted to the bar in Mississippi in 1841 and established a practice in New Orleans in 1844. Elected adjutant of the Sixth Louisiana Infantry in 1846, Reid resigned his commission to join McCulloch, explaining to his parents that "this is a spy company and will see the most active service, & one consequently will have more fun." His wide-eyed account of the Monterrey campaign, *The Scouting Expeditions of McCulloch's Texas Rangers*, was to become a best-seller and helped to thrust McCulloch into national prominence.[15]

George Kendall admitted that while on the Rio Grande he thought often and fondly of "the Saint Charles and the Verandah and Hewlett's and other cool oases in New Orleans," and Pvt. J. D. Brown of McCulloch's company remembered the service as "sometimes arduous." McCulloch's men called their quarters at Matamoros "Camp Maggot." The camp was downstream from the army's slaughter pens, and the offal thrown into the river often failed to clear the banks and was infested with immense swarms of flies. The rangers used the river water for washing, drinking, and cooking, and on some days they had to wade fifty or more yards beyond the bank to avoid floating maggots. Even after their arrival on the Rio Grande the rangers were not supplied with tents, except once, when a ranger died of illness. The camp was so plagued by flies that two men were required to keep them away from the sick man. "Even then," says Brown, "his blankets were flyblown." After two or three weeks in this dreadful location the company was ordered back across the Rio Grande to Fort Brown, where it was freed from flies, enjoyed the nightly serenades of the regimental bands and the company of the pretty Mexican girls, and "fared sumptuously on roasting ears."[16]

McCulloch's company remained encamped opposite Matamoros until 12 June, when it was mustered into Federal service and received orders to harass the rear guard of Mexican general Mariano Arista's retreating columns as far as practicable and to explore the country as far as Linares, 165 miles to the southwest, checking the condition of the road and the availability of food, water, and forage along the way. "We were fourteen days on the scout," recalled Kendall, "and it poured showers all the time." One night, he complained, he was awakened by water pouring into his mouth when the rain "came down in a chunk, like a water spout." Nevertheless, Kendall informed his readers, "there was not a minute at any time when any man's pistol or rifle would have missed fire, or he would not have been up and ready for an attack."[17]

After slight skirmishes with one or two groups of Mexican irregular cavalry, the thirty-five rangers pushed over rough, barren country to within thirty miles of Linares before determining that the route "is almost impracticable for an army [with] large trains and heavy baggage wagons." Arista, McCulloch concluded, chose it because the Americans, drawn farther and farther from their base of supplies, would have the most difficult time following it in pursuit.[18]

Having accomplished his reconnaissance mission, McCulloch struck across the desert, hoping "to obtain a fight or a footrace" with the Mexican partisan general, Antonio Canales, who was said to command six hundred ranchero cavalry in the region and with whom many of the Texans wished to settle the score for Mier. The "Chaparral Fox" was not in his lair, however. McCulloch's men reached the Monterrey road on the afternoon of the twenty-second only to learn that Canales had been there about a week earlier, "but of his present whereabouts we could not gain the slightest clue." Not wishing to follow a cold trail, McCulloch turned back to Fort Brown, where his company, looking to Kendall like "the rear guard of Peter the Hermit's crusading host," rested from 26 through 30 June and then pressed on to Reynosa, a town the rangers considered "the most rascally place in all Mexico." There they celebrated the Fourth of July at "Camp Nasty," consuming two horse buckets of whiskey and eating a feast of pigs and chickens "accidentally killed while firing in honor of the day."[19]

McCulloch's report of his company's scout convinced Taylor that "the direct land route from this point to Monterrey is much longer than the line from Camargo; in wet weather, impassable for artillery or heavy wagons, and in dry scantily supplied with water." Although it had been unable either to reach Linares or to catch Canales, for ten days McCulloch's command had operated with impunity in the triangle formed by Matamoros, Linares, and Reynosa. As important as the report itself was Taylor's discovery that when he needed knowledge of the enemy or the country, the rangers could bring it back, and on 16 July he announced McCulloch's promotion to major and his assignment to the commanding general's personal staff as quartermaster. As Kendall trumpeted to the world, "I have seen a goodly numbers [*sic*] of volunteers in my time, but Capt. Ben McCulloch's men are choice specimens."

Although pleased with the rangers' prowess as scouts, Taylor was much less happy with their discipline as soldiers. Taylor unquestionably esteemed McCulloch very highly, both personally and as a warrior and scout, and Walter P. Lane, a veteran of the Monterrey and Buena Vista campaigns, recalled having "often seen the two sitting by the campfire, late at night, talking to each other for hours." Nevertheless, Taylor lamented the rangers' behavior to Col. George T. Wood of the Second Texas Mounted Riflemen: "I fear they are a lawless set" and "too licentious to do much good."[20]

On 5 July the general sent his scouts out again, this time to reconnoiter the road up the Rio Grande as far as Camargo. The rangers were constantly on the alert for attack, rising shortly after midnight in order to travel during the cooler hours. They rested during the hot part of the day, sprawling under the sun. Kendall expressed wonder that anyone could ever sleep as they did, fully dressed, "belted round with two pistols and a Bowie, boots on and spurs to boot." "This thing of scouting in Mexico may be exciting enough, but is far from being agreeable any way it can be fixed," he informed his readers. "Not a sign of a tent do we take along, while shade and shelter are matters not pertaining to the country. You can form some idea of campaigning among the 'greasers' and then weep." However uncomfortable, this scout was able to report more positive results. The road to Camargo was passable, and food and water along the route were sufficient.[21]

Taylor fixed upon Camargo, at the head of navigation of the Rio Grande, as his base of operations against Monterrey, seventy-five miles south. Fearful of ambush from mounted partisans in the chaparral, Taylor ordered the Texans to screen the advance of his infantry from Reynosa to Camargo. McCulloch's mission as scout often rankled his command, and escort duty was worse. They had come to Mexico to fight, and the rare excursion against roving bands of Comanches did not satisfy that need. "Captain McCulloch was ordered not to fight," recalled one of his rangers, "but to survey various sections of the country and report. He was well known as a reckless fighter; but he knew how to obey orders, and he certainly did so. We begged him to give us a brush with the enemy, but he simply answered, 'orders.' "[22]

Perhaps his men did not realize that McCulloch, too, was chafing under the restraints imposed upon him by higher command and was begging his superiors to allow his men to slip the leash and come to grips with the enemy. Juan Seguín, now a colonel in the Mexican army and notorious among the Anglo-Texans as a supposed traitor, was reportedly nearby with a force of irregulars. From Camargo on 20 July McCulloch wrote plaintively to Taylor, "I am quartered in the town, and without your permission to move until my term of service will expire" on 18 August. McCulloch considered himself and his command to be "worthless." "If it would meet with your approval," he appealed to Taylor, "I would like very much to move in your direction," making a reconnaissance in force in the direction of Monterrey. He was convinced that Canales no longer posed a threat to Taylor's line of communication at Camargo, but he had been informed that "Seguin has forty men between this [place] and Monterrey; they are those cut throat fellows from San Antonio" whom McCulloch, in common with most Anglo-Texans, held responsible for murdering Capt. Nicholas M. Dawson and his men after they had surrendered near Salado Creek in September 1842 during the Adrian Woll campaign.[23]

Three days later McCulloch again wrote to army headquarters from Camargo, this time to Taylor's adjutant, Capt. William S. Bliss, requesting more active service. Ranger captain Richard A. Gillespie had just arrived from San Antonio with "forty well mounted men" eager for a scout, and McCulloch suggested that the new company take over his duties at Camargo, thus allowing McCulloch's men to search for Seguín. "I am extremely anxious to make one more trip into the country before my company is discharged," he wrote, "and wish you would be so kind as to mention this to the General." McCulloch reiterated his belief that his company was "of no use" where it was and "might explore the road toward Monterrey as far as the General wished, or we might visit some of those large Ranchos in the country and make impressions that would be favorable to our cause if the General will let us go."[24]

Still smarting, perhaps, from Taylor's rebuke regarding the company's behavior at Reynosa on the Fourth of July, where, Reid hinted, members of the company had assassinated one or more Mexican civilians, McCulloch pledged that Taylor's orders would be strictly observed. "Our orders were most strict not to molest any unarmed Mexican," Reid wrote. However, when certain citizens of Reynosa, identified by McCulloch's men as among those who had been responsible for the misuse of Texan prisoners after the battle of Mier or for cattle-thieving raids into Texas, "were found shot or hung up in the chaparral . . . the government was charitably bound to suppose that during some fit of remorse and desperation, tortured by conscience for the many evil deeds they had committed, they had recklessly laid violent hands upon their own lives! *¿Quién Sabe?*"[25]

The officers of the regular army took strong exception to the rangers' method of meting out justice. As Lt. William S. Henry of the Third United States Infantry observed, the behavior of the United States Army after its victories at Palo Alto and Resaca de la Palma was "as highly honorable as the victories themselves." At Matamoros, he was pleased to report, the army did not interfere "with either the civil or religious rights of the inhabitants" and had won the respect of the people, who were welcome in the American camps and sure of protection there. "Such conduct should make our country proud of their army," Henry maintained. One may surmise, therefore, that Taylor, for reasons both humanitarian and political, strongly disapproved of the Texans' behavior and told his chief of scouts so in no uncertain terms. "Were it possible to rouse the Mexican people to resistance," Taylor wrote later in the war, "no more effectual plan could be devised than the one pursued by our volunteer regiments." The commanding general did not have every volunteer regiment in mind but wrote specifically of "the companies of Texas horse." Of the infantry, Taylor had "little or no complaint; but the mounted men from Texas have scarcely made an expedition without unwarrantably killing a Mexican!"[26]

In response, perhaps, to a dressing down in this tone from the commander, McCulloch wrote to Bliss, "I know very little about how the people are disposed towards us off in the country, but presume they are under wrong impressions, as we have always found them [to be] upon first arriving among them." McCulloch's contention was that the average Mexican peon regarded the rangers first with suspicion and fear but later as liberators once the generosity and fairness of his men came to be known. Kendall illustrated an instance in which McCulloch's men responded to a call for help from a village beset by Comanche raiders. As the rangers approached, "the Mexicans who had remained concealed would crawl from their hiding places so soon as they were informed by the Captain that he had come to protect them." McCulloch did not conceal his contempt for the skulkers. "You d——n great big lazy greasers, why don't you turn out and whip these Indians?" he demanded. Nevertheless, McCulloch assured Bliss, only those who had committed crimes against Texas, such as the banditti, the guerrillas, and certain army officers who had harassed southern Texas for the past ten years, need fear the rangers' retribution.[27]

By most accounts, the rangers were loath to commit crimes against property. "The most of us had a little pocket change," recalled Reid, "and we drove a lively trade with the Mexicans for all the eatables they could bring to our camp. Our orders were most strict as regarded our intercourse with the Mexicans, and we were enjoined to take nothing without giving an adequate compensation." In most cases, Reid believed, the Mexican farmer got the better end of the bargain. Kendall noted that villagers offered eggs, which had sold locally at eighteen for twelve and a half cents, to the North Americans at a picayune each, and watermelons, "not larger than your two fists" and for which there was no local market, at two for a quarter. The rangers seem to have viewed the murder of Mexican citizens of a certain stripe, however, as just retribution for the Alamo, Goliad, the Dawson Massacre, and the decimation of the Mier prisoners. "The law of retaliation in war," wrote Thomas Jefferson Green on the eve of the war with Mexico, "the most salutary of all laws in preventing the excesses of an enemy—as yet has never been resorted to by the Texians; that law which should have been inflicted upon Santa Anna, and each and every one of his men at San Jacinto for his recent murder of Colonel Fannin and his four hundred, was permitted to sleep." Those scores the Texans now began to repay.[28]

Most eagerly sought was the man Ben McCulloch's brother once compared to Benedict Arnold and Judas Iscariot. "Seguin passed up the River San Juan a few days before we arrived here," McCulloch continued in his letter to Bliss, "and might have been overtaken. He had forty thieves and murderers from about San Antonio, to kill which would be doing God a service. It would be ridding the world of those that are not fit to live in it. They will never come to terms, because they would be condemned by the Civil Laws and executed. Accordingly, they must do the frontier of Texas no little harm by robbing and stealing from its citizens. Any orders the General may give will be thankfully received and obeyed to the letter."[29]

Perhaps in response to McCulloch's pleas for action, Brig. Gen. William Jenkins Worth, commander of one of Taylor's three divisions, ordered McCulloch's company back into the interior of Mexico to report on the condition of the roads and to eliminate Seguín if he could be found. On the morning of 3 August, to the "great joy" of the company, McCulloch's men set out for China, "not the great and celestial empire, with its Bangs and Whangs, its Tings and Lings," wrote Kendall, "but the little pueblo or town in Mexico." This village, sixty miles to the southwest, was thought to be the partisans' headquarters, and after two days of forced marching, the rangers arrived at midnight within a quarter of a mile of China. Here they camped for the night, expecting to surprise Seguín before dawn. Seguín had decamped on the previous day, however, and the rangers had to content themselves with the capture of only four of his men. Although the Texans pursued the retreating rancheros for some distance, the Mexican irregulars were soon lost in the hills and chaparral. The rangers spent the afternoon of the fifth in China, resting and enjoying the hospitality of the town. The next morning, after leaving a challenge to the partisan chief with the village alcalde, they began their ride back to Camargo. Not only had they been unable to force a fight with the rancheros, but, as McCulloch reported to Worth, Taylor's army would have to find another route to Monterrey. The road to China was impassable for artillery because of its "narrow passages and deep ravines," and the crossing of the San Juan River, about two miles above the village, was flawed by high and precipitous banks.[30]

Checked by the poor condition of the China route, on 12 August Taylor ordered McCulloch's rangers to reconnoiter an alternate course as far as Cerralvo, sixty miles through enemy territory. On the first night of the scout, Kendall reported, the rangers discovered a Mexican irregular, mounted on an American horse, near their camp. McCulloch ordered him to halt and then gave chase when the ranchero "broke through the chaparral and made a good race for his life; but McCulloch was too fast for him."

That afternoon a report reached Taylor's headquarters that McCulloch and his company had been captured by a band of rancheros. This piece of intelligence proved as groundless as a half-hundred others circulating about the war and the activities of Mexican partisans. "Rumors are as thick as blackberries, many not entitled to much credit," reported the Clarksville *Northern Standard.* McCulloch fell ill on the following day, however, and had to be escorted back to Mier while his column completed its scout. The rangers returned on the sixteenth to find their captain "nearly recovered from his illness" and to report favorably on the road to Cerralvo.

Worth's division marched for Cerralvo on 20 August with McCulloch's company again serving as vanguard, combing the chaparral for possible ambush. Pleased, no doubt, to be back in action, McCulloch's company was received back into Federal service at Camargo. The First Texas Mounted Riflemen, composed of three-month volunteers, had completed its term of enlistment on 30 August, but, according to James B. (Buck) Barry, a private in Hays's regiment, "some of us had traveled six hundred miles to kill a Mexican and refused to accept a discharge until we got to Monterrey where a fight was awaiting our arrival." Although the men complained that south of Camargo there was "scarcely a tree to be seen larger than a cherry" and that the rocky and sandy soil "produces spontaneously little else than burrs, briers, thorns, and all variety of cactus," they were nevertheless pleased to be heading toward Monterrey and a showdown with the elusive enemy.[31]

On 4 September McCulloch and Gillespie were ordered to prepare for another scout. The army was concentrated at Cerralvo and anxious for a description of the next leg of its route. By 4:00 P.M. the two companies were in the saddle, prepared to escort Lt. George Gordon Meade of the topographical engineers on a reconnaissance of the route to Monterrey. That night the column rode over the Cerralvo Mountains and arrived unexpectedly at the camp of Antonio Canales's 750 or 800 Mexican cavalry at Papagáyo.[32]

Not strong enough to dislodge the Mexicans, the rangers returned to the army on the fifth, having explored only thirty miles. Assured of his route that far, Taylor marched on 12 September. In the vanguard were his sappers, to repair the road, with McCulloch's company and a squadron of dragoons to protect them as they worked. The Texans' old adversary, Maj. Gen. Pedro Ampudia, now in command of the forces on Taylor's front, ordered one thousand cavalry under Brig. Gen. Anistasio Torrejón to harass the advancing American column. With a detachment of only fifteen men, McCulloch scouted well in advance of the pioneer company, skirmishing with

Mexican cavalry along the road and pushing as far west as Ramos, which he took from the enemy's scouts but gave up again when Torrejón arrived with two hundred troopers. After an exchange of volleys, the Texans set an ambush in the chaparral to draw a Mexican charge, but Torrejón withdrew. Reid considered this reconnaissance, the opening of the fall campaign, a great victory, declaring that "our little force of only forty men, and with only fifteen in the advance . . . chased and routed, for six miles, two hundred of the enemy!"[33]

Early on the morning of 15 September General Taylor dispatched McCulloch to scout closer to Monterrey, two days' march ahead of the main American column. On reaching a hill overlooking Marin, midway between Cerralvo and Monterrey, the rangers came in sight of a large body of the enemy's cavalry, drawn up in the streets eight hundred or a thousand yards distant and, according to Kendall, "evidently much flurried by our appearance." Their bright scarlet uniforms identified this force as Mexican regulars, and having only twenty-five men, McCulloch ordered a halt. The plaza was concealed by the church and adjoining buildings, making it impossible to tell whether infantry and artillery were in the town as well. The place offered every opportunity for concealing a force of thousands, however, and as McCulloch "was not so particularly certain that the Mexicans might not send an 18 pound shot . . . up our way on a flying visit," he ordered his men to deploy in an open formation along the brow of the hill, extend their flanks to prevent a surprise turning movement, and settle in to await developments. For an hour the rangers watched the movements of the cavalry in the town but were unable to interpret their intentions. "Horsemen," wrote Kendall, "were plainly seen dashing and cavorting about, while men on foot were jumping to get out of the way." Several of the poorer citizens of the town were either captured in the chaparral or simply came into the American lines to talk to the rangers. Torrejón, they said, had driven them from their homes, which he threatened to burn before allowing them to fall into American hands. "They pointed out their *jacales* and *casas* to us and implored our assistance in saving them! Singular war," remarked Kendall, "and more singular the people." In about an hour the Mexican cavalry moved off in good order, taking the road to Pescaria Chica, a small rancho east of the main road to Monterrey.[34]

Fearing an attack on his trains if the enemy horse were allowed to remain on his flank and rear, Taylor, once he had joined the spy company at Marin, ordered McCulloch's and Gillespie's rangers and Lt. Col. Charles A. May's dragoons to "make a dashing march in that direction and if possible

"Zachary Taylor at Walnut Springs" by William Garl Smith, Jr. Also portrayed in this painting are Braxton Bragg (standing bareheaded, sixth from left) and William Wallace Smith Bliss (standing to the general's left). (National Portrait Gallery, Smithsonian Institution)

disperse the party." They reached Pescaria Chica that afternoon, but Torrejón was gone. This was the last attempt of the Americans to draw the Mexican cavalry into a fight on the road to Monterrey, for that afternoon Torrejón and his men entered the fortifications of the city. With Torrejón out of harm's way, the rangers and dragoons proceeded up the Agua Fria River to San Francisco, an eastern suburb of Monterrey, where they found Taylor's army already encamped for the night.[35]

Monterrey was a city of nearly fifteen thousand inhabitants, situated on the main highway to central Mexico and guarding the strategic Rinconada Pass. Recognizing the vital importance of the city to the defense of the Mexican interior, General Ampudia concentrated all available forces there and fortified the already naturally strong position until he and many of his American adversaries considered it impregnable. Located in the foothills of the Sierra Madre range and on the northern bank of the swiftly flowing

Santa Catarina River, the city's eastern front was protected by three strong fortifications: the Citadel, the Tannery, and the Devil's Fort. To the west, the rear of the town was protected by a series of hills that made attack from that direction most unlikely. From this direction the vital road from Rinconada Pass, Saltillo, and San Luis Potosi entered the city between two commanding heights: Federation Hill on the southern side of the river and Independence Hill on the north. On the former, the defenders had constructed a stone fort known as El Soldado, and on the latter the crumbling ruin of the Bishop's Palace was as strong as the works devised by the military engineers. Earthen outer works and batteries of artillery supported both of these positions.

Despite these formidable obstructions, Taylor prepared his army for an assault on the city. McCulloch's Texans spent the afternoon of the nineteenth escorting engineer officers on their reconnaissance of the city's defenses and playing a daring game of "dodge the ball" with the garrison's gunners. To the horror of other United States troops, the rangers were "scouring over the plain," intentionally drawing the fire of the Mexican artillery. For sport they would gauge the trajectory of each cannonball and race their horses at the last minute from its path. The Mexicans might as well have attempted "to bring down skimming swallows as those racing dare-devils," wrote an awed officer of Ohio volunteers. Following the officers' report, and against all conventional military wisdom, Taylor divided his force in the face of a larger enemy and dispatched William Jenkins Worth and his division around the city to sever the Saltillo road and provide the anvil against which Taylor's two remaining divisions would hammer the city's defenders. In fact, it was to be Worth's men who would be the hammer.[36]

The Texas brigade was divided for scout duty, with former governor J. Pinckney Henderson's regiment remaining with Taylor while Hays's regiment accompanied Worth to the rear of the city. About noon on 20 September, with McCulloch's and Gillespie's companies in the vanguard, Worth's column feinted toward the city but soon struck off to the right, through the chaparral and corn fields, cutting first the Monclova and then the Pescaria Grande roads from the north. Late in the afternoon the Second Division turned south at the foot of the mountains beyond the city toward the Saltillo road, but a combination of fire from dismounted cavalry and artillery on Independence Hill, nightfall, and heavy rain caused Worth to order his men back to a group of jacales to bivouac for the night.[37]

The Texans had marched without blankets or supplies, and when they

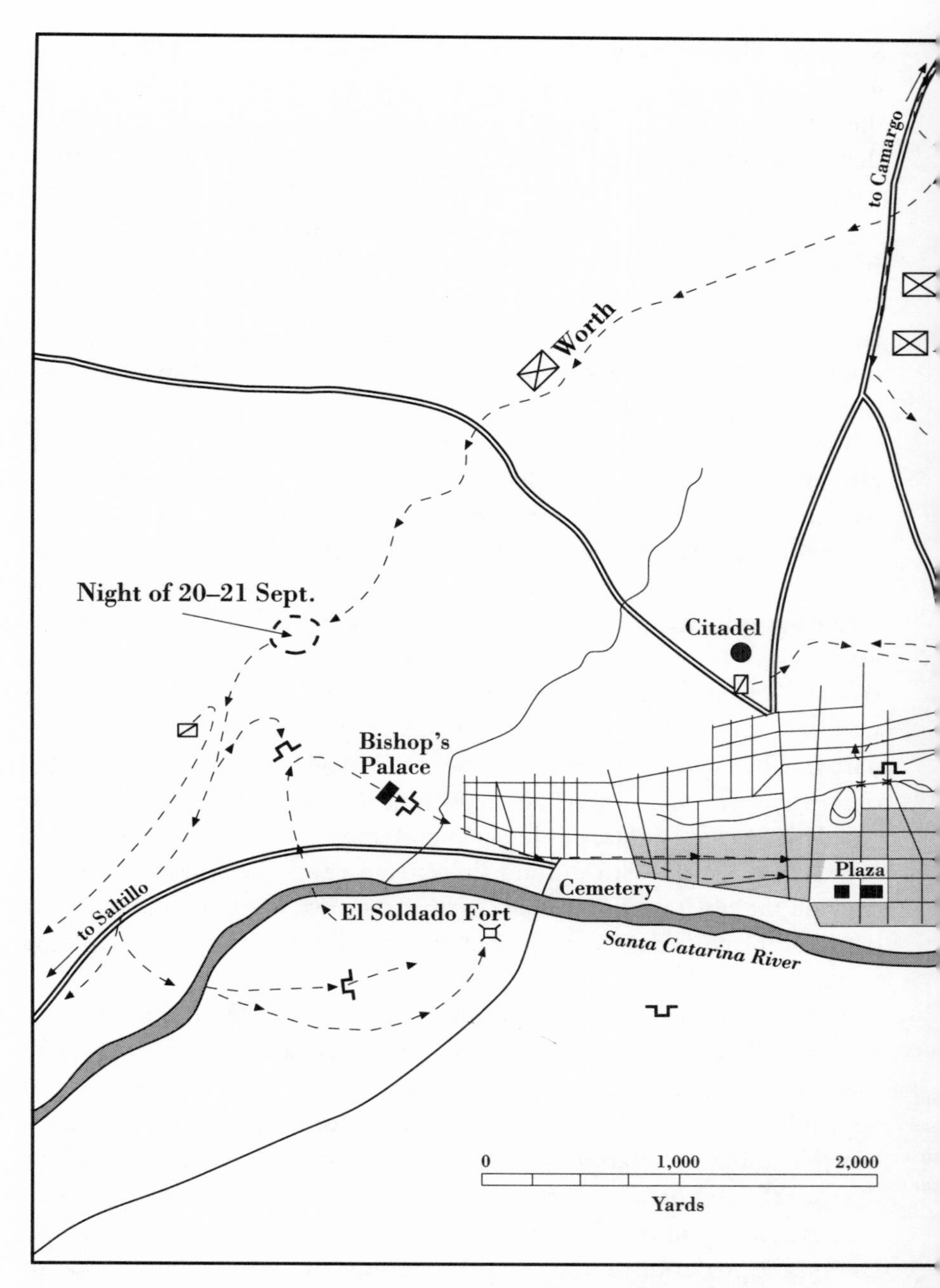

MAP 4. *Battle of Monterrey (adapted from Vincent J. Esposito,* West Point Atlas of American Wars *[New York: Frederick A. Praeger, 1959]; copyright © 1959, 1962 by Frederick A. Praeger, Inc. Reprinted by permission of Henry Holt and Co., Inc.)*

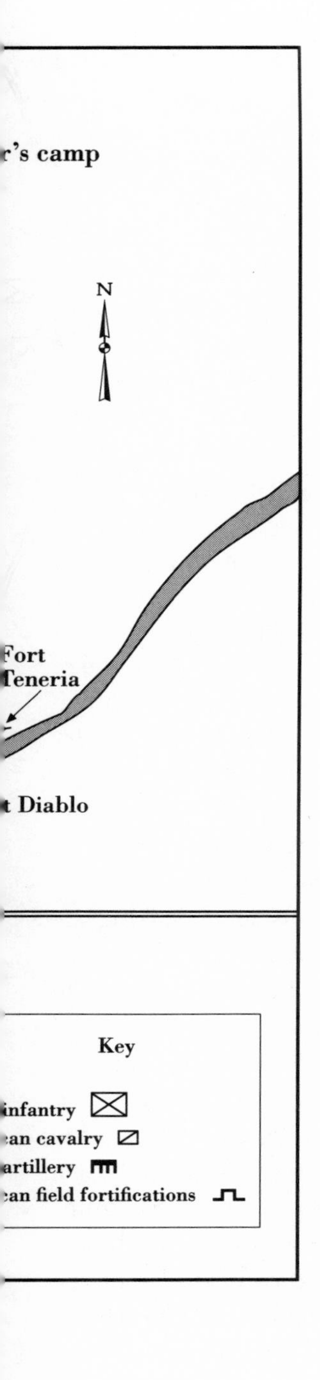

's camp
N
Fort
Teneria
Diablo
Key
infantry
an cavalry
artillery
an field fortifications

rode into a small farmyard, they immediately began to scramble for chickens, pigs, and *cabrito*. Hardly had they started their evening fires, however, when a sharp fire was opened on them from three or four hundred Mexican cavalrymen who had trailed the Texans and occupied a nearby hill. Capt. Christopher B. Acklin's company was sent into the chaparral as skirmishers while McCulloch's and Gillespie's men, behind the cover of a fence, awaited attack. Although the Mexicans eventually withdrew, the Texans were annoyed that they were not permitted to barbecue the meat they had foraged. During the subsequent five days of fighting in and around Monterrey, the ranger regiment lived almost exclusively on raw green corn. "We were too busily engaged in the day time to cook it," said Buck Barry, "and if we had built up a fire at night, a bombshell would have paid us a visit. It seemed," however, "that we did as well on raw green corn as if we had beefsteak and flour bread."[38]

At dawn, under a continuous but ineffective fire from the guns on Independence Hill, Worth's division set out once again to interdict the Saltillo road. When they had advanced a mile and a half, a turn in the road brought McCulloch's men face to face with an estimated fifteen hundred of the enemy deployed near the Hacienda San Geronimo. Lancers were drawn up across their route, while the road to the city swarmed with more cavalry and foot soldiers. Worth quickly deployed his division with Hays's regiment on the right. The enemy line moved forward, supported by the artillery on Independence Hill. Suddenly the *adelante* was heard from the Mexican line, and a squadron of lancers swept down upon the American right. "Each man had a Mexican flag waving from his lance, making the most beautiful spectacle of mounted men I ever expect to see," recalled Buck Barry. "Although everything was silent, these little flags told us in plain language they were after our blood." Hays ordered his regiment to move to the shelter of a fence and dismount. McCulloch's company, deployed in the chaparral at the extreme right of Worth's line, failed to receive the order to dismount and so, according to Worth, "received the heavy charge of cavalry" in the saddle "with their unerring rifles and usual gallantry." As the distance between the two bodies of mounted men diminished, the rangers fired a volley, "pouring in a perfect storm of lead from their rifles, double-barreled guns and pistols." The commander of the lancers, Lt. Col. Juan Najera, "a tall, splendid-looking fellow, with a fierce mustache and beautiful teeth," fell at the front of his men. The charge was broken midway. "The lancers tumbled from their saddles by dozens; yet with uncommon daring the survivors dashed onward, engaging, hand to hand, with the rangers still mounted." The Texans used their Colt revolvers and bowie knives with murderous effect.[39]

After experiencing appalling casualties, the Mexican cavalry retreated in disorder, carrying with them McCulloch and a portion of his men who had fought their way nearly to the enemy's center. Seeing their peril, the rangers began to fight their way back. Observers later characterized this as the hardest part of the fight. McCulloch, in a desperate effort to rejoin his company, put spurs to Tom, his sorrel war-horse, and "running everything down in his way," miraculously escaped unharmed. Although the engagement lasted only fifteen minutes, of the 180 men who made the charge, no fewer than 40 died, and nearly 100 were wounded. Only one Texan was killed, although several of McCulloch's men suffered lance wounds. Fire and shock—if not numbers—had favored the rangers. The heavier horses ridden by the Americans gave them a decided advantage over the Mexicans, who were mounted on mustangs. The rifles of the Texans emptied many saddles long before the lances could be brought to bear, and in cavalry melee no arm could match the Colt revolver, then the exclusive property of the rangers. Mexican bravery on this field was nevertheless superb, and the Texans considered it the best fight offered by the enemy during the war. Even the rabidly anti-Mexican Clarksville *Northern Standard* reported that the lancers fought "with a fierce desperation almost unparalleled amongst the Mexicans." "I have never called a Mexican a coward since," wrote Barry.[40]

As the remaining lancers were attempting to regain the safety of their lines, Capt. Charles F. Smith's light infantry dashed up, and a fieldpiece from Capt. James Duncan's battery unlimbered. Fire from these reinforcements sent the entire Mexican column, already demoralized by the slaughter of one of their finest cavalry units, reeling toward the defenses of Monterrey. The Saltillo road, Monterrey's last link with the rest of Mexico, was now in American hands.

The next morning, having gained this foothold on the Mexican rear, Worth sent his division toward the city. The advance was covered by about fifty Texas rangers acting as skirmishers. When artillery on Federation Hill, south of the Santa Catarina River, raked his right flank, however, Worth diverted the attack to take the battery. Federation Hill was nearly a thousand feet high and virtually perpendicular, defended by artillery and five hundred infantry and crowned by El Soldado, an imposing Mexican fort. At noon Worth gave the word: "Men, you are to take that hill—and I know you will do it." Under the command of Col. Persifor F. Smith, the assault force of two hundred rangers and four hundred regulars began its advance through a cornfield under the cover of rain and fog. As the Americans crossed the Santa Catarina River, hip deep and swift enough to wash a few men off their feet, the guns on the heights commenced a plunging fire. At the foot of the hill the attacking column came under fire from Mexican musketry. As Worth's men scaled the mountain, cut by hills, hollows, rocks, and brush, they "could not keep up any system," Barry recalled, and "every man had to assume the right to be his own commanding officer." Nevertheless the assault "was handsomely done," according to Lieutenant Meade. So quickly was the summit taken that the defenders were not able to save their artillery.[41]

"Without orders or system," said Barry, the rangers bore down upon El Soldado, some three or four hundred yards away, "well knowing that we had to take it or lose all the ground we had taken." When the Americans came under fire from the Mexican fort, a scratch force of gunners turned a captured fieldpiece and, on the first shot, disabled the enemy's last gun. The combined weight of the attackers' infantry and artillery quickly sent the defenders fleeing back into Monterrey. The storming of the heights lasted about one hour and thirty minutes. Mexican losses were severe, while Worth's men suffered only some eighteen wounded, two fatally. "When the advantageous positions which the enemy occupied and the difficulties which had to be surmounted on our part are taken into consideration," wrote Reid, "the small loss seems almost incredible."

At 3:00 P.M. the rangers were pulled out of the line and allowed to recross the Santa Catarina to care for their horses. They camped for the night two and a half miles from town on the Saltillo road, near the point of the morning's action. The remainder of the day was spent by the engineer officers reconnoitering, "a duty, I assure you," recalled Meade, who was later to gain fame as the Union commander at Gettysburg, "sufficiently hazardous."[42]

In the fighting of 21 September the American army, spearheaded by Hays's ranger regiment and most notably by McCulloch's company, had interdicted the Saltillo road and had seized the important works on Federation Hill, two of the most important objectives of the battle. Despite this strong foothold on the enemy's rear, however, the main objective remained to be taken. The formidable Independence Hill, dominated by the Bishop's Palace, loomed large beyond the Santa Catarina, commanding the final approach to Monterrey. At 3:00 A.M. on the twenty-second a storming party of some five hundred regulars and Texans was roused from its fitful sleep. Independence Hill, which Reid judged to be "between seven and eight hundred feet in height" and an "almost perpendicular ascent," was heavily defended by well-entrenched infantry and artillery, and the men who were ordered to take it held but a forlorn hope of either succeeding or surviving. The regulars, rangers, and other volunteers moved forward with great élan, however, and by daylight were at the summit, driving the enemy from their outer works and into the Bishop's Palace or Black Fort, as some of the rangers called it. From that stronghold, the Mexicans kept up an incessant but largely ineffectual fire of musketry. When the United States forces turned the guns of the captured battery on the Bishop's Palace, the Mexicans counterattacked in a desperate attempt to retake their lost artillery.

"In this they were defeated," Meade reported, "and on retiring, were so vigorously pursued by our people that they continued beyond the Bishop's Palace, leaving this work, with four pieces of artillery, in our hands, and they retired into the town." In his report on the storming of the hill and the capture of the palace, General Worth specifically cited Ben McCulloch for "distinguished bravery" and as one to whom his "thanks are especially due." United States infantry spent the night in the Bishop's Palace, but, as they had the night before, the rangers returned to their horses on the Saltillo road.[43]

On the morning of the twenty-third, McCulloch's company was again assigned to escort duty, accompanying Meade on a reconnaissance of the western approaches to the main plaza. They learned that the enemy had abandoned the city as far as the cemetery. They spent the middle part of the day with two other companies of Hays's regiment, guarding the pass on the Saltillo road west of Monterrey. From that direction, rumor held, reinforcements were racing to succor the beleaguered Ampudia. While McCulloch's rangers were pulled from the fighting to watch for enemy reinforcement that never came, their comrades continued to push the Mexicans back toward the center of the city. By noon Worth had occupied the plaza of La Purissima, from which he increased pressure on the already compacted garrison. The Mexican army still occupied the main plaza and some two squares around it in each direction that they had turned into a veritable fortress and defended with savage tenacity. Every street had been cut by a deep ditch behind which rose a solid masonry wall, each with its own embrasure from which artillery raked the approaches. Every house was garrisoned with infantry, and, as each had a flat cement roof above which loopholed stone walls extended three to four feet on all sides, every house

Assault on the Bishop's Palace, Monterrey. This is one of a series of primitive but colorful and detailed watercolors in which Dragoon Samuel E. Chamberlain portrayed the fighting at Monterrey. Note the Texas Ranger in the lower left corner.
(San Jacinto Museum of History Association)

became a fortress. Only the width of a street, and often only the width of a wall, separated the contestants. "Had we attempted to advance up the streets," said Meade, "all would have been cut to pieces; but we were more skillfully directed." With "every street a plain road to death," the Texans advanced toward the plaza by the same tactic they had employed in the capture of Bexar in 1835 and Mier in 1842: by breaking holes in the adobe walls of the houses and fighting room to room. As soon as the rangers had punched a hole through the wall, the Mexicans would begin firing through it. "It was nothing strange for the muzzles of the Texans' and Mexicans' guns to clash together," recalled Barry, "both intending to shoot through the hole at the same time." By nightfall this nightmare battle had reached to within one square of the plaza and seemed to guarantee a fight to the finish the next day.[44]

At daylight on the twenty-fourth McCulloch's company, now relieved of picket duty, dashed into the city on their horses. As the rangers approached the center of the city, admitted one of the citizens, "my heart almost failed me," for "the Texians, with their coarse hickory shirts and trowsers confined by a leather strap to their hips, their slouched hats, and their sweat and powder-begrimed faces, certainly presented a most brigandish appearance!" McCulloch's men galloped up the streets, "yelling like Indians and discharging their rifles at the Mexicans on the house-tops, a few of whom still continued to fire upon them as they passed along the street." As Col. Jefferson Davis of the Mississippi Rifles observed, however, "This was no place, sir, for the charge of horsemen."

Joining their comrades on the rooftops, McCulloch's men felt that the enemy was now in their grasp, to be dispatched at leisure. The old score of Mier was at last to be settled. Much to the Texans' displeasure, however, an hour-and-a-half truce, negotiated by colonels Jefferson Davis and Albert Sidney Johnston, was declared. Both armies used the time to improve their positions, fully confident that the fighting would soon be renewed. The Texans were at work with axes and bowie knives, picking holes through the parapet walls so that they could fire from a prone position, while the Mexicans were busy piling sandbags across streets and doors. At noon, however, the cease-fire was extended, and at 5:00 P.M. an armistice was announced. The city with all its public property was to be surrendered to the Americans, but Ampudia's army was to be allowed safe conduct beyond Rinconada Pass. "The Texians," says Reid, "were maddened with disappointment." "Old Rough and Ready," the rangers believed, had "committed a great blunder, with no justifiable excuse." As Big Foot Wallace had once observed, "Whenever [the Mexicans] hoisted the white flag and succeeded in persuading the Americans to 'parley,' they invariably got the better of them in one way or other." One of the general's guards remembered that for days afterward "Ben McCulloch's Texan Rangers were still loud in their expressions of indignation, threats were made against General Taylor, and the old hero deem'd it necessary to double the Dragoon guard around his

Rangers galloping through the streets of Monterrey, as depicted by Chamberlain. Chamberlain identified these four riders as "Cap. Baylee," presumably Samuel L. S. Ballowe, captain of Company D; "Mustang Grey," the redoubtable Mabry B. Gray; Col. John C. Hays; and "Old Reid," perhaps Samuel C. Reid, author of *The Scouting Expeditions of McCulloch's Texas Rangers.* (San Jacinto Museum of History Association)

Headquarters." Ampudia requested and was granted an escort of regular United States Army officers to protect him from the Texans.[45]

Yet, in his congratulatory order to his army for their victory at Monterrey, Taylor was effusive in his praise of the rangers, "assured that every individual in the command unites with him in admiration of the distinguished gallantry and conduct of Colonel Hays and his noble band of Texian volunteers—hereafter they and we are brothers, and we can desire no better guarantee of success than by their association." Worth, as well, attributed the American victory to the rangers, telling Hays, "It was the untiring vigilance, bravery, and unerring shots of your regiment that saved my division from defeat." So complete was the American success that no probability of another fight existed for months. Most of the ranger brigade, therefore, were content to go home. On 30 September the Texans were mustered out of the service, and the two regiments disbanded. McCulloch requested and received furlough, leaving the army sometime after 2 October, with the understanding that if hostilities were renewed, he would recruit a new spy company and return.

Taylor breathed a sigh of relief as the last of the rangers rode out of his camp. "With their departure we may look for a restoration of quiet and

U.S. soldiers observe the evacuation of Monterrey by Pedro Ampudia's troops. The disgust of regulars and rangers alike is evident in Chamberlain's painting on the faces of the two Americans observing the scene from a building overlooking the main plaza.
(San Jacinto Museum of History Association)

good order in Monterrey," he wrote to the adjutant general, "for I regret to report that some disgraceful atrocities have been perpetrated by them." A soldier of the regular United States army summed up the rangers' role and character perhaps best of all. "Gifted with the intelligence and courage of backwoods hunters, well mounted, and skilled in arms," wrote Luther Giddings, "they were excellent light troops." They returned to their "blood-bought state," however, with not only the good wishes of their former comrades but the hope "that all honest Mexicans were at a safe distance from their path."[46]

The legend of Ben McCulloch was now firmly fixed. George Wilkins Kendall's lavish coverage of his role in the Monterrey campaign, published in the New Orleans *Daily Picayune* and syndicated throughout the world, established McCulloch's reputation as a *beau sabreuer*. In 1847 Samuel C.

Reid, in his vastly popular account of his adventures with the spy company, intended to "give to the reader the continuation of the exploits of this daring partisan." *The Scouting Expeditions of McCulloch's Texas Rangers*, based on Reid's field diary, was reprinted four times before the Civil War and further buttressed McCulloch's romantic image, offering to a public avid for tales of American heroism and derring-do lively accounts of McCulloch's scouts, forays, skirmishes, and sprees. It also became the basis for chapters on McCulloch in the equally popular *General Taylor and His Staff*, published in 1848, *Pictorial History of Mexico and the Mexican War*, published in 1849, and *The Mexican War and Its Heroes*, published in 1857 and attributing to Taylor's chief of scouts "the intrepidity of a knight of chivalry."[47]

FIVE

In This Way We Did the Country Some Service

On 30 November 1846 McCulloch wrote to his mother from Galveston, "I hope this war will not last long as I am compelled to go again." Finding the terms of Taylor's armistice too liberal, the Polk administration had abrogated the agreement on 2 November 1846, and the army at Monterrey had begun preparing for further offensive operations. Although he had received instructions from the government not to attempt to hold territory beyond Monterrey, Taylor had marched through Rinconada Pass and on 16 November had occupied the strategic city of Saltillo. McCulloch was induced to return to the army, he told his mother, not so much by "the love alone for a soldier's life" but by a sense of duty. "My hand is at the plough, and I will not look back." Especially strong was the memory of his father, who had died the previous August. To leave the army in the midst of a war would be to disgrace his father's memory.[1]

By the winter of 1846, however, ardor for the war had waned even in

Texas, and McCulloch had difficulty filling his new company. Not only were fewer recruits willing to fight in Mexico, but those who did come to the colors were generally younger and less well educated than the men of his first company. Nevertheless, although in ill health, McCulloch raised twenty-seven men and by 31 January 1847 was back in Monterrey. Finding that the army had already moved south, he pushed on to Saltillo, arriving on 4 February. As they had paid their own expenses, the men requested that McCulloch offer Taylor their services for six months as regularly enlisted soldiers, or they would serve for food for themselves and their horses only until the prospect of a fight was over. Taylor at first replied that he could only receive the company for the duration of the war. The rangers held out, however, knowing, as McCulloch recounted, "that the General was in a tight place and the services very hazardous in as much as all the reconnoitering detachments sent out had been captured by the enemy." In a day or two, Major Bliss rode into town with the welcome news that the company would be mustered in for six months.[2]

Saltillo in 1847 boasted two cathedrals, a convent, four plazas, and hundreds of flat-roofed stone and adobe houses. The church and plaza of Santiago, wrote one of McCulloch's men, "are truly magnificent, covering a whole square." The town clock, the chimes, the column-supported arches, the groves of trees, and the fountains, "spouting forth the sparkling liquid into the basin below," charmed the weary and unsophisticated young rangers. After spending two weeks in this enchanting setting, recruiting their horses on government grain, McCulloch's company pushed on to Agua Nueva, where Taylor's army had occupied a forward position. "It is quite cold in this elevated situation, and we have suffered exceedingly," wrote one of the rangers of their new duty station. The view, however, was "truly romantic," presenting "some of the finest prospects" that the Texas boys had ever seen. Especially picturesque were the "extended plain, dotted with white tents, and the huge mountain piles," which, wrote Benjamin F. Scribner, "excite the loftiest sentiments."

The Texans did not long suffer the cold or enjoy the scenery. With almost all of northeastern Mexico in American hands and the Mexican government still disinclined to consider terms on which to end the war, the Polk administration decided to invade central Mexico by sea and march directly on Mexico City. In order to supply troops for this purpose, Taylor's command was stripped of many of its veteran regiments and was reduced to a dangerously low level of manpower. Taylor was ordered to stand on the defensive at Monterrey, but, believing that any potential adversary in

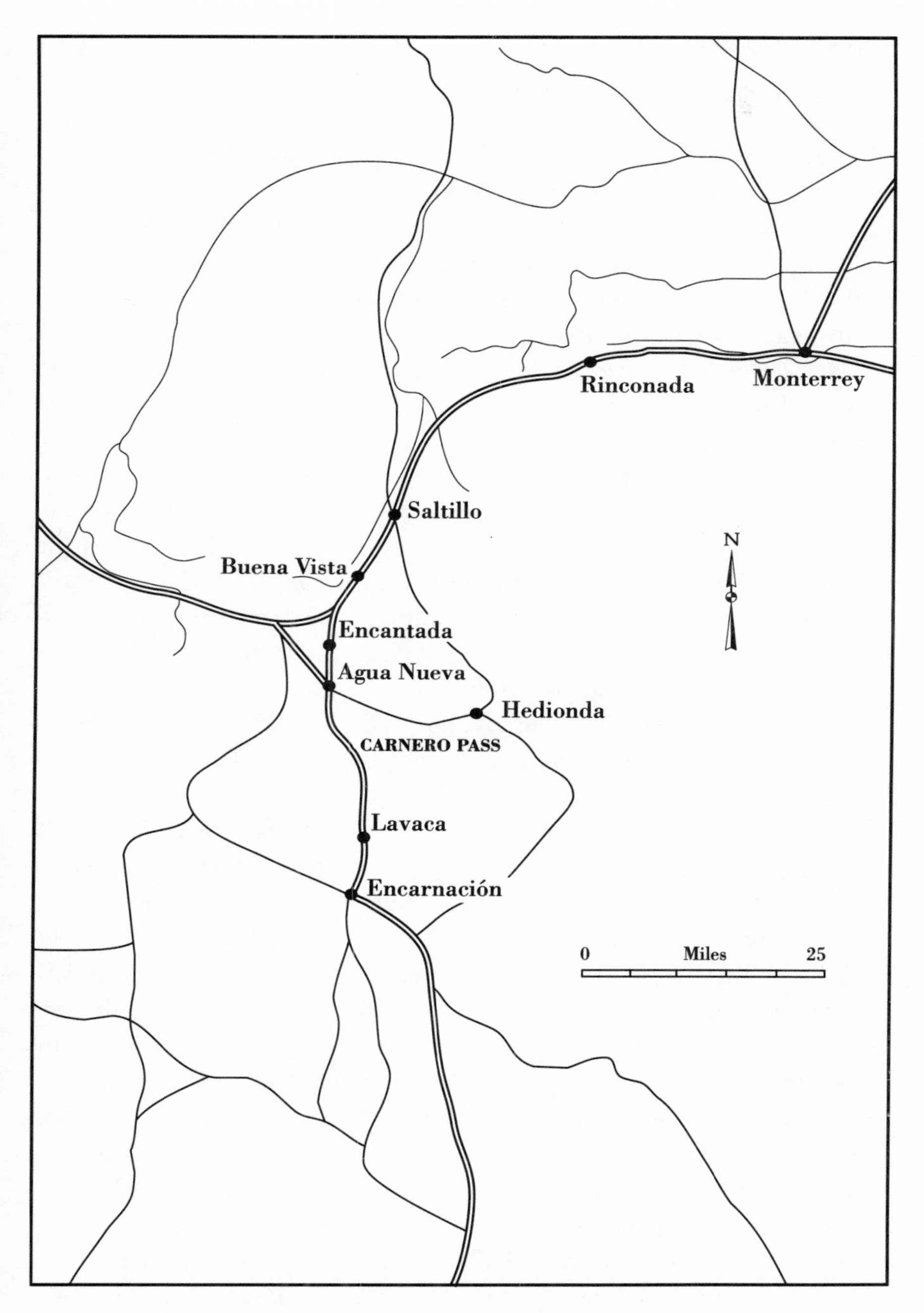

MAP 5. *Buena Vista Vicinity*

northern Mexico had been withdrawn to check the new invasion threat, he had extended his line twenty miles beyond Saltillo to Agua Nueva.[3]

Justifiably nervous in this militarily and politically indefensible situation, Taylor ordered McCulloch to make a reconnaissance of Rancho La Encarnación, some fifteen miles south. Leaving on the evening of 16 February McCulloch and fourteen companions approached the rancho near midnight. McCulloch and Maj. George T. Howard, formerly an officer in the Army of the Republic of Texas and now serving on Taylor's staff, riding in advance, captured one of the enemy's pickets, who told them that no Mexican soldiers were at Encarnación. Applying *la ley de fuga*, the custom observed by both the rangers and the Mexicans, which meant that prisoners were to be killed on the spot if a rescue were attempted, the captive was informed that if the patrol were ambushed, he would be shot. Nevertheless, McCulloch wrote, he "still persisted, as a brave man would, in saying there were no troops there." The ranger captain doubted the man's story, however. The picket claimed to have left his unit early in the day and to have ridden far from it on patrol; his canteen, however, was full and the country dry. It was not probable, McCulloch thought, that he would not have taken a single drink, "so we acted cautious accordingly."[4]

About one mile north of the rancho McCulloch and Howard, still in advance of the main party, passed a sleeping sentinel. At the sound of their horses he awoke, leaped on his horse, cut the rope, and rode for the rancho. McCulloch sent Howard back to halt the rest of the party while he trailed the fleeing picket. Through the dark night the ranger followed the Mexican to a group of ten or fifteen horses. He approached unseen to within ten yards before being challenged. "Like a 'true Yankee,'" he answered by asking who they were. "The Spanish I spoke not being the best Castillian, gave them to understand that I was an Americano. They testified their great respect for my nation by not firing, as one would suppose, a salute, but by taking to their heels as usual." McCulloch made a dash at the last fugitive, but his horse, leaping some chaparral, broke the strap by which his spyglass hung, and in trying to save the glass he lost both it and the Mexican.

McCulloch returned to the company, formed it in extended order with the center in the road, and moved on at a brisk pace, knowing the enemy would be waiting in ambush if it had time to bring up reinforcements from the rancho. Within four hundred yards of Encarnación, the rangers saw a dark mass, some one hundred yards long, lying across their path. Not knowing whether it was a line of cavalry or a brush fence, they approached cautiously until the demand "*¿Quién vive?*" was followed by a volley from the Mexican line. The blaze was such, said McCulloch, that "it completely blinded us for a moment." Instantly McCulloch gave the order to charge, which only about six rangers were able to obey; the rest were carried back by their frightened horses. "However, by the discharge of a few guns and pistols in their faces and some mighty tall yells, they were put to flight."

This was all the Texans desired, for McCulloch knew well that "if we could not make them run, we must ourselves, as both our *orders* and their *numbers* cautioned us against fighting." The rangers pursued the Mexicans far enough to hear their probable strength—"about two companies with a bugle each." Having learned this much, the patrol fell back, collecting scattered men as they rode. All of the Mexicans had escaped, including the prisoner. McCulloch regretted this very much but commented philosophically, "He was a noble fellow and deserved to live. Long may he do so."[5]

The patrol returned to headquarters, and McCulloch reported that he did not believe that the picket they had encountered at Encarnación belonged to the small screening force commanded by Brig. Gen. José Vincente Miñón, the only organized Mexican force then thought to be in the area. On the morning of 20 February Taylor summoned McCulloch and told him to take as many of his men as were well mounted and accompany Charles A. May and his dragoons on a scout to Hedionda, about twenty-five miles southeast. McCulloch inquired if the general intended sending anyone to Encarnación. When Taylor replied that he did not, McCulloch reminded him that he believed that the party with which he had skirmished at the rancho was part of a larger force, and if Taylor were to send anyone there, he would like to go. Having much faith in his chief of scouts' instinct for enemy activity, Taylor dispatched the Texans back to Encarnación.

McCulloch's party, consisting of 2d Lt. Richard H. Clarke of the Second Kentucky Infantry; ranger 2d Lt. Fielding Alston, recently recovered from a severe wound sustained at the storming of Monterrey; and four privates of the spy company, started at 4:00 P.M. and had proceeded eight miles when it encountered a Mexican deserter named Valdez. He gave McCulloch the startling news that Santa Anna himself was at Encarnación with twenty thousand men. The rangers turned the man over to a picket, with instructions to take him to Taylor, and rode on to determine the truth of this disconcerting claim.[6]

After a series of debilitating and demoralizing defeats, and now faced with the prospect of fighting a war on two fronts, Santa Anna realized that "if we did not move now we were dead. Victory was the only way out."

Believing that San Luis Potosi was "a strategic point in the campaign," the Mexican generalissimo slipped from Maj. Gen. Winfield Scott's front on the Gulf of Mexico and, by forced marches, traveled two hundred terrible miles hoping to deal a death blow to Taylor's weakened and unsuspecting army. With Taylor out of the way, reasoned "the Napoleon of the West," no organized American force would stand between him and the Rio Grande or, indeed, the interior of the United States. By destroying Taylor below Saltillo, he could turn the tide of the war, invade the United States, and perhaps reimpose Mexico's lost sovereignty over Texas. Taylor, of course, was blissfully ignorant of this plan.[7]

McCulloch, meanwhile, pursued his route to Tank Lavaca, twelve miles north of Encarnación. Believing the enemy would have a picket at least that far in advance if they were at Encarnación in force, he avoided the road as far as possible. This suspicion proved well founded, for within five miles of the rancho the light of Santa Anna's campfires was visible. Giving his horse to one of the men to hold, McCulloch edged close enough to count the Mexicans' lances by the "gleam of the light from their cigars." Returning to his party, McCulloch led his men toward the enemy's camp, encountering no other guard than that of the camp, which was very strong, "no doubt for the purpose of keeping their own troops from desertion," he thought. The rangers surmised that Santa Anna was preparing for a march, since his soldiers were up very late cooking the next day's rations.

Satisfied that Santa Anna was indeed at Encarnación in force, McCulloch knew his first duty was to get word to Taylor. About midnight he placed Lieutenant Alston in command of the little detachment and told him to return to Agua Nueva by the quickest route. McCulloch and a single volunteer, William I. Phillips, remained to "take a daylight view of the enemy" in order to determine the composition of the army in infantry, artillery, and cavalry. McCulloch's decision to remain "was thought by all the party to be extremely hazardous," he later wrote to his old friend William Reid Scurry, "owing to the country being destitute of any timber sufficiently tall to conceal the movements of a man on horseback." In addition, the road back to the American camp was made distressingly narrow by the mountains that ran for miles on either side. Even McCulloch admitted it was "indeed a risky affair." It was also the beginning of one of the great adventure stories of the Mexican War.[8]

After Alston and the others left, McCulloch and Phillips examined the enemy's camp and found it to be about a mile long and a quarter of a mile wide. Santa Anna had promised his soldiers that although they had marched without provisions, they would very quickly "be in possession of those of your enemy, and of his riches; and with them all your wants will be superabundantly remedied." Moving close enough to see the soldiers playing cards by firelight, the scouts were sure that they were "betting off their interest in the spoils of the American Army. If one was allowed to judge of their opinions of success by their hilarity," McCulloch wrote, "then they were certain of success, as a more jolly set of singers was never listed to by anyone." After seeing all that could be seen, the two rangers climbed the hill in the fork of the road leading back to the north, from which they would have a better view of the camp in the morning. Since they had seen a picket on one fork, however, they concluded that a guard might be on the other fork as well, and they decided to move from between the roads so they would have but one picket to contend with. As McCulloch and Phillips descended the steep hill, their horses dislodged some loose stones that made quite a noise—"sufficient," said McCulloch, "to create a suspicion on the part of the picket that all was not well."[9]

No sooner had the rangers reached the level ground and mounted than they heard Mexican cavalry coming in their direction. McCulloch and Phillips halted to listen; the Mexicans rode but a few yards and stopped to listen as well. As quietly as they could, the rangers unslung their canteens, which held all the water they had or could get that side of Agua Nueva, and laid them on the ground "as tenderly as if they were babies." For what seemed an eternity, McCulloch and Phillips played cat and mouse with twenty of the Mexican cavalry. "When they moved, so did we. If they stopped, we did likewise." At last the guards went back to their camp, and the scouts "got off without a race for it." They were still on the hill between the roads, however, certain they were between the enemy's pickets.

Making virtue of necessity, McCulloch selected a good vantage point on the hill and settled in to watch Santa Anna's camp. "It was *almighty* cold," he later recalled, and Phillips agreed "to keep a bright lookout" while the major caught a moment's sleep. "'Twas no go—entirely too cold for sleeping," and McCulloch rose in time to see the pickets building a fire at the foot of the hill, eighty yards away. Phillips begged to be allowed one shot at them, but McCulloch prudently moved himself and his man to a safer spot.

"Just at daylight, ah cracky, what an infernal din there was in the Mexican camp. Every fellow seemed to have a bugle or drum and was going it on his own hook." Still no chance to escape offered itself, and McCulloch's situation was truly critical. Below, only a mile away, were twenty thousand of the enemy; above, about half a mile distant on each road, was a picket of twenty well-mounted men. McCulloch and his companion were compelled to pass between them. "The chances were against us," said McCulloch, but then one of the pickets began to kindle a fire. This was the diversion, however small, for which the Texans had been waiting. Keeping the top of the hill between themselves and the other picket, they moved very slowly toward the fire starter. Only then did McCulloch remember that even if they successfully passed this picket, another waited at Tank Lavaca, eleven miles above. The attempt, however, had to be made. Holding their rifles under their legs on the off side of their horses to appear unarmed, they rode slowly toward the fire. Dressed as they were, much like Mexicans, the two men pretended to be horse hunters, occasionally mounting some small hill to point and look around the countryside. The Mexicans seemed to take McCulloch and Phillips for two of their own, for they allowed them to pass within two hundred yards of their checkpoint after being in their view for at least half a mile. "We felt like we had a new lease on life when we got fairly out from between these two pickets," McCulloch confided. "I don't think my feeling was ever wrought up to such a pitch." Only the presence of the outer picket at Tank Lavaca restrained him from "giving them a fire, raising the war-whoop, and breaking it up with a race."

Four miles from Tank Lavaca, McCulloch left the horses with Phillips and climbed a bluff on one side of the road. From that vantage point he spied four pickets in the uniform of regular Mexican cavalry. Passing them unseen seemed impossible because the gorge between the mountains at that point tapered to a very narrow gap. McCulloch and Phillips decided to wait, therefore, to see if the pickets would be called in. There they remained until about 11:00 A.M., with no indication that the guard would be relieved. To the south, however, clouds of dust clearly demonstrated that Santa Anna was on the march. McCulloch was painfully aware that Alston's party may have been killed or captured, and should Taylor's army be surprised at Agua Nueva, defeat was inevitable. No option remained but to attempt to pass. The two rangers clung closely to the rugged mountain on the western side of the road, intending, if discovered and cut off, to take to its rugged rocks. "We could have baffled them a long time," McCulloch told Scurry, "and killed many of them with our rifles ere we were captured, or I should say killed, surrendering being out of the question. To do so was to be hanged." Both men preferred to resist.

The ground was difficult, and though the mountainside was rocky, it offered some chance of concealment. The valley was occupied by a prairie dog town, over which running a horse would have been almost impossible. McCulloch was convinced, therefore, that "if we were discovered before reaching a certain point, we were lost to a certainty." Providence, however, seemed to favor the Texans. They traveled four long miles in full view of the Mexican pickets, seeing them all the time, yet going unseen, or at least unchallenged. After passing Tank Lavaca, they had nothing further to contend with but the distance to Taylor's army and the great thirst that came upon them as soon as they were out of danger.

Pushing their horses as hard as the heated condition of the animals would permit, McCulloch and Phillips reached Agua Nueva about 4:00 P.M. No sooner had they dismounted at the water hole than an officer of Taylor's staff rode up, saying the general wished to see McCulloch. Taylor had hoped for McCulloch's return but feared, after the Texan failed to reach camp by morning, that he was captured or slain, "for," wrote Jefferson Davis, "we well knew that he was as daring as he was skillful, and though we had great confidence in his resources, we had great fear that he had made his reconnoissance [*sic*] too closely and lost his life." The general "seemed right glad to see me," McCulloch later wrote, "saying, 'Major, I feared the Mexicans had caught you.'" The chief of scouts gave Taylor an account of what he had seen and what had detained him. This report satisfied the general, who said only, "You must be tired, Major. You had better repair to camp and take some rest and sleep." Taylor and his staff then mounted and rode for Buena Vista, where the army was now deployed on a ridge just behind a narrow pass through which Santa Anna's army must come. Alston's patrol had reported early that morning, and the army had fallen back immediately to that superb defensive position.[10]

The night of the twenty-first, McCulloch slept beside his company in line of battle. On the following morning, eleven years to the day since the Texan watchman in the tower of San Fernando Cathedral descried Santa Anna's army approaching the Alamo, McCulloch sent Lt. William H. Kelly with fifteen men toward Agua Nueva to see what the Mexican generalissimo was doing. Kelly had not gone more than two miles before he met the enemy advancing in great haste. The exchange of fire between the rangers and Santa Anna's vanguard notified the army of the Mexicans' approach. McCulloch galloped to Saltillo to inform Taylor, who mounted and rode for the army, followed by Col. William S. Harney's Second Dragoons, Capt. Braxton Bragg's battery of the Third Artillery, and Davis's Mississippi Rifles. The rangers did little else on the twenty-second, most of the day being taken by reconnaissance and parley between the opposing lines. Wishing to save Taylor from "catastrophe," Santa Anna offered the American commander the opportunity to surrender with all of the "consideration belonging to the Mexican character." Mindful, perhaps, of the Alamo, Goliad, and Mier, the Americans declined. "When night came on," says McCulloch, "those of us who were not out as pickets slept on our arms" in a cold, drizzling rain.

About 8:00 A.M. of the twenty-third, the long roll was beaten in both camps. Riding out with Brig. Gen. John E. Wool, the second ranking United States officer on the field, McCulloch thought the enemy line looked "like a great wounded serpent dragging its unwieldy length." To face the American line, Santa Anna's army was moving by its right flank up a ravine. "The sight," McCulloch recalled, "was grand."

With the first shots of the day Wool instructed McCulloch to anchor the right flank of May's First Dragoons several hundred yards in advance of the American line and to prepare for the Mexican assault. In a few moments the action was hot and general. "I was a good deal amused," McCulloch later recounted, at John Jasper Foster, "a lad about fourteen years old," who had claimed to be eighteen in order to enter the service. At the first volley from the Mexicans the boy was struck by a ball on the hand, his horse was wounded, and a moment later a ball passed through his hat, just grazing his head. McCulloch observed, " 'Japp, they seem to be after you.' 'And you too, Cap,' " he answered, as McCulloch's horse reared wildly with a ball in his breast.[11]

Since, as Capt. James Henry Carleton of the First Dragoons observed, it was "impossible for our handful of regular cavalry, then on the field, to gain any decided advantage by charging into such an overwhelming force, where, in one moment it would have been completely destroyed," the dragoons were ordered back to a ravine nearer the American infantry, and McCulloch's men took cover at the head of a gorge just in front of Taylor's headquarters. Almost simultaneously with this withdrawal, the Second Indiana regiment on the American left was broken, and enemy cavalry poured through the breach. May ordered his squadrons and McCulloch's company after the Mexican horsemen, but before they were overtaken, the enemy reached the American wagon train parked a mile to the rear at Rancho Buena Vista. Here the Mexican cavalry was shattered by fire from the wagoneers and United States infantry that had straggled from the front. May's dragoons arrived just in time to harry the broken cavalry from the field. McCulloch encountered a Mexican captain "dashing down our lines trying to escape back the mountain way. He was going full tilt one way, we the other." The chances of hitting him were slim, McCulloch thought, yet worth a try. "I just let slip at him with one of my barrels and had the luck to hit him in both hands and his horse on the side of the head, which brought him to his knees, and the poor fellow had to surrender." Then May halted the charge, an action the rangers did not understand. May claimed that the dust was so thick that the wagoneers and soldiers at the rancho might take the Americans for Mexican cavalry. For McCulloch, this was not reason enough, and he had missed a splendid opportunity to inflict heavy casualties on a shattered and routed enemy. The American horsemen, however, forced the Mexicans from the field and prevented most of them from rejoining their own army.[12]

After the charge of the Mexican cavalry was broken and repulsed, 2d Lt. Thomas John Wood of the Second Dragoons asked McCulloch to convince May to order a move against the enemy's right wing with the dragoons' two pieces of artillery. May agreed, on the condition that the ground between the two lines first be thoroughly examined. McCulloch and Wood rode forward to accomplish that purpose. Near the enemy line McCulloch discovered an officer of lancers making his way slowly on foot, having lost his horse at the rancho. Although within musket range of the Mexican line, McCulloch decided to try to capture him. "It was amusing to see the fellow try to run with his long saber on," said McCulloch. "It was no go." Realizing that he would soon be overtaken, the lancer stopped, at the same time holding up his bridle in token of surrender. Returning to his own lines with his captive, McCulloch met Maj. Andrew Jackson Coffee, paymaster on Taylor's staff, and gave him charge of the prisoner. McCulloch resumed his examination of the field, and in a few minutes Coffee rejoined him. The two attempted to take other prisoners, but by then the retreating lancers were too close to their own lines and were well covered by the fire of their infantry. McCulloch and Coffee fell back to a more respectful distance and waited for the arrival of Taylor, Wool, and May. During this lull, hail began to fall, and the Mexicans began their retreat. "The victory is ours," McCulloch told Coffee. "Then," said Coffee, "here is a bottle of champagne. We will drink to the success of the American armies." So saying, he took from his holster what McCulloch considered the best wine he ever tasted. They drank it between the two armies.[13]

Two other Ben McCulloch stories are associated with Buena Vista. The first, probably much exaggerated, puts a human face on this mythic warrior. Sarah Borginis, a notorious camp follower better known as the "Great Western," ran a boarding house–saloon–gaming establishment for the army near the rancho of Buena Vista and is credited with stalwart defense of the wagon trains parked there during the battle. After the battle, so the story goes, the well-known madam refused McCulloch a seat at her boarding house table because of his unkempt and dirty clothes. "Major McCulloch had not a ball dress on," observed one of his sergeants, and the hostess declared that she "kept no house for teamsters," though he might eat "after the gentlemen got through." As the hero of Encarnación was walking away, May informed the Great Western of his identity, whereupon she not only insisted that he return and have a meal on the house but opened a monte table and won $18 from him as well. "The next morning I saw Ben adjusting a shawl round her shoulders," reported his orderly sergeant.[14]

The second story concerns a scarlet sash reputed to have been that of Col. Jefferson Davis, worn on the day of battle and presented on the field to Ben McCulloch "in consideration of [his] distinguished gallantry on that occasion." If true, the tale is the first recorded encounter between these two great southern leaders and certainly the happiest. Davis later referred to McCulloch as "a highly meritorious . . . distinguished soldier[,] . . . a man to whom we all accord high qualities as a partisan officer, and credit for valuable services wherever employed." McCulloch's and Davis's future relations were not always so cordial.[15]

On 26 February the American dragoons reconnoitered Agua Nueva and found only the rear guard of the Mexican army. The next day the army reoccupied the town, and at noon on the first of March, Lt. Col. William G. Belknap, with four companies of dragoons, the Second Illinois Infantry, two pieces of artillery, and McCulloch's rangers, pushed on toward Encarnación. Leaving Agua Nueva at 3:00 P.M. to avoid observation and to arrive at Encarnación at daybreak, the task force marched thirty miles that night and bivouacked on the salt plain without water or tents. "Just at the first gray of morning" Belknap's command arrived at Encarnación but found that all but a light rear guard had fled. The advance guard of the First Dragoons under Captain Carleton dashed into the village as "some few officers and men" attempted to escape south. "The Texas spy company," recalled Carleton, "started in pursuit of them, and as it was a level and open plain, the whole chase was in view of the command. The Mexicans, one after another, were caught to a man, and conducted back to the hacienda." Ben McCulloch's special prey was a Mexican colonel, the commander of the rear guard who had tarried too long at the rancho, who "took off at speed." McCulloch and his first sergeant, George Henry Tobin, gave chase "and ran their game down in one mile." To lighten his load, to keep his treasure from enemy hands, or perhaps to create a diversion, during the chase the colonel jettisoned a bag containing fifty doubloons or gold *onzas.* This, wrote a dragoon, "was found and confiscated by the Rangers' chief."[16]

With no further prospect of action, McCulloch was granted leave to return to Texas on a recruiting trip and horse-buying expedition, and on 5 March he left his company under Alston's command. Upon his return to Taylor's headquarters at Monterrey on 31 July, with forty recruits and a herd of horses, he was surprised to learn that his company had been discharged in May at the end of the six-month period for which it had enlisted and that Taylor had no further need of his services. McCulloch and his men were mustered into service for a single day so they would qualify for the pay and travel allowance that the general "deemed it no more than just to allow them"; then they immediately returned to Texas.[17]

In his official report of the battle of Buena Vista, Zachary Taylor acknowledged that he and his army were "greatly indebted" to McCulloch and his scouts, who "rendered us much good service as spies. The intelligence which they brought caused us to leave the plains of Agua Nueva for a very strong and advantageous position." In battle and in scout, McCulloch and his Texans had been formidable, and without their timely report of Santa Anna's presence, Buena Vista might well have been an American disaster. McCulloch characteristically understated his Mexican War experiences when he wrote of them to Scurry: "In this way we did the country some service."[18]

SIX

California Is a Desirable Country

After returning from Mexico, McCulloch went back to surveying and locating lands on the Texas frontier and, according to Victor M. Rose, "sought recreation in an occasional skirmish with the Comanches." His chief ambition, however, lay in a military career. He read avidly in strategy, tactics, and military history and continued to correspond with his old military and political friends in hope of acquiring a regular commission in the United States Army.[1]

From Raleigh, North Carolina, where he was visiting relatives, McCulloch carried on a letter-writing campaign to Thomas Jefferson Rusk. Formerly the commander of the Army of the Republic of Texas as well as Houston's secretary of war and now a United States senator, Rusk was perfectly placed to aid McCulloch in attaining his chief ambition—the command of a regiment of cavalry. Hoping to sway Congress in favor of raising a new regiment of cavalry for service on the Texas frontier, and at the same time appointing him to its command, McCulloch visited Washington in the spring of 1848 but left with his mission unaccomplished. Brig. Gen. Franklin Pierce, with whom McCulloch had formed a friendship in Mexico, had "been very kind in making offers to place [him] again in service" if the Treaty of Guadalupe Hidalgo, signed on 2 February 1848, were not ratified. If a senior commission in the army were not forthcoming, McCulloch was willing to settle for an appointment as superintendent of Indian affairs in Texas, a position of which he was virtually certain if the law creating the office were passed. The congressional delegation from Texas was sure of the passage of the Indian bill, but McCulloch thought it doubtful "or by no means certain, to say the least." When Congress delayed debate on the Indian bill, McCulloch complained that he had "learned one thing since I have been out in the great east, and that is this, if you have business at Washington that you think will detain you one month, multiply it by four and you will be nearer the mark."[2]

McCulloch returned to his mother's home in Dyersburg in May, planning to remain in Tennessee until fall to assist her in arranging her affairs so she and his elder brother John could accompany him back to Texas. If he failed to be appointed superintendent of Indian affairs, he told Rusk, "any service, either in Mexico or on the frontier of Texas would be preferable to being idle." He besought his friend to do anything possible "to hasten my departure for Texas or the seat of war" as life in Tennessee was barely tolerable. "Crops are good in this region, money scarce, pigs plenty, corn low, and cetera," he concluded. "Such news is all that can, or ever could be sent from this glorious mosquito marsh. . . . I consider myself an exile."[3]

The best that McCulloch could do toward furthering his military career, however, was to enlist in November as a guide and scout under Brig. Gen. David E. Twiggs for $6 per day "and one ration for self and horse." With the beginning of the new year, McCulloch returned to Washington but was once again disappointed in obtaining either a commission in the United States Army or a position as an Indian agent in Federal service. By this time, vacancies in the commissioned ranks were going almost exclusively to West Point graduates. With the academy educating more cadets than it could commission, in fact, many of its graduates served as brevet second lieutenants until a post became available. Between 1812 and 1861 the number of academy graduates serving in the army rose from 89 to 744, and in 1856, of the 982 officers on active duty, 714 were West Pointers. The possibility of direct appointment from civilian life, therefore, was distinctly diminished.[4]

When Congress at last acted on an Indian bill, on 30 September 1850, the administration appointed three agents to Texas, all of whom were, according to Austin's *Texas State Gazette*, "strangers alike to our people and the character and conduct of the Indians whom they have been sent out to control." The editor considered President Zachary Taylor's "shameless disregard . . . of the true interest of our frontiers" to be but one more example of the administration's malignant neglect of Texas. "There are men among us of high character, energy and experience, who would have made good and efficient agents" but were overlooked, the editor complained, "and strangers selected and imported for the discharge of the most delicate and responsible trust that could be confided to any officer of the General Government stationed within our midst."[5]

By then, however, McCulloch was far away. Thoroughly frustrated with the law's delays, he decided, in common with John Coffee Hays and many other former rangers, to join the argonauts in quest of gold in California. According to Texas legend, McCulloch had already had one close and fruitless encounter with the gold bug when, as a ranger captain, he had led a patrol to the region of Packsaddle Mountain on the upper Colorado River. According to the tale, Comanches raided their camp in the night, driving away the rangers' horses. Attempting to recover them in the heavy morning fog, the men had become lost and, while searching for water, discovered a rich pool of gold. The rangers, wrote folklorist J. Frank Dobie, made their way back to the settlements, their pockets full of treasure. "On many a long ride in after years the rangers sought the golden pool, but though they were Ben McCulloch's own men—plainsmen and woodsmen right—they never found it again."[6]

Now, in the spring of 1849, although well advised that "it is all moonshine about one or two men digging fortunes," he decided to try his hand at the mines. "I think you are too fast and entirely on the wrong tack," John Washington Rose wrote to his twenty-one-year-old brother Preston Rose, a prosperous Victoria County planter who had determined to accompany McCulloch to the goldfields. As the elder Rose observed, "The traders have made all the money so far," while "the diggers have lived hard, gone naked, and been exposed to all kinds of suffering." Furthermore, the would-be argonauts were advised, a company going from Texas to California would require capital of not less than $1,000 per man after they arrived in the fields, *if* they arrived at all, "the risk of getting there without compass, chronometer, or guide" being, John Rose believed, almost overwhelming. "A sailor in the middle Atlantic without compass would be just as well or better off than a company in the middle of the western waste."[7]

Despite such dire warnings, Ben McCulloch transferred his power of attorney to Henry and departed Austin on 9 September 1849, bound for the gold regions "with a small party of gentlemen who, like himself, are bent on getting wealth . . . for the glorious privilege of being independent." McCulloch's plan was to pick up a few more men in San Antonio on the twelfth and head for Mazatlan on the west coast of Mexico. From there the company would sail up the coast to San Francisco Bay. Their route would lead them through settled country, and consequently, McCulloch believed, "we cannot suffer for provisions or animals." His party consisted of "some 8 white men and 3 or 4 Negroes," a sufficient number, he assured Rose, to guarantee a safe passage, and with all in "good health and spirits," McCulloch looked forward to "rather a pleasant trip."[8]

The next report of McCulloch's party was from Parras, Mexico, in November. There the company had grown to twenty men, all of whom were "splendidly armed and well mounted." McCulloch reported "quite a long trip, but not an uninteresting one." The company had traversed the last 150 or 200 miles of its journey on hired mules over what McCulloch called "the roughest road I have ever seen" and which Rose referred to as "the worst road in all the world." Often their path through the Sierra Madre was merely one foot wide "where the stumble of a mule would have precipitated one a thousand feet below." Such trails, wrote McCulloch, "were truly awful, yet they were interesting." He and his companions at first felt inclined to walk but soon became accustomed to the dizzying heights, "as a man will to anything," and only jested with each other as they threaded their way down the "ticklish places."[9]

The group reached Mazatlan on 9 November "without accident, all in good health and spirits." McCulloch had experienced "quite an agreeable trip, never having suffered a moment for water or provisions," and was able to boast that he and his comrades had "made a better trip than any party we have yet seen." He believed, in fact, that the route they had taken across Mexico was "the best land route, by far, that can be traveled from Texas." At Mazatlan, however, the company's luck began to turn. There, during the fifteen days they waited for a vessel to transport them to California, a cholera epidemic raged around McCulloch's party, "killing the poor Mexicans by wholesale." "You may imagine how comfortable we felt," Preston Rose wrote to his bride. Only one of the Americans died, however: Alex Martin, "a promising young man, age twenty years," who had followed McCulloch from Mississippi. "Poor fellow," wrote Rose. "We buried him far from home and in a strange land."[10]

After more than two weeks of frustrating delay in Mazatlan, with the constant dread of cholera compounded by the fear that all of the decent mines would be claimed before they could reach California, McCulloch's party broke up, with Rose and some of the other men opting for a slow but reliable schooner to take them north. McCulloch and the larger part of the company waited for the overdue steamer. Much to Rose's disgust, the schooner he chose to carry him to San Francisco was a slow boat indeed, taking nearly a month to reach its destination and arriving nearly two weeks after McCulloch and the men who started later.[11]

On 24 November, after fifteen days in Mazatlan, McCulloch and his mess sailed on the steamer *Oregon*, arriving in San Francisco on 1 December. Twenty days later, after "making all the inquiries of those that could be relied on from the mines," McCulloch wrote the first of his lengthy, detailed accounts of California to friends and relatives in the old states, a series that continued after he moved to Sacramento in the spring of 1850. "One who has seen as much of frontier life as you and I cannot be badly mistaken in things in a new country," he wrote to Henry. In San Francisco, he recounted, "the sound of a hundred hammers may be heard from the little room I am writing in." The city "sprang up more suddenly and is now growing more rapidly than anything within the knowledge of man," and McCulloch expected it to double in size in less than six months. He had been awakened that morning by a fire alarm and arose to witness the destruction of an entire square block "with the best tavern in the place." The loss was estimated at over $1 million, and only a favorable wind saved the whole town from the conflagration. "One of these days," he wrote prophetically, San Francisco "will be swept down as suddenly as an Illinois prairie."[12]

With the advent of the cold and rainy season in California, the miners had begun to come into the city in great numbers, reducing the supply of provisions and driving up the prices on what remained in stock. Flour, pork, beef, and potatoes were all very expensive due to the excessive cost of transportation. "In fact," wrote McCulloch, the merchants "make a lump business of it," charging $1 per pound "for everything that can be considered food." In short, although the city was "overflowing" with money, it remained "more easy to make than to retain." Real estate, McCulloch noted, was "up to the highest notch." Rents were exorbitant, with rooms no larger than ten feet by twelve feet costing from $100 to $300 a month. Lodging cost from $1 to $2 per night, and board cost an additional $25 per week. Everything else was proportionally high. Interest on loans was an astonishing 10 percent per month. A meal at a hotel cost from $1 to $3. Coarse boots, "no other kind are worn here on account of the muck," cost from $20 to $30 a pair. Wages, while astronomical in comparison with those paid in the older states, could not keep up with the cost of living. McCulloch at first assured his correspondents that the news from California "is of a very favorable character for labouring men," although "a great many of a different kind" were by then already returning to the States. Soon, however, he altered his assessment of the chances for a laborer to do well. Although carpenters earned between $12 and $16 per day, and common laborers commanded from $4 to $5, contrary to the custom in the East, they were expected to supply their own meals while at work. "Consequently they make nothing," McCulloch observed, "as no one can live here for less than $3.00 per day." In fact, he found, many men were willing to serve as waiters in the hotels without pay, working for meals only. "There is already a great deal of distress and will be more yet before spring," he predicted. Only those with sufficient "capital to operate on or houses to rent" were able to save any money. Such economic conditions, McCulloch predicted, could not possibly sustain themselves, and he was convinced that "a crash must come, and that in less than a year."[13]

Of the climate McCulloch had little good to say: it was "the worst I have ever felt." On Christmas he reported to his mother that he had "seen about eight days it did not rain out of twenty-five" since he landed in California. "Tis too cold of nights," he told Henry. "You must sleep under two or three good blankets to be at all comfortable." The evening air, he added, was as damp as "that of a cellar." Coughs and colds were pandemic, and dysentery, caused by exposure, want of fresh provisions, and an unhealthy water supply, was a leading cause of death. Equally lethal to the miners was "the powerful influence of the sun" in the intensely hot mountain ravines, where, "without any circulation of air, they stand over their shoes in cold spring water or in melted snow from the mountain tops."[14]

Despite his distaste for its climate, McCulloch was well pleased by the California countryside, finding it in appearance much like the hill country west of San Antonio. He was mightily impressed by the redwoods, "the finest timber in the world," which he found growing on the mountains "to enormity in height . . . having all the qualities of cedar without its knots." The region between San Francisco and Los Angeles he thought to be "the best stock country in the known world." On a trip to the southern part of the state he saw thousands of acres covered with wild oats as high as his shoulder, which ripened and fell to the ground "perfectly sound" to fatten stock through the summer and to spring up again of its own accord with the coming of the next rainy season. Three crops of wheat or barley could be reaped from a single sowing, he marveled, and the horses, cows, and hogs were always fat. "As to vegetables," he wrote, "no country in the known world can exceed or scarcely compete with this in that line." Thousands of acres of "the finest kind of mustard" grew wild to a height that "would be too incredible to mention without danger of being accused of romancing." Pears and grapes also did well, but apples, peaches, and figs were "only tolerable." This latter deficiency he attributed to lack of attention "as the Mexicans are both lazy and unskilled in all kinds of husbandry."[15]

McCulloch's opinion of California's population, both the native Californians and the Anglo-American and foreign newcomers, was generally unfavorable. To Sam Houston he reported, "There are more villains in this State than there is in half the States besides. All Queen Victoria['s] convicts from New South Wales as well as the worst thieves and burglars from the larger cities of the older States are among us." He could detect no lack of intelligence in the goldfields but found honesty to be a rare quality. "Men in this country," he opined, "might be well compared with a Mississippi boatman, who is a very clever and respectable man at home, but will, ere he reaches New Orleans, turn out as great a blackguard as any of the boat's crew." Scarcely ever had he loaned a dollar that was returned, he informed Houston—an indicator that few prospecters were doing well in the mines.[16]

The principal vice of the California populace, in McCulloch's opinion, was gambling. "Energetic young men will do well if they can live here without contracting a disposition to gamble," McCulloch advised, having perceived a higher incidence of games of chance in California "than anywhere in the known world." One could not "enter a house," he observed, "without seeing stacks of gold and silver on tables of chance of every description." As in the goldfields themselves, a few became rich, but many more were ruined. Not only in the gaming houses did such sports of hazard go on, however. "Speculation of every kind is gone into with recklessness that would be admirable in a cavalry charge," he wrote.[17]

He believed, however, that California progressed "as far in one year as any other state would in ten," and he expected that soon its society would be the equal of any state in the Union. From its hardscrabble beginnings, wrote McCulloch, "society is rapidly improving." As more immigrant families settled in California, "many substantial people" enriched the culture of the new state. Among these was the family of Senator William

McKendree Gwin, a Mississippi physician of staunchly pro-southern sentiment whose daughter Lucy was to become the principal romantic attachment of McCulloch's life.

By the fall of 1851, Sacramento had two well-attended theaters and several churches. McCulloch informed his mother that he had gone one Sunday to hear a Presbyterian service in which the sermon was "altogether about newspapers and journals" and the next Sunday to a Methodist service at which the minister preached "entirely upon politicks." "Is such the custom or fashion in the States," McCulloch wanted to know, "or have we got ahead of the times in religion as we have in everything else in this country?"[18]

McCulloch objected most strongly to the antislavery attitude that predominated in California. Although he generally wrote of "our Negro boys" with some fondness; sent his "best love to all, black and white," in his letters home; and regarded Aunt Lucy, his mother's maid, as "a second mother," he was zealous in his denunciation of free-soilers, feeling that "free Negroes and abolitionists will soon play the D——l with the best Negro in Christendom." Even in 1851, although he was never a planter and had little personal use for slaves, McCulloch seemed ready to fight for the institution of slavery. Of California he wrote, "This is fine country, and had [it] the right sort of constitution and people, I would like to live here, but as it now exists, never. Our own glorious Texas forever. I never can think of any other place as home, barring the [expulsion of the] abolitionists which render this unfit to live in."[19]

Of the topic no doubt most heavy upon his correspondents' minds, the mines, McCulloch could accurately report that "they are a perfect lottery." Prizes were indeed drawn, "but tis not everyone that does it." An average daily dig of $16 was considered good, with miners panning $100 on some days and nothing at all on others. A party might work for a month or more damming a stream while earning not a cent. Once dammed, a bed might yield a fortune or it might yield nothing. Some men, he recounted, had found pounds of gold in a day, and a few more had dug a fortune of $10,000 or $20,000 in a year. "This is by no means frequent," he cautioned.

"So," McCulloch concluded,

> after summing up the cost of everything, such as the expenses in coming out and those of traveling to get to the mines, (which are not inconsiderable, by any means,) the cost of provisions in the mines, the shortness of the time you are allowed to work between the time the

water gets low enough in the spring . . . until the rains set in in the fall, with probability of getting sick from exposure or want of proper food, being out of employment and on expenses during the winter—after all these things are summed up . . . I would, if I were asked, say to men who are married or to those who do not intend staying here but a year or two, if they are doing well, to stay where they are, particularly if they are not used to rough or frontier life.

If his health lasted, however, McCulloch did not doubt he would make money. "Whether the country will do to live in or not is another thing."[20]

While awaiting the dry season, McCulloch and most of his party had "gone at something to pay expenses." As "nothing can be done here at present that promises better profit," McCulloch made a mule-buying expedition to Los Angeles in the spring of 1850, where he observed "the most settled portions" of the territory. Returning from the south by the end of May, he began his search for his younger brother James Coffee McCulloch and Nat Benton, the husband of his younger sister Harriet Maria and the nephew of Thomas Hart Benton, who had preceded him to the gold regions. With his friend Daniel Gavan, McCulloch planned to go into partnership with James and Nat. These two had not been in San Francisco when Ben's party arrived, although he sought them diligently for his mother's sake. Their absence, however, was no surprise. "This is a very large country without mail," he wrote to her, and little traveling could be done during the rainy winter months. "One may be in this city a week with a friend and not meet him," he reassured her, "and how much worse in a country like the mines, where one scarcely knows the man digging next to him."[21]

Months later he found his brother and brother-in-law at Stockton on the San Joaquin River. Their luck, however, had not been good. They had arrived too late and found the best mines claimed and all "dug or crowded." What remained would yield no more than $10 per day through the mining season, so Nat Benton and James McCulloch determined to go north to Sacramento with Gavan. "The truth is," Ben informed his mother, "there is more difficulty in making money this year than last. The mines have been a good deal culled or skimmed over, so there is little of the cream left of those that have been discovered." Even so, he and his partners remained confident that "with ordinary luck" they would return to Texas "in better circumstances than we left."[22]

McCulloch believed, as did most others in California, that "the mines are inexhaustible" and would be worked profitably "for ages to come" but, he wrote to Sam Houston, the time had already passed when individuals might make fortunes by their own labor. This was because gold, he believed, had been uniformly distributed throughout the region at one time, but because of its superior weight, it had over the millennia become concentrated in the low areas, "the ravines, rivulets, and rivers." There the first wave of miners eagerly sought it and "in most cases found and worked out long since," leaving only the hillsides and other poor deposits for the latecomers. "There is no doubt of this country being one of the richest in the world in minerals and mines," he informed Houston, but the day of the forty-niner was past.[23]

McCulloch, therefore, chose to remain in Mariposa County, where Governor Peter H. Burnett had appointed him tax collector. Many of McCulloch's "Texican friends" were members of the California legislature, and they had won the office for him during his trip to Los Angeles, pledging to the governor that he would fill the position. "So you see," he informed his mother, "I was honor bound to accept." The office was considered lucrative because the legislature had recently passed a law taxing all foreigners $20 per month "for the privilege of working the mines." Although 15 percent of this assessment was to go to the collectors, McCulloch remained skeptical as to the value of the post, promising only to "hold it as long as it proves to be profitable, but not a moment longer." He disliked being separated "from the boys" but had vowed to do "anything honorable for money."[24]

McCulloch returned to San Francisco on 2 June after only two months as tax collector. The $20 levy on foreigners proved to be "more than they can pay and live, and if the law or my instructions are not altered, I shall certainly not return," he informed Henry. Although McCulloch protested the tax through official channels and through the newspapers, stating that "it is out of the question to make money collecting unless the tax is reduced," the law was not repealed, and in August McCulloch resigned his post. It had not "turned out as my friends anticipated. They thought it a fortune, it turned out a failure."[25]

Now "footloose," McCulloch made his way to "join the boys" on the American River some twenty-five miles above Sacramento. They had made little money but claimed to have located a site that would yield from $12 to $16 a day. The northern mines, McCulloch believed, were not yet so picked over, and some small fortunes had been made in them since he had been in the country. "So, you see," he wrote to his mother, "they have some little prospect." Yet, he warned her again, "tis all a lottery," and his Calvinist soul was repulsed by a calling in which "some do well while others equally industrious make nothing."[26]

As had been their fate on the San Joaquin, McCulloch's party arrived too late. Had they reached the American River a year earlier, thought McCulloch, they would have done much better. By August of 1850, however, if one found a place that yielded rich ores, he was "soon surrounded by men, so you get but a few days digging before you have to hunt another place." "If a man could keep steadily at work," McCulloch informed Houston, "he might make some money anywhere" in the mines, "but who can be content with ordinary wages in California?" As no one could, the miners "travel from place to place and so spend what little they do make hunting in vain for richer diggings." By the end of 1851 most of the argonauts had given up on the idea of finding fortunes and worked only "for money enough to get home on." Sadly, McCulloch reported, "many have despaired in doing even that, and not unfrequently take to the bottle or the gaming table, and not a few to robbing and stealing." Yet, McCulloch assured his mother, "we are content. We will do all we can to obtain success; the result is with Providence."[27]

By the end of summer Ben informed Henry that "the chances to make fortunes rapidly have all passed" and that the mines were no longer paying more than the average wage that men earned in the settlements. Therefore he advised his brother to "stay where you are. Tis a better country than this." Henry "might come here and stay here two years and not have more money than would take [him] back to Texas." No better evidence of the low rate of success in the mines existed than "the number who wish to borrow," McCulloch wrote to Senator Rusk. "There are many Texians in the country," he informed his old friend, "not one of which, to my knowledge, has enriched himself. The most of them speak of returning to Texas." Now disillusioned with the goldfields, McCulloch would advise no one but a gambler to try California except as a permanent home. "Take it all in all, I think Texas is the best country of the two, and will return there if I am allowed the time."[28]

Although longing to see Texas again, McCulloch determined to remain at the mines for one more summer. Since May of 1849, however, serious social unrest had been growing in California's central valley, and McCulloch was soon involved. John A. Sutter was one of the first Anglo-American settlers in California and one of its largest landholders. The huge influx of fortune hunters that followed the discovery of gold on his property in 1849 had, ironically, brought heavy pressure to bear on his holdings as squatters began to settle on his claims and to question his titles. Claim and counterclaim between Sutter and his unwelcome tenants filled the courts for a year while "squatterism" became a distinct party organization, and the threat of violence simmered below the surface of the legal conflict. When Sutter ordered the squatters forcibly removed in November 1849, the stage was set for serious civil insurrection.[29]

On 10 May 1850 the California court found in favor of Sutter's claims, and the Squatters' Association responded with a poster campaign stating that its members were "deliberately resolved to appeal to arms." True to their word, on 14 August forty armed squatters attempted to repossess certain of Sutter's lots in Sacramento and to free two of their fellows from the county's prison ship. There they were met by the mayor, who ordered them to disperse and disarm. He was shot four times and was dangerously wounded, and two of his companions were killed while three others were wounded by his side. Sheriff Joseph McKinney pursued the mob, killing one man and wounding three others. An alarmed state government placed the city under martial law, and volunteer infantry and artillery companies were formed throughout the territory. Five hundred police were called from California's other cities, and calm was at last restored only when Governor Burnett ordered Brig. Gen. A. M. Winn of the California militia to Sacramento with his entire command. A new mayor, Demas Strong, announced that "peace, order, and quiet have resumed their sway," and the Sacramento *Daily Transcript* proclaimed the rioters scattered, armed opposition crushed, and squatterism dead.[30]

Sheriff McKinney was awarded "a general expression of admiration" for his conduct during the police action against the squatters and was highly commended for his courage and discretion. On 15 August, however, McKinney and a posse rode to Five Mile House to arrest squatters. At a public house called The Pavilion the sheriff confronted a band of eight or ten squatters who opened fire on him and his party. In the general melee that followed, McKinney was struck by a load of buckshot. According to one witness, he "raised both hands and said three times, 'I'm dead.'" He then walked ten steps and fell.[31]

To fill the sheriff's place, an election was called for Monday, 2 September. "We understand that there will be no lack of candidates for this honorable and profitable office," read the Sacramento *Daily Transcript* of 23 August, and within four days no fewer than ten prospective lawmen were regularly advertising their candidacies in its pages. Ben had intended to go with

Daniel Gavan, James McCulloch, and Nat Benton on a prospecting foray to the Trinity River and remain there through the winter, but he "was induced by my friends" to become a candidate for McKinney's job. Only three days before the election he made up his mind, and on 2 September, the day of the election, he announced his candidacy. He considered his chance of winning only "a slim one," yet, as he wrote to his mother, "the office was worth the trial." In a field of ten plus a "scattering," McCulloch polled 678 of 3,938 votes—enough for a plurality of one vote over the nearest contender. The strength of his reputation as an Indian fighter and as the hero of Encarnación no doubt pulled him through, but, he wrote to his mother, "as Old Davy would say, 'tight squeeze.'" On the same day his old ranger comrade John Coffee Hays was elected sheriff of San Francisco.[32]

McCulloch expected the defeated candidates to contest his election, "but if it's thrown back to the people," he was certain, "I will beat them two to one or I am very much mistaken." Well aware of this, he expected his opponents to attempt to disqualify the precincts in which McCulloch received a large majority. The new sheriff was rightly confident they would not be successful, however, and so, he wrote to his mother, "I think the chances greatly in favor of my remaining sheriff of Sacramento County until April come year," after which time he planned to return to Texas. As sheriff, McCulloch expected to earn from $10,000 to $30,000 annually. The fearful toll of bankruptcy was expected to boost the fees he would collect, and, "at all events, it is much better than mining."[33]

Although never a member of any organized church, McCulloch demonstrated in a long, philosophical letter to his mother soon after his election as sheriff his profound belief in a benevolent providence and a predestinarian faith in a supreme being. Making light of the lack of success that had befallen him in the goldfields and attempting to cast a positive light on the last year's events, he pointed out that although he had failed to make his fortune as he had hoped, in comparison with newly arrived immigrants who "will be compelled to work for their board" and those still en route, suffering from cholera and the other distresses of crossing the plains, he was well off indeed. California, he wrote, "is good country and one of the most healthy in the world. Yet I prefer Texas, and most heartily wish we were all safely settled there at this moment." However, he wrote, "we must bide our time and console ourselves by the reflection none are completely happy, and we are much better off than many. So, let us be content to discharge our duty and trust to a wise Providence for success."[34]

Mindful, no doubt, of his missed Christmas rendezvous with Crockett at

Nacogdoches in 1835 and his bout with measles at Nashville that conspired to save him from death at the Alamo, McCulloch reminded his mother that "several times during my life had I . . . succeeded in what I fully intended, I would have been killed." Even his election to sheriff was a thing of fortune. Had James and Nat proceeded to the Trinity River the previous spring as he had directed them, rather than remaining in Sacramento, McCulloch "never could have been a candidate, much more possessed the office." The office of sheriff, unfortunately, proved only marginally more profitable than that of tax collector. The job did not pay "as well as I could wish," he confided to his mother after some months on the job, and he spent much time away from it through the spring of 1851, attending to "outside business." Still he found that it would "pay for attending to" and promised to give closer attention to its demands in the future.[35]

Having failed in the mines and now discontented with his job as sheriff, McCulloch thought increasingly of Texas and the military career he had sought unsuccessfully before coming to California. His strongest ally in his quest for a regular commission remained his old mentor, Senator Sam Houston, to whom he wrote on 6 April 1851. In this letter he recounted the "fair trial" he had given to the mines and told Houston how he had been "playing sheriff" of Sacramento County for the previous six months. He planned to continue in that office until winter, when he would return "to the Old States." He would then do one of two things: either "settle in Texas on a farm or join the army." Clearly service in the army was his first preference should a new regiment be raised for frontier defense, and to Houston he wrote that he would "be much gratified and assisted by your recommendation" for a commission. A bill was then pending before Congress to increase the size of the army in order to protect the Texas border, and McCulloch was perfectly willing, if Houston thought best, to speed back to Washington if "it would further my views." Always a well-informed observer of the newest technological innovations in military arms and tactics, McCulloch sent to Houston his views "as to the manner of arming and equipping of such troops" and hoped for the senator's approval. Hinting rather broadly that Houston might make a successful run at the presidency in 1852, McCulloch concluded, "with you to direct and I to execute," a regiment under McCulloch's command would be much more effective "than any troops now in the service."[36]

McCulloch also sent Texas's other United States senator and his second strong ally, Thomas Jefferson Rusk, long informative letters and petitions for help in furthering his military career. Having heard of the probability of one or two new regiments being authorized by the next Congress, McCulloch informed Rusk that he "would like above all things" to receive a commission in one of them and that he was more than willing to come to Washington "at such time as you may direct" if he might help his own chances of securing a command or have a voice in arming and equipping the troops with whom he hoped to serve. "No one knows better than yourself," McCulloch wrote, "the importance of this in rendering them efficient for frontier service."[37]

McCulloch's term as sheriff expired on 1 April 1852, and he did not run for reelection. The office had not proved profitable, and now, he told his mother, "the next legislature will ruin the fees by cutting them down" after he and his fellow peace officers had expended "a great deal of exertion" to see them set at what they considered a reasonable rate. More important, although he declared that "California is a desirable country," its "institutions" did not suit him, and if ever he was to settle himself he thought it "quite time to do so," vowing to "settle in Texas or not at all."[38]

Quite remarkably, considering all of the ill luck that his party had encountered in its quest for gold, new discoveries of gold-bearing quartz in the south caught McCulloch's attention, and he made one final foray into the goldfields. "Some of them have proved to be very rich," wrote the ever-optimistic McCulloch to his mother, "yielding a fortune in a single day." Accordingly, he journeyed down the central valley of California in the spring of 1851, spending several weeks looking at quartz mines and buying an interest in fourteen. Still he planned to start for the East by the first of December, when he expected Nat Benton back from the mines. He had earned enough money in the sheriff's office to pay their way back, even if Nat had no luck on the Klamath River, "without borrowing from our friends in the old states."[39]

McCulloch sold his claim on the American River for $100 and left Sacramento for the last time on 11 October 1851. He retained his interest in the quartz mines, however, still believing they might secure his fortune, and so ventured south to settle his affairs there. Winding up that chore, he departed California around 15 October "for the States," heading first to Texas to see Henry and Isabella and his favorite nephew and namesake, Ben Eustace McCulloch, as he had "very anxiously desired and prayed." Expecting to reach Henry's farm by 25 November, he proposed that the two brothers stop in New Orleans to arrange to have steam-powered rock crushers placed at his quartz mines and then make the trip up the Mississippi together, "which would make the trip double agreeable," to visit their mother in Tennessee in December. From there, on the advice of Sam Houston, McCulloch would visit Washington, where Congress would be in session and he might press his claim to a position in one of the new regiments then being debated. For all of his disappointment and loss since coming to California, McCulloch was not discouraged or rueful. "I, for one," he informed Henry, "do not regret in the least coming."[40]

SEVEN

The Marshal's Baton

By the end of 1851 McCulloch was back in Dyersburg attempting to settle his prodigal father's debts and aiding his seventy-one-year-old mother in her preparations to move to Texas. Although Alexander McCulloch's obituary stated that he "deliberately arranged his temporal affairs, set his house in order, and waited for the summons of his Lord in the comfortable assurance of a gracious immortality," Major McCulloch's want of providence would nettle his son for years as he attempted to make straight his father's estate and provide for his widowed mother. "I did hope to have a home for you both in your old age," he wrote to her from Mexico, "vain hope. I have none for myself yet, but if I am spared through this war I will settle myself."

Frances LeNoir McCulloch, since the death of her husband six years earlier, had been eager to join her sons in Texas. "I think if I go to your country," she wrote to Henry, "it may be the means of all my children going too, for I can assure you that it is my desire that they should leave this country and go to a new one, and there is none I would prefer before Texas." The brothers planned that she would live with Henry and his wife, with Ben to pay her expenses, "unless," Ben wrote, "some great good luck may befall me in the matrimonial line." Her move had been prevented, however, by the badly snarled condition of Major McCulloch's estate. Ben expected, therefore, to be detained for most of the summer closing his father's accounts, and he anticipated trips into middle Tennessee, North Carolina, and Alabama to do so. "The thing must be closed and the leak stopped," he wrote to Henry, "or all will yet go to waste."[1]

The task was a dreary one. To McCulloch, Tennessee remained an uninteresting "backwoods." "Everything and everybody are about the same in this country," he complained, "the men ignorant and the girls too modest to walk through the potato patch because the taters have eyes."[2]

Always a keen observer of the national political scene as well as an ardent Democrat, McCulloch noted with some disgust that Tennessee was "as usual, on the fence" and might be carried for Whig Millard Fillmore in the upcoming presidential election. In McCulloch's judgment, southern Whigs were unable to decide upon a viable presidential candidate, and he hoped that the Democratic convention would "make the issue between them and a certain Gentleman from Texas," namely his old friend Sam Houston. In the denouement, the Democrats wrangled through forty-nine ballots, with neither of the leading candidates—Stephen A. Douglas nor James Buchanan—able to secure a two-thirds majority. Finally, the prize went to one of the more obscure aspirants, Franklin Pierce of New Hampshire.[3]

"Politicks are at a low ebb in this region," McCulloch reported after the nomination was announced, but by October 1852 he had written to Henry of the "great excitement all through Tennessee" generated by the contest between the Know-Nothing and the Democratic candidates, "each giving barbeque dinners and c." McCulloch had attended two such Democratic rallies and found "more excitement in the present canvass than was ever before known in this state." He was now certain that Pierce would carry Tennessee as "the Democratic party will be the Great Southern Party in the next presidential election." He expected the Know-Nothings to "exert themselves to secure it," however, by nominating Millard Fillmore, a so-called doughface, a northern man with southern principles. "The South," McCulloch advised, "must all go one way or we will have a free soil President, and that will dissolve the Union to a certainty. . . . The South will never submit to the measures to be carried out by them should they get power."[4]

Probably because they had taken the strongest stand in favor of the Compromise of 1850, the Democrats won at the polls. With Pierce in the White House, McCulloch saw hope of exercising his sword in a United States effort to wrest Cuba from Spain. Such an undertaking would, of course, have been to McCulloch's personal benefit. American imperialism promised unemployed military men with southern sympathies and a penchant for adventure both a taste of glory and an opportunity for the expansion of slave territory into the "golden crescent" of Mexico and the Caribbean, creating the empire of which southerners had long dreamed. Not until 1854, however, did the Pierce administration make clear its intention to obtain Cuba, and this effort ultimately came to nothing.[5]

While waiting to hear from the president-elect, however, McCulloch spent July at the Virginia Springs, a fashionable spa just on the Virginia side of the Potomac River, with an eye, perhaps, to meeting a suitable woman to become his wife. Daniel Gavan had returned from California and had moved his family to Arkansas, where "he and [his] Lady, did me the compliment to name the boy after me," Ben informed Henry on 26 May. "I must endeavor to make arrangements this summer, if possible, to return the compliment that you and he have paid me."[6]

Quickly disillusioned with the beau monde, he wrote to his mother that he was sure that she "would feel very little pleasure in reading a detailed account of the ways and doings of fashionable people at a fashionable watering place. All can be given in a word: Vanity." Having grown up among the simple people of western Tennessee, reached manhood on the Texas frontier, and spent his most recent years in the raw California goldfields, Ben McCulloch was by no means prepared for the type of society he encountered at this favorite resort of Washington's social elite. All, he found, were "poor selfish creatures," seeking only their personal aggrandizement and pleasure. "When one looks at society at a place like this and sums up what it all amounts to, one cannot but wish for a more quiet place with a few friends." McCulloch found little to recommend the spa, as he was "neither deficient in health or desirous of making a display," the two sole reasons he saw for frequenting such a place. Its patrons, he wrote, were either sadly disappointed in not regaining their health, "or in other words, in not being made young again," or, if still young, "are sadly disappointed at the success of some more fortunate person of their own class, and conceive themselves quite neglected because there is not a crowd at their feet to admire their beauty, which in most cases can be summed up in dollars and cents." To McCulloch, only three other diversions were followed at watering places: "drinking, gambling, and making love." He observed that most patrons indulged in all three, but none of these activities was likely to prove profitable to a man like himself, "who is not handsome enough to marry to advantage or sufficiently dishonest to be a successful gambler." The only advantage he might hope to gain would be "an improvement in health and knowledge." His health was not in need of mending, but certainly from this experience among the upper class of Washington society he learned some valuable lessons about human nature.[7]

A wiser man, McCulloch started his journey back to Texas in August. Stopping first in Tennessee, he spent the latter part of the month at Lamar, Mississippi, visiting his brothers John and James. A slight case of yellow fever, then epidemic on the lower Mississippi, prevented his traveling to New Orleans, so he returned to work on the settlement of his father's estate, a chore that took him all over the Lower South. In mid-September he was in Florence, Alabama, only to "leave in a day or two for Georgia."[8]

Having failed at all else, McCulloch determined to go into stock raising and authorized Henry to purchase suitable land in Texas, inviting him and their nephew Eustace Benton to enter into partnership in the ranch. By selling his slaves, Ben had been able to raise $3,000 to invest in stock and advised Henry that he knew of no business "that will pay so well with a small capital." Henry quickly responded to Ben's request by offering his brother either of his own ranches, but Ben demurred. "Six months more will fix my destiny," he told Henry at the end of November, "and then I promise myself to be more settled at something or other." Still in Dyersburg in November, however, he decided to delay his return to Texas until spring. Cholera, to which he "never would be willing to expose Mother," was especially bad on the Mississippi that year, and once more he believed his best interest lay in Washington, where he intended to see Pierce inaugurated.[9]

When Franklin Pierce took office in March 1853, he was, at forty-nine, the youngest man to become president. Amiable and charming, he had been selected as the Democratic nominee largely for party harmony. In his short political career he had upheld few opinions and had made few enemies. His Mexican War record—he had been one of the five brigadier generals that James K. Polk had commissioned directly from civilian life—was also a credit. As president, however, he submitted to interference from the strong men of his cabinet, especially Secretary of War Jefferson Davis. McCulloch, who had become friendly with Pierce during the Mexican War, hoped that acquaintance would become an asset, although he wrote to Henry, "I do not know that I shall ask him for any office at present, but in the event Congress raised a new regiment for frontier protection, [I] do not know but what then I may. It will do no harm to renew my acquaintance with his Excellency, General Pierce."[10]

McCulloch's trip to the Federal City bore fruit, for on 16 April 1853 the Senate confirmed his nomination as United States marshal for Texas. McCulloch's appointment had received the unanimous endorsement of the Texas congressional delegation, but, reported the Galveston *Weekly News*, "such is his standing with President Pierce that apart from such recommendation, he could have had the office in preference to almost any other man." Equally important, Texas's editors were in agreement that "no one would have been more acceptable to the people of Texas" and that McCulloch's appointment had given "general satisfaction throughout the state."[11]

Marshals and their colleagues in the court system were part of an administrative network of lawmen that, by 1853, served twenty-one states and four territories from the national capital. Marshals were normally "persons of national consequence," appointed from among residents of the judicial district they were to serve. Appointed by the president with the consent of the Senate, marshals were authorized to execute "all lawful precepts" directed by the Federal benches. They were also responsible for the custody of Federal prisoners, the rental and provision of the physical needs of the court, and the disbursement of court funds, for which they were required to post a bond. When necessary, they were authorized to "command all necessary assistance" in the form of the *posse comitatus*. "Whether money, or whether any considerable amount of money, can or will be made by the office is yet uncertain," Ben confided to Henry, "but it will pay one man very well to attend to."[12]

The new marshal was still not above taking the law into his own hands, nor did he require the assistance of a posse when his personal honor was in question. While still in Washington, dining at the Brown Hotel on the evening of 5 May, he was insulted by Elias P. West, the United States attorney for the New Mexico Territory, who threw a glass of water into his face. McCulloch responded by knocking down West with a tumbler and then breaking over his head "a quantity of plates." He concluded the affray by beating West with a chair until his antagonist was "severely but not dangerously injured." In the future, wrote a correspondent to the Clarksville *Northern Standard*, "we would advise gentlemen from New Mexico . . . to beware of exciting the ire of old Texans."[13]

The judge under whom McCulloch served was John Charles Watrous, a bitter enemy of Sam Houston and one of the most controversial members of the Federal judiciary ever to grace, or disgrace, the bench. McCulloch arrived at Galveston from Washington on 16 April in company with John C. Hays, who was then on his way to California to take up his duties as surveyor general. Under instructions from Watrous, McCulloch repaired to Tyler on about 15 May 1853, where he took the oath of office and commenced discharging the duties of marshal. He spent the final week of May in Nacogdoches as the guest of Thomas J. Rusk, where the Nacogdoches *Chronicle* reported that the new marshal "looks as though he will be able to do this country much service yet."[14]

Marshals were required to make quarterly financial reports of their collections and to deposit them in a designated depository. Before each session of the Federal court the treasurer advanced a sum of money to the lawmen, who used it to pay jurors and to defray other expenses. The marshals submitted accounts of their expenditures with accompanying receipts that the treasurer carefully examined for unauthorized expenditures or other irregularities before making a settlement with the marshals. The treasurer required of them a bond of $20,000 with sureties, and "as the bond referred to the date of commission," McCulloch was delayed in posting it because his commission did not arrive until June. He was by that time in Brownsville preparing for the first session of the court there.[15]

On 12 June McCulloch forwarded his requisition for the June term of the court at Brownsville, but because he had not yet posted bond, he was uncertain as to whether the Treasury Department would forward the required funds. The marshal was compelled, therefore, "to become personally responsible" for the expenses of the court and requested of his superiors in Washington "the prompt attention of the Department to the matter." As the next session would begin in Galveston "as soon as we can get there," he was likewise compelled to "risk the necessary amount to pay the expenses of the same" from his own pocket and hoped that, "as I have been traveling all the while," the department would excuse the irregular manner in which he had been compelled to do business.[16]

At last, on 20 June 1853, Judge Watrous convened court in Tyler with McCulloch in attendance. The outgoing marshal, Joseph Bates, formerly a major general in the Alabama militia, mayor of Galveston, close personal friend of Henry Clay, and later colonel of the Thirteenth Texas Infantry during the Civil War, had received notification about the first of May of his removal and from that date had done no work in the office. His failure to serve papers, coupled with the personal legal problems of the judge, "conspired to prevent a protracted session of this, one of the most important and highest tribunals in the land."

At the close of the term at Tyler, Watrous and McCulloch departed for Brownsville, where on 26 March 1853 a band of Mexican insurrectionaries under A. H. Norton had crossed the Rio Grande, sacked Reynosa, Mexico, and held the alcalde for $30,000 ransom. On returning to the United States, Norton and his men were arrested, and the insurrection's leader, José María Jesús Carbajal, was likewise taken into custody.

McCulloch spent the first two weeks of July in Brownsville with the grand jury "engaged in enquiring into the offenses committed by Norton and others against the United States in the neighborhood of Reynosa." Norton and Carbajal, who since 1851 had been plotting the overthrow of Mexican authority in the states bordering Texas and the subsequent establishment of the Republic of the Rio Grande, were indicted for violation of United States neutrality laws and were scheduled for trial in Galveston the following January. Prosecution witnesses would be numerous, the Galveston *Weekly News* observed, and their travel and per diem compensations would "form no inconsiderable item of expenditure" to vex the new marshal.[17]

Following his investigation of the Carbajal disturbance, McCulloch changed his venue to Galveston to "give, in person, prompt and proper attention to each and every communication from the several departments." With the closing of the Galveston session of the district court on 26 August, the Brownsville *Flag* had only the highest acclaim for the district's new marshal. "Every praise is due the prompt, energetic, and strictly impartial manner in which the United States Marshal, Major Ben McCulloch, has discharged the many and arduous duties incumbent upon his office." The editor judged him "an eminent and zealous Texan, a brave and gallant officer, and the government could not have placed the marshal's baton in more worthy hands, or to one calculated to give more satisfaction."[18]

Despite the high marks McCulloch earned from the press and the officers of the court, his tenure as marshal was one of almost constant harassment by the Treasury Department for reports, receipts, vouchers, and other forms of bureaucratic red tape, so alien to McCulloch's natural tendencies toward adventure and direct action. On 18 December, for example, McCulloch wrote to Interior Secretary Robert McClelland from Galveston, assuring him that his accounts and vouchers for the July term at Galveston must have reached the first auditor before 5 December, because the marshal had his letter of that date acknowledging their receipt. Three days later McCulloch wrote again to McClelland, complying with the secretary's request that he make up and forward his accounts and vouchers of the expenses for the November 1853 Austin term. Those of the July 1853 term at Galveston, McCulloch wrote, had been forwarded, and their receipt had been acknowledged. "I have no motive whatever," he assured McClelland, "in withholding my accounts and will not delay them any longer than is absolutely necessary in procuring the proper signatures to the abstracts, vouchers, & *c*."[19]

The department seemed forever remiss, moreover, in forwarding to McCulloch the means required to support the sessions of court, thus obliging the marshal to keep up a steady stream of letters to Washington requesting necessary funds. Texas's remote location caused its marshal many administrative problems that were often aggravated by slow and uncertain postal and transportation systems. In a typical instance, on 30 October 1853 McCulloch wrote to McClelland from Galveston reminding him that the stipend due the court for its term in Austin was overdue despite the secretary's promise that it would be sent at once. However, only two weeks later he wrote to McClelland informing the secretary that he had just learned that the remittance for the November term at Austin had been delivered to the Texas capital rather than to McCulloch's Galveston office as he had expected. Despite the frustration with the department in funding the November 1853 judicial season in Austin, "the office of marshal seems to have been well conducted," Henry informed his mother, "and all that have had any business in the same seem well satisfied with the manner in which it has been attended to."[20]

McCulloch passed the remainder of 1853 with trips to Dyersburg; Lamar, Mississippi; New Orleans; Austin; and Washington, D.C., where he intended to "get [his] office a little more ship shape." Foremost on McCulloch's mind, however, as uneventful sessions of Federal court were punctuated by fruitless and frustrating trips to Washington, remained his dream of commanding a regiment of cavalry. In 1854, powerful friends in the Senate seemed closer than ever to bringing that dream to reality. According to his friend John Henry Brown, McCulloch "spent nearly all his time in the libraries of Washington City" during 1853 "studying military works." In fact, according to Brown, from 1836 until his death, McCulloch's spare time "was given to the study of works on the science of war." By 1861, Brown believed, McCulloch was "one of the most thoroughly posted military men in the United States," possessing a thorough familiarity with the campaigns and works of Caesar, Alexander, Turenne, Vauban, Frederick the Great, Napier, and Napoleon. "The popular impression was that he was a splendid scout and dashing cavalry officer," wrote Brown, but his closest friends, "our most eminent military men after the Mexican War," knew him as a dedicated and adept student of the arts of strategy and tactics.[21]

On 14 February 1854 Sam Houston took the Senate floor to press the issue of the defense of Texas's frontier. The Comanches, the Kiowas, the Cheyennes, and the other warlike Indians of the plains, Houston believed, could be "civilized" much more cheaply and easily than by the present efforts of the United States Army if troops were recruited locally and led by veteran frontiersmen. "There is one man within my knowledge," Houston told his colleagues, "who, with one thousand men, armed and equipped as he would suggest, in New Mexico and Texas—from his chivalry, for he is as brave as Pyrrus—from his integrity, for he is as just as Aristides—from his sagacity, for it is equal to any emergency—can civilize every border Indian in the course of ten years, if you will give him the means that can be withdrawn from other branches of expenditure and appropriate it to that purpose. I refer to Ben McCulloch, the Texas ranger, a man whose thoughts soar as high as Heaven, and whose impulses would adorn the proudest character that ever lived in the annals of history." Although Houston claimed that he had not conversed with McCulloch on the subject, he was certain that his protégé could accomplish all that he had set out for him. "I know his properties of heart, his readiness of hand, his manliness of soul."[22]

Similar endorsements came from western Tennessee as congressman and future Confederate general Benjamin Jefferson Hill and Governor William Trousdale assured Secretary of War Jefferson Davis of "the warm interest which is felt in his success and his fame in this portion of his native state." These supplicants only alluded to McCulloch's service and skill as an officer and as a frontiersman, acknowledging that Davis knew better than themselves "that merit which appertains to an able and successful soldier" and leaving to him the decision based upon his qualifications and "the high regards of his countrymen." The main thrust of their argument was that McCulloch's appointment to the command of the proposed new regiment of cavalry "would meet with undivided approbation among our people, and would give the friends of the Administration here additional reason to cherish an unshaken confidence in its trustworthiness and fidelity to Democratic principles."[23]

McCulloch spent the spring in Texas, handling his duties as marshal, but in the summer of 1854 he was back in the national capital, lobbying for the position Houston had advocated for him. As so many times in the past, however, Congress adjourned without raising the regiment Texans desired for the defense of their borders. "Yet," wrote McCulloch, "I trust the trip will not prove entirely without benefit in the future." He had been "most kindly treated by the President," he told his mother, having "stayed several days with him at the White House, rode with the Madam in her carriage, and *c.*"[24]

Despite his disillusioning experiences at the spa during the summer of 1854, McCulloch returned on 7 August to Greenbrier, one of the fashionable resorts at the White Sulphur Springs in Virginia, intending to remain there for several weeks before leaving for the West. At the springs he continued his friendly correspondence with President Pierce, whom he invited down to enjoy the waters and to discuss politics and the military situation on the Texas frontier. Pierce was "strongly tempted to break away from engagements here and participate with you in the enjoyment of the White Sulphur baths and the invigorating atmosphere of Greenbrier," but he found each day "some new obstacle is interposed."[25]

Although Pierce's correspondence was cordial and suggested a close friendship, no further preferment came that summer, and McCulloch returned west a few weeks later. He arrived in Texas in mid-October to find the border once more in turmoil, with rebel Mexican army officers having established their headquarters on the Texas border near Brownsville, where they organized a plot for "revolutionizing" Mexico's frontier states. McCulloch charged John N. Gary, his deputy at Brownsville, to "be on the alert" and to "take all *legal* and *proper* measures" to maintain United States neutrality and an amicable relationship between the United States and the Mexican governments in the affair. He cautioned Gary not to interfere with the right of American citizens to cross the border "under peaceable appearances" but to "ferret out" and suppress attempts to move "munitions or warlike implements" into Mexico. McCulloch authorized his deputy to call on the posse and, if necessary, the United States Army to assist him. The marshal did not yet see the threat of disturbance as sufficiently serious to require his presence in Brownsville, but he was prepared to go there instantly to "prevent a recurrence of those scenes which have so long disgraced the shores of the Rio Grande," if circumstances warranted. On 9

November, Secretary of War Davis responded to McCulloch's actions, expressing his gratification at the marshal's moves to prevent a violation of United States neutrality laws and declaring his faith in McCulloch's ability to see his plan properly executed.[26]

More vexing to McCulloch than the threat of renewed war on the border was the paperwork of the marshal's office. Plunged back into the administrative snarls of his job, McCulloch once more grappled with a seemingly inept Washington bureaucracy. From Galveston he wrote on 19 November to the comptroller of the Treasury, complaining that some months earlier he had submitted contracts to the Department of the Interior for the rental of buildings in Austin, Tyler, and Brownsville to be used as district courthouses. Having received no instructions from the department as to whether the contracts had been accepted, "and the parties now inquiring [of] me for payment of rents for the same," McCulloch was understandably anxious that Washington "advise and instruct" him as to the proper course of action. Exasperated with the endless paperwork his job demanded, McCulloch again turned those responsibilities over to his deputies and returned to Washington early in December, expecting to be there for the remainder of the winter "unless my matters are disposed of by Congress sooner."[27]

The winter of 1855, however, proved to be the most bitter and frustrating of McCulloch's life to that time, bringing into sharp focus the conflict between two American military traditions and two schools of thought about the United States military establishment. The first position was McCulloch's own, the belief that a talent for military leadership was a gift inherent in some individuals and discernible to their fellow citizens, who would readily call upon those so endowed in time of war. Although this skill might be enhanced by a program of readings in military history and science, and was certainly honed by experience in the field, it was essentially innate, and could not be taught in school. "At West Point Academy," Sam Houston stated bluntly, "they are drilled and taught—eyes right—eyes left; but if they haven't got the brains, it is impossible to make great men out of them. Unless Providence stamps the man of genius, depend upon it, education will not give it to him." The military academy could no more make a poor cadet into a good officer than it could "make a puddleduck into an eagle."[28]

The only function of such schools, McCulloch and his frontier neighbors and fellow Jacksonian Democrats believed, was to foster a privileged military caste—"presumptive, haughty, tyrannical and domineering"—

whose monopoly on army commissions represented a danger to the freedom of the republic. For proof of the efficiency of the traditional method of selecting the nation's military leadership, its adherents pointed to the examples of George Washington, Nathaniel Greene, John Sevier, Daniel Morgan, Andrew Jackson, Sam Houston, and Zachary Taylor, all of whom had established distinguished reputations as soldiers, none of whom had undergone any formal military training, and some of whom had enjoyed no formal education whatsoever.[29]

"This road is now blocked up," Houston observed in 1858, and "insuperable barriers are interposed to it." The "great path to glory, to honorable achievement," in his opinion, was barred by the United States Military Academy at West Point. Although the academy was founded during the Thomas Jefferson administration, ostensibly to break the Federalist stranglehold on the commissioned ranks, critics such as the McCullochs' old friend and neighbor David Crockett viewed the school as "not only aristocratic, but a downright invasion of the rights of the citizen" and a violation of the Constitution. In 1833, in fact, the Tennessee legislature passed a resolution calling for the abolition of the academy. Only by doing away with West Point, Houston and others of his mind believed, would the country "invite men of pride, of character, and of family to enter your Army."

Despite such savage criticism of West Point, the professionalization of the officer corps continued, and during the Pierce administration the military academy found its staunchest advocate serving as secretary of war. Jefferson Davis, an 1828 graduate of West Point and a successful commander of a regiment of Mississippi volunteers during the war with Mexico, had a grand vision of the United States military establishment as a powerful professional army manned by elite regiments and led by professionally trained officers—coincidentally his academy classmates, Mexican War comrades, and fellow southerners. Davis's attitude toward rangers and militia can perhaps best be summarized in his observation on Jack Hays's regiment in Zachary Taylor's army: "Our experience in Mexico would tell us that we wanted none but regular cavalry—no irregular mounted men of any kind."[30]

At last, after a decade of agitation on the part of the Texas delegation, Congress passed a bill on 3 March 1855 authorizing two regiments of cavalry, the First and Second, and two new regiments of infantry, the Ninth and Tenth. By Davis's estimate, 30,000 Comanches, Kiowas, and other "nomadic and predatory" tribesmen ranged nearly 2,000 miles of Texas frontier while lines of communication in that state ran through more than 1,200 miles of Indian territory. The army in that department numbered only 2,886 officers and men, a force the secretary of war considered "entirely inadequate for its protection and defense." Despite these daunting statistics and the Federal government's demonstrated inability to provide for the defense of the Texas frontier, Maj. Albert G. Brackett, the first historian of the United States Cavalry, considered this piece of legislation "an unheard-of thing in the history of the United States" and regarded it "as almost a miracle."[31]

The command of one of these regiments of cavalry was exactly the position for which McCulloch had been working, hoping, and preparing himself since leaving the army after the battle of Buena Vista, and while the administration policy was taking shape, his friends, as well as those of other aspirants for appointment or promotion, were at work in Washington. In addition to Sam Houston, Congressman Peter H. Bell of Texas, himself a former ranger and veteran of Buena Vista, was firmly committed to McCulloch's claim to the command, and Senator Rusk was sorely divided in his loyalties between McCulloch and Albert Sidney Johnston. The officers of the army, the members of the Texas delegation, and McCulloch himself all firmly expected that the command of one of the new cavalry regiments would be his.[32]

Indeed, Pierce personally promised McCulloch a colonel's commission, although, Ben wrote to Henry, "he thought it best to make the appointment and send it in without consulting Davis, as he was disposed to be in favor of making appointments from the line of the army." The president also advised McCulloch that no further letters of recommendation or endorsement were required. McCulloch, however, found himself "woefully deceived by the President." The opposition to McCulloch as a nonprofessional was too great, and the partisanship in favor of fellow Texan Johnston was insuperable. Johnston's wife, Eliza, and Congressman William Preston of Kentucky, brother of Johnston's first wife, skillfully pressed his cause. Their "diplomacy" on Johnston's behalf was "crowned with success," Preston wrote to Mrs. Johnston, after he "made Mag [Preston's wife] write her prettiest possible letter to Mr Jeff Davis, the moment I felt convinced the regiment would be created." Mrs. Preston also did "rare electioneering" when the army's commanding general, Winfield Scott, was their guest for seven weeks prior to the passage of the bill. "Now you may rest assured," Preston told Mrs. Johnston, "that all the rest except yours and Mag's letters were mere Cotton & prunella."[33]

Albert Sidney Johnston, general of the Republic of Texas, colonel of the Second United States Cavalry, leader of the Mormon expedition, and commander of all Confederate forces west of the Allegheny Mountains
(Archives Division, Texas State Library)

Another possibly decisive factor was the stance of the Texas legislature. After debating sharply whether to endorse Johnston or McCulloch, the legislature at last dispatched a memorial to Senator Rusk recommending that he back Johnston, an old political rival of Sam Houston's, and Governor Elisha M. Pease concurred. It is doubtful, however, that the ladies' electioneering or the legislature's preference would have availed Johnston much had he and Davis not been West Point classmates.

As Adj. Gen. Samuel Cooper informed one successful candidate for promotion to one of the new regiments, "Political influence did not have much weight in the selection of officers of the army to these new regiments; in fact, I think it was detrimental in many instances. You owe your promotion to the Secretary of War." Johnston's son and biographer rightly observed that "the Secretary of War and Johnston were not strangers." Rather, Davis was "a friend who had known him from boyhood and who esteemed him as highly as any man living." The two Kentucky natives had been classmates at Transylvania University and cadets together at the United States Military Academy; they had served together during the Black Hawk War, and both had been on the United States team that negotiated the much-vilified terms of the surrender of Monterrey during the Mexican War. Thus, Davis "was able to present the subject so strongly to the President, that he was allowed to make his selections, for the most part, from the army."[34]

On Saturday, 3 March, Pierce sent for McCulloch to inform him that he would receive a lieutenant colonel's commission only. McCulloch stated frankly that he could not accept without first consulting Rusk and Bell. McCulloch spent the balance of the day in consultation with his friends and returned to the Capitol about 8:00 P.M. to inform the president that he would "leave it with Rusk and Bell and himself whether I should accept," but he added that an appointment for Henry to his old position as Federal marshal would incline him to favor the commission. If the president and the Texas legislators determined that McCulloch should accept a commission as lieutenant colonel, then Pierce "would confer a favor by giving me one of high grade." Somewhat ill, McCulloch left the Capitol and heard no more until about 10:00 A.M. the following day when Davis called at his rooms at the Brown Hotel to say that he would be tendered only a major's posting with the First rather than the elite Second Cavalry, "and the lowest on the list, at that." Bitterly disappointed, McCulloch contended with Davis, as he had earlier with the president, that "the country had some claim upon these appointments, and that they ought not to fill them all from the army." He would again confer with Rusk before rendering a final decision as to whether or not to accept a commission he had begun to view as an insult, but his first impulse was to tell Davis that he "would be obliged to him if he would say to the president that I would prefer to have my claims passed over than to accept such an appointment."[35]

The roll call of officers of the two new cavalry regiments was most impressive and was to become a virtual roll call of Civil War generals. Edwin Voss Sumner was appointed colonel of the First Cavalry, and Joseph E. Johnston, lieutenant colonel. Of field officers, McCulloch alone was appointed from civilian life. It was a nomination, however, McCulloch could not in good conscience accept. His friends Houston and Rusk felt that he, and they, had been slighted by the president, and under their advice he refused the commission. His place was filled by Capt. William H. Emory, who had distinguished himself in the topographical engineers, conducting boundary surveys and writing scientific treatises. On 9 March Davis formally notified Johnston of his appointment to command the Second United States Cavalry, "Jeff Davis's Own." Robert E. Lee was named lieutenant colonel, and William J. Hardee and George H. Thomas, majors. Among the unit's company-grade officers were Earl Van Dorn, Edmund Kirby Smith, George Stoneman, and John Bell Hood. Winfield Scott, despite Mrs. Preston's electioneering, thought that the positions of Johnston and Lee should have been reversed. Johnston had never held a cavalry command; but his professional knowledge was wide, and according to his son "his special tastes inclined him to that arm of service, so that he felt no difficulty in accepting the promotion."[36]

No personal animosity seems ever to have existed between McCulloch and Johnston over the appointment. Years later McCulloch said that Johnston was the right man for the command, and Johnston represented his former rival as "a gallant and enterprising leader of partisan troops" who "deserved well of his country." McCulloch's nomination to the rank of major, Johnston took to be "a high compliment," because, although a total of 116 lieutenants and captains were appointed to the four new regiments from civil life, McCulloch was the only civilian tendered a field-grade commission.[37]

This pattern of selecting leaders for the new regiments, however, stood in stark contrast to previous instances in which new units had been formed, for in the past large numbers of officers had been commissioned directly from civil life. During the Mexican War five civilians received appointments directly as brigadier generals and two as major generals, and

President James K. Polk, "Young Hickory," even attempted to revive the rank of lieutenant general for Thomas Hart Benton, one of West Point's bitterest antagonists. McCulloch, Houston, and a host of other interested observers from the frontier regarded Davis's sudden shift in military policy as a betrayal and a usurpation of power by a federally subsidized military elite. The Constitution, they argued, at least implied that offices of honor, trust, and emolument should be open to all.[38]

In an open letter to Pierce, printed on 10 March in the Washington *National Intelligencer*, McCulloch stated his reasons for declining the proffered post. He firmly believed, he wrote, that civilians had a right to expect some of the appointments as field officers of the new regiments. "Out of all the gallant men who led our troops to battle and victory in Mexico, surely some could have been found competent and worthy to command a regiment or battalion," he argued. He was certain that Congress would not have authorized the creation of the new regiments had it known that, with a single exception, all appointments to high rank were to be made from the army, and he felt sure that any future congressional appropriation for additional regiments would "carefully provide for the protection of the equal rights of citizens in civil life" to fill the commissioned ranks at all grade levels.

Davis's appointments, it appeared, were either merely "made to benefit those who were already in service" or were based on the assumption that no one who was not of the West Point–trained professional officer corps was competent to command troops in the field. In either case, McCulloch's acceptance of a commission would have placed him in "an awkward position." If the former criterion had been applied, he reasoned, "I have no claims, not being in the army." Had three or four civilians been appointed as field officers, he wrote, the administration would thereby have demonstrated that something was "due to the country, and *something* had been given and of right belonged to those appointed, and no jealousy or bad-feeling could have arisen." Under such circumstances he would have joyfully accepted the proffered commission. As the sole field-grade appointment from civil life, however, he feared that his subordinates might view him as an interloper, "occupying a position that they were better entitled to." McCulloch was proud of his friendly relations with the officers of the regular army "wherever we have met, whether in rough conflict with the enemy or in the peaceful walks of quiet life," and he did not wish to see those friendships disturbed. "War may once again come upon our country," he reflected, "and I again have the pleasure of seeing them in the field. If so, I wish to meet them not only as brothers in arms, but also in feeling."

If the appointments were made on the grounds that only the West Point–trained were worthy to wear the epaulet, moreover, he believed that his acceptance would have implied to his "gallant countrymen" that he alone was worthy of a field-grade commission. "This superiority I do not claim," he told Pierce, "but, on the contrary, I believe there are many who would not only have been good appointments, but would have rendered eminent service against the Indians in the cavalry regiments, which are created for that particular duty."[39]

With the publication of this letter, McCulloch assumed he had fallen under Pierce's displeasure and saw no reason why he should seek "to conciliate an administration that has treated others as well as [himself as badly] as this has." With no further business in Washington, he planned to return to Texas in time to attend the spring session of the Federal court in Tyler if, as he feared, he were not first removed as marshal. "If such should occur," he would try to "leave things as favorable as possible" for Henry's appointment as his successor. Pierce, however, seems to have been truly saddened by McCulloch's decision, and on 9 March he wrote to the marshal expressing his concern. "I just received your note of yesterday," wrote the president. "I regard the determination expressed by you with much regret." Pierce had just learned that McCulloch intended to leave Washington that day, and he hoped that McCulloch would "if at all practical" allow the president to see him at the War Department prior to his departure. Whether the two men met again is unknown, but McCulloch was back in Texas by mid-April, having resumed his duties as marshal.[40]

From Tyler he wrote to McClelland, again battling his old nemesis, government inefficiency and red tape. McCulloch was already out of patience with Washington, and his temper with the Treasury Department was especially short after he learned that he must support the courts with his own money. His 13 March requisition for $5,000 had been cut to $4,000, and even that had not yet been forwarded from Washington, probably because his deputies had made errors in preparing vouchers or because his request was late in reaching Washington. "It is well known to the Department that the proceeds of the marshal's office does not enable me in all cases to employ the best men to be found in the Country to attend courts," McCulloch snapped at the secretary, whom he also reminded that "the courts being held at four different places in the State, and they remote from Galveston, is and must remain my excuse for any delay in making returns at an early period after the adjournment of the courts."[41]

Only for a brief time in June was a hint of excitement in the air. "The revolution is again broken out in Mexico," wrote the marshal. Following his release from imprisonment for his 1853 Reynosa raid, José María Jesús Carbajal had been reported as crossing far up the Rio Grande with five hundred to one thousand men. By December 1854 Juan N. Almonte, Mexican minister to the United States, informed the American secretary of state, William A. Marcy, that the Mexican revolutionary was again contemplating invasion and insurrection in northern Mexico, and by summer he was reportedly massing troops near Brownsville. "I shall proceed at once to the Rio Grande," McCulloch wrote to McClelland, "and use all means in my power to preserve that neutrality so necessary to the peace of both nations. There will doubtless be much work for the Grand Jury, and additional expenses incurred in arresting and bringing offenders to justice." Because of a change of plans or because of McCulloch's swift action, however, Carbajal marched his forces into the heart of Mexico to do battle with Santa Anna's centralist dictatorship and never again troubled the Rio Grande frontier.[42]

EIGHT

Mission to Zion

As 1855 drew to a close, Ben McCulloch continued to find himself ensnarled in the bureaucratic coils of the Federal marshal's office. Once more he was writing lengthy and detailed letters to Secretary McClelland concerning payments for witnesses, bailiffs and criers, fuel and lights, stationery and furniture, "and *c*., besides $1,000 rent to be paid quarterly, which is always done," for courthouses at Galveston, Austin, Tyler, and Brownsville. Costs always seemed to be rising, and the Treasury Department seemed always to be tardy with its payments, leaving the marshal typically "somewhat embarrassed for the want of funds to close up the expenses of the term." The fact that Secretary McClelland leaned notoriously toward the free-soil faction in the struggle for Kansas also made McCulloch's dealings with him barely tolerable.[1]

McCulloch's interest in the economics of slavery was only slight. He never owned more than a few slaves at any one time and never participated in the plantation economy. His treatment of his few bondsmen seems to have been relatively benign. He wrote fondly of old Aunt Lucy, a house servant who had helped to raise him, and he freed in California the two men who had accompanied him to the goldfields. Fannie McCulloch Driver, one of the McCulloch family slaves Ben brought from Tennessee, remembered McCulloch as "a reasonable master." Her mother was Ben's and Henry's cook, and Driver recalled that "de workers had all kinds ob things to eat; meat, bacon, eggs, soups ob all kinds, biscuits and corn-pones," in general a better diet than that enjoyed by other Texas slaves. "Our Mawster McCulloch," in fact, "was putty good to us." Nevertheless, at age eighty Driver recalled that "he did whoop some ob de slaves some-times," and although the practice of educating slaves was not forbidden by Texas law, "us slaves was never allowed to learn our A B C's." Whatever his personal and financial interest in slavery might have been, Ben McCulloch was a product of his culture: the son of a slaveholding family and a proud citizen of a region increasingly embattled by northern and European foes for its dedication to the "peculiar institution." McCulloch was fiercely committed to slavery in the abstract and looked upon the abolitionist assault on the institution as an affront to southern honor. He therefore took an avid interest in the political crisis that the question was forcing upon the nation.

Increasingly contemptuous of the North and its institutions, and set in his belief that an abolitionist conspiracy was in place not only to end slavery but to destroy the South's political liberties, Ben recommended to Henry, then a member of the Texas legislature, that he introduce a joint resolution appointing commissioners to negotiate with the owners of Mount Vernon for its purchase by the state of Texas. "It would be a proud day for our state when it was proclaimed that she owned the Tomb of Washington. Besides," he wrote, "we may want a campaign ground near the city in the event of the election of a Black Republican candidate."[2]

During the final weeks of June 1856, with Pierce's term of office drawing to a close and the great regional controversy over the expansion and perpetuation of slavery reaching its crisis, McCulloch took his first trip into New England. After spending no longer in Boston than required to visit "the monument on Breeds Hill, Faneuil Hall, the Commons, etc.," Ben reported to Henry that "the whole population looked as though they were just returning from a funeral. Too puritanical in appearance to be good neighbors or patriotic citizens."[3]

Back in Washington on 2 July, McCulloch was able to observe firsthand the maneuverings of the upcoming political campaign and perhaps hoped to enhance his own chances of acquiring a more congenial position in the Federal government as well. Writing to Henry soon after his arrival, Ben assessed the strengths and weaknesses of the various candidates. The American or Know-Nothing party was beginning to break apart on the inevitable rock of sectionalism. At the party's convention in Philadelphia, many northern delegates withdrew because the platform was not sufficiently firm in opposing the expansion of slavery. The remaining delegates nominated former president Millard Fillmore, whose candidacy was endorsed by the sad remnant of the Whig party, which could not support either James Buchanan or John Charles Frémont. Fillmore's nomination, however, "falls on the ear of the country still born," Ben wrote to Henry, with the only apprehension entertained by the Democrats, who met in Cincinnati on 2 June to select their nominee, being that Fillmore might decline the nomination. "No fears are sustained as regards the election of the nominee of the Cincinnati convention." Fillmore, nevertheless, had McCulloch's good opinion due to a speech he had recently delivered in Albany. There, according to Ben, he had told the North that the South "would not permit a sectional president of the north to govern them." McCulloch shared this opinion most earnestly, and he vowed to be "the first to volunteer my services as a soldier to prevent it, and would rather see the streets of this city knee deep in blood than to see a black republican take possession of that chair."[4]

The Democratic delegates in Cincinnati were making "great efforts," Ben reported, "to secure that nomination for their own particular favourite." McCulloch had been asked to add the weight of his name to the cause of one or more of the Democratic contenders but declined to do so. "I have my preference as well as others," he told Henry, "but will waive them and go with all my might with the man selected by that convention, provided he is solid on Southern rights, and I don't think it possible for any other to get the nomination." The Democrats, he believed, were the only party that could be considered "a national party—the only one that has the power or inclination to do justice to all parts of this great union and hand down to posterity the priceless gift bequeathed us by our forefathers."[5]

The Democrats adopted a platform that endorsed the Kansas-Nebraska Act and defended popular sovereignty. The leaders wanted a candidate who had not made many enemies and who was also not closely associated with the explosive issue of "Bleeding Kansas." James Buchanan of Pennsylvania, a reliable party stalwart who as minister to England had been safely out of the country during the Kansas-Nebraska debate, therefore became their leading contender. A reaction to what McCulloch described as "the manouvering of the friends of the prominent men North" made him at first believe, however, that the nomination would be thrown to "some Southern man." Were Buchanan not nominated on the first ballot, he believed, "no Northern man will be."

The Republicans, engaging in their first presidential contest, faced the campaign with confidence. They denounced the Kansas-Nebraska Act and the expansion of slavery. Eager to present a safe candidate, the Republicans nominated John Charles Frémont, who had made a national reputation as an explorer of the Far West. McCulloch did not see much likelihood of the election of Frémont, "notwithstanding his friends in the North are sanguine." Rather, he foresaw a reaction against the Republican candidate "unless they can keep up the Kansas excitement or occasionally get a man's head broken by some Southerner." Kansas, opened to settlement by the Kansas-Nebraska Act of 1854, had by 1856 become the battleground of the proslavery and the antislavery camps. On 19 and 20 May 1856 Senator Charles Sumner of Massachusetts delivered an intemperate attack on the pro-southern Kansans, and on the following day a group of these so-called Border Ruffians destroyed a free-soil center at Lawrence. On 22 May Preston Brooks of South Carolina, a nephew of Senator Andrew Butler, whom Sumner had vilified in his speech, strode into the Senate and broke his gutta-percha cane over Sumner's head. Two days later the scene shifted back to Kansas, where John Brown and his band of radical abolitionists hacked to death five proslavery settlers on Pottawatomie Creek. The Republicans, McCulloch lamented, "made at least 100,000 votes out of the Sumner and Brooks affair, and would rejoice at another occurrence of the kind." Having only contempt for individuals who would submit to being "whipped like dogs so they may go home whining and make political capital out of it instead of giving blow for blow like men," McCulloch hoped "never to be a member of such a society as will countenance such arrant cowards and poltroons as Sumner and his associates."

Although he professed to be "really uneasy about the office," McCulloch chose to skip the judicial term at Tyler rather than miss the political action in Washington. His deputy in Tyler reported that all his officers were "getting on very well," and he was increasingly restive under the administrative problems associated with the office. Although he did "not expect to make much out of it" and wished to be soon rid of the appointment, McCulloch did hope that when he was finished, he would "be done with it altogether" and not, like his predecessor, "bothered by harassing law suits." In addition to his political interests, Ben still had Lucy Gwin on his mind and was thinking strongly of "trying to get married this summer," although, as he told Henry, he had "said nothing to any lady on the subject." While Ben was observing the political affray and courting the ladies that summer, an act "to create the county of McCulloch (in honor of Captain Ben McCulloch)" was introduced to the Texas senate on 29 July and was passed on 27 August. On the "gloomy subject" of politics, however, Ben was far less happy. From the White Sulphur Springs Ben wrote to Henry on 14 August that "many talk of disunion that never spoke of it before, and in the event of Frémont's election, the Union is a dead letter." Even should Buchanan be elected, McCulloch felt that the country would be "so shaken by this contest as to render its continuance precarious. God in His wisdom may preserve us. Nothing else will, I fear."

For most southerners, the threat of honor lost was as much an inducement to secession as was the defense of slavery, and as much as McCulloch dreaded a disruption of the Union, he was ready, even eager, to dissolve the alliance that bound the states rather than "submit to such degradation" as to allow the North to "force Frémont upon us." Such an insult to the region's concept of self-worth could not be tolerated, and violence alone, southerners of all classes felt, could erase the stigma of interference and condescension from the North. In common with John C. Calhoun and increasing numbers of southerners whom he met on his travels, McCulloch believed that conventions should be held throughout the South at which the slave states might "agree upon some course." Personally, McCulloch stood for "open opposition" and recommended that in the event of a Republican victory the South should "at once march an army to Washington" to prevent Frémont's inauguration on southern soil. The North should be informed, he wrote, "that we should not interfere with them, nor should they with us in any government we might think proper to establish for ourselves." If Frémont were to be inaugurated, he concluded, "I am for secession with Texas. I will not be treated as their inferiors."[6]

Election day, 4 November 1856, saw Democrat James Buchanan the winning candidate, polling 1.838 million popular votes to 1.341 million for Frémont and 874,000 for Fillmore. Always a friend of the South, Buchanan was a happy choice for McCulloch, who, according to Texas governor Francis Richard Lubbock, was "one of the most intimate friends of Mr. Buchanan" and who was "at all times a welcome and honored guest at the executive mansion." Ominously, however, only a slight shift of votes in Pennsylvania and Illinois would have thrown those states into the Republican column and elected Frémont.[7]

As for his matrimonial prospects, Ben confided to Henry, "they stand status quo," although he intended "to move them from that point even if they progress backwards." As he had written to Henry two years earlier, he had met "a great many pretty women in these mountains," but none struck him as the right one to bring home to Texas. "All such places are dull unless a man could take an interest in some particular Lady. Which happens not to be my case at this particular time." Therefore, he resolved not to remain long at the springs but to "wend my way to other posts and other people more to my liking just at this moment." "He is still a bachelor," the Galveston *Weekly News* reported on 25 November, "but there is doubtless time enough yet" for him to marry.[8]

McCulloch's long sojourn in Washington and the North had, as he feared, left the marshal's office in considerable disarray. Returning to Tyler on 17 December, he found his affairs "in rather bad trim." His deputy there, who was "not worth his salt," was sick, and his clerk was nowhere to be found. His books were literally "thrown together," the result of a recent fire near the Federal courthouse. Worse, his chief deputy had allowed the other deputies to keep all the money they had collected, "being too lazy to send papers by mail to other deputies at a distance."[9]

Despite his frustrations with the Pierce administration and with the office of marshal, McCulloch decided early in the Buchanan administration to reapply for his old position. Among those recommending his reappointment was Congressman Peter H. Bell, who wrote to President Buchanan that McCulloch "has discharged his duties as marshal with fidelity and ability. His antecedents as a good citizen and a distinguished military man of Texas commend him to your excellency, and I trust he may receive this appointment or any other which you may choose to give." Senators Thomas J. Rusk and Sam Houston seconded Bell's nomination; "His reputation is too well established to need further commendation," they wrote. Buchanan was moved to reappoint McCulloch, who, back in Texas, received his new commission on 12 May and by summer was once again engaged in the monotonous chore of accounting for money spent on rental of buildings and otherwise caring for the needs of the court.[10]

McCulloch spent part of the following July on "a flying trip to Kansas" on business for the government. "The whole Utah movement of the Army depended on my report," he wrote to his mother, and "once it has been followed to the letter," as he predicted it would be in the fall, a column of two thousand soldiers would be dispatched for the Utah Territory and another one thousand would be sent to Kansas. "Kansas," he reported, "is a beautiful country," reminding him in many ways of eastern Texas, but lost to the South. "The pro-slavery men all give it up," he lamented, only meaning to remain long enough to "make it a Democratic, sound constitutional state and not a black Republican state."[11]

McCulloch intended to return to Austin for the next meeting of the legislature because his name had been frequently mentioned as a potential candidate for the United States Senate at the expiration of Sam Houston's term. Although the Senate seat would not become vacant until March 1859, it was being filled by the Texas legislature in November 1857. President Buchanan expressed the hope that McCulloch would be chosen senator. The new secretary of war, former Virginia governor John B. Floyd, had more than once done the same, and "other distinguished men" had mentioned the subject to him as well. McCulloch, however, expected by 1859 to be in the army, so that even if appointed or elected to the Senate, he "would never expect to enter upon its duties." Therefore he attempted to suppress the notion that he was "at all prominent before the people of Texas," regretting, he wrote to Henry, that his name ever got into the papers in connection with the senatorial election, since he did not wish to be interpreted in "a false position" and felt the publicity more likely to do him harm than good. He believed that his "prominence now and defeat eventually" would be unfortunate or that his election would prove "at most, but a compliment" because he would most certainly not take a seat in the Senate if he were offered the command of a regiment, an eventuality he felt quite certain would come to pass—"both as to the raising of some additional regiments and having the command of one of them tendered me." Thus, he reasoned, "there is little to be gained and much to be lost" by having his name placed before the public in regard to a Senate seat.[12]

George Washington Pascal, editor of Austin's *Southern Intelligencer*, believed, however, that "none who have been named," including McCulloch, would be loath "to take the senatorial robes, provided the coast was clear—and that they could beat all the other candidates." Indeed, Ben hedged his bets somewhat, advising Henry that by tacit agreement the Senate seat held by Thomas Jefferson Rusk belonged to eastern Texas and that of Sam Houston to the west. A caucus of the western members was likely to determine Houston's successor, and there McCulloch's appointment might be assured, although he predicted "a warm contest between certain gentlemen for this nomination," John Hemphill, chief justice of the state supreme court, and Isaiah Addison Paschal, a representative from San Antonio, among them. "If the legislature should think proper to confer the office upon me," McCulloch felt that he "should most certainly esteem it the highest compliment that had ever, or, in all probability, ever would be paid" him. He cautioned his brother, however, that if he were unable to reach Austin in time for the meeting of the legislature, Henry must see that Ben's name was not "used in that connection if there is a single chance for defeat." All speculation ended on 9 November 1857 when Hemphill was elected to fill Houston's seat.[13]

At that time McCulloch was in Galveston, settling accounts for the previous court session in Brownsville and preparing for the term to begin there. His correspondence with Washington was rendered somewhat less odious, perhaps, by the presence of a new interior secretary, Jacob Thompson, a genial Mississippian whose states' rights views were more in accord with McCulloch's principles. Nevertheless he was still plagued with such nuisances as finding that the clerk had failed to furnish the marshal a copy of the order for the payment of petty jurors, thus necessitating another long delay in remittance and, no doubt, additional outlay of McCulloch's personal funds. As during the Pierce administration, he continued his refrains of "please remit as early as convenient," "forwarded to the First Auditor of the Treasury Department the accounts of expenses," "vouchers forwarded," and "delay in getting off the accounts."[14]

Back in Washington a month later, McCulloch received more disappointing news. Although the previous autumn he had been certain not only of seeing the creation of a new regiment for the defense of the Texas frontier but also the command of it for himself, by the end of January he could see "no chance for an increase of the army, and consequently no opportunity of my getting a permanent position in its ranks." Although he claimed to have no regrets and to foresee "other fields for enterprise about to offer," this was a bitter blow. A war between Spain and Mexico, which was then brewing, would give the aspiring soldier "a much better chance for usefulness and distinction," he believed; but more important, McCulloch felt that his region was "on the eve of a rupture with the North," and were it to come, his "services may be needed at home."[15]

A third possible exercise for his sword, an expedition to the Utah Territory to suppress a growing Mormon insurrection there, would, he feared, "again be a failure," because he believed Congress too dilatory to act with any decisiveness. "Betwixt the Black Republicans of the North and filibusters of the South, I fear our glorious country will be for the first time disgraced in the eyes of the world as well as in those of her own patriotic citizens." That autumn, despite his disparaging remarks about armed southern adventurism, McCulloch seriously contemplated joining William Walker's ill-starred filibuster to Nicaragua, and had he done so, no doubt many other Texans would have followed him.[16]

A brief but severe illness slowed McCulloch in the winter of 1857–58, but, nursed by his niece Rush and medicated with a remedy compounded of "one-third beef gall and two-thirds French brandy," he was sufficiently recovered by early February to return to Washington "ready for anything that will give me a chance to increase my reputation or purse." Even at this late date, the matter of the defense of the Texas frontier was not a dead letter, and McCulloch still had a very powerful and committed partisan in Congress arguing the cause of both a new regiment on the western border and the command of that unit for Ben McCulloch. On 1 February 1858 Sam Houston again informed the Senate that "Texas desires to have a more efficient force."

As early as 1849 McCulloch's old comrade George Wilkins Kendall had written to the Austin *Texas State Gazette* that if Col. William S. Harney, commander of the Second Dragoons, then stationed in Texas, had his way, he would call in "McCulloch, and all the frontier men, and pursue the Comanches to the heads of the Brazos, the Colorado, and even up under the spurs of the Rocky Mountains. . . . Harney can take the dragoons along with him," Kendall opined, "but for the light work he must have Texas Rangers—without them even he . . . can effect but little." Houston concurred absolutely. Texas, he contended, demanded soldiers who understood Indians and the mode of warfare that must be waged against them. Rather than an increase in the number of Federal troops stationed in Texas, Houston called for a regiment of Texas Rangers to protect the frontier. Granted that, the United States Army could withdraw "every regular soldier of the artillery, infantry, and dragoons" from the state. A single regiment of rangers, he asserted, "will give more protection than all the regular Army of the United States." The Second Cavalry, "though well designed," was unaccustomed to frontier life and therefore "utterly incompetent" as an Indian fighting command, said Houston. It had "not accomplished the purpose for which it was intended" and was "comparatively useless" at keeping the Comanches and Kiowas away from the border settlements and isolated farmsteads. Texas Rangers, on the other hand, would be men who could ride as well as the Indians and who understood "their disposition," their "inclinations," and "their points of foray and attack." They would be capable of taking the war to the enemy in their own territory and could "track them as the beagle would the deer."[17]

Taking up the refrain, familiar since the days of Andrew Jackson, of attacking West Point–trained officers and professional soldiers in favor of a well-regulated militia led by homegrown officers familiar with the terrain on which they would fight as well as with the enemies they would naturally face, Houston raised the example, still fresh in American memory, of the service of the volunteer regiments in 1846–48. "Who achieved the glories of the war with Mexico?" he asked rhetorically. "Were they regular soldiers?" The regulars, he conceded, "fought well and could be shot down," but "the efficient men," those who exhibited the most "gallant and daring" behavior on the battlefield, were the volunteers. Speaking, no doubt, directly to his old antagonist Jefferson Davis, now returned to the Senate after his term as secretary of war, Houston pointed out for special commendation not only Hays's regiment of Texas Rangers but the Mississippi Rifles, which Davis himself had led. "Yet they tell me," Houston went on, "that volunteers are not to be relied upon"—a reference, no doubt, to Davis's attack on the rangers' record. "If you have no reliance upon them, the country is not free." Free men, he argued, constituted the pool from which American volunteers had always been drawn. They had always been ready and capable. They were fully acquainted with frontier life and cost no more than regulars. "Rely on them in every emergency," Houston concluded, firing a Parthian salvo at the United States Military Academy and its reputation as a nursery for tyrants, "and you place your reliance, not on a broken reed, but on a strong, firm staff, that will not deceive you or wound the hand that presses on it."[18]

McCulloch, who was in Washington as a keen observer of the debate on Texas frontier defense, wrote to his mother soon after Houston's presentation. Although "some fighting in Congress" had taken place, he reported, no action had yet been taken on "those matters in which I feel an interest." He did not believe the size of the army would be increased, and because of the urgency of "the Kansas question," he felt sure nothing would be done soon toward launching the rumored punitive expedition to Utah. He did believe, however, that the "probability of raising a regiment of Rangers for our state" existed, and if the regiment were raised, he promised to do all in his power to see that its command devolved upon Henry. "It will suit him," he wrote to their mother, "and he will suit it."[19]

The Kansas question, however, remained foremost, not only in the mind of Congress but of all America. A proslavery constitutional convention had met in Lecompton, Kansas, on 28 October 1857 and had drafted for the territory a constitution highly prejudicial to the rights of its free-soil citizens and of questionable legal authority. When the plebiscite on ratification was boycotted by the free-soilers, the constitution was carried by a large majority, and the Buchanan administration supported it in an effort to bring Kansas into the Union as a slave state. In Congress, however, it was destined for severe scrutiny. As the date for a legislative decision neared, the nation became increasingly polarized, with North and South for or against the proposed constitution with equal intensity. "If they reject the Lecompton constitution," McCulloch rightly observed, "there will be trouble in this Union." The states of the Lower South, he believed, would meet in convention and in all probability would withdraw from the Union, and Texas would be among them. If this were to come to pass, he wrote to his mother, "I have no disposition to fight the battles of the North against the Mormons, but will most willingly turn them over to their friends, the Black Republicans, who are now sustaining them by throwing obstacles in the way of the administration so as to prevent a vigorous and successful campaign being carried out against them." The vote on the Lecompton constitution, which would come on 2 August 1858, McCulloch believed, would set the course of his personal fate as well. Although he was uncertain of his future, he assured his mother that "we are on the eve of troublesome times, and every Southern man should be at his post and ready to act promptly."[20]

Three days later Sam Houston again took the Senate floor to plead for rangers to protect the Texas frontier, and to lash the regular army, then patrolling its borders. In the harshest speech he ever directed against the professional military establishment, he attacked West Point as incompetent to produce officers capable of dealing with the Indians of the Texas frontier and insisted that the academy undermined the liberties of American citizens. In a heated debate with Jefferson Davis, Houston reminded his colleagues that "the Senator from Mississippi" had praised the achievements of the dragoons under Harney and Capt. Henry Heth against the Sioux at the 1855 battle of Blue Water in the Nebraska Territory. "A single company of rangers would have done all that," Houston insisted. "Jack Hays, Ben McCulloch, and [Robert] Gillespie achieved more than that, and I believe they never had more than seventy-five men, and those for a few days only. Give us rangers in Texas."[21]

Davis fiercely rebutted Houston's argument, replying that no army had ever been "more favorably composed for desperate service" than that on the Texas frontier. "The Senator from Texas," Davis maintained, "spoke in language well calculated to feed the vanity of his state, but not as a historian." Citing Zachary Taylor's observation that the Texas Rangers had created a serious problem of discipline in his army in Mexico, Davis insisted that "if the General had gone further, and said that irregular cavalry always produce disturbance in the neighborhood of a camp, he would have said no more than my experience would confirm."

Although a ranger regiment was ultimately raised at Federal expense, Col. John Salmon (Rip) Ford was called to its command. When Jefferson Davis, never one to forget a friend or forgive a foe, became president of the Confederate States, the memory of his exchange with Houston over the efficiency of his prized Second Cavalry no doubt further disinclined him to reward Ben McCulloch, the man most closely associated with Houston's attempts to reshape the frontier military establishment that Davis had built as secretary of war.[22]

Second only to Bleeding Kansas among the troubles of the American republic in 1858 was President Buchanan's "war" with the Mormons. The Church of Jesus Christ of Latter-day Saints, one of the numerous new religions that had flowered in America in the 1820s and 1830s, had originated in western New York, with splinter communities located in all parts of the United States. Seeking a more congenial environment under the leadership of their prophet, Joseph Smith, they moved to Ohio, then to Missouri, and finally to Nauvoo, Illinois. Everywhere they met with resentment, largely caused by their economic and community organization. At Nauvoo they particularly outraged their neighbors by introducing polygamy. Their troubles came to a climax when a mob lynched Smith. Smith's successor, Brigham Young, a radical separatist, decided that if the Mormons were to escape further persecution, they would have to move outside the United States.[23]

In 1846 almost the entire Mormon community left Nauvoo. Their destination, selected by Young, was the Great Salt Lake basin in Utah, a territory so arid and barren that no other people had any desire to live there. By 1850 more than eleven thousand people were settled in and around the Mormon metropolis of Salt Lake City. With the aid of irrigation they made the desert bloom, establishing a thriving agriculture and building a profitable trade with immigrants on the way to California. Once in Utah, the Mormons occupied an inland mountain fortress, a thousand miles beyond the Kansas frontier. There they established a theocracy they called the State of Deseret, complete with constitution, governor, currency, and army and a social and economic system based upon collective labor and centralized planning and authority. Federal officials who had entered the Mormon state after it passed into the hands of the United States as a result of the Mexican War returned to Washington denouncing Brigham Young's government as a church state, fundamentally disloyal to the United States. Although the Mormons claimed to be loyal to the American Constitution and acknowledged the status of their home as United States territory, they intended to pay little attention to Washington or its officials. When Young publicly proclaimed the doctrine of polygamy, which had been practiced in private for more than a decade, outraged reformers, ministers, and politicians reacted to destroy his authority. Buchanan, feeling the need to appease this powerful segment of his constituency and to establish Federal authority in Utah, ordered the army to prepare to march on Salt Lake City.

By April 1857 Buchanan had removed Young as governor of the Utah Territory on suspicion of insurrectionary designs and hoped to stifle the secessionist movement in Utah by appointing a gentile in his place. The role required a tactful and courageous man capable of controlling an isolated community that had a history of treating Federal officers roughly. Ben McCulloch was the administration's first choice for the job. After a month of deliberation, however, McCulloch declined the office so little suited to his taste and temperament.[24]

Although he invariably turned down the offer of that and other territorial governorships, always holding out for a military appointment, McCulloch accepted a delicate mission to the Mormons "to try and settle the matter with Brigham Young without bloodshed." On 6 April 1857, under pressure to avoid a military confrontation, Buchanan signed a proclamation emphasizing the offenses of the Mormons and the malign influence of their leaders and declaring the territory to be in a state of rebellion. On 27 January 1858 a joint resolution was introduced in the Senate proposing the appointment of two commissioners to the Mormons. The task of the commissioners would be to find a peaceful solution to the controversy, and they would be authorized to grant the rebellious church elders a full presidential pardon if the commissioners thought conditions warranted. McCulloch and senator-elect Lazarus W. Powell of Kentucky were chosen as Buchanan's official representatives. As the president's emissaries, the two were to offer pardon for "seditions and treasons heretofore committed," provided the Mormons would pledge acceptance of Federal authority and obedience to Federal officials. The commissioners were ordered to set out at once for Utah, circulate the proclamation throughout the territory, and acquaint the Mormons with their "unfortunate relations" with the government and "how greatly it would be to their interest" to submit promptly and peacefully to its laws.

The commissioners were to reach Salt Lake City as soon as possible in order to treat with the Mormon leaders before Brig. Gen. Albert Sidney Johnston could launch the punitive expedition against the home of the Saints. McCulloch and Powell were to assure the Mormons that the army's mission in Utah had no reference to their religious tenets and that if they resumed their allegiance, no power in the United States had either the right or the will to interfere with their religion. "To restore peace in this manner," wrote Secretary of War Floyd in his instructions to the commissioners, "is the single purpose of your mission."[25]

McCulloch was perhaps not the most tactful ambassador whom Buchanan could have chosen, but if the president's intention was to convince Utah of his resolve, McCulloch was probably the sternest. "I had much rather he had gone at the head of a gallant regiment," wrote Henry to their mother, "as it would better suit his taste and habits," but after preparing his will in Washington on 3 April 1858, Ben McCulloch set out for the Far West, bearing the olive branch instead of the sword.[26]

McCulloch and Powell reached Fort Leavenworth, Kansas, by way of St. Louis "without accident or delay." There the commissioners were furnished with five ambulances, each drawn by four excellent mules, and with three saddle horses each for themselves and their escort—one sergeant and five dragoons, a wagon master, five teamsters, and a guide. Other than carrying forage for their animals, the party traveled lightly and found the ambulances so comfortable that tents were unnecessary. They began their crossing of the plains on 25 April, expecting to make thirty-five miles a day and to reach Johnston's camp "at the earliest possible moment."[27]

McCulloch's party was particularly well armed. A part of their mission was to test six Springfield rifles and as many Sharp's carbines for the army, and McCulloch took singular delight in riding ahead of the party for several hours each day to shoot antelope, thus giving the men "a supply of the best of fresh meat." True to his lifelong penchant for arms and arms collecting, upon his return to Washington McCulloch reported to G. W. Morse, inventor of one of the new carbines, that the commissioners and their escort "met with no gun or carbine that equaled it in accuracy or length of range." The former ranger was sufficiently impressed with the carbine's reliability that he considered it, with its new primed metallic cartridge, "for all practical use, the best that has yet been invented."[28]

On 2 May 1858 McCulloch and Powell arrived at Fort Kearney, Nebraska. Two days later they pushed on for Fort Laramie, Wyoming, and on 27 May, one month and two days after leaving Fort Leavenworth, the commissioners and their party entered Camp Scott, exceedingly anxious and apprehensive about the health and condition of the soldiers there. In the East, rumors had circulated of subsistence on mule meat and even of outright starvation among Johnston's men, and the commissioners "wished to read the story on each soldier's face." As McCulloch passed through the camp, however, he remarked that "these men don't look as though they were suffering from hunger," and closer inspection revealed that their discipline and morale were quite high. If McCulloch ever harbored any resentment toward Albert Sidney Johnston over McCulloch's failure to gain command of the Second Cavalry, it was certainly not reflected in his assessment of Johnston's capacity as leader of the expedition to Utah. "Never," he declared, had he seen troops "better disciplined, better disposed, or better prepared for the field." Unstinting in his praise of Johnston and his little army, McCulloch reported to Floyd that "the best order and most cheerful feeling prevail" despite the "severe trials and difficulties" the soldiers had undergone, and that all at Camp Scott conducted themselves "in a manner becoming American soldiers." He was pleased, also, with the full and free nature of the commissioners' relations with their commander, reporting that Johnston cooperated "most heartily and cordially" with him and Powell, doing everything in his power to facilitate their mission.[29]

On 1 June McCulloch and Powell reported the arrival of the advance guard of Lt. Col. William Hoffman's command, the remainder of his column being seven or eight days away. Johnston was of the opinion that Capt. Randolph B. Marcy was fifteen or twenty days behind, and that upon his arrival the expeditionary force would be ready to march to Salt Lake City fully prepared to quickly disperse "the best army the Mormons can bring into the field." The grace period provided by Marcy's delay gave the commissioners time to treat with the people of Utah before the military would be united and ready to strike a punitive blow.

Despite the fact that Alfred Cumming, whom President Buchanan had appointed as Utah's new governor, had recently returned from Salt Lake City and informed his colleagues that the Mormon army had disbanded, the commissioners remained suspicious of Brigham Young and other Mormon leaders and feared treachery. The Mormons had by this time abandoned their northern settlements and had moved their women, children, and supplies to Provo, fifty miles south, leaving only about fifteen hundred men to protect the abandoned capital and to burn it if hostilities commenced. This move indicated to the commissioners the Mormons' intention to leave the territory, to prevent their families from coming into contact with the army and the civil authorities of the United States, or to "place themselves in an attitude to fight the army when it shall enter the valley." Young, one Salt Lake City woman informed Lt. John Van Deusen DuBois of the Mounted Rifle regiment, had told his people that the army "would tear down their houses, kill all the men & reserve the women for prostitution. What a character to give an army free from every crime of that kind for fifty years," DuBois remonstrated. In hopes of preventing outbreaks of violence between the army and the Mormons, McCulloch and Powell pledged themselves to "use every effort to see and confer with the Mormon people, and to make known their intentions to General Johnston by the time he is ready to march."[30]

The commissioners intended to leave for "the Great Salt Lake City" on 1 June, but McCulloch was stricken with a bout of "mountain fever" and was unable to ride until 2:00 P.M. the following day. After McCulloch recovered, he and Powell started for the Mormon capital, expecting to arrive in three or four days. Slowed by McCulloch's illness, however, they did not reach there until 7 June. Their intention on arriving had been to establish communication with Young and the other leaders of the Mormon people in the "strong hopes" that they would be induced to "submit quietly to the authority of the government." Dissident Saints had informed them that "great disaffection" existed among the Mormons and that large numbers of them would leave Utah but for their fear of the so-called Danite band, a secret Mormon society gentiles believed to be a terrorist organization dedicated to the preservation of church hegemony. These citizens, McCulloch and Powell reported, desired and deserved "the protection of the flag."[31]

With Young and his lieutenants at Provo, McCulloch and Powell opened direct communications with the people of Salt Lake City, informing them of the purpose of their mission. On the evening of 8 April, however, a committee of citizens informed the commissioners that the people of the territory desired that they confer with Young, a request with which McCulloch and Powell gladly concurred. The following evening the committee called again to inform McCulloch and Powell that Young was ready to meet with them and would be in Salt Lake City on the evening of 10 June. Upon Young's arrival, McCulloch and Powell met informally with Young; Counselor Herber C. Kimball and the Mormon military commander, Lt. Gen. Daniel H. Wells, who constituted the first presidency of the church; several of the twelve apostles; and other church leaders, explaining to them the object of their visit. On the following morning they opened formal negotiations at the council house.[32]

At this meeting McCulloch and Powell restated the object of their mission and informed the Mormon leadership of President Buchanan's views and intentions: that "the authority of the United States be maintained in Utah and that the Constitution and laws of the nation should be enforced and executed in this Territory." In accordance with their instructions, the commissioners sought to induce the Mormons "to submit quietly and peaceably to the authority of the United States." Failing that, they warned, the president would send the army of the United States to the Utah Territory "in such numbers, at such times, and to such places" as necessary to maintain national sovereignty and would establish military posts to protect emigration to and from the Pacific, prevent Indian depredations, and secure the cooperation of the people.

Informed that if they would accept the laws of the United States and receive the Federal officials appointed by Buchanan, no necessity would remain for the army to enforce civil authority, the Mormon leaders responded with bluff and bluster. "God was our general and had preserved us at Nauvoo and still would continue to do so," Young retorted. "If He is still your General, you have nothing to fear," McCulloch responded. Maj. Warren Snow of the Mormon army, according to McCulloch's recollection, "commenced to abuse the President," whereupon McCulloch replied that he "did not come here to hear the Government abused." "It was unpleasant to me," he later recollected, "but if forced to would do so with what patience I could." Snow then denounced the president's proclamation as "a tissue of lies from beginning to end." On this assertion McCulloch assured him that he was in error. Referring the elder to the final paragraph of the document stating that "the military forces now in Utah and hereafter to be sent there will not be withdrawn until the inhabitants of that Territory shall manifest a proper sense of the duty they owe to this Government," McCulloch promised that it was true and that "the army would come."

Realizing that their bluff had been called, Young, Kimball, and Wells shifted their stance and expressed gratification that the president had sent commissioners to Utah and stated that they were "attached to the Constitution and government of the United States." They spoke harshly, however, of many of the officials who had held office in the territory and of "the wrongs and injuries heretofore done them." Expressing a desire to live in peace under the Constitution of the United States, they denied that they had driven any official from Utah or prevented any civil officers from entering the territory. They did, however, admit to having burned army wagon trains and to having driven off army cattle during the previous fall, for which they accepted the president's pardon.

The seemingly amiable course of the meeting was severely shaken, however, when O. Porter Rockwell, one of Young's principal lieutenants, entered the council chamber and whispered a message to Young. The prophet rose and demanded of the commissioners, "Are you aware, sir, that those troops are on the move towards the city?" Powell denied the possibility of such a move, but Young insisted that he had received a dispatch to that effect and insisted, "My messenger would not deceive me." As the commissioners puzzled over the meaning of the news, Young commanded, "Brother Dunbar, sing 'Zion.' " Immediately the council house echoed with a favorite Mormon hymn:

> Sacred home of the prophets of God;
> Thy deliverance is nigh,
> Thy oppressors shall die,
> And gentiles shall bow
> 'neath thy rod.

Unintimidated but thoroughly frustrated, the commissioners withdrew from the chamber. "What would you do with such a people?" asked Governor Cumming. "Damn them! I would fight them if I had my way," replied McCulloch.[33]

Although he had told McCulloch, Powell, and Cumming before they left Camp Scott that he would not move before hearing from them, Johnston had, indeed, put his army on the march. The general had not believed that the army would be able to move before negotiations were complete, but a combination of Marcy's speed and Brigham Young's delaying tactics made him able and eager to advance. Cumming later upbraided Johnston for his provocative action, but Young knew that, having failed to dislodge or starve the United States expeditionary force during the winter, the Mormons had not the means to carry out their implied threat and so would not resist the army's advance. After a session of several hours on the eleventh, the conference adjourned until 9:00 A.M. the following day, when they again met at the council house. A large number of citizens were present, and elders of the church and officers of the Mormon army made speeches, in "general tone and sentiments" averse to Johnston's entry into the Salt Lake valley. Nevertheless, they were pleased to state that "the conference resulted in their agreeing to receive quietly and peaceably all the civil officers of the government, and not to resist them in the execution of their duties." Young and his followers promised they would offer no opposition to the army. At the close of the conference McCulloch and Powell made a short address to a large audience, expressing their gratification at the outcome of the negotiations and reiterating their promise that the army would "not molest or injure any peaceable citizens, in person or property." All present, they concluded, "appeared gratified at the result of the conference."[34]

Finally, disguising their capitulation behind a flood of face-saving rhetoric, the Mormon hierarchy accepted Buchanan's terms. On 12 June the commissioners invited Johnston to bring his army into the valley of the Saints. The commissioners had assured the Mormons of their safety and full civil rights but suggested that Johnston issue a proclamation stating that the army "would not trespass upon the rights or property of peaceable citizens." Such a proclamation, they assured him, "would greatly allay the existing anxiety" and would aid them in their task of returning civil life to normal in the Utah Territory. Somewhat surprised by the apprehension of the citizens of the territory, Johnston assured McCulloch and Powell that "under the twofold obligations of citizens and soldiers," his men "may be supposed to comprehend the rights of the people, and to be sufficiently mindful of the obligations of our oaths and not disregard the laws which govern us as a military body."

Johnston was not the only soldier to express bitterness at the result of the campaign. At Buchanan's pardon of the Mormons, Lieutenant DuBois lamented that "all the authorities seem to have separated the army from the government & joined another unholy alliance against it." Speaking for his fellow officers, he maintained that "we are all disgusted. If the Mormons are rebels, they should sue for pardon instead of its being given to them unasked. If they are not rebels this campaign is unjust." Despite the army's, and perhaps some of their own, misgivings, McCulloch and Powell assured Mormon leaders that "no person whatever will be anywise interfered with or molested in his person or rights, or in the peaceful pursuit of his avocations; and should protection be needed, they will find the army . . . as ready now to assist and protect them as it was to oppose them while it was believed they were resisting the laws of their government."[35]

With their regimental bands playing "Going over Jordan," Johnston's troops entered the valley and peacefully encamped near Salt Lake City. On 26 June the commissioners reported to the president, the secretary of war, and the general commanding the United States forces in the Utah Territory their pleasure in having settled "the unfortunate difficulties existing between the government of the United States and the people of Utah."[36]

With this accomplished, McCulloch and Powell visited Provo and the settlements to the south, to which most of the territory's people had fled. There they informed the citizens that the troubles between the Latter-day Saints and the government of the United States were past and attempted to induce them to return to their homes. On the evening of 16 June the two commissioners addressed a large crowd at Provo and another on the following evening at Lehi. The people of those places "seemed pleased that peace had been restored," they reported to Buchanan, and by the twenty-sixth they could tell their superiors in Washington that the governor, the secretary of state, the chief justice, the marshal, the superintendent of Indian affairs, and the postmaster had once again entered upon the duties of their respective offices. With their mission successfully completed, McCulloch and Powell planned to set out for Washington in a few days.[37]

Before leaving for the East, however, McCulloch was asked to assist Johnston's men in locating a permanent camp. "Gratifying his adventurous backwoods spirit," he set out with Johnston and his staff on 28 June, passing to the west of the Great Salt Lake, winding around the foot of the West Mountains, and then turning south toward Rush Valley. Detaching himself from the party and going into the mountains on a private reconnaissance, McCulloch, for perhaps the first time in his life, became lost. Rather than attempt to find his way back to Johnston and his escort, the old ranger reckoned the position of the army and struck across the mountains in that direction, arriving in camp early on the morning of 1 July "after a fatiguing journey."[38]

The following day he returned to Salt Lake City to find a sealed document, six pages long, from Brigham Young, "purporting to contain remarks" that McCulloch had made but stating neither when nor where. Young had promised the commissioners a copy of the transcription of the conference proceedings of 11 and 12 June, and McCulloch was "left to infer they were intended for the remarks" that he had made on those occasions.

"With one or two slight exceptions," he protested, "there is not a single sentence correct," and according to Capt. Jesse A. Gove of the Tenth Infantry, "the first sentence in the report is the only one Major McCulloch used. All the rest of the report is false, fraudulent, and suppositions." Gove, who read the report soon after McCulloch received it, reported that "such a jumbled up mess I never saw" and claimed that "the Saints are making a determined effort to traduce the character of the commissioners."[39]

In an angry letter to Young, whom he suspected of attempting to falsify the record of the negotiations, McCulloch first drafted and then struck through an assurance that his statements at the council house were still fresh in his memory and as Young's recorder failed to render them accurately, he would do so. He then recalled, as nearly word-for-word as possible, his remarks and their contexts from the two days of meetings nineteen days previous that he claimed had been "wholly omitted" from the Mormon transcript. McCulloch's remarks had been "few and brief," yet even they were either omitted or incorrectly taken down, leading McCulloch to suspect that Young's recorder "is totally incompetent or intends to grossly misrepresent me." In conclusion, McCulloch accused Young of breaking his promise to supply the commissioners promptly with a full and accurate report of the proceedings and of allowing enough time to elapse between the meetings and the time that the transcriptions were turned over to him and Powell that errors had been intentionally introduced. Before the controversy could be cleared up, the commissioners started east, arriving in Washington on 24 August. President Buchanan reported to Congress that McCulloch and Powell had "conducted themselves to my entire satisfaction, and rendered useful services in executing the humane intentions of the Government."[40]

NINE

My Allegiance to the South

Upon his return from Utah, McCulloch had to stand for reappointment to his office as United States marshal. Although he remained one of the most popular men in Texas, his reappointment was not without opposition. One rival from Chappell Hill wrote to "His Excellency James Buck Hannon" that "it is rumored that Maj. McCulloch will [resign] his present position and if that is the case the Democratics of this State are willing to indorse me. . . . I do not wish to put dirt [on any] man for my selfe owen benefite but the peopal are dissatisfied for one man to hold two federal appointments at one time and the bisness in the hands of a know nothing Depity."[1]

McCulloch, too, hoped to "get some other place" but saw Henry, who was then serving as a state senator, as his choice as successor to the marshal's office. From Washington Ben wrote to his brother on 8 September 1858, alluding to "an offer made me by the Secretary of War" to serve as superintendent of the United States arsenal at Harpers Ferry—an excellent appointment given McCulloch's penchant for arms technology—and to securing the marshal's appointment for Henry, since he had "made up [his] mind to accept the office" if it were offered.

Also of immediate interest, Ben had recently bought a half interest in a patent for an "apparatus to bore wells," which he planned to see into production. McCulloch was delighted with his new project, as he always was with technological innovation and a chance to make money. He had become a full partner for $500, he boasted, without "paying one cent more than my portion of the expenses." As he had been with California gold, he was sure that "there is money to be made out of my purchase." Always fascinated by mechanical devices, McCulloch described the drill in loving detail. "It is a punch auger 8 or 10 inches square," he informed Henry, "which brings up the earth as fast [as] it fills by being dropped which fall is regulated by machinery. It is worked by a rope, and can be elevated and lowered in a few minutes to and from any depth." Its inventor claimed it was capable of drilling "200 feet per day for a week if there is no rock" and of boring rock ten times as fast as an ordinary auger. "If this be so, there is a deal of money in it."[2]

As so often before, McCulloch's hopes of professional advancement came to disappointment. The appointment as superintendent of the Harpers Ferry armory did not come to fruition, and on 14 September 1858 he received from Attorney General Jeremiah L. Black his commission for a second term as United States marshal for eastern Texas. Somewhat reluctantly McCulloch accepted, but by the end of the year some excitement quickened his days when President Buchanan once more dispatched him on government business, this time as a "secret agent" to the Mexican state of Sonora. Border relations between the United States and Mexico were especially volatile at that time, and recurrent rebellion in Sonora often negatively affected the peace and prosperity of the Arizona Territory. In the long and brutal civil war in Mexico, reported Buchanan, local military governors often paid no allegiance to either party, making friendly relations with that country impossible and exposing Arizona to "outrages of the worst description . . . committed both upon persons and property." So perilous did life become in Sonora that the president dispatched McCulloch, "a reliable agent," to that province to observe "the actual condition and prospects of the contending parties" and to report on the feasibility of committing United States military forces to the province to preserve the peace.[3]

At the end of November McCulloch passed through Galveston on his way to Arizona. Although he told the local press that he was going only to purchase land in Sonora for a mining company, the Galveston *Weekly News* reported more accurately that McCulloch was armed "with important powers for our government." McCulloch's passage through southern Texas gave rise to considerable speculation "that the territory in question," Sonora and perhaps Chihuahua as well, "will shortly be added to the United States."[4]

McCulloch recommended the establishment of a protectorate over the northern parts of Sonora and Chihuahua in order to secure the lives and property of the citizens of both nations. To accomplish this task, he suggested that three thousand United States troops garrison Arispe, Sonora, until order was restored and the administration was assured that local authorities could keep the peace.[5]

As a consequence of McCulloch's report, Buchanan requested of Congress the authority to "enter Mexico with the military forces of the United States . . . in order to protect the citizens and treaty rights of the United States." Unless this power were given him, Buchanan argued, "neither the one nor the other will be respected in the existing state of anarchy and disorder, and the outrages already perpetrated will never be chastised." Not coincidentally, McCulloch's recommendations also offered the Texan an exercise for his sword and for financial speculation. In recommending that Congress authorize him to invade Mexico, Buchanan refrained from recommending either regular or volunteer forces but, with McCulloch no doubt in mind, pointed out that if volunteers were chosen, "such a force could easily be raised in this country among those who sympathize with the sufferings of our unfortunate fellow-citizens in Mexico, and with the unhappy condition of the republic." McCulloch would no doubt have been only too happy to lead them. In addition to this chance of military service on the Mexican frontier, McCulloch seems to have had some "private speculation" in view, hoping to procure the concession to build a railroad through Sonora in partnership with Judge Robert Rose, the United States consul to Guaymas.[6]

When Sam Houston introduced Buchanan's resolutions to establish a protectorate over Mexico to the Senate, however, they were defeated by southern votes as "a free soil scheme." Once more, with no military command forthcoming, the president offered McCulloch a prestigious civilian post. As Buchanan informed a joint session of Congress on 6 December 1858, Arizona, with a population of ten thousand American citizens, was "practically without a government, without laws, and without any regular administration of justice," and he strongly urged Congress to establish a territorial government there with Ben McCulloch as governor. McCulloch declined the governor's chair, however, and neither the protectorate nor the railroad ever became a reality. The months following his return from Mexico, therefore, were again filled with the tedium of accounts and receipts, of rents and remittances.

After the court term at Galveston closed in February 1859, McCulloch reported to Secretary Thompson its expenses paid and on 7 March 1859 submitted his resignation to James Buchanan, to become effective 1 April. On 16 March Attorney General Black wrote to Henry McCulloch, informing him of his appointment as marshal. "Please have the kindness to inform the President that I will accept the office and enter upon its duties on the first of next month," Henry responded.[7]

On 26 April McCulloch tendered to Thompson his final accounts and his "grateful acknowledgments for the favor and kindness throughout my terms in office." His final settlement with the government allowed him $2,046.21, $18.06 more than he claimed. "This difference in amount," wrote the editor of the Galveston *News*, "may be considered as pretty close, considering the amount disbursed by him on account of the government during the past seven years of his official duties has been about $160,000."[8]

"I hope the people of my state are content and satisfied with the manner in which I conducted the office," Ben told his mother, but he added that "if they are not, I care but little as I feel conscious of having done all that was necessary to the proper administration of the office." The people of Texas were pleased indeed, and the *News* claimed that McCulloch had conducted his office "more to the entire satisfaction of the departments than almost any other marshal in the Union," a feat "worthy of notice in these degenerate days." The editor added that "the gallant major has acquitted himself in his civil duties with as much honor to himself and fidelity to his country as he always has in his varied services on the battlefield." Somewhat more modestly, Ben told his mother that "this is doing better than any of my predecessors, who have all been sued by the government."[9]

With no Federal appointment to fall back on, Ben McCulloch was, he wrote to his mother, "perfectly free" and ready to "go into anything that offers." He intended to "touch no little thing" for the present, however, but like Dickens's Mr. McCawber, resolved "to take the chances for something to turn up." Yet, he assured his mother, "I shall not want for employment when I wish it, but don't be surprised if I decided in favor of playing the gentleman this summer." Even that, he joked, might be made to pay.

"Suppose, for instance, I was to meet and win some good woman. It might prove the best year's work that was ever done by me."[10]

Again off for Washington, New York, and New England in the spring, McCulloch entertained "fair prospects of being above want and out of debt." There, Ben informed his mother, he was "engaged at several projects which may turn out well or not as chance or fortune favors." Still casting about for the best prospect for future employment, McCulloch was confident that he would "never be out of employment of some kind" and saw "hundreds of plans laid before me out of which to choose. The great difficulty is to know which to select." In New York he spent two weeks selling half of his interest in the Sonora mine he had purchased the previous winter. Another company wished to commission him to sell railroad iron to Texas, and "if they will put it in the proper shape," he would consider taking the job. Otherwise, he had business that would compel him "to be at this city when Congress meets."

Footloose for the present, McCulloch confessed that "there is no telling what I will do or where I will go." He thought of going to Canada for the summer and planned to return to Virginia's White Sulphur Springs by 8 August, when the Knights of the Golden Circle, a paramilitary organization dedicated to the expansion of slavery into Mexico and the Caribbean basin, would be holding their first and only national convention there, but conceded that "a few days may start me to Europe." Waxing philosophical, he declared that whatever the future held in store, he would not find himself either "miserable or perfectly happy." Such is the nature of "human life and existence," he observed, that having done "the best we can under the circumstances," nothing more might be expected or required of one.[11]

After spending most of July at the Virginia Springs, where he discussed his future with Secretary of War John Floyd, McCulloch at last laid his hand on something that combined his great interests in soldiering, technology, and building his fortune. On his trip to Utah he had been tremendously impressed with a newly patented carbine, a modification of the Springfield rifle manufactured by the United States arsenal and one of the first breech-loading weapons to be tested for military adoption. George Washington Morse had adapted the flintlock rifle by cutting off the top of the barrel at the breech and installing a rear-hinged breech block and a bolt containing a firing pin. The jaws of the original hammer were cut off, leaving a dummy hammer to cock the arm. The Morse carbine fired a .58 caliber, rim fire, metallic cartridge and was finished with a butternut stock, full length forearm, and a brass frame and heelplate. Sometime in late July

McCulloch obtained an interest in the rifle and plunged into an effort to market it in the United States and Europe.[12]

Repeating a refrain that must have grown flat after so many disappointments, Ben wrote to his mother that "much money can be made out of it if well managed." The venture would, however, require all of his attention and financial resources through the fall and winter and, he predicted, would probably send him to Europe before the end of the year. Very much in his favor was his friendship with Secretary of War Floyd. McCulloch was convinced that Floyd's influence would help to sell the rifle to the United States Army and to many state militias, and such sales in America would improve his chances of finding foreign markets as well. Floyd's health was very poor, however, and many at the capital did not expect him to live long enough to affect the adoption of the weapon. "One of two things will be the consequence of my connection with it," McCulloch prophesied, "I will either be rich or flat broke in one or two years."

In spite of his excitement over the arms project, McCulloch could not help but be despondent at being forty-seven years old and unemployed. Although in New York City that summer a fortune teller informed him that he would die by a bullet on the battlefield, McCulloch seemed increasingly unlikely ever to have the thing that he wanted most, the command of a regiment of cavalry. "I will soon be old," he wrote to his mother. "I can scarcely realize it, and must try and make enough money to prevent being a burthen to my kin or friends."[13]

As so often before, McCulloch's plans were dashed by unforeseen circumstances. From New York on 23 October he wrote, "Matters about the gun are more complicated than I first thought." Unknown to McCulloch at the time he bought his share of Morse's patent, "some other parties" had also purchased shares, making both his control of the rifle's marketing and his share of the profits much slighter. Although his disappointment was keen, he told his mother that "it will make no great difference, as there are plenty of other things that offer themselves for my acceptance." His trip to Europe he dismissed with a garnish of sour grapes. The Old World was "a great humbug," he wrote, "everything being overrated by our people who go there with more money than brains."[14]

Back in Washington in early December, McCulloch was "making nothing and spending rapidly." Nevertheless, he intended to winter at the capital, where Congress was about to convene. As the fateful year of 1859 drew to a close, McCulloch was increasingly fearful of the collapse of the Union with the rise of the Republican party. The "black republicans" were on the verge of electing their first Speaker of the House, and McCulloch predicted that if they were to elect the president in 1860, "the union is gone and civil war will follow." "May God prevent such a calamity from falling on my country," he prayed, "but if it does come, I was born on Southern soil and owe my allegiance to the South and will fight her battles, no matter who may be her enemies."[15]

On 22 December, hearing of "a great Union meeting in Austin," he wrote to Thomas H. Duggan, state representative from Seguin, what was in effect a personal manifesto. Duggan, without McCulloch's knowledge or consent, gave the letter to the Austin *Texas State Gazette* for publication. Written in haste and decidedly not for the general public, the letter nevertheless fairly represented its writer's beliefs concerning the crisis of the Union, and McCulloch was hopeful that it "may do good in our State and be instrumental in making Texas take a bold stand among the Southern States should it ever become necessary."

McCulloch considered Union meetings "well enough and all right" but insisted that their theme must be "what is to be done to preserve the Union?" Dreading the loss of equality that he was certain would attend the election of a Republican president, McCulloch asked rhetorically if Texas were prepared to tell such a president that "we are ready to submit." Rather, he echoed John C. Calhoun, saying Texas "will have equality in the Union or she will go out of it." Although he was committed to the preservation of the Union so long as it should remain "consistent with honor," he was equally committed to "a proud position in a Southern Confederacy" if the North should fail to guarantee southern equality under a Republican administration. "A crisis has arrived in our country," he warned. "A storm is lowering," and he prayed that it might pass "with only a lesson that may make us wiser in future." From what he heard daily in Congress, however, McCulloch was convinced that the South would not allow the inauguration of a Republican president. The only question that remained was which course the cotton states would pursue in the event of a Republican's election. "Shall they await an overt act, or will it be wiser in them to consider the overt act already perpetrated at Harpers Ferry?" he asked in reference to the recent John Brown raid.

In McCulloch's judgment, the Republicans would not act against the South until the South was no longer in a position to effectively resist. "They understand their game too well to make a mistake," he warned the citizens of Austin. Southerners would first be divided and weakened at home as Federal offices would be given to abolitionists and opportunists from the "lower classes" of the region. "If a man was mean enough to hold office in the South under such a president, and was denounced for so doing, as he would be, would he not be mean enough, also, to say it was because he was not a slaveholder?" Once the patronage system had filled the post office with abolitionists and their sympathizers, he warned, "their emissaries and incendiary documents" would further divide southern opinion. Then, "first only gently," no more slave states would be allowed into the Union. This, McCulloch thought, southerners "might be inclined to yield to," as only the Indian Territory among unorganized territories might be adapted to slavery and the plantation economy. Then would follow the repeal of the Fugitive Slave Act and the abolition of slavery in the District of Columbia and on all military installations in the South. By then the institution would be so thoroughly sapped as to fall almost of its own weight, without the fearfully awaited "overt act."

"It will be folly, it will be suicidal, for the South to await an overt act," he concluded. Rather, he urged, "let the South meet her danger. Let Southern men look it in the face and take prompt action to meet it, and this great and glorious union can be saved." The southern members of Congress, he advised, should immediately draft an article calling on the people of the North "not to inflict this great wrong upon them." Should the northern states continue to circumscribe southern institutions and values, however, by electing "Mr. Seward or one of like politics," the southern representatives should call "a Convention of the Southern States for the purpose of forming a Southern Confederacy" and at the same time urge the southern states to organize and arm their militias for the coming crisis. "This," he admonished the people of Texas, "will do more to prevent the election of a Black Republican president than all the Union meetings that ever have or ever will be held, either North or South."[16]

McCulloch also urged the legislature and Sam Houston, who had been reelected governor in 1859, to purchase arms for the state. "The South is in a manner defenseless, for the want of arms," he observed, and as the other cotton states were beginning to arm themselves, so should Texas. Perhaps not coincidentally, on New Year's Day 1860, McCulloch wrote to his mother from Washington of "a little better prospect of my doing something with the gun now than of late."

While the thought of arming Texas cavalrymen with the finest of modern breech-loading, metallic cartridge carbines was much on his mind, so were two guns from the state's heroic past whose value to the morale of the Texas soldier might have been as great as that of the Morse rifle. Near the end of 1859 McCulloch informed Sam Houston that he had just learned that the famous Twin Sisters of San Jacinto were in the Federal arsenal at Baton Rouge and could be had from the United States government "in lieu of other arms due the State of Texas, at their appraised value." The governor immediately applied to Secretary of War Floyd for possession of the guns. "It is a matter of pride with the state," he wrote, "and particularly with those who participated at the battle of San Jacinto, to procure those arms for the State. They should never have been given up by the State in the treaty of annexation. They are worthless to the general government, but would be highly prized by the state as a relic of her revolution." As McCulloch and Houston had envisioned, the Twin Sisters were to prove a potent rallying point for Texas soldiers in the coming conflict. For Houston, a devoted Unionist, however, the great psychological value of the guns must have been a matter of bitter irony as he saw them help to destroy the dream that they had helped him to create.[17]

With the coming of the new year, McCulloch was in a somber and a philosophical mood. Although he was more committed than ever to the idea of a southern confederacy, the threat of disunion and war troubled him, and the reality of his unemployment and long string of disappointments and failures began to play upon his mind. "Another year has commenced its round and one more has been numbered with the past," he wrote. "How different time seems to pass now than when I was a boy. . . . We don't realize we are men until we are growing old."[18]

By the end of the month, however, the future appeared brighter than at any time since before his loss of the command of the Second Cavalry. The owners of the Morse patent received an order from the secretary of war for 1,000 carbines at $35 each. "This makes the neat sum of $35,000," Ben wrote to Henry. He admitted that the sale was consummated in part through his influence, although "in a manner that will not benefit me a cent." The profits would go to the other owners, who would in exchange give McCulloch a clear title to the patent. "The Secretary says they shall do it or he shall never give them another order of any kind." Once the patent was in his own hands, McCulloch was convinced, he would be able to "do something handsome with this gun."

In the face of the looming crisis over secession, volunteer military companies were forming all over the South and demanding "the best improved arms," ironically enough, from the Federal government. In addition, many of the southern states were purchasing arms against the eventuality of a northern embargo. "No time could be more favorable than the present," Ben told Henry, to make a success of the arms trade. A bill allowing the states to purchase arms from the United States government at cost had recently been introduced into the Senate, and McCulloch was confident it would pass. "Then if an appropriation can be also passed for the purpose of altering them in the Government armories for the states, I can do well, I think."

Suddenly an incident occurred that offered the potential for diverting Texas's, and, indeed, the nation's, attention from regional factionalism and secession and giving to McCulloch the best chance in years at a military command and a venue to achieve great good and great glory. "The territory of Texas has been invaded," Governor Houston telegraphed John B. Floyd from Austin on 13 February. For some months Juan Cortina, a Texas citizen of Mexican parentage, had defied state and Federal authority along the lower Rio Grande, attracting to his headquarters near Brownsville a small private army and engendering the persona of a Tejano Robin Hood. Seeking to drive the Anglo-Americans back beyond the Nueces if not to the Sabine, Cortina briefly occupied Brownsville and twice repulsed Anglo-Texan attacks on his nearby camp. When a force of United States regulars and Texas Rangers at last drove the rebels across the border on 27 December 1859, Cortina retaliated on 3 February, firing into the steamer *Ranchero* from the Mexican side of the Rio Grande. Sixty Texas Rangers under Rip Ford crossed the river in a retaliatory strike and, according to Houston, engaged and routed some two hundred "bandits," inflicting a loss of twenty-five or thirty on the enemy. Houston called for the immediate interposition of the army. "Unless prompt measures are adopted by the Federal Government," he warned, "circumstances will impel a course on the part of Texas which she desires to avoid. Texas cannot be invaded with impunity. If thrown upon her resources, she may not only resist, but adopt means to prevent a recurrence of the outrage." Houston, however, was not seeking only a defensive cordon along the southern border of his state; he demanded an offensive war against Mexico, with the occupation of its northern tier of states as a minimum objective. "There is no security for Texas until the Government occupies the right bank of the Rio Grande."[19]

Mexican banditti who raided cattle ranches in southern Texas and sold their plundered herds south of the Rio Grande had for years recruited and resupplied in Matamoras, more or less in the face of the authorities there. The game of raid and counterraid by the lawless element on both sides of the border was ancient, and one may justifiably wonder if the staunchly pro-Union Houston had not contrived this incident as a ploy to draw national attention from the growing tendency toward disunion by provoking a foreign war against a common enemy. In addition, he had long favored the establishment of a protectorate over northern Mexico by which American standards of democracy and stable political institutions might be imposed and that would serve as a buffer between Texas and a traditionally hostile Mexico.

Whatever his motive, on 13 February the governor fired off a telegram to McCulloch, announcing that "there will be stirring times on the Rio Grande ere long. What are you doing? See the President and Secretary of War. Reply at once." McCulloch responded swiftly, "I am at all times ready to serve Texas." As Houston instructed, McCulloch quickly consulted with Buchanan and Floyd and soon had their assurances that the government would concentrate troops on the Rio Grande. Orders for these troops, however, were so restrictive that "no officer (unless a very bad man) will cross the River in pursuit of the enemy," McCulloch reported to Houston. More importantly, a bill to provide a new regiment for Texas would make its way quickly through the legislature. Ben McCulloch, of course, had every expectation of being its colonel.[20]

"We understand that Major McCulloch has been telegraphed to return to the State," the Galveston *News* reported. "When we see the governor calling around him the military men of the State, and organizing the militia, it looks to us as if something of moment was threatening." McCulloch was at that very time preparing to return to Texas. "There is trouble brewing on her frontiers," he told his mother, "and I wish to participate in any war in which she may engage." Reminding his mother that she had taught her sons "never to refuse to serve your country when it becomes a duty" and promising her that "no son of yours will ever disgrace himself on the battlefield," he speculated that the Federal government would soon order its troops to follow Cortina across the river if necessary. "This looks like war, and if so, one of your sons ought to be in the field. None can be spared so well as myself," he assured her, and if he should be killed, he "could not fall in a better cause."[21]

On receiving Houston's call for Federal aid, Floyd acted immediately to carry out the governor's wishes. On 28 February the secretary of war informed Houston that "such measures as the means and powers of this Department could command have been taken for the defense of the Texas frontier on the Mexican border" and that Col. Robert E. Lee, "an officer of great discretion and ability," had been sent to take command of the Department of Texas. In addition, strong reinforcements were to be sent to

Texas as soon as the season would allow. Five hundred troops left Carlisle Barracks, Pennsylvania, on 22 February en route to Indianola and Brazos Santiago, and one hundred more infantry and five companies of the Third Artillery were moved from the Jefferson Barracks in St. Louis to Ringgold Barracks at Brownsville. Elements of the Second Cavalry were moved from the western to the southern frontier of Texas. In addition to these two thousand United States regulars, Lee was to have command of the Texas Rangers, "should the President deem it necessary to call them out."[22]

While the Federal buildup was under way on the Rio Grande, large numbers of Knights of the Golden Circle had assembled at Gonzales, much as volunteers had come to San Antonio after the Woll raid of 1842, with plans for a counterstrike against Mexico and an assumption of government sanction. Fearful now that such extralegal activities might jeopardize Federal sympathy for the Texan cause, Houston, on 21 March, called on the men at Gonzales to return to their homes. Already, he told them, he had offered five thousand Texans to the secretary of war to protect their border. "Neither freedom can be extended or glory achieved," he warned, by such "rash action," and he reminded them that "the most calamitous disasters that have befallen Texas have grown out of expeditions not sanctioned by law and disobedience of order."

On 6 April McCulloch wrote to Governor Houston that the volunteers at Gonzales were without the necessary means to carry out their designs and had for the present abandoned their intended campaign into Mexico. "This is fortunate for them and the Mexicans," thought McCulloch, "as there seems to be no leader among them of sufficient experience and ability to carry out successfully so great an enterprise. In truth," he assured Houston, "no one could succeed so easily as yourself." McCulloch was sure that at Houston's promise of good government and continued independence from the United States, more than half of the people of Mexico would joyfully welcome him as "their savior from their own leaders, who are no better than so many robbers." Houston, McCulloch believed, could "redeem Mexico," and Ben hoped that he would choose to do so "when the time comes."

If the time became right "to do this great thing for that oppressed people" and Houston failed to lead a filibuster into northern Mexico, McCulloch counseled, other less scrupulous and less skilled men would, and "there is no telling the effusion of blood" that would result. McCulloch, of course, was eager to serve his old chief in any capacity in the projected incursion and protectorate and begged Houston to "reflect gravely; reflect well." "You need not fear for wanting men or money. Thousands of men and millions of money will be placed at your disposal. To do this will be the crowning act of your life and will make your name greater than if you had been President of the United States."[23]

Lee, however, moved in a timely and resolute manner to suppress the lawlessness along the border, and by March the so-called Cortina War was over before plans for invading Mexico or establishing a protectorate over its northern states could crystallize. McCulloch was disappointed by this turn of events, but his hope for the future was not extinguished although somewhat dimmed. "The Governor has no use for me," he told his mother, "having abandoned the idea of crossing the Rio Grande for the present." Yet when the editor of the Austin *City Gazette* interviewed the "honored old Ranger," McCulloch admirably concealed not only his frustration at the failure of his mission but the purpose of it as well. The editor thought it a mistake "setting him down in any way with designs against Mexico" but found McCulloch interested only in "a breech-loaded gun." He still believed, however, that a new regiment was to be formed and he still believed that he would, with Houston's help, find his place in it.[24]

While awaiting developments on the border, McCulloch's attention returned to politics and the impending national election. When the state Democratic convention met at Galveston on 2 April, "every man present could write his name and had on a clean shirt," and Ben McCulloch, who had made the trip from Washington to attend, was hailed as "a hero as well as one of the most glorious men in the world." Very much concerned about the possibility of a Republican victory, McCulloch counseled Democratic party unity and moderation. "Let Texas send men of sense, not passion," he told Henry, for "the convention should select a man who could be elected. The permanence of the Union depends on their choice." He considered this convention the most important ever and urged that the delegates leave "the little quarrels among ourselves" at home in order to present a united front to the rest of the nation. "We have no hopes, save in its nominee and must go for him, be he whom he may." Much to McCulloch's satisfaction, the state convention took a decidedly secessionist stance, electing Guy M. Bryan as chairman of the Texas delegation to the Democratic National Convention and sending as well the equally militant Hardin R. Runnels and Francis Richard Lubbock.[25]

Although not a delegate, McCulloch attended the Democratic National Convention in Charleston in the latter part of April, and despite his earlier declaration that the party must stand together against the Republican threat, he walked out of the convention with the fifty Lower South delegates rather than support Stephen A. Douglas. On 10 June he was in Baltimore, where he again walked out of the Democratic convention when it refused to adopt a slave code for the territories and joined the 230 ultrasouthern delegates at the Maryland Institute. This splinter group organized itself under the leadership of such fire-eating secessionists as William L. Yancey and Edmund Ruffin and nominated John C. Breckinridge for the presidency. No longer even hoping to win the election, the ultramontane wing of the Democratic party now sought only to speed the secession of the southern states by further splitting the anti-Lincoln vote, thus assuring a Republican victory.[26]

If his hope to save the Union consistent with his concept of southern honor was now in vain, at least McCulloch's efforts at marketing his rifle seemed to be on the verge of bearing fruit. As an agent of the state of Alabama in July, he was unsuccessful in finding a manufacturer willing to produce arms in the quantities desired by only one state. He suggested to Governor Andrew B. Moore, however, that if Alabama joined with Mississippi in placing an order for a total of ten thousand rifles, "it might be an inducement." On 28 July Governor Houston applied to the War Department for an advance of five thousand stand of arms against Texas's quota for the next year, specifying the Morse carbine as the arm best adapted for Indian warfare. The War Department initially replied that Texas was entitled to only 169 muskets, but Senator Louis T. Wigfall persuaded Floyd to allow Texas its quota of arms for two years instead of one and to furnish Morse's rifles instead of muskets. As Wigfall wrote to the editor of the *Texas State Gazette*, it was McCulloch who first drew his attention to Morse's patent and recommended it as "the best arm ever invented for mounted troops." Regarded as far superior to Colt's carbine, the Morse rifle was simpler, more reliable, more accurate, and at $13 each, only half as expensive as its competitor. "With these arms in their hands," wrote Wigfall, "the men of the Frontier will be able to protect themselves. When they will get protection from the Federal Government, God only knows."[27]

While McCulloch's arms sales seemed to be progressing favorably, Houston was again scheming for a Mexican protectorate with McCulloch as head of its military arm. Once more the Knights of the Golden Circle were to be called upon. Twelve thousand southern men, according to one former ranger who was urged to join but declined, were to be recruited to seize Nueva Leon, Chihuahua, Coahuila, and Tamaulipas. These filibusterers were to be paid $18 per month while under arms, and "all the great estates in Mexico were to be confiscated to secure fortunes to the adventurers" when the prize was won. English capitalists, wrote James Pike, a Texan of strong Unionist sentiment who chose not to be a party to the scheme, were to underwrite the expenses of the campaign and to pay Houston "a fabulous sum for accomplishing the work, and then settle an annuity upon his wife." On 27 August Houston wrote to Col. Charles L. Mann, a former ad interim adjutant general of Texas who had also served as a captain in William Walker's filibustering expedition to Nicaragua, seeking funding by way of a bond sale to raise, arm, and equip his expeditionary force. Advising Mann of his choice of McCulloch as commander of the military column to invade Mexico, Houston assured his co-conspirator that "Ben will do for a very 'big Captain' as my red brothers say." To McCulloch himself, Houston wrote, once again in the vein of the kindly mentor that he had used before the star-crossed Moore expedition of 1842, "I am for some work if it is undertaken. We look on it as a mission of mercy and humanity, and it must not sink into the character of spoil and robbery. It must be to elevate and exalt Mexico to a position among the nations of the world." All was contingent, however, on a successful meeting of McCulloch, Mann, and John Hancock, a Texas state representative of strong Unionist loyalties, with the New York financiers. Cautioning McCulloch to secrecy, Houston warned that "if this question should be asked and get out, it would do no good, and it might create a thousand foolish or silly rumors. So best keep it sub rosa."[28]

That fall, while awaiting developments on the Mexico incursion, McCulloch toured the South, proselytizing for secession and demonstrating the Morse rifle to those whose influence might guide it into more state armories. "I hope he will succeed," Henry wrote to their mother. "Not that [I] care so much to see him make money as to see him have something to engage his mind and make him satisfied with his life and keep him out of dangerous and hard trips, campaigns, and cetera." In Milledgeville, Georgia, on 22 November McCulloch, with fire-eaters Robert Barnwell Rhett of South Carolina, Edmund Ruffin of Virginia, and Gideon Pillow of Tennessee, was invited to a seat on the floor of the senate chamber when Governor Joseph E. Brown delivered a special message in reference to the choice of presidential electors. By that date, Brown and virtually all of the members of the legislature were "fully up to the mark of secession and independence for Georgia," and the legislature passed an act appropriating $1 million for arming the state's militia.[29]

Two days later the Milledgeville *Herald* reported that several men had been observed "handling firearms of a new patent" near the river a few days before. "A tall, muscular and self-possessed individual" owned the guns, it reported. He remarked to the bystanders that "to show what a man could do, he must fire without a rest; but to show what the gun could do, he must fire with a rest." Showing off his weapon's aim rather than his own, the gentleman fired some thirty or forty times at a rock twelve hundred feet across the river. Each shot struck within a space of about a foot in diameter. The editor reported the "long shots" on the first page, not only because they were in themselves remarkable, but in order "to inform our readers that the tall marksman was no other than Captain Benjamin McCulloch, the celebrated Texas Ranger."[30]

TEN

Jeff Davis Does Not Intend to Give Me Any Show

By the beginning of 1861, Ben McCulloch was one of the most celebrated Texans, and his reputation as a scout and an Indian fighter was known throughout the United States. As the editor of an Austin newspaper wrote, McCulloch "is unique, original, and always himself—the same old plain, unpretending 'Ben.'" This editor did not claim that McCulloch did not "adumbrate a shadow, like the great Corsican," but he was certain that the ex-ranger had "no model." McCulloch, he claimed, "has killed more bear than Davy Crockett, fought more Indians than Daniel Boone, and in Mexico he was simply incomparable." Yet, he marveled, "there is nothing about him savoring of the backwoodsman, as one would expect." More wondrous yet, in that age of near universal indulgence in tobacco and strong drink, McCulloch was "strictly temperate." Rather, McCulloch was a man of "vigorous mind, fine sense, big views, and thoroughly posted on all questions that enter into the political controversies of the hour." If war were to come, he concluded, "you will hear from him or I am much mistaken."

While in Austin that winter McCulloch continued to demonstrate the virtues of the Morse rifle, holding an impromptu shooting exhibition on the banks of the Colorado River every morning at 10:00, while spending the rest of his days closely observing the activities of the secession convention, which, on 1 February, voted to take Texas out of the Union. McCulloch realized that if the expected war for southern independence were to take place, the arms and military stores located in San Antonio would be of major significance. Since the days of Spanish colonial Texas, San Antonio had been regarded as the most strategically vital point in the region, and when the United States assumed responsibility for the defense of Texas's southern and western frontiers, it also took over the Alamo and the city's other military installations as departmental headquarters. There it located not only the principal concentration of soldiers in the state but also a massive arsenal and supply depot. Three days after the passage of the secession ordinance, therefore, the convention appointed commissioners to confer with Brig. Gen. David E. Twiggs, commander of the Department of Texas, at his San Antonio headquarters. At the same time, the Texas Committee on Public Safety was instituted by the convention to prepare the state for war. This committee was empowered to demand, "in the name of the people of the State of Texas," those United States arms, stores, and munitions under Twiggs's control.[1]

Twiggs, who had taken over the command of the Department of Texas from Robert E. Lee on 13 December 1860, was a native Georgian, seventy years old, and a strong states' rights advocate. Certain, after Lincoln's election, that the Union would be dissolved, this veteran of the War of 1812 and hero of the battle of Monterrey was resolved never to fire upon American citizens. Repeatedly he had asked Washington for instructions, stating that he did not assume the government desired him to carry on civil war in Texas and that he consequently would turn over the army property in his department to the government of the state after Texas seceded. On 13 January he had requested that he be relieved of command, but orders to that effect were not issued until 28 January, and then the necessary papers were sent by mail rather than courier. Confronted with a situation in which he could not reconcile his duties as a soldier with his belief in the state's constitutional right of secession, Twiggs appointed a military commission to meet the Texas commissioners.

David E. Twiggs, commander of the United States garrison at San Antonio. For his unwillingness to fire upon Texans in the streets of their own cities Twiggs was mercilessly vilified in the North. To Albert Brackett, he "was guilty of a treason blacker than that which shrouds the name of Benedict Arnold . . . and his name has gone down to posterity loathed by all good and honest men." He was dismissed from Federal service by order of President James Buchanan on 1 March 1861. (Library of Congress)

Fearing, however, that Twiggs might refuse to surrender the Federal property to the commissioners, the committee appointed Ben McCulloch to the rank of colonel of cavalry to be prepared to "raise men and munitions of war whenever called on by the commissioners." He was ordered to station himself at Ranger's Home, Henry's ranch near Seguin, and there await further orders. Ben began to contact former rangers, Knights of the Golden Circle, and other central Texans upon whom he could call when the committee should send for him. "To Texans," he wrote, "a moment's notice is sufficient when their State demands their service."[2]

McCulloch and his volunteers had not long to wait. On 8 February the commissioners at San Antonio reported that although Twiggs was willing to "deliver all up" to the committee when the state ratified its secession ordinance, he "expressed a fixed determination" to march the troops under his command out of San Antonio under arms. The commissioners, "being desirous of avoiding if possible the necessity of collecting a force around the city for the purpose of compelling a delivery," deputed Samuel A. Maverick to obtain Twiggs's promise in writing. When Twiggs refused this demand, the commissioners sent a rider to McCulloch with orders that he "bring as large a force as he may deem necessary, and as soon as possible to San Antonio."[3]

McCulloch called upon his command, "the real bone and sinew" of central and southern Texas, to meet him at the earliest possible moment on the Salado Creek, five miles above San Antonio, "with all firearms to be had." Upon receiving McCulloch's instructions, "nearly all the men able to bear arms and to do military duty"—variously estimated at five hundred, twelve hundred, or four thousand men—"started with a rush," recalled James Knox Polk Blackburn, later a lieutenant in the famous Terry's Texas Rangers, "riding continuously without rest or sleep until we reached the place of gathering."[4]

"It was a formidable force mustered in that camp," wrote volunteer Robert H. Williams, "for though it couldn't boast much discipline, all the men were well mounted, most of them expert rifle and revolver shots. With just a little training, what a brigade of irregular cavalry it would have made!"[5]

The question of what Twiggs's men could take with them when they evacuated the state was close to settlement when, on 15 February, Twiggs received the order relieving him of command. Col. Carlos Adolphus Waite of the First Infantry, next senior officer in the department, was named his successor. Waite, a New Yorker, was a strong Unionist, and the Texans reasoned that he would not surrender the Federal property. The Committee on Public Safety, therefore, abandoned diplomacy for force, conferring upon McCulloch command of the District of Texas and ordering him to move on San Antonio. If Twiggs's command "should express a desire to depart the country peaceably," McCulloch was instructed to allow them to do so under honorable terms. In all matters not stated explicitly in his orders, McCulloch was to exercise his "best judgment and discretion in any emergency which may present itself."[6]

Receiving the word from Maverick on the evening of 15 February, McCulloch prepared to march at once. The editor of the San Antonio *Herald* found "the gallant old Ranger" camped on the Salado with a portion of his command and other volunteers from as far away as Lavaca County continuing to pour in as late as 2:00 or 3:00 A.M. "It was really interesting to look upon the busy throng," he commented. "Some were engaged in feeding their horses or mules, some in discharging and cleaning their pieces, and others talking over the chances of war, while all appeared to be anxious to consummate the grand objects of their mission." McCulloch himself, the journalist found alone, "engaged apparently in cogitating upon the most feasible plan of operation."[7]

About 3:00 on the morning of the sixteenth, McCulloch moved toward San Antonio. "The movement," Blackburn recalled, "was made with much caution and secrecy," for, as Williams later wrote, "we of the rank and file expected a sharp tussle." Although many northern observers believed then and later that Twiggs was party to a conspiracy to surrender the garrison and its stores without a struggle, McCulloch, wrote Williams, "played the game as though it were in earnest, and occupied every commanding position as we advanced." On entering the outskirts of the city, he ordered ninety men to dismount and proceed on foot. These he posted on the surrounding rooftops to command the buildings occupied by Federal troops as well as the artillery emplacements on the corner of Soledad and Houston streets. The remainder of McCulloch's men then entered the city on horseback.

Suddenly roused by screams of "We're all going to be killed!" from black people coming home from market, the United States soldiers looked out onto the main plaza to see "the revolutionists approaching, two by two, on muleback and horseback, mounted and on foot." McCulloch had commanded his men not to fire unless fired upon, and in a very short time he was sure that no resistance would be offered.

Caroline Darrow, wife of a clerk at Twiggs's headquarters, thought McCulloch's men "a motley though quite orderly crowd" as they approached the Alamo, "carrying the Lone Star flag before them." Although the February nights were cold, only some of them wore coats. Others were in shirt-sleeves, and not a few were wrapped in old shawls and saddle blankets. All, however, had stitched onto their coats or shirts a simple red insignia to serve the place of a uniform. Indeed, as Williams later recalled, "we were not encumbered by our supply train, for each man was his own commissariat, and carried his rations in his 'malletas.'" "Their arms," reported Darrow, "were of every description." Yet so great was the enthusiasm generated by their appearance that two fiercely pro-southern women dressed in male attire thrust pistols into their belts, mounted their horses, and rode out to join them.[8]

At a quarter of four Capt. Larkin Smith of the Eighth United States Infantry received a message from Capt. John H. King, the officer of the day, informing him that a large armed force was entering the city. Smith, a Virginian who was to serve the Confederacy as its assistant quartermaster general, repaired to his company barracks where he found his men assembled but under orders to remain in their quarters. Proceeding to headquarters, Smith found his fellow officers "awaiting developments rather than orders," as they understood that no resistance would be made. Very shortly some eighty of McCulloch's men took position across the street while another company formed in a nearby lot. While returning to his company quarters, Smith found a strong party of Texans on the street leading to the plaza, some of whom were climbing to the roof of the ordnance building. As Smith approached the Texans, McCulloch himself halted him. When Smith informed McCulloch that the house on the corner was occupied by soldiers, McCulloch replied that "he could not help that." Smith then asked what McCulloch's intentions were and was told that "his force was in commanding positions, and would take possession of all the public property, after which, if anything was wanted, it would have to be asked of the commissioners." He assured Smith, however, that "the persons of [Smith's] men were secure, and would not be molested."

Continuing on his rounds, McCulloch climbed to the roof of the Veramendi House, formerly the residence of the Mexican governor and then Twiggs's headquarters. There he found one of his men, a Knight of the Golden Circle, warming himself at the chimney. As McCulloch raised his head above the parapet, the volunteer trained his pistol on it. "Halt," the man demanded, "Against orders for anyone to come up." "All right, sir," McCulloch replied. Then he said, "Good boy. I'll go see the officer of the day," and continued on his way, sure that that position was secure.[9]

Ambrotype thought to be of Ben McCulloch's volunteers atop the Veramendi Palace on Soledad Street in San Antonio, 16 February 1861 (Archives Division, Texas State Library)

By 5:00 A.M. the men were in positions around the arsenal, the ordnance building, the Alamo, and the quarters in the commissary building occupied by Smith's company of Federal troops. Having heard that McCulloch intended to demand the surrender of his men's arms, Smith sought McCulloch to ask him if this were true and to inform him that "they would consider their persons very much molested if their arms were interfered with." McCulloch replied that the question of side arms was one for the commissioners to determine, and Smith assured him that an attempt to disarm his men "would be followed by serious consequences, which would be painful to all concerned." The Federal officer suggested that McCulloch should confer with his commissioners on that subject "if he had not been instructed upon it." McCulloch, no doubt rankled at having his duty told to him by a prisoner and an enemy, retorted that he intended to obey the instructions of the commissioners, "whatever they might be," and added, "Some of you had better arrange this matter quickly, or my men will do it for you."[10]

The Alamo, San Antonio, Texas; *Harper's Weekly*
(author's collection)

When daylight came, a little before 7:00 A.M., McCulloch approached Smith with a letter addressed to the commander of the Department of Texas. Smith referred him to the commander of the post, Lt. Col. William Hoffman, whom McCulloch had met on the Mormon expedition three years earlier. Under a flag of truce, McCulloch called Hoffman's attention to the hopelessness of his situation and requested that the Federal troops keep within their quarters until the commissioners should agree upon terms by which their arms and other government property should be surrendered to the state.[11]

Meanwhile a strong detachment of McCulloch's men was picketing Twiggs's quarters, a mile outside of town, to prevent the Federal commander from communicating with his forces in San Antonio. Seemingly unaware of what had transpired while he slept, Twiggs arose on the morning of 16 February, ordered his carriage, and started for San Antonio. Two of McCulloch's guards met him as he rolled away; they presented their shotguns, told him he was their prisoner, and escorted him into San Antonio. There McCulloch met Twiggs and his adjutant, Maj. William Augustus Nichols, on the main plaza. The mounted volunteers ringed the plaza and sent up a cheer as McCulloch required Twiggs "to deliver up all military posts and public property held by or under [his] control." Al-

McCulloch's Texas volunteers hold the main plaza, San Antonio, on the morning of 16 February 1861; homeograph by William DeRyee and Carl von Iwonski
(author's collection)

though willing to surrender the other public property, Twiggs repeatedly assured the Texans that "he would die before he would permit his men to be disgraced by a surrender of their arms." Wishing to avoid a bloody confrontation, the commissioners were willing to compromise on that issue. After what Surgeon Edgar H. Abadie reported as "a stormy conference between the department commander and the commissioners," Twiggs agreed that the 160 United States soldiers in San Antonio would surrender all public property, an inventory estimated at $1.3 million in value. Twiggs and the commissioners further agreed that all forts in Texas would be turned over to Texas state troops, and their garrisons were to march from Texas by way of the coast. Cavalry and infantry commands were authorized to retain their arms, and light artillery companies were permitted to retain two batteries of four guns each. Necessary transportation and subsistence were also allowed the departing Federals.[12]

With the negotiations finished, the hapless Twiggs confronted McCulloch. "Ben McCulloch, you have treated me most shamefully," he

Surrender of Twiggs to McCulloch's Texas troops in the Gran Plaza, San Antonio, 16 February 1861; *Harper's Weekly*, 23 March 1861 (photograph courtesy The Institute of Texan Cultures, San Antonio)

protested, "ruining my reputation as a military man and now I am too old to reestablish it." McCulloch's reply was characteristically simple: "I am serving my state, the State of Texas, sir." Twiggs, nearly beside himself with anger and frustration, remonstrated, "If an old woman with broomstick in hand had come to him having authority from the State of Texas demanding his surrender he would have yielded without a word of protest. 'But you, sir, without papers, without any notice, have assembled a mob and forced me to terms.' "[13]

By 8:00 A.M. the Stars and Stripes had been furled, and the Lone Star once again flew over the Alamo. The San Antonio *Herald* found "our usually quiet city . . . full of soldiers" with "all the important streets . . . guarded" and the main plaza looking "like a vast military camp." By that hour, Maverick and his colleagues estimated, McCulloch commanded no fewer than eleven hundred men, "and a more respectable looking or orderly body of men than the volunteer force it would not be easy to find." Caroline Darrow, no friend of the secessionists, had much to say about the disarray of their costume but little about their conduct. Nights had been cold and comfortless on the Salado, she admitted, and those circumstances "had not added to their valorous appearance." In the excitement all of the city's stores were closed, but the citizens of San Antonio brought coffee and other refreshments for McCulloch's men and distributed blankets and clothing. Men, women, and children armed themselves in anticipation of a fight; but McCulloch's volunteers maintained order throughout the day, and their leader expressed "admiration for their orderly conduct whilst we held the city."[14]

McCulloch was authorized to enlist "any portion or all of the Federal troops in the district in the temporary service of the State" at their current rank in the United States Army. However, only one officer, Capt. Alexander Welch Reynolds, a native of Virginia who was later to become a brigadier general in the Army of Tennessee, threw in his lot with Texas.[15]

At 2:00 that afternoon an ambulance bearing Robert E. Lee from Fort Mason drew up in front of the Read House. Immediately the vehicle was surrounded by a crowd of Texas volunteers. Observing Caroline Darrow crossing the plaza toward him, he inquired, "Who are these men?" On being informed that they were McCulloch's and that Twiggs had surrendered the post to the state, he wondered sorrowfully, "Has it come so soon as this?"[16]

At 3:00 P.M. the two companies of United States infantry marched out of San Antonio. With the departure of the Federal troops, McCulloch released his volunteers, "there being no necessity for their remaining away from their ploughs and other peaceful avocations." They left immediately for their homes, McCulloch reported to the Committee on Public Safety, "conscious of having rendered service to their State, and giving offense to no one save their enemies."[17]

Had Robert E. Lee rather than David Twiggs been in command of the Department of Texas, the American Civil War might very well have commenced in San Antonio on 16 February 1861 rather than two months later at Fort Sumter. Although fond of Texas and as unwilling as Twiggs to fire upon Americans, Lee's first loyalties were to Virginia and to the United States Army. Never a secessionist and still undecided about the rectitude of the southern cause even after Virginia left the Union, Lee would almost surely have made at least a token resistance at San Antonio and perhaps, as some observers suggested at the time, would have tried to fight his way north of the Red River. Blood would have been spilled on both sides, and the nation might well have been hurled into its fratricidal war before the secession of the Upper South and before the week-old southern Confederacy had established the means to fight. How this might have affected the course of the war and subsequent American history is only the subject of speculation, but surely the restraint exercised by the armed men on both sides of the conflict at the Alamo is commendable and bought a precious little time for statesmen to attempt to avert the coming disaster.[18]

McCulloch was especially embittered by the unwillingness of the officers and men of Twiggs's command to join the forces of Texas, and as the nation hurtled toward civil war, he was more inclined to abrogate the terms of the San Antonio agreement and intern all United States soldiers still in the state. "They will do nothing to benefit the South," he wrote to John H. Reagan, a member of the secession convention and soon to become postmaster general of the Confederacy. "Many of the officers, who are Southern men, say they will not serve Mr. Lincoln," McCulloch reported, "yet they will neither resign nor do anything else to assist the section that gave them birth. I hope the Southern Confederacy will aid them as little in the future as they are helping her now."

McCulloch could see little advantage to the South in the resignations of these officers once they had maintained the integrity of their commands and returned them "with arms in their hands to Lincoln" to garrison southern coastal forts or to where they might be "otherwise used to coerce the Southern people." Therefore, McCulloch argued, the Union regiments should be immediately disbanded and their soldiers enlisted into Confederate service. If the men of Twiggs's command were offered proper pay and inducements, he was sure, "Mr. Lincoln will never get many of them to leave this State." Not until Col. Earl Van Dorn arrived to assume command of the Department of Texas in mid-April, after the firing at Fort Sumter, did the Confederates in Texas make an effort to secure "the adhesion of the US troops to the Confederate cause" or make them prisoners of war. As McCulloch rightly predicted, however, "All who are at the [Matagorda] Bay will be off as soon [as] they hear he is raising men." The recruiting effort, therefore, was largely unsuccessful, and McCulloch would soon face many of these same men and guns on the field of battle.[19]

Of equal concern to McCulloch was frontier defense and the proper arming of state troops. He urged the convention to station cavalry regiments on the western frontier against the Indian threat and to post infantry on the fords of the Rio Grande to guard against potential Mexican incursions. Although he had captured a huge stock of arms at San Antonio, he feared that they were "not such as will be much use to the State, particularly in defending her frontiers." Left behind when Twiggs evacuated Texas, for example, were more than fifty sabers, which Henry speculated "might be of service to Texas rangers in a snake country" but of little further benefit. Ben recommended the purchase of weapons more suitable to the irregular nature of Indian warfare and suggested the Colt revolver and the Morse carbine as superior, "if we can get them." If Virginia were to secede, he proposed to go at once to Harpers Ferry and acquire for Texas the Morse rifles stored there "in time to be placed in the hands of the men who have to march against the Indians."[20]

On 4 March 1861 Confederate secretary of war Leroy Pope Walker wrote to McCulloch expressing his concern for the safety of the frontier now that United States garrisons had been withdrawn from its forts. Although the Confederate States had not yet formed a regular army, Congress had passed an act "to raise provisional forces," and Walker, with the concurrence of President Jefferson Davis, requested that McCulloch accept a commission to raise and command a regiment of mounted riflemen in Texas, the first Confederate commission offered to a Texan. This was perhaps the crowning irony of McCulloch's life. The one ruling ambition of his career, to command a regiment of cavalry in the defense of Texas's frontier, was now achieved, and at the moment of its achievement it was turned to gall. Texas, only a year ago the cockpit of the country's military activity, was now a strategic backwater, and every man with an ambition to glory looked east to Virginia and Kentucky for what was sure to be the seat of the war. "In the event it should not be agreeable to you to undertake the duties of the position hereby tendered," Walker had written, "you are authorized and requested to designate some suitable person for that duty, and transfer this communication and accompanying act to him." Hoping for a higher calling, in either Texas or regular Confederate service, McCulloch passed Walker's commission on to Henry and looked to Austin and Montgomery for a more visible command.[21]

Although Ben had declined command of the First Texas Mounted Riflemen, hoping for a more exciting commission in the eastern theater of the war, he was by no means unmindful of the threat to the Texas frontier or unhelpful in filling his brother's regiment. On 20 March he published a circular in the Texas newspapers encouraging "those who wish to enter into the service of the State" to enlist immediately in Henry's regiment. "Let it not be said," he urged, "that Texas cannot defend herself as she did in the days of the Republic." Two regiments of rangers, he wrote, "will drive the Indians from our borders and make them beg for peace." Every volunteer, he advised, should report with "a good horse, a Colt's pistol, and a light rifle or double-barreled shot-gun that can be used on horseback," and when the regiment was thus armed and mounted, "the Comanches will know 'The Ranger Is at Home on the Prairie' again."[22]

One of the saddest aspects of McCulloch's stand in favor of the Confederacy was his growing estrangement from his old friend and mentor Sam Houston. When, on 8 March, Governor Houston ordered Edward Burleson, Jr., to take possession of all the military property surrendered by Federal forces in Texas, he exceeded the authority granted him by the secession convention, and McCulloch was forced to override Houston's order. In Austin at the time and not informed of Houston's instructions until the following morning, McCulloch left immediately for San Antonio to prevent the execution of the orders and to maintain the authority of the convention. This was evidently McCulloch's final involvement with Houston, and it was the only time in his life that he raised his hand or his voice against his former commander. Houston soon thereafter refused to take an oath of allegiance to the Confederacy, and on 16 March the governor's office was accordingly declared vacant. Lieutenant Governor Edward Clark was sworn in two days later to replace Houston.[23]

So potent in the land was the name of Ben McCulloch that no sooner had Texas left the Union than rumors spread through the North that he was encamped in northern Virginia with five hundred Texas Rangers prepared to dash across the Potomac on 4 March, murder or kidnap Lincoln in the inaugural parade, and take over the capital. Even high-ranking government officials believed him to be flitting in and out of Washington, hiding by day in the home of California senator William McKendree Gwin, with whose daughter Lucy, also an ardent secessionist, he had long been romantically linked. On 11 April Attorney General Edwin M. Stanton reported to President Buchanan, "It is true . . . that Ben McCulloch has been here on a scouting expedition, and he carefully examined all the barracks and military posts in the city and said that he expected to be in possession of the city before long." The *New York Herald* reported on 27 May that McCulloch was within fifteen miles of the Capitol "with a body of troops," and the *Richmond Whig* speculated that it was a matter of a very short time before he "takes his siesta in Gen. Sickles' guilded tent." According to many eastern newspapers, only the precautions of Maj. Gen. Winfield Scott prevented McCulloch from carrying out his mission. Remarkably, another popular report found him in Washington declining a commission in the United States Army.[24]

As late as 13 June, Col. Edward D. Townsend, assistant adjutant general of the United States Army, informed Maj. Gen. Robert Patterson at Chambersburg, Pennsylvania, that "Ben McCulloch has two regiments of sharpshooters coming from Texas" and that McCulloch was presently posted in the Shenandoah Valley preparing to meet Patterson's column advancing from the north. General-in-chief Winfield Scott advised Patterson that McCulloch's "sharpshooters be met by sharpshooters." Right up to the eve of the first battle of Manassas, *Harper's Weekly* located McCulloch in Richmond with one thousand "half savage" rangers, each "mounted upon a mustang horse" and "armed with a pair of Colt's navy revolvers, a rifle, a tomahawk, a Texan bowie-knife, and a lasso."

The Houston *Telegraph* reported that spring,

> Our distinguished fellow-citizen, Ben McCulloch, appears by all accounts to have achieved the difficult faculty of ubiquity. If all reports are true, he is at one and the same time in the neighborhood of Alexandria, at Richmond, near Lynchburg, at Montgomery, at New Orleans, at or near Memphis, and in Texas somewhere between Galveston or Austin, or for all we know he may be all over that space. However this may be, one thing is morally certain, the powers that be at Washington and the abolitionists throughout the North entertain a wholesome dread of Ben McCulloch, and they appear to apprehend his terrible presence in every shadow and every shaking bush. Wherever he may be, or whatever doing, they are sure it bodes them no good.[25]

Because the commissioners had "very kindly" relieved him of "many duties common to officers commanding," and being responsible only for organizing and commanding the tiny force guarding the public property in his division, McCulloch returned to Austin and reported himself "ready to perform such service as shall be assigned" to him by the Texas Committee on Public Safety. Texas's greatest need and one of McCulloch's greatest talents coincided. The arms taken at San Antonio were soon issued to Texas volunteers, and the committee urged citizens to turn over their personal arms to state ordnance officers. When this expedient fell short of supplying the needs of the new regiments being raised for Confederate service, John A. Wharton, Brazoria County's delegate to the secession convention, introduced an ordinance on 9 March to purchase "or otherwise obtain" one thousand Colt revolvers and one thousand Morse rifles, and the convention appointed McCulloch as the state's commissioner to purchase the arms. Two days later McCulloch resigned his commission from the Committee on Public Safety and began his new assignment.[26]

From Richmond, where his presence excited "much interest in army circles," McCulloch contracted with his old friend Samuel Colt for one thousand revolvers. Although frustrated in his attempts to purchase suitable carbines for cavalry service, he was most pleased with the Colt navy-style revolvers, finding them to be "of a very superior quality" and "much lighter and better adapted to our service than the old model Army size pistol." Since the state was unable to pay for these handguns, Texas sold them to the recruits at cost, with the sum deducted from the soldiers' pay. McCulloch left Montgomery for New Orleans on 1 April to see that the arms he had secured "reach the Rangers before they take the field against the Indians."[27]

With the firing upon Fort Sumter only three days away, the first 250 pistols arrived in New Orleans on the night of 9 April, and McCulloch telegraphed Colt to send the others by Addams Express. From his room in the St. Charles Hotel, McCulloch wrote to Governor Clark that he would transship the pistols to Port Lavaca, from where they could most easily be forwarded to Austin, San Antonio, or wherever else the governor might wish, so that they would be in the hands of Henry's regiment as soon as possible. With the outbreak of hostilities, however, McCulloch had the arms shipped instead to Galveston, fearing their capture if they were landed at Indianola.[28]

Not yet giving up the hope of securing carbines suitable for frontier service, he "thought of giving Mr. Morse a contract to make a thousand" and sought Governor Clark's approval. Although he was "very anxious to introduce his arms into the frontier service," Morse would contract for no fewer than two thousand rifles since he would have to go to Belgium to have them made. McCulloch, therefore, had first to "get any other state or the Confederate States to give him a like contract." Despite the fact that the rifles would cost between $25 and $30 each and the state would have to pay an advance bonus of $10,000 to the contractor in Europe before he would begin work, McCulloch highly favored the proposal. "We want this arm in Texas to be used against the Indians, and I hope the State will do all in her power to obtain them at once," he urged Clark. This was the only means by which Texas could acquire good cavalry arms "for a year or two," and he believed that Morse could deliver them in six months. Soon, he told Clark, they would become unavailable at any price because, he predicted, the North would impose "a blockade if no more." The contract, however, never materialized.[29]

Still in New Orleans on 14 April, the day Maj. Robert Anderson's garrison surrendered Fort Sumter, McCulloch wrote to Henry that Samuel Colt had sent him a carbine of which he was "anxious to sell me 1,000 for Texas." McCulloch still favored the Morse carbine but would rather have the Colt than none. "In truth," he told Henry, "the state would do well to purchase a thousand of his and a thousand of Sharps also." Remarkably, he believed that both could be had and that he could arrange for their delivery if the state were willing to pay for them. "Otherwise," he warned, "they would never get South." McCulloch sent the Colt model to Henry as a present to Eustace Benton, providing that he was "in the service and likes the carbine." Otherwise, "if Nat is in the field," Henry was to give it to him. "Let it be in the hands of someone who will use it against the enemy."[30]

After learning of the outbreak of hostilities at Fort Sumter, McCulloch was sure that "the vigilance of the Federal government" would prevent delivery of any additional arms, so, with all of the Colt revolvers that he had been able to order on their way to Texas, McCulloch prepared to travel first to Pensacola and then to Montgomery to seek further service in the Confederate cause. At Pensacola, Confederate brigadier general Braxton Bragg was confronting the Union garrison occupying Fort Pickens in Pensacola harbor. Hardly less than Fort Sumter, Fort Pickens was one of the most volatile crisis points in the South, and McCulloch was avid to participate in the expected battle there. From Pensacola he planned to push on to the Confederate capital at Montgomery, where, he wrote to Henry, he "fully determined to put Jeff Davis to the test in regard to appointments of civilians." His first request was to be the command of a regiment of Texas cavalry in Virginia. If Davis denied him that position, he planned to ask for command of the Department of Texas. If the president failed to favor him with either of these alternatives, he wrote to Henry, he was willing to do anything required of him "to be useful until the war is over" and then to "subside quietly into private life, married or not as the case may be."

One alternative that caught McCulloch's attention was a political rather than a military office. John Marshall, the influential editor of the Austin *Texas State Gazette* and the leader of the Democratic party in Texas, was encouraging McCulloch to run for governor when Clark's term expired in November. Fearing that he would be spurned by the Davis administration, McCulloch seemed inclined to do so. Because of the controversy over the command of the Second Cavalry and the Confederate chief executive's preferment of West Point–trained officers, McCulloch saw "little chance for me with Jeff Davis as President" and thought "it would be well to secure the other position if it could be done." He therefore wrote to Marshall to announce his candidacy "if he thought proper for the Governorship of our State," and he requested that Henry confer with Marshall on his prospects before Henry left with his regiment for the frontier.[31]

A position in the army remained McCulloch's first choice, however, and only the rumor of counterrevolution in Texas delayed his departure for Pensacola and Montgomery. Many Texans gave credence to the report that the Lincoln administration planned "to aid Old Sam in reestablishing his power" by landing Federal troops on the Texas coast. Although their views on secession had diverged absolutely, McCulloch still refused to believe that Sam Houston would betray Texas to the North. "Yet," he wrote to Henry, "there are men in our state who are both knave and fool enough to mislead Lincoln and who would like to bring trouble on our state and people. Let them do it. It will result in our getting clean of all suspicious characters before tis done with. Our State will be all the better in future for the attempt." If Texas Unionists were to try to take the state out of the Confederacy, he vowed, "you will see your humble servant there in short notice."

At last satisfied that the secession movement was safe in Texas, McCulloch telegraphed Louis T. Wigfall and Thomas N. Waul, members of the Provisional Confederate Congress from Texas, to determine whether Secretary of War Walker would "accept an armed regiment from Texas, to pay its own expenses to Virginia." When Waul replied that the War Department was not prepared to receive such a regiment, the disappointed McCulloch telegraphed the information to the editor of the Galveston *News*, hoping to "prevent many gallant young men from leaving Texas at this time to hunt a fight." Rather, McCulloch urged his fellow Texans, "let us organize and be ready. We may yet be needed. Let them call. Texas will respond, and when the hour comes, will take her place in the picture near the flashing of the guns."[32]

Although the Davis administration had refused his offer of a regiment for service in Virginia, McCulloch held out hope that he would be appointed to command the Confederate forces in Texas. On the afternoon of 14 April, however, just as he was preparing to depart for Montgomery, McCulloch encountered Earl Van Dorn in the lobby of the St. Charles Hotel. Van Dorn, like Davis, was a West Point graduate and Mississippian. He had just arrived in New Orleans, he informed McCulloch, on his way west to take command of the Department of Texas, an assignment that the president had made without consulting any of the state's political leaders. "So you see," McCulloch wrote to Henry, "Jeff Davis does not intend to give me any show."[33]

ELEVEN

The Army of the West

McCulloch's relationship with Davis had indeed been characterized by "a qualified coolness" since the days when McCulloch, as Houston's protégé, had been recommended to and rejected by Secretary of War Davis for various frontier commands. Davis "knew McCulloch very well" in Mexico, however, and admitted that "he rendered very valuable service and displayed vigilance, judgment, and gallantry where ever those qualities were required." Davis was especially familiar with McCulloch's great contribution to the United States victories at Monterrey and Buena Vista and was well aware of what John Henry Brown called "his splendid intuitive intellect, his severe studies, and the great hold he had upon the people of Texas, Arkansas, and the Southwest." Indeed, the echoes of McCulloch's Mexican War service still reverberated throughout the South, where volunteer companies were naming themselves after him and where many people expected that he would be promptly appointed to high command.[1]

"Jefferson Davis and His Generals." Ben McCulloch stands at Jefferson Davis's right hand—an unintended irony on the part of the unkown printmaker (courtesy T. Michael Parrish)

Despite this almost universal acclaim, Davis, with a stroke of ironic genius, finally gave McCulloch the command that for years Houston had sought for him, "the district embracing the Indian Territory lying west of Arkansas and south of Kansas," now the darkest backwater of the Confederacy, yet also a command involving, perhaps, "more vexatious questions for solution than any other in the Confederate States." On 11 May 1861 Davis appointed McCulloch a brigadier general, the first commission as brigadier general issued to a civilian in the Confederate States Army and among the first issued to anyone. Only four officers with field commands outranked him. These were Albert Sidney Johnston, Joseph E. Johnston, P. G. T. Beauregard, and Braxton Bragg. Not only was he the first general-grade officer in the Confederacy who had not attended West Point, he was 1 of only 11 of the 425 general officers to serve the Confederacy who had received no college training whatsoever.[2]

Departing in great haste to take command of the Indian Territory, McCulloch informed Clark that his force, known as the Army of the West, would consist of two regiments of mounted men (the Third Texas Cavalry and a regiment from Arkansas) and one regiment on foot from Louisiana. Additionally, teacher-poet-lawyer-editor Albert Pike was assigned to Mc-

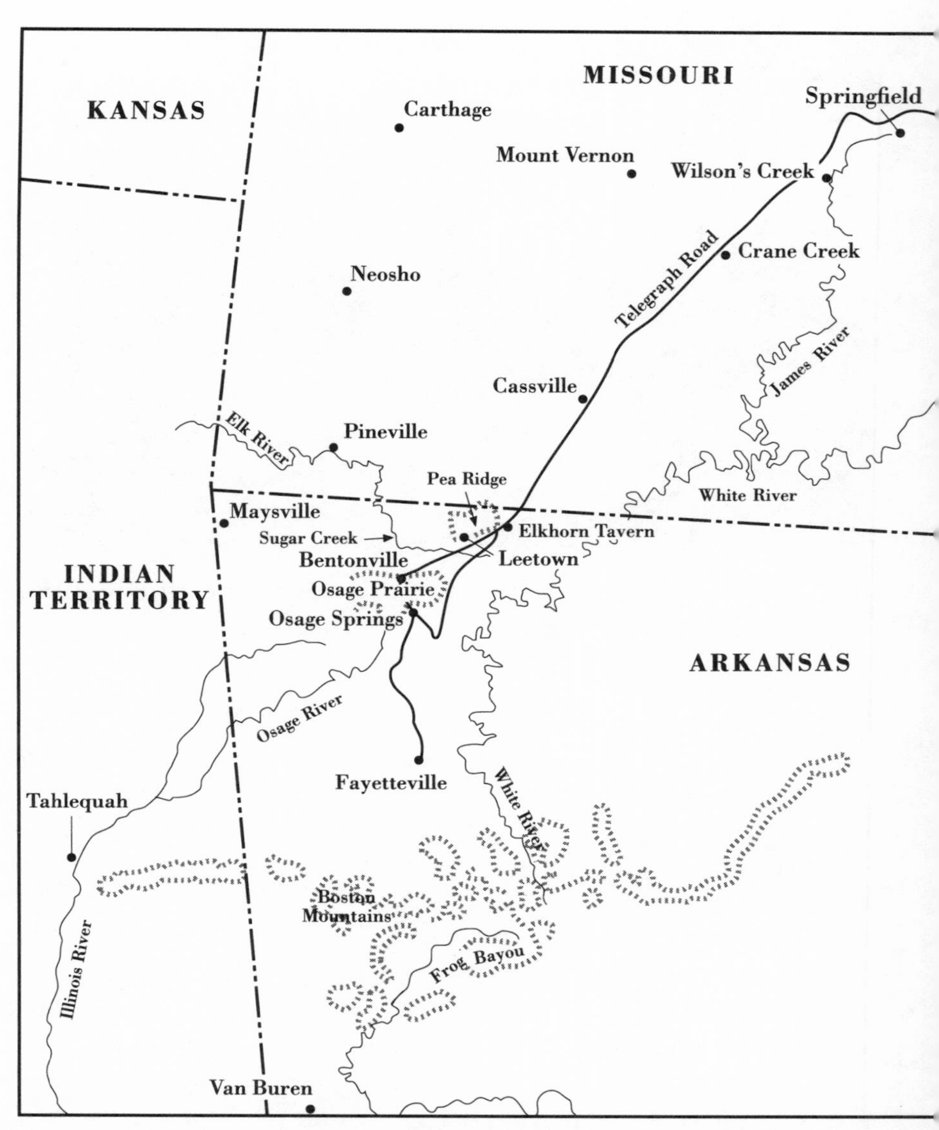

MAP 6. *Arkansas and Missouri Theater of Operations*

Culloch's staff with instructions to raise two regiments from among the "civilized tribes" of the Indian Territory. "This force," wrote Confederate adjutant and inspector general Samuel Cooper, "should you be able to obtain it, you are authorized to receive and organize as part of your command, for such service as your judgment may determine."[3]

The new Confederate government desired a strong alliance with the Indians of eastern Oklahoma but feared that what Secretary of War Walker regarded as "the agrarian rapacity of the North" would soon drive the Indians from the reservations north of the Red River. Accordingly, on 13 May Walker called upon Maj. Douglas H. Cooper, a Mississippian who had been the Federal Choctaw and Chickasaw agent in the 1850s, to raise and command a mounted regiment of Choctaws and Chickasaws for McCulloch's army. With two similar regiments the War Department hoped to raise among the Creeks, Cherokees, Seminoles, and other friendly tribes, this force was thought ample "to secure the frontiers upon Kansas and the interests of the Indians." The latter, Walker identified as being in "common with that of all the Southern States entering the Confederation."[4]

The gravest immediate threat to the northern flank of the trans-Mississippi Confederacy was perceived as the United States garrison at Fort Washita, Indian Territory. Samuel Cooper suggested that this force "be captured with the least practicable delay" and ordered McCulloch to organize an expedition to take the fort and capture its garrison. Elkhanah Greer, of Marshall, Texas, who had served as a private in Jefferson Davis's Mississippi Rifles in the Mexican War and more recently had been the head of the Texas division of the Knights of the Golden Circle, had arrived in Montgomery about the same time as McCulloch and was at the same time commissioned as a colonel of cavalry. Together with Davis and Walker, the two Texans planned an expedition to southern Kansas. "This will protect our northern border," McCulloch assured Governor Clark, "and consequently I had to accept though I would have preferred going to Virginia at present." By then, however, it was too late. Already Lt. Col. William H. Emory, who had accepted the major's post in the First United States Cavalry turned down by McCulloch in 1858, had moved all Federal forces in the Indian Territory to Fort Leavenworth, Kansas, as McCulloch learned on about 20 May. His agents reported, however, that "the notorious General [James] Lane" was rapidly organizing an army in Kansas to invade the territory, and he was sure that jayhawker leader James Montgomery was also "hovering near the border." He made his plans, therefore, to proceed to Fort Smith as rapidly as possible in order to organize his new command and "put them at once in the field."[5]

McCulloch and his adjutant, Capt. William R. Bradfute, formerly of the Second United States Cavalry, wasted little time, leaving Little Rock for Fort Smith on 23 April. Arriving in early May "without a dollar, a man, or a gun," they began to build the Army of the West. "He came unannounced," wrote volunteer aide John Henry Brown, "without bluster, fuss, or feathers, in the garb of an earnest citizen who meant business and realized the difficulties and responsibilities of his position." Near old Fort Smith, on slightly rising ground in the middle of a large prairie, McCulloch's men established a camp of instruction called Camp Walker, erecting rows of wooden barracks around a parade ground featuring "a very high flag pole, carrying an enormous Confederate flag." As more troops came from Texas, Louisiana, and Arkansas, the fringes of the prairie filled with their tents, and the parade ground swarmed with the drilling of horse, foot, and guns.[6]

Fifty years of age, although often considered ten years younger, McCulloch was a figure whose training, experience, and habits of mind might well inspire the confidence of his followers. Although never formally trained in the art of war, he was what Sgt. William Watson of the Third Louisiana called "a thoroughly practical general." His penchant for personally scouting Union dispositions became legendary in his little army, and Col. E. I. Stirman of the Arkansas brigade was only one of many who "often saw him riding through our camp alone in citizen's garb, with a small breech-loading rifle swung across his shoulders, going in the direction of the enemy." From his days as an Indian fighter with the Texas Rangers and as Zachary Taylor's chief of scouts in Mexico, he had learned to pay closest attention to the topography of his field of operations and, according to Watson, "made himself acquainted with every road or passage through which an army with trains could pass or operate in. He examined every river, creek, ford, or bridge where an enemy could be checked or met to advantage. He took care to know where forage and supplies were to be procured readiest, and noted where a pass could be guarded, defended, or stopped up."[7]

In common with almost all of the untutored leaders on America's military frontier, he was "not so particular about clock-work movements in drill or in having ranks dressed straight as an arrow," but he knew and insisted upon the importance of proper alignment and distancing and demanded, above all, that his men be expert in the use and care of their arms. Of the latter, at least, he had little to fear, for few of his men had grown up far from the frontier, and all were seasoned hunters if not veteran soldiers. In common, too, with his models Andrew Jackson, Sam Houston, and Zachary Taylor and such contemporaries as Nathan Bedford Forrest, who "generally whupped the hell out of" a West Point graduate "before he got his tune pitched," McCulloch had what Watson characterized as "an utter abhorrence of all red-tape and bureau government."[8]

From Camp Walker, McCulloch called upon Confederate recruiting officers throughout the region to complete the formation of their units as soon as possible and to forward them to Fort Smith. The rumor mill reported that Union general-in-chief Winfield Scott had sent fifty thousand stand of arms to Kansas and that Lincoln had ordered James Henry Lane, the highly controversial leader of the abolitionist faction in Kansas, to capture Fort Smith and the other Arkansas and Indian Territory military installations now in Rebel hands. McCulloch, according to popular report, would receive five new regiments from Texas to thwart the invasion. "We again tell our Texas boys," wrote the editor of the Dallas *Herald*, "put yourselves on your muscle, in good fighting trim for advance movement upon Kansas."

The paper saw the occupation of Kansas as "a military necessity, which President Davis will not long overlook to give security to our whole border from Missouri to Texas." An army under McCulloch, it argued, should be immediately raised in the trans-Mississippi to "take the field and sweep Kansas." This move, the editor believed, would relieve Missouri of Federal occupation and give "absolute security to Arkansas, the Nations, and Texas."[9]

Among the first units to report was the Totten Light Battery, commanded by Capt. William E. Woodruff, which arrived at Fort Smith on the steamer *Lady Walton* in mid-May. This Arkansas artillery unit had received its two six-pound guns and two twelve-pound howitzers from the former United States arsenal at Little Rock, which had been seized by Col. Patrick R. Cleburne at about the same time McCulloch was taking San Antonio. Woodruff proudly reported that "the company was thoroughly drilled in the Rifle Manual on the hurricane" deck of the steamer during the cruise up the Arkansas River. McCulloch was a passenger on the *Lady Walton* on its trip to Fort Smith, and he came to know the officers and many of the men of the battery during the journey. When they arrived at Camp Walker, McCulloch requested that the Little Rock battery camp next to his quarters, and its officers were housed in rooms adjoining his in the barracks. While at Camp Walker the name of the battery was changed from Totten to the Pulaski Light Battery.[10]

With most of his units, however, McCulloch was not nearly so fortunate. Col. Thomas J. Churchill, commander of the First Arkansas Mounted Rifles, informed McCulloch that his regiment would be delayed because of the difficulty in finding men willing to enlist for so indefinite a period as the duration of the war. His companies were ready to enlist for twelve months, however, and McCulloch besought Walker to allow him to accept them for that period. The "great want of arms for mounted service" was also a serious impediment to putting a force in the field. From his arrival at Fort Smith, McCulloch had been aware that, although the Arkansas secession convention had authorized him to draw upon all the stores taken in the Federal arsenal at Little Rock, the great majority of guns and ammunition had been dispersed by state officials without proper authorization and were "scattered over the state in every direction." Virtually none of the weapons available were suitable for mounted service, leaving the regiments of Arkansas cavalry almost destitute of arms. McCulloch called earnestly for rifles or carbines, pistols, and sabers. The Arkansas River was then "in fine navigable order," and he urged Walker to send arms, tents, and rations at once before the river fell; but Walker had none to send.[11]

The problem of arming his regiments was by no means limited to Churchill's. "There are no arms suitable for the regiments of Indians that I am authorized to muster into service," McCulloch complained, and although some of them were expected to "present themselves with their rifles," the majority would be entirely unarmed. In order to maintain their loyalty, the Indians would have to be speedily supplied. Without the Indian regiments, McCulloch informed Walker, he would have only "an insignificant force" to defend the Indian Territory. Finally, to complete his logistical worries, McCulloch pointed out to the War Department that he had "neither officers of the quartermaster's nor commissary department," and because he considered a staff familiar with these duties "absolutely necessary for a successful campaign," he called upon Walker to send them at once. Although many months would pass before he was able to assemble the staff necessary to run an army efficiently, McCulloch was ultimately able to assemble what Col. Dabney H. Maury characterized as "five or six working men, and all about them bespoke the stern seriousness of soldiers trained to arms."[12]

McCulloch's staff. Two of them, Lunsford L. Lomax (seated at far left) and Frank W. Armstrong (standing at right), would themselves become Confederate generals.
(courtesy Dr. Tom Sweeny)

On 22 May the Arkansas convention passed an ordinance to provide for cooperation with the forces of the Confederate States of America in defense of the western frontier and "authorized and requested" Nicholas Bart Pearce, the brigadier general commanding the nearly two thousand state troops in northwestern Arkansas, to cooperate with McCulloch "to the full extent of his ability." Five days later, amid rumors of Federal troops crossing Arkansas's northeastern border, Governor Henry Massey Rector dispatched a courier to McCulloch requesting that he take command of all of the state's military forces. Although deeply concerned about the Union invasion of their state, the people of Arkansas placed great reliance upon the man in whom they had trusted for their defense. As the editor of the Van Buren *Press* wrote on 5 June, "The name of Ben McCulloch, wherever it is known, is a guarantee of itself." So popular was McCulloch in the state that when the Second Arkansas Infantry was ordered to Virginia at the end of May, its colonel, Thomas C. Hindman, protested that he had raised his companies "for Ben McCulloch's command." He assured the Confederate inspector general that his men were "anxious to go with McCulloch into the northeastern frontiers of this state. I may not hold them [if] ordered elsewhere," he warned Cooper.[13]

In response to the fears of Governor Thomas Overton Moore of Louisiana that his state was in peril of invasion by way of Forts Cobb and Washita, Walker assured him of McCulloch's strength and also called upon him for a regiment of infantry. Moore designated the Third Louisiana, commanded by Col. Louis Hébert, to join McCulloch's army. Recruited from among the young men of the planter and professional classes, this elite unit had anticipated being ordered to Virginia, and on learning that they were to be shipped to Fort Smith, their morale suffered a stunning blow. Nevertheless, remembered a Louisiana sergeant, the men "were eager to see their future leader, already so famed as a Ranger on the Texas frontier," and soon this regiment was to become the Old Guard of the Army of the West and one with which McCulloch shared a mutual love and respect comparable to that of Robert E. Lee with Hood's Texas Brigade or Thomas J. Jackson with the old Stonewall Brigade. Capt. John J. Good of the Texas artillery characterized the regiment's officers as "very clever gentlemen," although he saw the men as "turbulent" and "desperately fond of whiskey." Nevertheless, "there was not a braver regiment in the entire Confederate Army than the Third Louisiana," wrote an Arkansas soldier, and Good admitted that "all are good fighters" and that in battle he would "rather be with them than any regiment in the service."[14]

With the Confederacy's deep concern over a threatened invasion of the Indian Territory from Kansas, binding treaties of friendship and mutual aid with the "civilized" tribes of the territory became paramount among McCulloch's responsibilities, making him, in the words of one of his officers, "as much ambassador as general." These five tribes—the Cherokees, the Creeks, the Choctaws, the Chickasaws, and the Seminoles—shared enough values and customs with white southerners for the Confederacy to deem them worthy as allies. Each tribe was in fact a nation, with recognized boundaries, written constitutions, and other political institutions rooted in both American democracy and tribal tradition. In what is now the eastern half of Oklahoma, a fertile, well-watered land, they farmed individual homesteads in the manner of the white yeoman farmer or, like the southern planter, managed plantations worked by black slaves. Most of them prospered. They understood the value of learning, and during the 1850s they developed public school systems superior to those in Arkansas and Missouri. They were a Christian people, primarily embracing the

Methodist, Presbyterian, and Baptist creeds. Finally, they drew their leadership from an extraordinarily gifted elite: some were full-blooded Indians, and others were descended from alliances between native women and English or Scottish traders half a century or more earlier.[15]

Upon his arrival at Fort Smith, McCulloch began to gather intelligence regarding the disposition of the tribes. He soon ascertained that the Choctaws and the Chickasaws were eager to join the southern Confederacy, leading him to believe that Colonel Cooper would have no difficulty recruiting a regiment among them. The Creeks, too, he counted on for a regiment, but he learned that among the Cherokee were two factions. One group, made up in the largest part of those with some Anglo-American blood, was very much in favor of joining the southern Confederacy. The other, the majority, consisting of "all the full bloods and part of the half-breeds," favored a neutral status. "These two parties," McCulloch reported to Walker, "are kept apart by bitter feuds of long standing, and it is possible that feelings of animosity may tempt one party to join the North, should their forces march into the Indian Territory." His most urgent priority, therefore, was to meet with John Ross, the seventy-two-year-old chief of the tribe, and attempt to enlist him in the southern cause.[16]

McCulloch and Capt. Albert Pike left Fort Smith on 30 May for a tour of the Indian nations designed to cement alliances with the various tribes, to select a site for McCulloch's permanent headquarters, and "to get a force into the nation that will prevent any force from the North getting a foothold and enlisting the sympathies" of the Cherokees. Although the irony of McCulloch's commission as an ambassador to the tribes was at least as great as his mission as peace commissioner to the Mormons—"How he hated Indians!" Mary Chesnut noted in her diary—he and Pike were successful in negotiating treaties with the Choctaws, the Chickasaws, and the Creeks, and these Indians began immediately to raise and organize units for the Confederate army. Even before the treaties were signed, Douglas Cooper had recruited many Choctaws and Chickasaws, and from 10 July to 4 August McCulloch and Pike negotiated treaties of alliance with the Creeks, the Seminoles, the Comanches, the Chickasaws, the Choctaws, the Wichitas, the Osages, the Senecas, the Quapaws, and the Shawnees. On 10 June the Choctaw National Council authorized Principal Chief George Hudson of the Choctaw nation to raise seven companies of mounted men to be designated the First Regiment, Choctaw and Chickasaw Mounted Rifles. Factionalism among the Creeks caused some difficulty in the organization of a regiment from that tribe, but McCulloch solved this problem by accepting two battalions, one from the Upper Creeks and the other from the Lower Creeks, rather than a unified regiment, allowing each to elect its own officers.[17]

Negotiations at the Cherokee capital of Tahlequah were less satisfactory. In council with the Cherokees, Pike's splendid rhetoric fell upon unresponsive ears, while McCulloch, as taciturn as he had been in the Texas legislature or as a commissioner to the Mormons, listened quietly, convinced from the beginning that Ross would not be moved. McCulloch had found the only suitable site for the posting of his army in the Indian Territory to be in the Cherokee nation and "determined to take the first opportunity of moving [his] command to it." McCulloch informed the Cherokees that he had been sent by his government to take command of the Indian Territory and to guard it from invasion from the North. He assured the tribal chief that the Confederate government wished only to assist the Cherokees in defending their own rights and territories, and he made known its desire that the Cherokees "unite their fortunes with the Confederacy" against "a people who are endeavoring to deprive us of our rights." Further, he promised that Cherokee regiments would never be marched out of their own country to make war. The Cherokees' true interest, he assured them, lay with the South. A Union invasion would deprive the Indians of their land, he argued, while the Confederacy wished only "to maintain them as they are in all their rights," their lands, and their slaves. While holding out the olive branch of friendship and a mutual defensive alliance, McCulloch also revealed that if the Cherokees were to remain neutral and "sit idly by, and ingloriously refuse their aid" in defense of the Indian Territory, then the annuities promised them by the Confederate government would not be paid. More forcefully, McCulloch assured the Cherokees that his government would never consent to an alliance between the Indians and the Federal government or allow the Cherokee nation to be "settled or governed by abolitionists."[18]

Although McCulloch reminded Ross that "he that sits between two stools comes to the ground," the old chief resolved to take no part whatever in the pending conflict between the two American republics and admonished the Cherokee people to pursue the same course. "Our country and institutions are our own," he told McCulloch. "We have done nothing to bring about the conflict in which you are engaged with your own people, and I am unwilling that my people shall become its victims." Were the North to launch an invasion of the Cherokee nation, however, Ross assured McCulloch that, "old as I am," he would "put himself at the head of his people and march to repel it." Time was on the side of the Cherokees, and they had no desire to rush into an incautious alliance with the losing side of the white men's war.[19]

Convinced, however, that Ross had already concluded to make a military alliance with the Union and was merely stalling for time, McCulloch returned to Fort Smith and considered sending troops into the Cherokee nation to guarantee Ross's neutrality. Deciding, however, that "to give offense to this party now by marching into their country would injure our cause" and perhaps precipitate the Cherokee nation into the Union camp, he satisfied himself with surrounding the Cherokees with Cooper's First Choctaw and Chickasaw Mounted Rifles and Col. William Cocke Young's Eleventh Texas Cavalry to "force the conviction on the Cherokees that they have but one course to pursue—that is, to join the Confederacy."[20]

Accordingly, McCulloch wrote to Ross on 12 June that his people's neutrality would not be molested "without good cause." For the present, he insisted, those Cherokees who favored the Confederate cause must be allowed to organize into "Home Guard" companies to defend themselves "in case of invasion from the north." In the event of such an invasion, or if Ross invited the Federal military occupation of his territory, McCulloch assured him that he would at once advance into Ross's country. With such threats coupled with the pressure of a virtual siege by Confederate troops, McCulloch at last had his way. By the end of July, Stand Watie, a pro-southern Cherokee and a recently commissioned colonel in the Confederate army, had recruited a large Confederate Cherokee force to protect the northern border of the Cherokee nation "from the inroads of the Jayhawkers of Kansas," and once a treaty with the Cherokees was consummated, McCulloch accepted a second Cherokee regiment commanded by Col. John Drew.[21]

Despite the tribes' sobriquet as "civilized," many Confederates found the new alliance a good deal less than reassuring. Even their friend Pike described the Indian troops as "entirely undisciplined, mounted chiefly on ponies, and armed very indifferently with common rifles and ordinary shot-guns." One Louisiana soldier described them, "in all the hideousness of their war paint," as armed with long rifles, tomahawks, and scalping knives and "apparently as savage as when, in years long past, they alone inhabited the North American continent."

Others, however, were well pleased with their new allies. Capt. Charles A. Bruslé of the Third Louisiana, whom McCulloch had appointed mustering officer and had ordered into the Creek nation to swear in the new battalions, confided to his diary that they were "nearly as white as I am, they are educated gentlemen, and are polite as any of our own race." The Creeks, in fact, "would certainly stand the test of civilization" better than the people of Arkansas, Truslé believed. Furthermore, "in feeling and sentiment they are truly southern. They would rather scalp a Yankee than eat." While crossing through the Chickasaw and Choctaw nations on their way to join McCulloch's command at Fort Smith, troops from Greer's Texas cavalry regiment and Good's Texas battery perceived the Indians to be loyal to the South and found Cooper's regiment "keen for a fight with the Abolitionists."[22]

Although McCulloch's commission from the Confederate government stressed the defense of the Indian Territory against invasion from Kansas, the Federal threat to Arkansas from bases in Missouri loomed ever larger in the formulation of southern strategy as the spring of 1861 wore on. Missouri's moderate faction, although in a majority, failed to maintain the state's neutrality when, on 10 May, Capt. Nathaniel Lyon's United States regulars seized Camp Jackson, a pro-southern camp of instruction near St. Louis. Lyon's move secured the state's arsenal and made a refugee of the state's pro-southern governor, Claiborne Fox Jackson, and a majority of the legislature. It also polarized the citizens of Missouri, causing bloody rioting in St. Louis. Moving the state government from Jefferson City to Neosho, Jackson called for fifty thousand troops "to repel the invasion" of his state.

On 26 June 1861 the Confederate War Department authorized McCulloch to render whatever assistance he thought proper to the Missourians as long as it was consistent with his mission to protect Arkansas and the Indian Territory. At the same time, Secretary Walker cautioned him that Missouri's position as "a Southern State still in the Union" required him to behave with "much prudence and circumspection." Only "when necessity and propriety unite" should McCulloch consider crossing the national boundary to render "active and direct assistance" to Jackson's Missouri State Guard.[23]

The command at McCulloch's immediate disposal would hardly have warranted such an advance, even if the secretary of war had ordered it. "My embarrassment here has been very great," he wrote to Walker on 29 June. "Sent here without a force, without transportation, and without arms," McCulloch had found himself "very much crippled." With little or no aid from the Confederate government he had organized a staff and the logistical support necessary to maintain his small army. He had, on his own initiative, recruited new units in northwestern Arkansas and could only hope that the War Department would sustain him in his decisions. Most of the supplies he had requisitioned had not yet arrived, and although the Third Louisiana and seven of Churchill's companies had reported at Fort Smith, the Arkansas cavalry regiment was "armed with old muskets, flint and steel locks, and bayonets" and had "no cartridge-boxes, bayonet scabbards, or belts." It was in great need of ammunition and was "entirely without tents or camp equipage of any kind." To his desperate plea for more and better weapons, Secretary Walker replied that the War Department had none to send.[24]

The Eleventh Texas Cavalry, which had been destined to join McCulloch in Arkansas, was assigned instead to garrison the forts in the Indian Territory. Equally unfortunate, Greer's Third Texas Cavalry (also known as the South Kansas–Texas Cavalry), was delayed in Dallas for want of supplies and would not be available until too late to assist McCulloch in his contemplated thrust into Missouri or to aid in the early defense of Arkansas. Some of Greer's companies were "well mounted and armed to the teeth" with revolvers taken at San Antonio, double-barreled shotguns brought from home, and "a good many chop knives." Those without firearms had bowie knives, some three feet in length, which, according to one trooper, were "heavy enough to cleave the skull of a mailed knight through helmet and all." Although such knives had done fearful execution among the Mexican ranks at San Jacinto and perhaps bolstered the Texan cavalrymen's view of themselves as a new incarnation of the knights of Walter Scott's novels, they were to prove next to useless on the battlefield. Even after reaching Arkansas, some of Greer's troopers took it upon themselves to procure arms locally, placing advertisements in the Fort Smith *Daily Times and Herald* for carbines or other weapons. Two-thirds of the Third Texas Cavalry were said to have purchased shotguns from private sources in Fort Smith.[25]

A. B. Blocker, a private in Greer's regiment, was outfitted in a full Confederate uniform of cadet gray and armed with a new Colt repeating rifle. Other soldiers, however, were not uniformed at all, wearing only their normal civilian clothing with a strip of white muslin around the left arm to signify themselves as Confederate soldiers. "It would astonish you to see how common some men are clad here," Captain Good wrote to his wife. "Men worth half a million clothe themselves with suits they would not purchase for a Negro."[26]

Nevertheless, rumors were rife that the army would soon take the offensive. "I do not know as yet where Old Ben McCulloch will take us or what the plans of his operations are," Capt. David Pierson of the Third Louisiana wrote to his father, "but I can give you a guess and will do so." Pierson and his messmates believed that the army was bound for Missouri "as soon as our division is ready for marching." In response to this persistent report, Nathaniel Lyon, promoted to the rank of brigadier general for his capture of Camp Jackson, informed Maj. Gen. George B. McClellan, commander of the Department of the Ohio, that "the rumor which has been so long prevalent in regard to the contemplated movement from Arkansas under Ben McCulloch appears to me to [have] assumed shape and consistency, and it is no longer to be doubted that such an enterprise is on foot." Fearing that Governor Jackson's and Brig. Gen. Mosby Monroe Parsons's Missouri cavalry brigade would soon unite with McCulloch, giving the Rebels ten thousand to twelve thousand men in the state, Lyon dispatched a large force to face the supposed incursion.[27]

Governor Jackson urgently requested McCulloch's assistance in recovering his capital and providing a rallying point for the pro-secessionist element of the Missouri population. After carefully considering the governor's proposition, McCulloch recommended it to Secretary Walker on 14 June, seeking his permission to advance a force into southeastern Kansas and to capture Fort Scott. This action, he believed, would "force the conviction on the Cherokees that they have but one course to pursue—that is, to join the Confederacy" by completing the circle of Confederate units drawn around them, and it would, at the same time, free southern Missouri of Federal units and "give heart and countenance to our friends in Missouri." McCulloch was satisfied that Lane had not yet recruited or organized a force of any importance, and since all the border counties on the western line of Missouri were considered pro-southern, he hoped to be able to draw supplies from them. From Fort Scott, after receiving reinforcement from Missouri, he proposed marching to the Kansas River. To make such a move, he calculated, would require a minimum of seven thousand troops, for whom he applied to Walker. Indians, he reported prophetically, would not do, as they would object to service outside their own country and "would be difficult to restrain" if moved into Kansas. McCulloch feared, as well, "the censures that would be heaped upon our government by employing them."[28]

On 26 June Adj. Gen. Samuel Cooper authorized McCulloch to advance on Fort Scott and to "give such assistance to Missouri as will subserve the main purpose" of his mission to "conciliate the Indian nations" and "obtain their active co-operation" against the Union. Events in Missouri, however, quickly altered McCulloch's strategy. Only one day after Cooper's wire left Richmond, McCulloch learned that Jackson's three columns of pro-southern Missouri militia were falling back into Arkansas. McCulloch's scouts reported on 28 June that Sterling Price, the newly appointed commander of the Missouri State Guard, was at Maysville, some eighty-five miles north of Fort Smith, with "1,000 men, poorly armed." Governor Jackson, 50 miles behind Price, had an estimated 1,500 men, and James S. Rains, a brigadier general in the Missouri State Guard, had a force of 3,000. From Fort Smith, McCulloch sent "reliable men" to urge Jackson and his generals to join him on the Arkansas line.[29]

The Federal force that drove them from their state had left Lexington on the morning of 20 June at a reported strength of 4,000 or 5,000 men. An additional 3,000 to 5,000 Union troops were said to be at Springfield, and two more regiments were at Fort Scott. Worse, Lyon and an additional 9,000 men were reported advancing from St. Louis. Although all of those numbers proved to be wildly overestimated, McCulloch wrote to Pike that "we must meet and rally the forces of Missouri and turn this invading tide back if possible," adding that "Arkansas must make the selection between her own soil and that of Missouri for a battlefield."[30]

Although desperate for arms, ammunition, and reinforcements, McCulloch marched from Fort Smith on the morning of 30 June with the Third Louisiana and the First Arkansas Mounted Rifle regiments en route to Maysville on the northwestern frontier of Arkansas. There Brig. Gen. N. Bart Pearce was waiting with nine hundred to twelve hundred men of the Arkansas State Militia. To meet an enemy force reportedly several times the size of his own, McCulloch issued a proclamation calling all the men of western Arkansas to "rally upon Fayetteville" to meet the emergency and another calling on the men of Texas to "Look to Your Arms, and be ready for any emergency!" Although unauthorized to recruit new units, McCulloch reminded his fellow Texans that they must be prepared to defend their state. "Let your horses and arms be kept in good condition," he advised them, and be ready for the call. "The Black Republicans boastingly say they have conquered Missouri and will now overrun Arkansas and Texas. Will you permit it? Let those States now stand by each other, and the victory is ours!"[31]

With new recruits from Texas and Arkansas, he hoped to have sufficient means to check the Union incursion at the Arkansas border and then to "strike them a blow in Missouri." "I go at once to meet the enemy," he wrote to his brother John, "We shall have some hard fighting, but will beat them." Some twelve miles from Fort Smith, McCulloch and Pearce met Sterling Price and offered to "serve him or Missouri." Price replied that he and his men, only a part of whom were armed, were attempting to effect a junction with the columns of Governor Jackson and General Rains. Lyon, Price informed McCulloch and Pearce, was pressing them hard from the north while Col. Franz Sigel, born in Germany and educated at the Karlsruhe Military Academy before becoming a fugitive following the unsuccessful revolution of 1848, was menacing their front. Jackson's "disorganized, undisciplined men would probably be cut to pieces," McCulloch believed, "and Missouri [would] fall entirely under the control of the North" if he did not march to their aid.[32]

McCulloch and Pearce at once agreed to aid Price in Jackson's rescue. "It will depend upon his fate what my future movements will be," McCulloch wired Walker, and he assured the secretary that his "great object" in entering Missouri was "to relieve the governor and the force under him." Accordingly, on 4 July McCulloch led Churchill's mounted riflemen and Pearce's Arkansas brigade from Camp Jackson, Arkansas, into Missouri. The following day McCulloch learned that Jackson and his band were in imminent danger of being overwhelmed, and he concluded that if he were to rescue them, he would have to "move with more celerity than infantry and artillery could march." Leaving his slower units, therefore, McCulloch pressed on with only his cavalry. Upon arriving within twelve miles of Neosho, the Confederates learned that Sigel had recently passed through, closing in on Jackson. The Federals, however, had left a rear guard of 137 men, and McCulloch sent two columns of cavalry—six companies under Churchill and five companies under Col. James McQueen McIntosh, each by a different road—to capture the detachment. McIntosh's column made the trip in much less time than expected, however, having taken the shorter route, and found itself at Neosho a full hour before Churchill's companies were due to arrive. Fearing that word of the Rebels' presence would reach Sigel's garrison, McIntosh determined to attack at once. Dismounting his battalion about a quarter of a mile outside of town, he sent the troopers at the double-quick to within two hundred yards of the courthouse. There they encountered a company drawn up in line of battle. McIntosh sent one of his companies around the Union flank and rear while he, with his remaining three companies, pinned the enemy in place. Finding himself surrounded, the commander of the Union company "made an unconditional surrender." McCulloch reported the movement as "entirely success-

Sterling Price, commander of the Missouri State Guard and perpetual nemesis of Ben McCulloch as commander of the Army of the West (Archives Division, Texas State Library)

ful," bagging 137 prisoners, 150 rifles with saber bayonets, a quantity of ammunition, a stand of colors, an ambulance, and a train of seven subsistence wagons loaded with provisions. In later years General Pearce recalled how the contents of the wagons "were freely distributed and generously consumed by the young soldiers of the Confederacy. Having marched most of the night and all the day before, they had emptied their haversacks of rations. They rejoiced over their first capture."[33]

McCulloch was now within twenty-five miles of Governor Jackson, whose beleaguered command had been fighting its way toward him throughout the day. "I will push a portion of my force (now nearly 4,000 men) as near to him as possible tomorrow and do all in my power to relieve him," McCulloch vowed. During the early part of the night, however, McCulloch and his men heard a heavy cannonading in the north and determined to march toward the sound of the guns. He immediately mounted his remaining cavalry and rode toward Jackson, whom they met before midnight near Cassville "after a rapid march of twenty miles."[34]

McCulloch's appearance "was hailed with great joy," wrote Col. Robert S. Bevier of the Missouri State Guard, bringing "the assurance . . . of the friendly feeling and intentions of the Confederate Government." McCulloch was popular with the Missouri soldiers "from the first." Bevier recalled how "the slightly bent, spare form, sallow face and old slouch hat of the famous Texan Ranger were always greeted with shouts, while his kindly grey eye had a friendly gleam for all." At their first meeting with McCulloch and his command, in fact, the Missourians, "seemed to out-demonstrate all the demonstrations we had yet seen." Wrote one of the Louisianians, "In their excitement of cheering and firing salutes, they exploded a barrel of gunpowder, which blew some of themselves into the air." McCulloch's astonished men never learned whether the human cannonball act was intentional or accidental but "considered such displays of zeal to be quite overstepping the thing."[35]

At Cassville, McCulloch learned that Jackson, at the head of the state guard, that very morning had defeated Sigel's eleven-hundred-man column in a small but encouraging engagement at Carthage. As Union brigadier general John M. Schofield derisively informed his superior, Maj. Gen. Henry W. Halleck, at the "celebrated 'battle of Carthage' " Sigel had about two regiments of infantry, "most of them old German soldiers," and two good batteries of artillery. Jackson had about twice Sigel's number, most of them mounted and armed with only "shot-guns and common rifles" and "a few pieces of almost worthless artillery." The Missourians

James McQueen McIntosh, commander of the cavalry brigade of McCulloch's Army of the West
(Library of Congress)

were "entirely without organization and discipline," Schofield maintained, a "miserable rabble." After a desultory bombardment and a halfhearted assault on Jackson's line, Sigel withdrew toward Springfield. Now fearful of McCulloch's approaching column, the Federals dared approach no nearer. With one jaw of Lyon's trap thus wrenched off, the Missouri State Guard was free to make its way southward unimpeded, for the time being. In a hurried conference, the Missouri generals concluded not to pursue Sigel but to retire to the southwestern corner of their state to organize their volunteers, many of whom were not formed into regiments or even companies.[36]

With the immediate threat from Sigel and his command removed, and having gone into Missouri without the express authorization of the War Department, McCulloch returned to Camp Jackson, seven miles below the state boundary, while Price established his headquarters on Cowskin Prairie, just twelve miles inside the Missouri line and within easy supporting distance of McCulloch. There Price began to organize the Missouri State Guard, a task McCulloch considered beyond his capacity. According to one trooper in the Third Texas Cavalry, four-fifths of the Missouri army was on horseback and featured "generals, horses, and mules enough for 50,000 men." The Missourians refused to give up their horses despite the dire need for infantry, the unsuitability of the terrain for mounted operations, and the great difficulty in obtaining grain and fodder for so many animals. Most of Price's seven thousand to eight thousand men were without weapons, and those who were armed had only shotguns and squirrel rifles. Critical as McCulloch's own arms situation was, Price's was worse, and McCulloch "loaned" the Missouri State Guard some 615 muskets with ammunition.[37]

The Army of the West had gained much valuable experience and even more valuable confidence from its incursion into Missouri. In his report to Walker, McCulloch praised his little command extravagantly, assuring the secretary that "they bore themselves like men, and their only regret seemed to be that they could not prove their strength against their Northern foes." With their morale heightened by their new military skills, reinforcements, and supplies, "the men grew hilarious over the anticipation of an active campaign, and rejoiced at the prospect of a change from an idle camp life to scenes more worthy [of] the spirit which had led them this far from home." Not all of the acclaim for the Neosho raid was visited upon McCulloch's officers and men. Secretary of War Walker hastened to commend McCulloch on "the brilliant operation" in Missouri, assured him that he "could not receive too high praise," and approved his conduct "in every particular." "Your future operations will be looked for with great interest, and in every emergency this department confides fully in your ability, courage, and skill."[38]

Slight as the brush at Neosho had been, coming early in the war, it provided much sensational material for southern newspapers and, as in the days when Kendall of the New Orleans *Daily Picayune* was riding with his ranger company, contributed to the legend of Ben McCulloch. According to the Dallas *Herald*, the Neosho raid was "the most characteristic thing of Ben we have seen yet." Typical of the stories circulated about him was one that characterized his Missouri exploit as "Ben McCulloch all over." Among the prisoners, so the story ran, "was a regiment or so of Dutch," as nineteenth-century Americans were wont to characterize Germans. This apocryphal regiment had captured a party of 150 unarmed Missourians who had been on their way to join Price's command. On learning that these men were "in possession of the Hessian infidels," McCulloch rode to their camp and asked the leader of the Missourians "why he allowed himself to be captured by a pack of Dutch." The would-be Rebel replied that "he could not help it" because his men were both unarmed and outnumbered. "Well," said Ben, "if you had arms, would you fight for the Southern Confederacy?" "Of course I would, if I could," the Missourian replied, but explained that he was bound by his oath not take up arms against the United States. "Did you do that?" McCulloch demanded of the "Dutch" captain. " 'Oh, yas, I dun that,' said Dutch, 'but I vas only doing my duty.' 'Doing your h——l!' " thundered McCulloch. " 'Do you call it your duty to make a man swear against his country?' 'Vell, I can't help dat, I vas only obeying orders of my zuperior officers.' 'Well, I want you to obey me now,' said Ben. 'So take that Bible and unswear every one of them back into the Southern Confederacy.' "[39]

Another story current in the army was viewed by Victor Rose as "altogether characteristic of McCulloch." Disguised as a drover, the tale went, McCulloch had visited Neosho some days previous to the raid, offering a herd of beeves for sale. As he had spied out Woll's camp on the Medina in 1842 and Santa Anna's encampment on the eve of Buena Vista, he was said to have satisfied himself of the Federals' numbers and dispositions and ridden back to his own camp in perfect safety. Although both of these stories are no doubt fanciful, they do indicate the high regard in which southerners in general and Texans in particular held their general and, although smacking of the broad humor so popular in the old Southwest, are based on characteristics and past exploits of their hero. "Of undaunted courage, iron nerve and will, never for a moment losing his self-control under the most trying circumstances," Willie Tunnard said of McCulloch, "he delighted in such perilous adventures."[40]

Waiting for McCulloch when he returned to Camp Jackson was the War Department's official approval of his "conciliatory" Indian policy and his plan for an invasion of Kansas as well as his foray into Missouri. Admonishing McCulloch to keep "steadily in view the great object of [his] command," Walker allowed him to exercise discretion when cooperating with Missouri, encouraging him to collaborate with Price's army "when it is quite clear that co-operation will be likely to avail." Walker cautioned, however, that border crossings would require "much prudence and circumspection," and he reminded McCulloch to exercise his option to make common cause with the Missourians without prior approval of the War Department only "when necessity and propriety unite."[41]

With orders so vague and contradictory, ideal circumstances would have been required for a close and healthy cooperation between Confederate and Missouri armies on the northwestern frontier. Reality proved less than ideal. The southern army in Arkansas and Missouri was in fact a loose alliance of three armies: the Missouri State Guard, belonging to a state of the Union resisting what it considered Federal usurpation and commanded by Sterling Price with his major general's commission from Governor Jackson; the Arkansas state troops, commanded by N. Bart Pearce, with a state brigadier general's commission but with instructions to cooperate with McCulloch; and McCulloch's own command of the Provisional Army of the Confederate States. Although McCulloch was only a brigadier general, his commission was from the Confederate government, and he therefore presumably took precedence over officers of greater rank commissioned only by their states.

More serious was McCulloch's distrust of the ability of the Missouri officer corps to discipline its troops and to lead them wisely on campaign. Although as eager as the Missourians to drive the Federals beyond St. Louis, he had serious doubts about the military efficiency of the state guard and its commander. "I find," he wrote to the War Department on 18 July, "that [Price's] force of 8,000 or 9,000 men is badly organized, badly armed, and now almost entirely out of ammunition. This force was made by the combination of different commands under their own generals. The consequence is that there is no concert of action among them, and will not be until a competent military man is put in command of the entire force."[42]

The Missouri volunteers had been raised primarily in the hill country south and southeast of Springfield and were, as Col. Thomas L. Snead, Governor Jackson's adjutant general, understated, "a unique body of soldiers." The most loyal of the Missourians freely admitted that very few of their officers had any knowledge whatever of the principles or practices of war and those few had "only the most superficial experience in company tactics." Colonels, Snead observed, "could not drill their regiments, nor captains their companies." In a force too democratic for its own good, officers and men messed together, and soldiers lounged around headquarters, taking part in every phase of military decision making. Regimental commanders were approached without a salute and addressed not as "colonel" but by the only honorific the hill people knew, "Jedge."

Their only arms were their hunting rifles, but these they knew how to use with deadly accuracy. "A powder horn, a cap-pouch, 'a string of patchin,' and a hunter's knife completed their equipment," and Snead doubted that a man among them had ever seen a piece of artillery. "But, for all this," he rightly insisted, "they were brave and intelligent. Like all frontiersmen, they were shrewd, quick-witted, wary, cunning, and ready for all emergencies, and like all backwoodsmen, their courage was serene, steady, unconscious."[43]

Although Price and his officers agreed that McCulloch was "one of the bravest men and best of scouts," their pride and the innate mistrust their hill-bred followers had of "outsiders" made them loath to unite their army with that of the Confederacy, even under McCulloch's command. Although McCulloch never used derogatory language in any written communication, the Missourians were not far wrong when they assumed that he "saw in the Missourians nothing but a half-armed mob, led by an ignorant old militia general."[44]

Perhaps the best assessment of the great personal and philosophical differences growing between McCulloch and Price was rendered by their mutual antagonist, Union general Franz Sigel. In Sigel's estimation, "Although serving the same cause, there never existed an *entente cordial* between the two champions of Missouri and Arkansas; the two men were too different in their character, education, and military policy to understand each other perfectly, to agree in their aims and ends, and to subordinate themselves cheerfully one to the other." McCulloch, in Sigel's opinion, was a "rough and ready" soldier, "not at all speculative, but very practical, to the point, and rich in resources to reach it. . . . He was a good fighter, energetic in battle, and quick in discerning danger or espying the weak point of his antagonist; an excellent organizer, disciplinarian, and administrator, indefatigable in recruiting and equipping troops." As a strategist, McCulloch was committed to the defense of Arkansas and the Indian Territory, the district the War Department had placed under his command and protection.

Price, like McCulloch, had acquired some military experience in the war with Mexico, which, combined with his popularity as former governor of Missouri and his "irreproachable personal character and sincere devotion to the cause which he embraced," had made him the natural choice to command the state guard. "Brave and gifted with the talent of gaining confidence and love of his soldiers, he was undoubtedly the proper man to gather around him and hold together the heterogeneous military forces," wrote Sigel. "His army," however, "was an ever-changing body, varying from week to week, advancing and retreating, without stability of quarters and security of resources, and therefore not disciplined in a manner to be desired. No wonder then that in spite of the great popularity of the champion of Missouri, McCulloch became disgusted in meeting the half-starved 'State Guards' of Missouri with their 'huckleberry' cavalry and their great crowd of unarmed, noisy camp-followers."[45]

TWELVE

McCulloch Has Made a Clean Platter in Missouri

Despite the myriad problems besetting the Rebels on their northwestern frontier, the Missourians and the Confederates gamely attempted to make their unstable alliance work. McCulloch's hesitancy in moving to support Jackson, Pearce later recalled, was not the result of his not wishing to fight, "for then he was in his glory," but occurred because Jefferson Davis "was very scrupulous in his state's rights ideas." Missouri had not passed an ordinance of secession and thus had not been admitted to the Confederacy. Davis, therefore, was hesitant to allow Confederate forces to enter Missouri territory until the legislature requested southern aid. Missouri officials tried to hammer out a more binding agreement with the Confederate government that would allow McCulloch greater freedom to cooperate across the Arkansas line. Brig. Gen. E. C. Cabell, a member of the pro-secession legislature that had fled St. Joseph with Jackson, urged Jefferson Davis, "if not inconsistent with [his] views of constitutional powers," to issue more specific instructions to

McCulloch authorizing him to enter Missouri to engage the Federals. "None but the enemies of the Confederate States and Missouri will protest," he assured the president.[1]

McCulloch, for his part, was eager to accompany Price back into Missouri in search of Lyon. Missouri citizens had reported that Lyon was in Springfield, the principal town in southern Missouri and the point at which the roads from Kansas, the Indian Territory, and Arkansas converged and led north toward St. Louis, with nine or ten thousand men said to be "busily engaged in fortifying." Nevertheless, McCulloch was confident that, if his troops could be successfully united with those of Arkansas and Missouri under his unquestioned command, they could defeat Lyon and recapture southwestern Missouri.[2]

By 18 July the Rebels were astride the Springfield road, seven miles above Bentonville, Arkansas, with a patchwork army of 13,500 men. McCulloch's Confederates numbered 4,000, "all healthy and in good spirits," according to their commander. "They are a fine body of men," he reported with justifiable pride, "and through constant drilling are becoming very efficient. I place a great deal of reliance upon them." Pearce commanded 2,500 Arkansas state troops, who, if properly armed and supplied, could be relied upon, and Price led 7,000 of the Missouri State Guard. Of the latter, only 4,500 were even indifferently armed, and its cavalry was "very inefficient." However problematic their organization, supply, command, and discipline, though, Price's men, as Pearce said, "were clamorous and fretful at the delay. They wanted to drive the vandals from their homes."[3]

McCulloch saw no present threat to the Indian Territory and maintained close communication with "trusty men" there who would inform him of Union activity. "Should any movement be made in that direction I will have timely notice of it and will be prepared," he assured Walker. Maj. Gen. William J. Hardee had recently taken command of a Confederate brigade at Pitman's Ferry in northeastern Arkansas, thus opening a broad window of opportunity for a Confederate offensive into Missouri. Hardee was encouraged to move north to Ironton, Missouri, and there unite with Brig. Gen. Gideon J. Pillow, who was poised to move into Missouri with six thousand men from western Tennessee. McCulloch and Price, advancing into southwestern Missouri, would at worst hold Lyon until the three Confederate columns converged to overwhelm him and then march victoriously into St. Louis.[4]

The strategic concept was never formalized, however, and when Maj. Gen. Leonidas Polk, commander of the Confederate military district embracing the upper Mississippi River, learned that Governor Jackson had consistently overstated the strength of the Missouri State Guard, he withdrew his support from the project. The crowning failure came, however, when Hardee and Pillow, both situated on Missouri soil and facing only shadow opposition, refused to support each other in an attack on Ironton, thus collapsing the eastern wing of the invasion.[5]

Nevertheless, McCulloch, Price, and Pearce, still hoping for the cooperation of Hardee and Pillow, started out together to beard Lyon in his den at Springfield. When the allies reached Cassville, Missouri, on the afternoon of 29 July, Pearce went to Price's headquarters to work out "some definite understanding as the rank and command of the combined forces." The column of southerners was approaching Lyon's army and was likely to encounter it at any moment, and Pearce "was not satisfied to have so many separate and independent commanders." He was, he said, quite willing to serve under Price or McCulloch but wanted "a head to the army." Price agreed with Pearce and suggested that the two generals visit McCulloch. At McCulloch's headquarters, Price addressed McCulloch "in his dignified and courteous manner" and informed him of the purpose of their errand. "Voluntarily, before McCulloch replied," Pearce later recalled, Price "proffered in his own name and mine" the command of the allied armies. Thomas L. Snead, Price's adjutant and loyal partisan, recorded that the Missouri general, "in compliment to the Confederate States, and desirous only of how he could best serve Missouri, willingly waived his rank and placed himself and command under the Confederate commander." McCulloch agreed that the success of the campaign was perhaps dependent upon achieving unity of command and accepted the offer with thanks and "in the same kind and earnest manner in which it had been tendered him."[6]

Despite the apparent cordiality of the meeting, McCulloch privately suspected that Price had offered him the command only to throw the responsibility of ordering a retreat upon him if the want of supplies should mandate a retrograde movement. The army's commissary situation was critical. The Missouri division was entirely out of bread, and only the corn that was just beginning to ripen saved the troops from starvation. Although McCulloch and Pearce were somewhat better off, they were, as McCulloch said, "by no means burthened with commissary's stores." "Since crossing the Missouri line," Pvt. A. W. Sparks of the Ninth Texas Cavalry wrote, "each man had acted as his own purveyor of supplies, and those supplies consisted almost exclusively of green corn." The Rebels, consequently, were "wolfish," and one private, roasting a dozen ears of green corn when the enemy were heard approaching, swore he would not leave them "for all the damn Dutch in hell." All "indulged in bright fancies of capturing the Federal army, bag and baggage."[7]

In accordance with the terms of his agreement with Price and Pearce, McCulloch drew up the order of march to Springfield and submitted it to the Missouri and Arkansas commanders, offering each the option of amending it if he wished. Both men approved without comment. The three columns, united as one, moved north out of Cassville "as early as practicable" on 31 July. A battalion of Rains's Missouri cavalry, especially organized at McCulloch's request because of its knowledge of the southwestern Missouri countryside, constituted the advance guard, riding ten miles ahead of the infantry and maintaining continual communication with the main body. McCulloch's division led the infantry, with Hébert's Third Louisiana in the van. The Second Division, the infantry of Price and Pearce, marched on 1 August, and the remainder of the cavalry, designated as the Third Division, under McIntosh, moved out on 2 August.[8]

The campaign began inauspiciously with a test of wills between the Confederate and Missouri commanders and a show of insubordination in the state guard. Before setting out, McCulloch had insisted and Price had agreed that all of the unarmed Missourians and their camp followers, a total of about two thousand men and women, were to be left in camp "and under no circumstances permitted to march with the army." Although many of his own men were imperfectly armed, Pearce loaned the Missourians one thousand flintlock muskets with bayonets, and McCulloch gave Price enough ammunition "to warrant them in again taking the field." These loans and donations so depleted McCulloch's own supply that it had became "very limited," and he was forced again to call upon the War Department for replenishment.[9]

Despite McCulloch's and Pearce's generosity, fewer than 5,500 of Price's men could be considered effectively armed. When the armies formed their junction at Cassville, however, McCulloch discovered to his extreme distress that "the whole crowd of camp followers had arrived also." He remonstrated with Price on the violation of their agreement, and Price promised to leave his ineffectives at Cassville. Only after the allied army was again on the march did McCulloch learn that Brig. Gen. John B. Clark, a former member of the Missouri house of representatives, had refused to obey the order to leave his unarmed men. McCulloch at once rode back down the line and urged him to set a better example for the army. "Knowing the danger of a divided command when brought in contact with one well united, well drilled, and under one efficient leader," McCulloch "considered it of vital importance to rid the army of these men until after the battle was fought." The acute scarcity of supplies and the danger of a panic among unarmed men on a battlefield further motivated McCulloch's pleas. Clark still refused to obey, and Price would not or could not enforce his orders. Meanwhile the unarmed troops continued to tag along—an unruly, plundering, and encumbering mob.[10]

Some thirty miles below Springfield the army bivouacked for two days on Crane Creek, "a fine clear stream," along whose banks "was a good deal of level ground suitable for camping." McCulloch's pickets were soon skirmishing with those of Lyon's army and informing him that the Federals had left Springfield and were advancing upon him. McCulloch's position was admirably suited for defense. It was approached from the north by a broad road commanded on both sides by high ground, "steep and rugged in many places and covered with small wood of oak, hickory, and hazel." On these slopes McCulloch formed his lines, with the Pulaski Battery stationed on a hillside covering the ford. There he hoped the enemy could be drawn into ambush. On 2 August McIntosh pushed forward as far as Dug Springs with "a thousand more or less" of Rains's Missouri cavalry as bait for McCulloch's trap. One Louisiana soldier recalled that day, "the first time the command was ever called out in line of battle," and as the "long roll" was beating to form his regiment, word passed down the line: "Steady, men, General McCulloch is loading the cannon himself."[11]

Early in the afternoon of 2 August, McIntosh and the Missouri cavalry encountered the advance guard of Lyon's army at Dug Springs, some seven miles from the Rebel camp. The result, according to General Pearce, "was a sprightly skirmish for a short time." Pearce, it appears, was being kind. Captain Woodruff recalled how, after receiving but a single cannonball from the Union vanguard, Rains's Missourians, "in seeming hordes," rushed south across the ford "with any imaginable style of vehicles and people, mounted and on foot." As they swept "in hot haste" through the southern camps, "coming as hard as whip and spur could urge the horses," the terrified horsemen announced that the enemy had advanced in great force and had cut off and killed McIntosh. "The disorder was terrifying," reported Woodruff, "and had well nigh panicked the unattached and unarmed Missourians."[12]

At this point McCulloch dashed up the road, "fairly foaming with rage" and "exhausting his whole vocabulary of vituperation" ("no meager one," according to Sgt. Willie Tunnard of the Third Louisiana) in denunciations of Rains's cavalry. They had been put to rout, it was learned, with the loss of only one man "who died of overheat or sunstroke." They returned with no reliable information and were never afterward "of the slightest service as scouts or spies," declared McCulloch.

Their retreat at last arrested, the Missourians were anxiously questioned about the fate of Colonel McIntosh. Finally, said Tunnard, "one old fellow" was found who had seen a man answering to McIntosh's description as he rode by. "Well! what was he doing?" demanded McCulloch. "Cussin' the Missourians," the old man replied. A roar of relieved laughter and then a cheer arose from the Louisianians, "for the identification was certain and satisfactory." Every hope of ambushing the enemy had now evaporated, however, and as McCulloch rode past the Third Louisiana, he called out, "The enemy have stopped to take dinner. Come on, boys, we will go and take dinner too."[13]

Although the Missourians repeatedly promised reliable information on Lyon's strength and position, such intelligence was never forthcoming. Rather than bring on an engagement with an unknown enemy, McCulloch halted within thirty miles of Springfield, ignorant of "whether the streets were barricaded or if any kind of works of defense had been erected by the enemy," and finally threatened to order the whole army back to Cassville.[14]

According to Snead, Price approached McCulloch on 4 August, furious that no further advance had been made on Lyon. In what Snead described as a "loud, imperious tone," Price delivered an ultimatum to McCulloch.

> I am an older man than you, General McCulloch, and I am not only your senior in rank[.] I was a brigadier-general in the Mexican War, with an independent command when you were only a captain; I have fought and won more battles than you have ever witnessed; my force is twice as great as yours; and some of my officers rank and have seen more service than you, and we are also on the soil of our state; but, General McCulloch, if you will consent to help us to whip Lyon and repossess Missouri, I will put myself and all my forces under your command, and we will obey you as faithfully as the humblest of your own men. We can whip Lyon, and we will whip him and drive the enemy out of Missouri, and all the honor and glory shall be yours. All that we want is to regain our homes and to establish the independence of Missouri and the South.

If, however, McCulloch should choose to retire into Arkansas, Price intended to push on against Lyon with only his own command, "for it is better that they and I should all perish than Missouri be abandoned without a struggle." Vowing to attack Lyon on the morrow, the quixotic Price dared McCulloch to "fight beside us, or look on at a safe distance."[15]

In all likelihood, McCulloch planned that evening to pull out the Confederate and Arkansas forces and to abandon Price to his folly. The Missouri division was clearly little more than a rabble in arms, and by all reports Lyon's force, consisting largely of regular regiments from the old army, was vastly superior to the allied southern armies in numbers, arms, supplies, and discipline. The Federals were concentrated only a few miles distant, with Springfield and its stockpiles of supplies close behind them. McCulloch, on the other hand, was 150 miles from his base of operations and had but few supplies even there. "A wild country and almost impassable roads" lay between McCulloch and Springfield, and his draft animals were almost exhausted. With green corn the chief subsistence of the army, diarrhea was rapidly becoming epidemic, and perhaps worst of all, McCulloch could expect no reliable intelligence from the Missouri cavalry. Providentially, however, a messenger rode into McCulloch's camp with a message from Leonidas Polk stating that Hardee and Pillow were advancing from Pitman's Ferry and New Madrid toward Rolla, Missouri, with twelve thousand men to intercept Lyon. Although this intelligence proved false, McCulloch realized that he must cooperate with the right wing of the Confederate offensive and defeat Lyon or at least hold him in position until Pillow could administer the coup de grace. Price, informed of McCulloch's decision to advance, issued orders placing the Missouri State Guard under McCulloch's command. McCulloch once more specified that all unarmed men should remain in camp. Combatants, however, were to immediately "put their guns in condition for service, provide themselves with fifty rounds of ammunition, and get in readiness to take up the line of march by twelve o'clock at night."[16]

McCulloch's army was "thrown into a ferment of suppressed excitement." "Orders were quietly given to the captains and orderly sergeants of companies to have arms inspected and the men supplied with ammunition and be ready at nine o'clock to march forward and attack the enemy," recalled Watson. Elkhanah Greer's Third Texas Cavalry, the self-styled Ironsides, having just arrived after its forced march from Fort Smith, received word from the regimental sergeant major to "cook up three day's rations, distribute all the ammunition they can get, and be in their saddles." With the enemy so near, the advance was to "take place in quietness" with "neither shouting nor beating of drums." Canteens were filled, one day's rations were cooked, and, as so often before, the unarmed men were admonished to remain in camp.[17]

Wearing a white badge on each arm to distinguish him on the night march, McCulloch addressed his men. "Look steadily to the front," he told them. With the news of the Confederate victory at Manassas on 21 July still green, he reminded them that "the eyes of your gallant brothers in arms who have so nobly acquitted themselves in the East are upon you." McCulloch's plan of battle was a simple one and somewhat naive. Rains's cavalry, leading the line of march, was to fall in on the left wing of the southern army as soon as contact with the enemy was made. The four regiments of Texas and Arkansas cavalry under McIntosh were to anchor the Rebel right. Price was to command the left wing of McCulloch's line and Pearce the center. Once the line was formed, and assuming that Lyon remained passive, the right wing cavalry was to ride around Lyon's left "and endeavor to take the enemy in the flank." The men were reminded to take careful aim once engaged, and, confident of victory, McCulloch called upon his colonels to rally their commands for further orders "as soon as the enemy is driven from their first position."[18]

Federal scouts, however, had served Lyon far better than the Missouri cavalry had served McCulloch. The Union commander was well enough informed to estimate that McCulloch had fifteen thousand Missouri and Arkansas soldiers, most of whom were "ill-conditioned," in addition to his own four thousand Louisiana and Texas troops. However poorly armed and organized a large portion of his enemy's army was, Lyon calculated his own command was sufficiently outnumbered to place him "under the painful necessity of retreating," and he was fearful that his retiring army would be overwhelmed. Reluctantly, therefore, he ordered his army to fall back toward Springfield.

Although unable to explain the Federal withdrawal, McCulloch assumed Lyon had either overestimated southern numbers or was attempting to draw him further from his supplies or into a trap to completely annihilate his army. Nevertheless, McCulloch made his decision quickly. He ordered his weary column forward at dawn. With the embarrassment of his army on Crane Creek, McCulloch recognized "the total inefficiency of the Missouri mounted men" and, therefore, was three miles in the van with his staff, acting as his own intelligence. McCulloch pursued Lyon on 5 August, skirmishing through the early forenoon with the enemy's rear guard cavalry, but could not overtake him. Characteristically, McCulloch made several such reconnaissance excursions on his own, and, according to

Pearce, "had on more than one occasion tried the effect of his breech loading rifle on the advance pickets of the enemy, much to their discomfiture and greatly to his amusement."[19]

About sundown on 7 August, the Third Texas Cavalry, having been transferred to the vanguard in consequence of Rains's incapacity, reached Wilson Creek and went into camp to await the arrival of the main body of the army. The next morning the remainder of the Rebel army joined Greer's regiment, with McCulloch's division encamping on the eastern side of the creek and Price's on several grassy ridges on the western bank. That night, for the first time in many nights, the army enjoyed a fair rest.[20]

Wilson Creek was similar to the half-dozen other creeks that the army had recently crossed, but perhaps a bit larger. The Springfield road ran for some distance parallel to the stream, crossing it near McCulloch's headquarters. The ground on either side was higher and was cut with ridge lines, the highest terminating in a hill about half a mile west of the creek. Its top was covered with scrub oak trees and so bore the name Oak Hill. The site's principal recommendation, at least so far as the soldiers were concerned, was the several large fields of green corn that grew conveniently nearby and from which the men supplied themselves. The troops had not eaten for twenty-four hours and had been supplied with only half rations of green corn for ten days previous. The absence of the baggage train was severely felt, and McCulloch swore that if supplies were not moved forward by that evening, he "would hang every wagon-master and commissary in the division upon the oak trees."[21]

At the Oak Hill camp the army spent two days, "rather inactive," while its commander was frustrated in his attempts to gather intelligence, the best of which he found "very conflicting and unsatisfactory." Evidently much out of patience with McCulloch's cautious advance over unexamined terrain, Price called at the general's headquarters and demanded loudly, "General McCulloch, are you going to attack Lyon or not?" When McCulloch responded noncommittally, Price replied, "Then I want my own Missouri troops, and I will lead them against Lyon myself if they are all killed in the action, and you, General McCulloch, may go where the devil you please!"[22]

Price's ill temper and impetuous ardor to close with the enemy probably had little positive influence, but, as McCulloch later told Adjutant General Cooper, he was now left with the option of "a disastrous retreat or a blind attack upon Springfield." Therefore, on 8 August McCulloch sent a company of Arkansas cavalry under Capt. A. V. Reiff toward Springfield to map the approaches to the town and the position of the enemy. At 3:00 P.M. on the following day two secessionist women gained Lyon's permission to pass through Union lines, and they delivered a detailed report on the condition of the enemy at Springfield. Lyon, they told the southern generals, was not half so formidable as they had been led to believe. McCulloch therefore determined to attack at once. Shortly before 9:00 P.M. on 9 August, Captain Reiff found McCulloch and McIntosh in the general's tent, "with a pencil sketch of Springfield, showing the location of the Federal forces, and three roads leading from our encampment." Price, McCulloch informed his scout, was to take the main road to Springfield while Rains, with the Missouri cavalry, would take a smaller road, somewhat to the west, by way of Pond Springs. McCulloch and McIntosh were to advance by another route, slightly to the east. All of the Rebel units, he insisted, must be in sight of Springfield and ready to attack by daylight.[23]

After receiving their marching orders, McCulloch's men ate what food they could find and began to see to their horses, guns, and ammunition. As General Pearce observed, "The question of ammunition was one of the most important and serious." McCulloch's ordnance department was "imperfectly organized and poorly supplied," and Price's was nonexistent. The men, therefore, set about improvising ammunition for their antiquated arms. "Here," Pearce saw "a group . . . molding bullets—there, another crowd dividing percussion-caps, and, again, another group fitting new flints to their old muskets. They had little thought then of the inequality between the discipline, arms, and accoutrements of the regular United States troops they were soon to engage in battle, and their own homely movements and equipments." So undaunted were these amateurs at the art of war that, once fed and satisfied that their arms were as well prepared as they could make them, impromptu dances were begun and continued around many of the campfires until the hour of march was at hand.[24]

When 9:00 came, however, a slight rain was falling, and the night was exceptionally dark and threatening. After conferring with Price, McCulloch delayed the advance. The Rebel troops had an average of only twenty-five rounds of ammunition with "no more to be had short of Fort Smith or Baton Rouge," and only the Louisiana regiment was furnished with anything better than cotton cloth bags in which to carry their cartridges. Some men carried their handmade cartridges in their pockets, and others had only loose powder in ancient powder horns. "The slightest rain or wet would have almost disarmed us," reasoned McCulloch.[25]

With the order to move out, Rains's pickets on the north and Churchill's on the south and east of the Rebel camp had been called in. When the order delaying the movement "until further orders" was given, these pickets were not sent out again because their commanders expected the order to advance would come at any moment. The Louisiana infantry slept on their arms, and the Third Texas Cavalry "stood to horse" all night. "Of course our men became weary with standing and waiting, lay down at the feet of their horses, reins in hand, and slept," recorded Pvt. Samuel Barron of Greer's regiment. The officers and men of the Pulaski Battery were ordered to remain at their guns, "with teams harnessed and hitched, parked at full instance, and remained so all night." In the camps of the Missourians, however, "the dance before the camp-fires was resumed and kept up for some time with a merry earnestness."[26]

Between 1:00 and 2:00 A.M., after ordering the army to delay its march to Springfield, McCulloch dispatched Lt. William (Buck) Brown and twenty-five men from an independent Arkansas cavalry company, then serving as his personal bodyguard and scout company, to investigate reported enemy activity on the Pond Springs road between the Confederate army and Springfield. Returning from patrol before dawn, 10 August, Brown's party encountered a battery of Federal artillery rolling toward McCulloch's army, only a mile and a half from its camps on Wilson Creek. Dashing back to camp, the scouts rode through what they took to be a regiment of the enemy, who "shouted something in a Dutch brogue." Brown hastened to McCulloch's headquarters to report that "the enemy is almost in your camp." McIntosh was incredulous, demanding, "What now, Brown—another Missouri humbug?" McCulloch, however, "partly dressed and bare headed," quickly ordered an aide to warn Price of impending attack. When the aide instructed a servant to catch his horse, McCulloch thundered, "Catch him yourself, and be quick about it." He then returned to his tent and immediately came out wearing his coat and hat. After commanding his Third Louisiana to "Fall in there!" he walked swiftly to Woodruff's battery to have it ready for action at once.[27]

About the same time, Sergeant Hite of General Pearce's bodyguard, who had gone early to a spring for water, was challenged by the Federal advance. He escaped and at once reported the presence of the enemy to Pearce's headquarters. Pearce sent him to McCulloch with the news, but before Hite reached the general's tent, Lyon had opened his attack upon Rains's camp atop Oak Hill. While McCulloch was conferring with Price, Col. John F. Snyder of Rains's command came running up and cried, "Thirty thousand Yankees are attacking Rains' line!" Almost simultaneously Rains's panic-stricken regiments, "a great crowd of men on horseback, some armed, others unarmed," rushed down toward Wilson Creek. Mixed with them were wagons, teams, and led horses, "all in dreadful confusion." At the same time, Capt. James Totten's Company F of the Second United States Artillery appeared on Oak Hill, less than three-quarters of a mile distant, and before the company could throw the first shell, Sigel's battery, on the opposite side of the Rebel camp, fired into Price's camp from the rear.[28]

Rains later reported that by sunrise his pickets had sighted the enemy advancing in force on the western side of Wilson Creek and within three miles of camp, and Maj. John M. Schofield of the United States Army reported similarly that at about 4:00 A.M. his troops had made contact with Rains's pickets, who "fled upon our approach." Nevertheless, the Rebels were taken almost completely by surprise and, as McCulloch later wrote, ran a terrific risk of panic "being communicated to the fighting men of the army by having such material among them." According to Rose, McCulloch "had personally the night previous designated a company of Missourians who lived in the vicinity, and who were of course acquainted with the country, as the guard to be picketed on the Springfield road." These men, he wrote, were drawn in without McCulloch's knowledge. Considerable controversy ensued over who ordered the pickets in and who knew of their withdrawal. McCulloch professed never to have been able to learn who, if anyone, ordered the pickets to leave their posts, but he claimed that "the fault was theirs and not mine that the enemy was allowed to approach so near before we were notified of it."[29]

Daylight had found some of the men up, starting little fires to prepare coffee for breakfast, while the majority were sleeping on the road in line of march. "Numbers of our horses, having slipped their reins from the hands of the sleeping soldiers, were grazing in the field in front of the camp." McCulloch's fear of Price's unarmed men proved justified, as the Third Texas Cavalry, attempting to form its ranks, was almost engulfed by "the hundreds of unarmed men" who had accompanied the Missouri division now "rushing in great haste from the battlefield." Private Barron recalled that the road was "so completely filled with the mass of moving trains and men rushing pell-mell southward" that "a heroic effort" was required to cross it to reach the regiment's assigned position in the line of battle. Henry Clay Neville of the Arkansas brigade also remembered that the camp followers were "a great encumbrance" to the army and that Price "had to get his unarmed men out of the range of the Federal guns before the other troops could do much effective service in resisting the attack." Pearce, too, calumniated the “stampede” of the Missourians, maintaining that it threatened disaster in his brigade when Lt. Col. Dandridge McRae’s battalion “was literally run over by this rabble trying to get out of the way (of harm).”[30]

The situation in Lyon’s camp had been remarkably similar to that in McCulloch’s. Like McCulloch, Lyon believed his army to be confronted by a larger force, and like the southern commander, he would have preferred to retire from the enemy’s front and avoid a battle he did not think he could win. Both generals, however, believed that a retreat at that time would prove disastrous and therefore resolved to attack rather than cede the initiative to the enemy. Hardee, Lyon believed, was marching with nine thousand men to cut the Federal line of communication. “It is evident that we must retreat,” Lyon informed his officers on 8 August, but asked rhetorically if they should “endeavor to retreat without giving the enemy battle beforehand, and run the risk of having to fight every inch along our line of retreat.” Rather, he suggested, they should attack McCulloch where he stood and hope to disable him from pursuing the Federal withdrawal.[31]

Three significant factors influenced Lyon’s decision. First, the enlistment period of several of his volunteer regiments was about to expire. If his army was to fight at all, it would have to fight now. Second, he had but slight regard for the Missouri and Arkansas troops of McCulloch’s command and thought they would count for little in battle. Finally, Lyon was aggressive by nature and could not tolerate the idea of retreat without a trial of arms. Bevier rightly sized up Lyon as “an able and dangerous man—a man of the times, who appreciated the force of audacity and quick decision in a revolutionary war.”[32]

Lyon executed a daring envelopment of McCulloch’s position on Wilson Creek. Franz Sigel, with about one-third of the Union army, swung around the southern camps to the east and struck up Telegraph Road from the south while from the north Lyon himself led the larger part of his army in a direct assault on Price’s cavalry camp on Oak Hill, the eminence that came to be known as Bloody Hill. Facing imminent disaster, McCulloch and Pearce quickly returned to their commands. Price swung his 250 pounds into the saddle and galloped off to rally his men while McCulloch, “furious with excitement and rage,” dashed back to the camp of the Third Louisiana and shouted, “Colonel Hébert, why in hell don’t you lead your men out?” The question, Tunnard recorded, did not have to be repeated. Conversely, Victor Marion Rose, then a trooper with the Third Texas Cavalry, remembered years later McCulloch’s “cool, calm, and unruffled demeanor, and silent, busy, serious air” as he set about recovering victory from apparent disaster. Indeed, McCulloch "never considered anything lost by their manner of attack as we were never in a better condition to make battle, every man being ready, gun in hand, to receive the enemy when at other times thousands of our men would be miles from camp, hunting something to eat for themselves and horses."[33]

In fact, Captain Woodruff believed the Federals would have had an easy victory if Lyon and Sigel had attacked without first firing their artillery, for their cannon gave notice of their presence. Woodruff quickly passed his caissons to the rear and ordered his guns into battery quickly enough to answer Totten's third or fourth shot. McCulloch and McIntosh rode to the eastern side of the creek, where the infantry of his own command and the infantry and artillery of Pearce were awaiting orders. McCulloch was soon beside Woodruff, urging him and his gunners to sustain the artillery duel until the southern infantry lines were established. Woodruff and Totten exchanged fire for half an hour or more, checking Lyon's advance and allowing McCulloch to dispose his troops to meet the Union attack. He posted J. G. Reid's Fort Smith Battery on the bluff opposite the mouth of Skegg's Branch. John R. Gratiot's Third and Thomas P. Dockery's Fifth Arkansas regiments he sent further north to a position along the bluff that forms the eastern bank of Wilson Creek, running from Skegg's Branch northward to the ford. With this disposition, McCulloch commanded the Skegg's Branch ford, which Sigel would have to cross if he attempted to attack Price in the rear.

Observing that the extreme left of Lyon's line had crossed to the eastern side of Wilson Creek and had moved down its left bank to the Ray family farm, threatening to outflank Woodruff's battery, McCulloch sent McIntosh with some companies of the Third Louisiana and the Second Arkansas Mounted Rifles and McRae's Arkansas battalion north of Gratiot to oppose it. Just at daylight McIntosh galloped up to the Third Louisiana and called, "This way, boys," leading them rapidly toward the front. Coming into contact with the enemy, he placed the Louisiana and Arkansas companies abreast of the fence to the south of the Ray cornfield. There elements of the two southern regiments exchanged volleys with Capt. Joseph B. Plummer's battalion of United States regulars. Greatly harassed by Maj. John Van Deusen DuBois's battery of horse artillery, which was delivering an enfilading fire into his left flank from the eastern slope of Oak Hill, McIntosh ordered his men to charge the Union infantry. The charge was made with great élan, driving Plummer back across the creek to the base of Oak Hill, where Lyon's main body lay. In the ardor of their pursuit, however, the

Confederates came within close range of DuBois's battery and Maj. Peter Joseph Osterhaus's infantry battalion, which drove the attackers back in some confusion. "Fortunately," recalled Sergeant Tunnard, "we were not in very compact order at the time, and not much damage was done." The Louisiana and Arkansas troops then rallied behind some rising ground and "took a breathing space" until McIntosh rode up and informed them that they "had made a good beginning, but the day was not yet won," and ordered them back into line.[34]

The Missourians, in the meantime, were directly in Lyon's path at the southern foot of Oak Hill and were in danger of being overrun by the Union assault. McCulloch considered Price's position to be the key to the battle and quickly moved Col. Frank A. Rector's and Gratiot's Arkansas regiments, five companies of Dockery's regiment, and a two-gun section of Reid's battery supported by Greer's Texas cavalry to anchor his left. Together they checked the primary Federal thrust with what McCulloch described as "an incessant fire of small arms." About 7:30 A.M. Brig. Gen. James H. McBride led his Missouri division around the right wing of Lyon's position but failed to dislodge the enemy from Bloody Hill.[35]

While McIntosh was repulsing Plummer's flanking movement across Wilson Creek and Price and Pearce were holding the center at the foot of Bloody Hill, Sigel's detachment was advancing on the Rebel rear and throwing shells into the backside of Price's line. Since his brush with Rains's pickets at dawn, Sigel had crossed Wilson Creek and had moved up Telegraph Road from the south with only the feeble First and Fourth Missouri regiments and Hiram M. Bledsoe's three-gun Missouri battery to oppose his progress. Sigel had halted his column, some twelve hundred men, on a bluff south of Skegg's Branch, overlooking and commanding a large part of the field. In the center of Sigel's line was a six-gun battery of Frank Backoff's First Missouri Light Artillery Battalion, posted to command the road and harass Price's rear, and his infantry was drawn up on both sides of the battery with mounted men on each flank. Although Reid's battery was raking his right from a ridge beyond Wilson Creek, causing it some discomfort, Sigel planned for this commanding position to serve as the anvil against which Lyon's hammer would smash the Rebel army.[36]

Just as McBride was withdrawing his men from the slopes of Oak Hill, however, McCulloch, with two companies of the Third Louisiana, swept down Telegraph Road to reinforce the hard-pressed Missourians on Skegg's Branch. Riding swiftly back to the scene of McIntosh's victory over Plummer, McCulloch had commended the Louisiana troops for their bravery and called on them to follow him back to Sigel's front. "Come, my brave lads, I have a battery for you to charge, and the day is ours!" he called to the Third Louisiana. The regiment was still in some disarray from its retreat across Wilson Creek, but about three hundred men followed McCulloch "with steady, regular tread along the valley."[37]

Approaching Skegg's Branch, McCulloch halted the Louisianians before Backoff's battery and surveyed the front through his field glasses. Coolly he turned in his saddle, waved his hand, and called "Come on!" "His actions and features were a study for the closest scrutinizer of physiognomy," remembered Tunnard. "Not a quiver on his face, not a movement of a muscle to betray anxiety or emotion. Only his grey eyes flashed forth from beneath his shaggy eyebrows a glittering, scrutinizing, and penetrating glance." Giving the order to "keep down and trail arms," McCulloch led his "Pelicans" through the battle smoke face to face with Backoff's battery—near enough that Watson remembered seeing quite plainly the muzzles of the guns. "What force is this?" called McCulloch. "Sigel's brigade," came the reply. At the same time the Union soldier raised his rifle and took deliberate aim at the Confederate commander. The sharp crack of a Mississippi rifle cut short his purpose, however, as Cpl. Henry Gentles of Company K of the Third Louisiana dropped the Federal to the ground. McCulloch remarked simply, "That was a good shot."[38]

Now within forty yards of the battery, close enough to make a dash for the guns, McCulloch turned to Capt. John P. Vigilini of Company K and said, "Captain, take your men up and give them hell." The Louisiana troops wore bright new gray uniforms, and their equipment was the best in McCulloch's army. Sigel's Fifth Missouri saw the advancing line and, unable to see Oak Hill and know of Lyon's check there, mistook the Louisiana troops for the First Iowa, one of Lyon's regiments that wore gray uniforms. Thinking that Lyon had succeeded in breaking through the Confederate line, Sigel too late realized, "They are carrying the secession flag." The Third Louisiana fired a volley into the face of Sigel's line and, with McCulloch leading, rushed the enemy with a wild Rebel yell, sweeping them at the point of the bayonet. Reid's battery on the east and Bledsoe's on the west opened fire at almost point-blank range. Sigel confessed that it was "impossible . . . to describe the consternation and frightful confusion which were caused by this unfortunate event." The Federal gunners could scarcely be brought to serve their pieces, and the infantry would not level their arms. In five minutes the Unionists were routed, streaming into a cornfield and along the road to the south, a panic-stricken mob.[39]

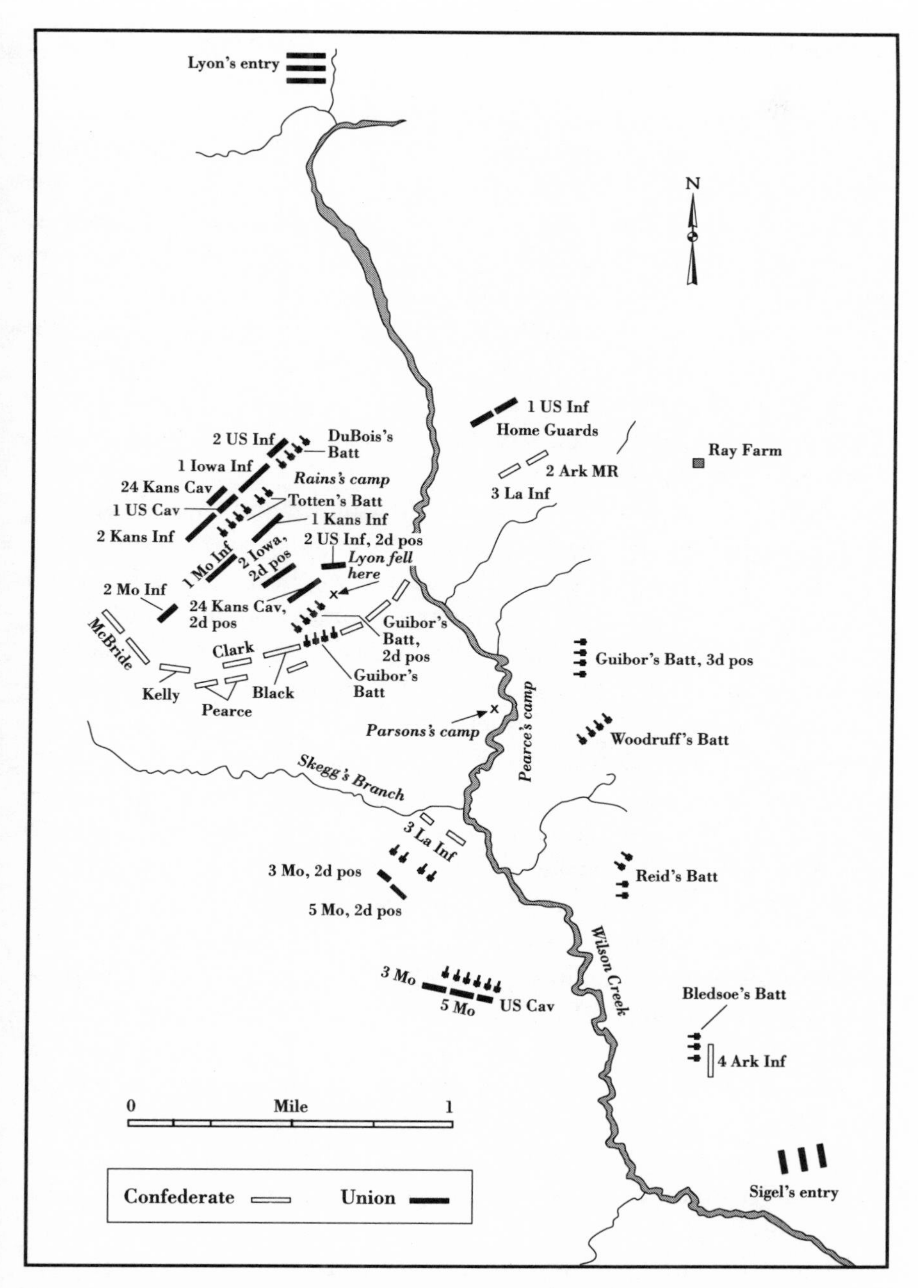

MAP 7. *Battle of Oak Hills (adapted from Calvin D. Cowles, ed.,* Atlas to Accompany the Official Records of the Union and Confederate Armies *[Washington, D.C., 1891–95])*

Abandoning five of his six guns, Sigel, with about two hundred German-born Missourians and Capt. Eugene Asa Carr's Company I of the Fourth United States Cavalry, tried to make his way back to Springfield via the same route by which he had arrived. As Sigel's troops scattered and fled, two companies of Texas cavalry under Capt. Hinche Parham Mabry and a portion of Lt. Col. James P. Major's Missouri cavalry pursued the fugitives, capturing their single remaining piece of artillery. As Pvt. Henry Clay Neville recalled, "The daring riders who had done service for years on the Indian frontier now did deadly execution with their carbines and big revolvers." Abandoned by Carr, who was to be breveted lieutenant colonel for his "gallant and meritorious service" that day, most of the men of Company I were either killed, wounded, or made prisoners. Sigel got into Springfield with only one man.[40]

With the threat to his rear removed, McCulloch and the Louisianians again changed front and marched toward the sound of the guns on Bloody Hill, where the climax of the battle was drawing near. As the Texas and Missouri cavalry were harrying the fugitive Federals from the field, Colonel Snead galloped up to McCulloch with a message from Price. His chief was sorely pressed, Snead reported, and his and Pearce's line could not hold unless reinforced. McCulloch ordered the Third Louisiana to secure the captured guns and battery horses and to prepare for action on another part of the field. "You have beaten the enemy's right and left wings," he told the Louisianians, "only their center is left, and with all our forces concentrated upon that, we will soon make short work of it."[41]

At 8:30 A.M., with McCulloch in the van, the remnant of the Third Louisiana set out for Oak Hill and the showdown with Lyon. Joining their Arkansas and Missouri comrades on the brow of Bloody Hill, the Louisianians surged forward, and by 9:00 the reinforced southern line was again pushing the Federals. The wounded Lyon, sensing that the battle was at its crisis, threw in his reserves and halted the Confederate advance. Lyon then counterattacked at the head of the Second Kansas Infantry. Wounded in the head and with his horse shot from beneath him, he swung his hat in the air and called on the Kansans to follow him. A moment later he was dead, a bullet in his heart. At this point the command of the Union forces devolved upon Maj. Samuel D. Sturgis, who continued to press the attack. McCulloch described this devil's din in his report to Walker: "The terrible fire of musketry was now kept up along the whole side and top of the hill upon which the enemy was posted. Masses of infantry fell back and again rushed forward. The summit of the hill was covered with dead and wounded—both sides were fighting with desperation for the day."[42]

Perceiving that the advance of the First Iowa and the First and Second Kansas regiments had left Totten's guns unprotected, McCulloch ordered Col. Charles A. Carroll's Arkansas cavalry and five companies of Greer's Third Texas Cavalry—then placed on the extreme left of the southern line—to "form in column of platoons, and drive them in." At approximately 10:00 A.M. the mounted column, under Greer's command, slipped around the Federal right and, when Greer believed that they were far enough behind Sturgis's line, charged. "This was done with a shout for Texas," Greer recorded, and the enemy was thrown into considerable confusion. Initially taken badly by surprise, the Union troops gave ground. The terrain was ill suited to cavalry operations, however, and when the Federals rallied and Totten turned his guns on the Rebel horsemen, Greer was driven back with considerable loss.[43]

Greer's impetuous charge had turned Sturgis's attention from the front, however, long enough for Price to rally his badly punished command and for McCulloch to call to the front the last two regiments of Pearce's brigade. "The battle then became general," wrote McCulloch, "and probably no two opposing forces ever fought with greater desperation." Contesting every yard, the Federals fell back before the weight of the renewed Confederate assault until the withdrawal became a retreat all along the line. Finally, at 11:00 A.M., with his soldiers exhausted and his ammunition almost gone, Sturgis withdrew his badly mauled army toward Springfield. For seven hours the battle had seen no pause. Having entered the battle with 5,500 men, the Federals reeled away with 4,200, having suffered a 24 percent rate of casualties. McCulloch and Price had begun the day with a combined army of 10,000 effectives, of which 1,200 became casualties, a rate of 12 percent.[44]

McCulloch, Pearce, and their staff officers met on the top of Bloody Hill. Together they watched the retreating enemy through their field glasses "and were glad to see him go." Their ammunition was exhausted, their units were shattered, and because they still believed that reinforcements were coming to the Federal army, the risk of pursuit was too fearful to contemplate. Only the next day did McCulloch and his generals learn that the disaster to the retreating army was greater than they had supposed and that "a few fresh cavalry troops could doubtless have followed and captured many more stragglers and army stores." McCulloch, however, was content

Battle of Oak Hills. At the climactic moment of the battle, Samuel D. Sturgis reported, "every available battalion was now brought into action, and the battle raged with unabated fury for more than an hour; the scales seeming all the time nearly equally balanced. . . . [Brig. Gen. Nathaniel Lyon] mounted, and swinging his hat in the air, called to the troops nearest to him to follow. The Second Kansas, or at least a portion of it, gallantly rallied around him, headed by the brave Colonel Mitchell. In a few moments the colonel fell, severely

wounded; about the same time a fatal ball was lodged in the general's breast, and he was carried from the field a corpse. Thus gloriously fell as brave a soldier as ever drew a sword, a man whose honesty of purpose was proverbial, a noble patriot, and one who held his life as nothing when his country demanded it of him." Lithograph by Louis Kurz
(author's collection)

to hold the battlefield and to allow his troops to return to their campsites for sorely needed food and rest. His few cavalrymen capable of following the enemy reported that "they were last seen at twelve [midnight], retreating among the hills in the distance." Sigel, taking charge of the remainder of the Union army, retired to Springfield and at 3:00 A.M., 11 August, commenced his retreat for Rolla, one hundred miles north, the nearest Federal garrison town.[45]

In the haste of their retreat, the Federals left Lyon's body on the field. An hour or two later Snead delivered it to a flag-of-truce party that had been sent to ask for it. He saw it again the next day in Springfield, where it had again been abandoned. Sometime later the Dallas *Herald* ran a story typically untrue but nevertheless revealing the image McCulloch projected to his men and to his state. "Ten thousand tales of the genuine 'raw head and bloody bones' stripe of Ben McCulloch are told among the Unionists and Lincolnists of Missouri," the paper read, and this one "contains so much characteristic *diablerie*" that the *Herald* could not refrain from printing it. When southern troops recovered Lyon's body, the story went, McCulloch, "with that refined chivalry so much remarked among Southern soldiers," ordered a detachment to guard it and "protect it from the touch of friend or foe." Mary Whitney Phelps, wife of former Missouri congressman John Smith Phelps, a strong Unionist, searched the battlefield for her friend's corpse and, finding it, "fell upon it and wept." When she ordered her attendants to place the body in her carriage, however, "a large, raw boned Arkansasian stepped up, leveled his gun, and said, 'Nary a bit, Miss. You can't come nigh doin' that theer. General McCulloch eats a Dutchman for supper every night, and has ordered us to save that old cuss for tonight; so just let it alone, if you please.'"[46]

So fearsome had McCulloch's reputation become, in fact, that for days after the battle the road to Rolla was crowded with Union refugees "fleeing in mortal terror from Ben McCulloch and his Texians," and Missouri Unionists called loudly for "men and artillery without fail if this place is to be held and Sigel succored."[47]

"The battle," McCulloch wrote, "was well fought throughout, skillfully managed and stubbornly contested on both sides." He attributed his victory to a number of causes, "of which fortune no doubt formed some part." Generous to a defeated foe, he credited Lyon with "no lack of skill, or his troops of bravery." Still emotionally attached to the old army of the United States, of which he had longed for so many years to be a part, he remarked that "nothing could excel the bravery of the United States regular troops" who fought against him at Oak Hills.[48]

The Federals, he reported to Walker, "were superior in discipline and arms and had gained a strong position." Too, the Confederates "were at great disadvantage on the account of their inferior weapons." Captain Woodruff agreed that because all of their infantry were armed with long-range rifles, "the Federals could pick their distance out of range of our old muskets, squirrel rifles, and shot guns, when the two lines clashed." This difference in quality in armament explained to him the heavy loss of the Confederates. McCulloch, however, believed that Lyon played into his strength by attacking him in the wooded hills around Wilson Creek. There the fighting was, of necessity, at close range or hand to hand, and the Federals' long-range rifles were hardly more effective than the Confederates' smoothbore muskets and shotguns.[49]

Want of discipline among the Missouri regiments "made my number comparatively small," wrote McCulloch. Nevertheless, he conceded, "they fought generally with great bravery," and this courage on the part of all of his regiments he considered the principal factor in the Confederate victory. Roger Q. Mills, a private in the Third Texas Cavalry, agreed that "never did men fight more fiercely or stubbornly than did the Missourians," and Governor Oran M. Roberts later wrote that the Third Texas Cavalry "fought with the old Texas spirit." Certainly the Third Louisiana Infantry and the Second Arkansas Mounted Rifles more than distinguished themselves.[50]

To other observers and participants "the great advantage in favor of the Confederate troops was their practical skill as marksmen." Accustomed, as many of them were from boyhood, to hunting and other field sports, "their certainty of aim was acquired by instinct," Watson believed. Interestingly, Pearce believed that it was the Missourians' very lack of discipline, their ignorance of "this regular way of shooting by word of command," that made them so effective. Instead of discipline and textbook tactics, their reliance upon "the old-accustomed method of using rifle, musket, or shotgun as gamesters or marksmen" helped them win the battle when they were pressed into close quarters with the enemy.[51]

Not the least of advantages to the Confederates at the battle of Oak Hills was the performance of Ben McCulloch. Although Capt. A. V. Reiff, commander of McCulloch's bodyguard company, contended that Lt. William Brown's reconnaissance on the morning of 10 August had furnished intelligence that enabled McCulloch to alert the Third Louisiana and

Woodruff's battery in time to save the army "from utter rout and gave us the victory," the general had been caught uncharacteristically off guard and was thoroughly surprised by the dawn attack. Nevertheless, McCulloch and his men performed remarkably well under desperate circumstances. With the handling of untested armies in two other early Civil War battles—the first battle of Manassas and the battle of Shiloh—McCulloch's leadership compares quite favorably. Ironic as it was that the man who had detected the presence of Santa Anna's army at Encarnación and prevented a United States debacle at Buena Vista should have been failed so badly by his scouts as a commanding general, he fared no worse in this regard than Grant and Sherman at Shiloh. McCulloch recovered more quickly than Grant, however, and placed his units well and led them with flawless courage.

Like most early Civil War commanders, North and South, McCulloch considered the offensive his primary tactic, and storming enemy batteries with bayonet or saber was the ideal. Even Lee, Jackson, Sherman, and Grant were long in learning the horrible cost of the frontal assault against modern rifled musketry and well-served artillery. McCulloch's extensive reading in military history and tactics, like the readings of his peers at West Point and the common experience of military leaders in Mexico, had been in what were essentially Napoleonic tactics, in which the *arme blanche* was still a match for the short-ranged and inaccurate musket. Joseph E. Johnston, P. G. T. Beauregard, Irvin McDowell, Albert Sidney Johnston, and Nathaniel Lyon all planned complex offensive battles with their half-trained armies, expecting native courage and personal example to overcome deficiencies in training and discipline. It is not surprising that Lyon and Albert Sidney Johnston were struck down at the heads of their armies in their first battles and that Joseph E. Johnston was severely wounded in his second campaign at Seven Pines. In 1861 and 1862, however, trenches were not yet for gentlemen volunteers, and Plum Creek and half a hundred other skirmishes against the fleet Comanche had taught McCulloch the absolute value of mobility on the battlefield. Months passed and thousands of lives were lost before commanders fully realized the effectiveness of the minié rifle fired from a well-prepared defensive position against advancing masses of troops, and southern officers, especially, continued to lead by personal example until the end of the war.

Like McCulloch after Oak Hills, the victors of First Manassas and Shiloh were censured in the press and by any number of armchair strategists for failure to follow their defeated enemies and destroy them. Like the victors of Manassas and Shiloh, McCulloch was commanding an army as disorganized and impaired by victory as his enemy was by defeat. As Pearce pointed out, the Confederates were out of ammunition. "The bullets they had molded the evening before the battle had been expended in the fight, and there was no ordnance department to furnish a fresh supply." He "never doubted for a moment," he wrote after the war, "that, had there been a supply of ammunition . . . McCulloch would have captured the entire Federal army—not having it, he could not." Perilously low on ammunition, exhausted by seven hours of uninterrupted fighting, and faced with reorganizing units badly depleted by casualties and stragglers, McCulloch felt himself in no better position to pursue Sturgis and Sigel than Johnston and Beauregard had been to follow McDowell or Grant and Sherman were to pursue Beauregard. Ideally, all of them would have followed their victories with a swift march—on Washington, on Corinth, or on Springfield and beyond. Circumstances were far from ideal, however, and none of the three armies had the strength or the will to move from the fields they had won.

McCulloch's men and the people of the South were well satisfied with the job the general had done at Oak Hills. McCulloch's decision not to follow Sturgis and Sigel "proved to us," wrote Pvt. Douglas John Cater of the Third Texas Cavalry, "that he was a safe commander and worthy of our confidence and support." In the words of Private Sparks, he had "displayed the high qualities of a commanding general. . . . He comprehended the situation at a glance and decision came as if by intuition. He shared all the dangers of the field with the meanest of his men." Coming so soon on the heels of the Rebel victory at Manassas, the news of Oak Hills filled the South with the confidence that the war would soon be over. "The news of McCulloch's victory in Missouri came today," Congressman T. R. R. Cobb of Georgia wrote to his wife on 13 August. "If it is not exaggerated I look upon it as the finishing stroke of this war." Mary Chesnut, writing in her Richmond diary on 18 August, confided, "Ben McCulloch has, they say, swept all the Yankees from Missouri." At first she believed the news "too good to be true," but three days later she accepted the report that "McCulloch has made a clean platter in Missouri."[52]

In addition to clearing southwestern Missouri of Federal occupation, McCulloch's victory at Oak Hills had produced the end of Cherokee neutrality, a welcome result. On 24 August John Ross informed McCulloch that the Cherokee people had determined to form an alliance with the Confederate States. In accordance with McCulloch's wishes, Ross authorized the organization of a regiment of mounted men under Col. John

Drew for the defense of the Cherokees' northern border and requested that it be armed at Confederate expense. "Having abandoned our neutrality and espoused the cause of the Confederate States, we are ready and willing to do all in our power to advance and sustain it," Ross pledged. McCulloch replied warmly, noting that the interests and institutions of the Confederate States and the Cherokee nation were the same and that the two peoples should cooperate against their common enemy. He would "most gladly" receive Drew's regiment and pledged to protect the northern border of the Cherokee nation until it was raised, armed, and trained.[53]

After the battle of Oak Hills, the legend of "Old Ben McCulloch" continued to grow. As was his custom, he made his headquarters near the camp of the Third Louisiana, and a private in Capt. Charles A. Bruslé's Company A wrote to his uncle in New Orleans that McCulloch "is no ordinary man, although very much so in looks." To the Louisiana soldier, he seemed remarkable for his taciturn nature, his habits of dress, and his penchant for leaving camp alone dressed in civilian clothing. "He was absent some time ago," the soldier reported; he had left camp in patched clothing, "and subsequent accounts report him selling chickens all over Missouri." One rumor had McCulloch "walking leisurely along the road" and another "making tracks through the woods." Some days later he reportedly rode into camp on a mule, dressed quite decently. "No one can understand him, no one can keep account of his movements. He is the most mysterious man I ever saw, and Abe will find him hard to deal with."[54]

Authorities in Richmond believed so as well. At Oak Hills, McCulloch and his men had proved "that a right cause nerves the hearts and strengthens the arms of the Southern people, fighting as they are for their liberty, their homes and firesides, against an unholy despotism." The Confederate Congress averred, and on 21 August it passed a vote of thanks to McCulloch and his army for their victory "in a portion of the country where a reverse would have been disastrous" and for saving "the families of the good people of . . . Missouri" from "the unbridled license of the brutal soldiery of an unscrupulous enemy." Secretary of War Walker added his personal congratulations, informing McCulloch that the War Department "cannot sufficiently express to you the thanks of the Government and of the country" for his victory, and assuring him that "the day and the field of Oak Hills have become historical in the annals of our young Confederacy, and will be mentioned in accents of gratitude not only in Missouri, probably liberated by your arms, but throughout the entire Confederacy, whose glory has been illustrated by the achievements of that day."[55]

THIRTEEN

A Campaign That Failed

At daylight on the morning following the battle of Oak Hills, McCulloch ordered Lt. Col. Walter P. Lane of the Third Texas Cavalry to take four companies and "see what the enemy was doing" in Springfield. Lane approached the town with caution, believing the enemy there in force, but when he entered the suburbs, he met a man coming out "with a gun on his shoulder and a big loaf of bread in his hand, which he was gnawing away on." Lane asked him "who the d——l he was and what he was doing there." The man replied that he was "one of you-uns and belong to General Price's company." He had been on picket duty the previous night, and, as he got "mighty hungry," he concluded to "drop into town and see what them federals was up to, and get something to eat." Incidents such as this failed to inspire McCulloch's confidence in his Missouri allies.[1]

Lane secured the evacuated town for the Confederacy and hoisted the battle flag of the Third Texas Cavalry over the Green County courthouse.

Later in the day a detachment of Price's troops marched into the city, and, "as they were Missourians, and the city belonged to their state," Lane turned over to them everything that the Federals had left, including large stores of provisions and quartermaster supplies. The wounded of both armies were speedily moved into Springfield and were distributed among the public buildings, hotels, and private houses. The courthouse and several churches became hospitals, and "almost every woman in Springfield, of either side, who could endure the sight of mangled soldiers," found service as a nurse. McCulloch visited the hospitals and spoke personally with every one of his wounded men. As for his prisoners, after exchanging for the few Confederates in the hands of the enemy, he dismissed them, saying that "he had rather fight than feed them."[2]

Woodruff, viewing the abandoned Federal fortifications at Springfield, surmised that the Rebels "should have had a much more difficult fight had the original plan of battle been carried out" and that Lyon had gravely erred in leaving his prepared position to attack. Less concerned with fortifications than with the "architectural wonders of the old Green County Courthouse," some of Price's youthful recruits who had never been "upstairs" before coming to Springfield spent the day exploring the wonders of a three-story building.[3]

Soon after arriving at Springfield, Price called on McCulloch, urging him to march into central Missouri. McCulloch, Price, and Pearce spent 11 and 12 August in heated conference over plans. Price favored an offensive to the Missouri River designed to destroy the Hannibal and St. Joseph railroad, thus crippling the Federal resupply effort in Missouri and Kansas. In Price's estimation, the greatest concentration of Kansas Unionists was on the Missouri River, and there, he told McCulloch, they should strike. Although assuring Price that he was willing to aid Missouri "at all times to the fullest extent" of his power "consistent with the interest of [his] government and the condition of [his] force," McCulloch, for several reasons, declined to accompany the state guard on its intended raid.

First, his mandate from the Confederate government remained the protection of Arkansas and the Indian Territory. The Federals in Kansas, he believed, had designs on the Cherokee nation, and his whole effective force was required to block an enemy move south. Second, he had very little ammunition. Some of his officers, in fact, had informed him, "when ordered to be ready to pursue the enemy on the 10th of August, that some of their men had fired their last cartridge in the battle." His quartermaster and commissary stores were also exhausted. Third, he believed that the "undisciplined condition" of his men required considerable training in drill and tactics at a camp of instruction "not so far from his resources" before he once again could take the field.

Most important, as McCulloch warned Jefferson Davis, "little can be expected of Missouri. She has no military leader or arms." Price's command, he complained to Hardee, was "undisciplined and led by men who are mere politicians," and he perceived "not a soldier among them to control and organize this mass of humanity." In McCulloch's opinion, the Missouri forces were in no condition to meet an organized enemy and never would be so long as Price commanded them. "I dare not join them in my present condition for fear of having my own men completely demoralized," he wrote.[4]

McCulloch was also convinced that the southerners "could never maintain a position on the Missouri River for any length of time" because their supply line would extend over three or four hundred miles of inadequate and obstructed wagon roads and destroyed bridges, while railroads and steamboats could supply their enemies, giving the Federals the means "to do as much in twenty-four hours as we could in as many days to supply a want of men or means to make war." Fifty thousand to a hundred thousand United States troops, drawn from seven of the largest western states, McCulloch believed, could be concentrated by rail at St. Louis, transported by boats on the Missouri River, and thrown on the rear of any invading force. Even were the roads in better condition, McCulloch's transportation was deficient, and he was much too far from his base of operations to have forwarded even the scant supplies in his Arkansas depots. His men were ill clothed and ill shod, and the people of the region "if not hostile, were not to be depended upon."

McCulloch agreed with Price that the capture of Lexington, with its garrison and valuable stores, was indeed possible and would induce thousands of volunteers from central Missouri, where southern feeling was strong, to rally to Price. He contended, however, that Price would only be able to raise troops "under the fallacious belief that he was going to hold the country"—troops that he could not arm. Once he withdrew, as he inevitably must, the unarmed recruits would return to their homes "to be plundered, persecuted, and hunted down as public enemies by the Union home guards." Missouri would not only become "a land of scourge" but would be lost to the South as well.

Finally, neither Hardee nor Pillow could be expected to cooperate with such a move. Pillow, in fact, had already fallen back into Arkansas, and

The disorganized and undisciplined condition of the Missouri State Guard is evident in this painting of the unit. Note the Van Dorn–style battle flag, characterized by a red field with white stars and a crescent moon. “Close Up, Double Quick” by Samuel J. Reader
(Kansas State Historical Society)

1865.
FEB. 13. 65

Hardee was convinced that the country between Greenville and Rolla, where the Federals had rallied, was too poor to support his army and offered no roads or rail links by which his army might swiftly travel.[5]

McCulloch offered a counterproposal to fortify Springfield and hold it with his infantry and artillery while ranging his cavalry west to interdict the incursion of jayhawkers from Kansas. This done, McCulloch believed, Governor Jackson could call the Missouri legislature into session at Springfield where an ordinance of secession could be drawn up and passed. Missouri's army would then pass to the control of the Confederate States, under which it could be properly armed and trained to march to the Missouri River. There and then, he argued, the strong secessionist element on both sides of the river would rally to the army, making it strong enough for a move against St. Louis. Although both men protested that they had "ever been of the most friendly terms personally," Price refused even to listen to McCulloch's proposal.[6]

The crowning blow to hopes for a southern offensive into Missouri came within two weeks of the battle of Oak Hills when the period of enlistment of Pearce's Arkansas regiments expired and they left for home, taking their arms with them. McCulloch appealed to their patriotism and bravery, but "Home!" was their only response. The Arkansas troops had been in the army from two to five months and had never received any pay or clothing. When Arkansas's military board offered them the option of honorably leaving the service, "the natural impulse to each individual was, 'I must go home,'" Pearce wrote, and "despite all persuasion and appeals, this unfortunate decision could not be overcome." By 31 August only twenty of Pearce's men remained with McCulloch, and the arms of the old Arkansas brigade were being redistributed in other parts of the state.

The ruinous effects of organizing state troops outside Confederate authority were nowhere more evident. McCulloch's army, when he might have used it to great effect, was almost fatally crippled. McCulloch returned from his fruitless mission to the Arkansas troops "furious with anger at his failure." Even Woodruff's crack Pulaski Battery voted to return to Arkansas, leaving McCulloch with only the Arkansas regiments of Churchill and McIntosh, the Third Louisiana Infantry, the Third Texas Cavalry, and Capt. John J. Good's First Texas Battery, a total of twenty-five hundred men fit for duty. Therefore, as Tunnard assessed the situation in classic understatement, a campaign deep in Missouri "probably did not seem to General McCulloch to be a very prudent movement."[7]

Appealing directly to President Davis on 24 August, McCulloch urged that "a large force ought to be organized at once." His sole reinforcement following Oak Hills was Evander McNair's Fourth Arkansas Infantry. McNair, who had served as orderly sergeant in Jefferson Davis's Mississippi Rifles during the war with Mexico, had been a merchant in Washington, Arkansas, when his state left the Union. He raised his regiment in southwestern Arkansas and marched the two hundred to three hundred miles into southwestern Missouri, but he arrived too late to take part in the battle.[8]

Having failed to secure McCulloch's cooperation, on 14 August Price issued orders revoking McCulloch's command of the Missouri State Guard, and Price himself resumed "the command-in-chief of the Missouri forces in the field." Eleven days later Price and his men marched north alone into central Missouri. With them went the battery of artillery the Third Louisiana had captured from Sigel at Oak Hills, "by what authority was not discovered." Only after fierce remonstrance from McCulloch was the battery returned and then without the battery horses and most of the harnesses. The injury of this unauthorized appropriation was not so grievous, McCulloch maintained, as the insult that accompanied it. "I would not have demanded these guns had General Price done the Louisiana Regiment justice in his official report," he later informed the War Department, but Price had implied that the battery had been captured by his men instead of the Louisianians. At last Price agreed that "the several pieces of artillery captured from the enemy on the 10th instant will be given to Brigadier-General McCulloch," without admitting that he had attempted to take them without justification. The anger inspired by the incident haunted the two camps for almost a year and rendered cooperation between them yet more difficult.[9]

McCulloch also maintained that Price's camp followers "had robbed our dead and wounded on the battlefield" of three hundred rifles and muskets as well as taking enemy armaments without offering McCulloch or Pearce even the smallest share. His and Pearce's attempts to recover their own arms were in vain, and Price returned to Pearce only 10 of the 615 muskets the Missourians had borrowed from Arkansas prior to the invasion. As a final outrage, the Missourians appropriated the tents McCulloch's men left at Cassville to speed their march and had the temerity to pitch them the next day near the Confederate camp. "In a word," McCulloch informed Hardee, "they are not making friends where they go, and from all I can see we had as well be in Boston as far as the friendly feelings of the inhabitants are concerned."[10]

With the remainder of Lyon's command reduced to a cipher in the Missouri strategic equation, Federal authorities in the trans-Mississippi began to show considerable concern for McCulloch's next move, all fearing that it would be in their direction. The commander at Fort Scott, Kansas, warned his superiors that one thousand Rebels had left Greenfield for his position on 20 August and that McCulloch was "sending 4,000 picked men from Springfield, all armed with Colt's, Sharp's, and minnie rifles." Brig. Gen. Ulysses S. Grant admitted on 25 August that he had no reliable information as to the movements of McCulloch's forces but reported a rumor current at Jefferson City that the Confederate general was moving toward the Missouri capital. Col. P. E. Bland, commander of the United States garrison at Ironton, Missouri, reported on 27 August that "the more intelligent Southern sympathizers" there believed that McCulloch was advancing in that direction in great force. Finally, Grant reported to his superior, Maj. Gen. John Charles Frémont, on 12 September that McCulloch was reported to have been in Columbus, Missouri, within the last few days but admitted that "he is such a ubiquitous character that I place no great reliance in it."[11]

McCulloch's assessment of the strategic situation in Missouri was not nearly so bright for the Confederacy. Both Hardee and Pillow evacuated the southeastern corner of the state. Price's march to the Missouri River would surely draw Federal troops back to Springfield, and McCulloch had neither the arms nor the men to prevent it. Nevertheless, after Price's move north, McCulloch determined to remain awhile in southwestern Missouri, waiting for the Missouri legislature to make a move toward secession, watching over the Indian Territory, observing Federal movements in Missouri and Kansas, and shielding northwestern Arkansas. Moving his truncated army about twenty miles northwest of Springfield, on 14 August he established a camp at Mount Vernon, "a beautiful little town, situated in a picturesque country, favored with fine apple orchards" and what Private Cater described as "the biggest spring I ever saw."[12]

Of great consternation to the Rebel soldiers, however, was the popular attitude of that corner of Missouri. Union sympathy remained strong there, and according to Capt. John J. Good many of the citizens threw "every obstacle in our way in their power." Merchants, he claimed, hid their goods and would sell to the soldiers "at no price." Good also maintained that "the Missourians have treated our troops miserably bad" and that at Mount Vernon the commander of a Missouri regiment "closed every store until he could cull and pick for his men." Good remonstrated that as the guests of Missouri, having marched "many hundreds of miles to assist them in their struggles," his men needed clothing and deserved an equal chance in the stores. When reason failed, he threatened "to shell the damned place if the stores were not opened to my boys."[13]

Despite this lack of local cooperation, McCulloch issued a proclamation to his soldiers on 16 August decreeing that the reputations of Arkansas, Louisiana, and Texas were in their hands and calling on his men "to restrain the vicious." A "single trespass upon the property of the citizens of Missouri," he said, would darken the honor of all and wither the laurels of Oak Hills. He called upon them, therefore, to rely upon their quartermasters for "all that can be had in the country for your use," so that it might not be said that "we are not gentlemen as well as soldiers."[14]

Among the southern sympathizers of the region, one of Greer's troopers wrote, "the utmost confidence is expressed in General McCulloch's abilities and courage. The best feeling prevails toward Texas and Texians, and everywhere on the road thousands of questions were asked about the Texas Rangers." The name Texas Ranger carried a magic of its own, according to Missourian H. Clay Neville, coming as it did "from the Indian frontier with the fame and paraphernalia of the resistless hero." Tales of the ranger's prowess and skill in fighting "the wily savage on the Western plains" were enhanced in the eyes of southern partisans by "the marvelous feats of horsemanship exhibited by the bold Texan as he dashed about camp," and none doubted that "the knight of the lasso would perform new wonders in driving back the 'hireling foe.'" While encamped in southwestern Missouri, the Third Texas was visited by an old woman who said she wanted to see a Texas Ranger. On being shown a squad of Greer's troopers, she gazed upon them for some time "with mingled feelings of curiosity and wonder; then turning to her conductor and giving vent to a deep sigh, she remarked in a long whining tone, 'why, Lors a Massy, they's just like our folks, for the world; I thought from what I hard, they was as big as three on 'em and could pull up saplings by the roots.'"[15]

While occupying the southwestern corner of Missouri, McCulloch called upon the people of the state to formally sever their ties with the Union so that they might join the Confederate States and thus alleviate the problem he and Price had experienced in operating as mere allies rather than as a united army. On 15 August he issued a proclamation assuring the Missourians that he was in their state "simply with the view of making war upon our Northern foes" and to "give the oppressed of your state an opportunity of again standing up as freemen and uttering their true sentiments." No citizen, he pledged, "whether Union or otherwise," need fear for his life, his rights, or his property. He urged refugees of both allegiances to return to their homes and promised to release all political prisoners who fell under his command and to administer "no oaths binding your consciences."[16]

By the end of summer, however, McCulloch could see no prospect of an imminent secession convention in Missouri and felt that he was exceeding his instructions from Richmond by remaining outside his assigned theater of operations. He remembered, too, the words of Sam Houston. "Let us act on the defensive," he had counseled the Texans in 1842. "If the enemy chooses, let them run the risk. A wise man will wait for the harvest, and prepare the reapers for when it comes." So, with his ammunition supply perilously low and his quartermaster and commissary departments scarcely able to keep his army supplied, McCulloch shortened his line of communication by falling back to Camp Jackson, Arkansas. There he filled his arsenals, prepared fortifications, and set about creating what John Henry Brown called "an army of Spartans."[17]

McCulloch took special pains to drill and train the newly raised regiments so they would be at peak efficiency to take the field with the coming of spring. The Scottish-born William Watson "wished that some of the military critics of Europe could have seen them at this time if just to show them something of volunteers and what an efficient army can be produced from raw material in a few months." With the men responding perfectly to the kind of training and spirit a frontier democracy created for its military organizations, he was convinced that "a nation has nothing to fear for its defense that can raise an army of volunteers and knows how to treat them and bring them into the field without having their enthusiasm dampened or their progress obstructed by fastidious deference to rank, official formalities, and red-tape restrictions."[18]

During this period, J. H. Robinson, a Missouri-born private in the Third Louisiana, found McCulloch to be "as vigilant as a tiger" in keeping his camp of instruction performing properly. "Perhaps the character of none of our public men is so misunderstood as that of General McCulloch," he posited. Robinson, who had "fancied him a perfect devil, a backwoodsman, a ruffian, an unpolished desperado," found McCulloch unfailingly kind and ever on friendly terms with all of his men. McCulloch did enjoy the goodwill and confidence of his men, but he was also credited with keeping firm order and discipline in camp. One evening Lt. William Harris of Good's battery saw the general passing the battery's camp with a small detachment of men and inquired what was afoot. McCulloch, he learned, was out to destroy a barrel of "bust-head" reported in the camp. "I suppose some of the men had been drunk and acting disorderly," wrote Harris. McCulloch's attitude toward liquor in his camps was generally moderate. The soldiers were well aware that their commander "was not a total abstainer," but as Sergeant Watson observed, "no man knew better how to use and not abuse" strong drink. McCulloch trusted that his men, as well, would show enough "resolution and strength of mind" to use alcohol only in moderation, saying he "would be ashamed to say that a canteen could not be attached to a regiment." For those who habitually overindulged, however, McCulloch exuded only contempt. Regarding them as "unfit for the companionship of respectable men and true soldiers," he did not want such men in his army and believed that "the sooner they drank themselves off the face of the earth the better."[19]

Life for the Confederate soldiers at the camp of instruction, however, was not all drill and punishment. Private Sparks of the Third Texas Cavalry remembered "doing little else than cooking and eating the wholesome and abundant rations furnished them by the commissariat," and Captain Good agreed. "We fare abundantly here," he wrote of Camp Jackson. Flour, bacon, coffee, sugar, beans, salt, soap, candles, and "fine peaches and apples" were available in abundance within a half-mile of the camp that September, but he noted as well that the season of plenty could not last long and predicted that "fearful holes will be made in our subsistence department soon. In the army it is feast or famine."[20]

On 30 August the war took on a radical new aspect when Frémont, Federal commander of the Western Department, issued a proclamation placing Missouri under martial law and ordering all slaves to be declared freemen. Acting upon Walker's authorization, McCulloch issued a proclamation of his own on 10 September calling on the men of Arkansas, Texas, and Louisiana "to drive back the Republican myrmidons" now in Missouri threatening to "confiscate your property, liberate your slaves, and put to the sword every Southern man who dares to take up arms in defense of his rights." Assuring the people of the Old Southwest that the enemy was making "every exertion" to retrieve its losses at Manassas and Oak Hills, McCulloch reminded them that a large force must be "thrown into the field on this frontier" to protect the fruits of those victories. He called upon the men of the region to enlist at once in one of the five regiments of infantry being raised in each of the trans-Mississippi states.

In issuing his call for fifteen thousand men from Arkansas, Louisiana, and Texas, McCulloch inadvertently stirred up one of the many controversies over states' rights that plagued the Confederacy and eventually contributed heavily to its ordeal. Governor Henry Massey Rector, although assuring Secretary Walker that he had only the highest admiration for "the gallantry and patriotism of General McCulloch," protested the general's call for volunteers. "The authorities of Arkansas were neither consulted as to the propriety of making this call nor advised in any manner that such was the purpose of the general," he complained, and he expressed his disapproval of what he considered a usurpation of the rights of the individual states by the Confederate government and its generals in assuming the prerogatives of the governors in calling for volunteers. "My idea of the rights relatively belonging to the States and to the Confederate Government is that those pertaining to the former were by no means abridged by the withdrawal from the old confederacy and a union with the new government," he told Walker, and the governor could find no precedent for "the raising of men by proclamation emanating from generals commanding nor from the President." Although McCulloch was fully sustained in his actions by the Confederate government, he later confessed to Albert Pike his distress over the contretemps. "Having done all in my power to avoid getting into any kind of disputes or contentions with any person whilst on the frontier," he wrote to his subordinate in the Indian Territory, "I am grieved to find at last that I am to share the fate of others."[21]

Despite his pleas to Richmond and the promises of an adequate supply of arms from the War Department, McCulloch had received only "1,600 single-barreled pistols and a few sabers from the arsenal at San Antonio" and was "also much crippled for the want of necessary funds." Governor Edward Clark of Texas informed the secretary of war that his state was "destitute of arms," those seized by Texas from United States troops having been transferred to the Confederate government, and was therefore unable to supply its regiments. The Texas and Louisiana troops, therefore, were "expected to equip themselves with the best arms they can procure."[22]

With winter approaching, the men began to fear also for their wardrobes. The Confederate government promised to provide each recruit "two suits of winter clothing and two blankets, also tents, if they can be procured." Like the weapons, however, these were not forthcoming, and few of the men could afford to buy decent clothing, even if it were available in Arkansas. "Some of the boys are badly in need of clothing now," Good wrote to a friend in Dallas, "and nearly if not quite all will be by the time cold weather sets in." The troops, he wrote, "must be clad or disorganized," for disease and death were otherwise inevitable. Good informed the Dallas *Herald* that “the patriotic who desire to send clothing” should do so without delay, since McCulloch had warned him that each company “had better look to our counties for comforts of that character.”[23]

With his troops thus ill clad and Price deep in Missouri without a line of supply and subject to raids from Federal cavalry and jayhawkers alike, McCulloch took the ill-advised expedient of allocating to his own command a wagon train of clothing, paid for from a special congressional appropriation for the relief of “our suffering brethren in Missouri.” McCulloch was exercising the prerogative granted him the previous May by the War Department to take charge of “such supplies of the ordnance, quartermaster’s, and commissary departments in Texas and Arkansas as are under the control of the War Department.” When Judah P. Benjamin replaced Walker as secretary of war on 17 September, however, McCulloch lost one of his staunchest allies in Richmond and found that the new secretary, neither having known McCulloch before the war nor remembering his services or his instructions through the summer of 1861, was more inclined to take the part of the Missourians than had been his predecessor. Benjamin failed to understand the need for winter clothing in McCulloch’s army, was apparently unaware of the general’s authorization to take control of the supplies in his district, and sharply rebuked him for having “subjected the government to annoyances and embarrassments that paralyze its best efforts for the common defense.”[24]

Confined to its base of operations by want of arms and clothing, the army was nonetheless alive with rumors of imminent offensive movements. Pvt. David R. Garrett of Col. B. Warren Stone’s Sixth Texas Cavalry, then en route to the Confederate camps, wrote to a friend in Texas that “Ben McCulloch says he will winter in St. L[ouis] or heaven or somewhere else.” Good, however, reported to his wife that his men “expect to have some fun at Fort Scott,” because talk was then running high of an invasion of Kansas. His only fear was that they would miss the action if “Price and Rains of the Missouri State Guards cut us out.” “Confound these Missourians,” he wrote. “When we free them I think they will do their own fighting without assistance from Texas, Arkansas, or Louisiana.” Only a few days afterward Good was equally sure that the army would be marching east across northern Arkansas.

At last, on 12 September, the Kansas rumor was verified when McCulloch ordered the Third Texas Cavalry toward Fort Scott. Following in Greer’s wake, McCulloch planned to lead his army on “a dash into Kansas,” where it would spend a month "ravaging the Territory," and then return to winter quarters in Arkansas. McCulloch urged "the propriety of destroying Kansas as far north as possible," based on his belief that the trans-Mississippi Confederacy could "never have quiet or safety among the Indians so long as Kansas remains inhabited by its present population." McCulloch was quite prepared to use his Indian troops against the Kansas jayhawkers.[25]

By mid-September the Army of the West was on the march to Kansas, there to "penetrate as far as we can with our forces and burn and desolate the whole country." On 28 September Governor Jackson of Missouri visited McCulloch's camp and informed the men that in ten days McCulloch's army was to unleash upon the Unionists in Kansas "the most ruthless invasion known to man since the razing of Jerusalem to the earth, and burn the accursed land from Dan to Beersheba!"[26]

Lawrence Sullivan (Sul) Ross, major of the Sixth Texas Cavalry, considered this to be "cheering news to us who feared that our campaign was destined to be a fruitless one," and he anticipated "a great deal of sport" in Kansas. Although Ross hoped it would keep the jayhawkers so busy defending their own homes that "they will not find time to plunder others," others in the army were less pleased with the idea of carrying out a campaign against civilians, even in so volatile a theater as the Kansas-Missouri border. Kansas, Captain Good assured his wife, "will be the theatre of war in all its horror, and what distresses me is that innocent women and children must suffer for the conduct of trifling and villainous husbands and fathers. The scenes in Missouri are nothing to what they will be there." David Pierson of the Third Louisiana wrote to his father that the Kansas jayhawkers "have committed many depredations in the joining counties of Missouri, have overrun two or three counties, burning houses and towns, killing every Southerner they could catch, and taking away all the horses and cattle and provisions. It may be that our army will adopt this mode of warfare and lay waste their country in the same manner. If so, I hope that Louisianians will not be part of such bloody work." McCulloch, Ross wrote, was "driven to this course from a variety of circumstances." The Unionist partisans, first of all, could "claim to be nothing more than a band of horse thieves," whose object it was to bring fire and sword among the secessionist Missourians, and "the adage directs to 'fight the Devil with fire.'" More important, as he had only about six thousand men fit for duty—and roughly half were cavalry—McCulloch could not risk a pitched battle with the enemy, and yet "he must do something—inactivity would be inexcusable under the circumstances."[27]

McCulloch's "Kansas frolic" was delayed, however, when measles, "the terrible scourge of all armies," broke out in the army. Unaccustomed to communal life, "nearly every man that had not had the disease was attacked." Surgeon Washington Lafayette Gammage of the Fourth Arkansas reported "more sickness amongst the men than I have ever known in one command in so short a time," observing in his regiment alone thirty deaths in thirty-six days. Measles often gave way to pneumonia and other complications, killing many of the regiment's "strongest and most robust men—all good soldiers." For a time the effective strength of McCulloch's army fell from 6,000 to 1,100 men.[28]

Not until 8 October was the Army of the West sufficiently recovered to continue its advance. "The long looked for time has come at last," Captain Good wrote to his wife the night before the army was to march. "All the boys in camp are in high glee. Some are singing 'Dixie' with a perfect vim, while others are writing letters to their sweethearts. . . . I never saw the boys happier of an order in my life. 'To Kansas' is the watchword, and McCulloch swears he will devastate the whole country before winter sets in if possible." First Lt. James P. Douglas, Good's second-in-command, was equally avid to "march into the enemy's country and attack him wherever we find him." Douglas observed that the men of the battery, sure that a fight was imminent, were "manifesting great joy at the prospect of an engagement." Even as Douglas wrote to his wife, they were "talking and laughing merrily and singing war songs around me." McCulloch himself was "in fine spirits" and sure of "routing Montgomery and his minions."[29]

McCulloch's plans were frustated, however, by events in Missouri. Price, since leaving McCulloch after the battle of Oak Hills, had pushed into central Missouri and had accomplished the improbable, capturing the Union garrison at Lexington on 20 September. As McCulloch had predicted, however, Price was unable to arm all of his enthusiastic new recruits despite the capture of 3,000 rifles. Their morale sagged and desertion became epidemic. Soon Price's command dwindled to the 12,000 men with whom he had commenced the invasion, and Frémont's strong, new, 38,000-man army once again began to move against him. Price "deemed it prudent not to risk being hemmed in" and abandoned the Missouri River to fall back south for a junction with the Army of the West. On 14 October McCulloch received a note from Governor Jackson informing him that Jackson and Price had retired from Lexington with an army of about 12,000 and the rump of the Missouri legislature, ready to vote the state out of the Union.[30]

McCulloch quickly altered his plans and called for Price to take up a strong position in the neighborhood of Springfield and there hold Frémont in check while McCulloch advanced to the northwest, operating against the Federals' right flank and rear, cutting off their supplies. Price suddenly evacuated Springfield, however, and on 20 October the Missourians entered Neosho, "directly severing [McCulloch's] force in twain." The Army of the West was totally surprised by the sudden appearance of the state guard, which Good described as "little else than a rabble." This radical shift in the military equation canceled McCulloch's plan for a campaign in Kansas, "much to the general regret of all who understood it." McCulloch's "retaliatory programme" was fatally smashed when Frémont occupied Springfield, leaving McCulloch's base of supply at Fayetteville "liable to be destroyed by a few bold horsemen."[31]

In response to Frémont's sudden appearance, McCulloch evacuated Neosho and fell back to Cross Hollows, a favorable defensive position twenty miles below the Missouri and Arkansas line and astride Telegraph Road connecting Springfield with Fayetteville. McIntosh's cavalry reported sixty "quite large" Federal regiments in and around Springfield, "pressing transportation and grain" and preparing for an immediate advance. Price was eager for a fight and urgently solicited McCulloch to join him in an attack on Springfield to "thrash the Hessians." McCulloch, however, believing himself outnumbered five to one, had no intention of turning his command over to the rash Price or of leading his men against the fortifications of Springfield. "For us to attack them in their present position would be to lose a battle," McCulloch wrote to Secretary Benjamin, as most of the Confederates were cavalrymen and thus "unfit to attack a strong position or to be of great use in a general engagement with heavy forces." Concerned, as always, about the efficiency of his Missouri allies, McCulloch reported that Price's army was "getting weaker daily by men leaving for their homes." The enlistment term of many Missouri companies was near expiration, and he predicted that "nothing but a battle within the next ten days" would keep more than four or five thousand of Price's men in the army. Such a battle, he said, could only be precipitated by a general advance of the enemy.[32]

McCulloch's own strategy was to resort to the defensive. He dispatched McIntosh to devastate the country between the two armies, and "everything that would or could aid them was destroyed—corn, fodder, oats, hay, and wheat stacks—while the roads were thoroughly and completely blocked by felling timber across them." Certain that Frémont was strong enough to drive him from the Missouri border, McCulloch reported to Benjamin that he hoped, "by resorting to the partisan mode of warfare, to make them withdraw ere they reach Fort Smith."[33]

On 8 November, three days before his fiftieth birthday, McCulloch wrote one of his rare personal letters to his mother from a "camp in Missouri near the line." In a tone reminiscent of Travis's final letter from the Alamo, McCulloch reported that his scouts had been near the enemy for the last ten days and had located them "some sixty miles off"—forty to fifty thousand strong and "reinforcing all the time." Although he believed that these numbers were exaggerated, he confessed his own command to be very small. "Be that as it may, I have but one duty to perform, and that is to oppose them in every way possible as long as we both live or until this war is brought to a successful close." With some bitterness, he explained that he had called on the people of Arkansas to join him in resisting the Federal invasion and had not raised even a thousand men. "They may have their homes laid in ashes ere they can rally to their own defense," he predicted. If Texas, "our own gallant state," were thus threatened, "how different it would be with them." As McCulloch commented to Good, "If he is not reinforced, 'damned if he don't retreat.' "[34]

McCulloch invited the Missouri forces to retire with him some sixty miles south to fight Frémont as a united force from the formidable ramparts of the Boston Mountains. Remembering Sam Houston's San Jacinto campaign, McCulloch remonstrated that even a victorious battle in their present position would amount only to "a repulse of his infantry," but if the enemy could be lured deeper into Arkansas, a southern victory would net "all his cannon—one hundred and twenty—and most of his army with their arms" as well as his baggage wagons and sutlery. Price still demurred, declaring that his men would not consent to go so far from Missouri, so McCulloch at last agreed to fight at Cross Hollows, "though I believed it would result in little good to Missouri."[35]

The army's position at Cross Hollows "was a very advantageous one," according to Watson. The Confederate line of battle extended along a wide ravine commanding Telegraph Road, down which the Yankees were expected to advance, and with his rear secure and his base of supply near, McCulloch was confident of giving the Federals "a warm reception." "From all indications we will have a fine chance to test our mettle," Sul Ross wrote to a friend in Dallas, and, McCulloch wrote to Brown, "never were men more keen for a fight" than his. Although deprived of his raid into Kansas, Ross was "fully satisfied [McCulloch] can find a more formidable adversary much nearer home," who could "be accommodated to fight upon his own terms." Lieutenant Douglas promised that "even with our small force, McCulloch will dispute every inch of soil from the line of the Confederacy to Texas."[36]

Frémont advanced toward Cross Hollows but, as Watson said, "did not seem inclined to attack us in this position." To the contrary, Frémont mysteriously dropped from sight and could not be located. Sul Ross, from his conversations with Price and his officers, found the Missourians' knowledge of Frémont's movements and his whereabouts "was very limited and contradictory" and correctly assumed that "General McCulloch came to the same conclusion." McCulloch, therefore, mounted a scouting expedition under Ross who, he said, "would find Frémont's army if they were still on Missouri soil." Approaching Springfield with some caution, Ross sent captains Hinche Parham Mabry and Adam Rankin Johnson, both destined to become Confederate brigadier generals, into town. They were discovered in the Springfield hotel; Mabry was wounded in the arm, and Johnson's hat was riddled with bullet holes. Nevertheless, the two men returned to report only a single company of Federals in the town. Frémont, "having rusticated sufficiently," it seemed, had withdrawn to the north. To clear Springfield of Frémont's rear guard, McCulloch sent thirty men under command of Lt. Frank Daniels into the town. Returning to issue his report, Daniels, although a lion in battle, was too bashful to utter a word. McCulloch, noticing his embarrassment, asked, "Well, Lieutenant, they tell me you have been to Springfield and charged with your squad right through the town. Is it so?" McCulloch's genial humor overcame the young man's shyness, and with a pardonable breech of military decorum he blurted, "You bet, General, we have, and the . . . Yankees there thought that Ben McCulloch's whole army and the devil to boot was after them!" After this, Gammage recalled, "You bet, General" became a byword in the Third Texas.[37]

Unknown to McCulloch, Maj. Gen. George B. McClellan had maneuvered Maj. Gen. Winfield Scott into retirement and, on 1 November 1861, had become the general-in-chief of all United States forces. Among his first acts was the reorganization of the high command west of the Appalachians. He replaced Frémont as commander of the Western Department with Maj. Gen. David Hunter and subordinated Hunter to Maj. Gen. Henry W. Halleck as commander of the Department of Missouri. Hunter suspended all offensive operations, taking his own division to Sedalia while Lane took his troops back to Kansas and Sigel and his men retreated toward Rolla. Not yet privy to this news, McCulloch could only speculate that the Federal army was either not so strong as his scouts had reported or that the Union general had overestimated the size of the southern armies.[38]

While the motive for the Federal withdrawal remained a mystery in the Rebel camps, Price again set out in a drive into the heartland of his state and sent McCulloch a note requesting his cooperation. "Let us then move . . . upon the Missouri River," Price pleaded, where he expected to find abundant supplies and where McCulloch's "name and fame and that of your gallant men would bring to our standard an army of full 50,000 men." Although McCulloch had been willing to come to Price's aid when the Missouri State Guard had been threatened with attack, he considered this move equally rash and pointless as Price's last foray into central Missouri.[39]

With only five thousand men, five hundred of whom were too ill to take the field, and most of the rest new to the service and "badly organized, armed, and equipped, and poorly provided with clothing and blankets," McCulloch still believed himself too weak to mount an extended pursuit deep into Missouri. His ammunition supply was sufficient for a campaign into Kansas, but his army lacked the wagons and draft animals to transport ammunition for his artillery. Both Rolla and Sedalia were garrisoned by Union troops, and both were terminals of railroad lines from St. Louis. Both towns could be easily supplied and swiftly reinforced by the Federals, while McCulloch's army would have been forced to traverse two hundred miles of bad road to approach them.

McCulloch, furthermore, had only three days' rations for his men and no shoes for his horses. The latter was a special problem because, with winter fast approaching, the frozen ground would immobilize the army's horses and mules. Additionally, the great number of animals belonging to the two commands—"not much short of 15,000"—had to be supplied with grain and fodder from a poor country already picked over by the ebb and flow of armies. The men, likewise, would have fared most poorly on what could be gathered on a march through a country already laid waste by the armies of both sides.[40]

Another important factor in McCulloch's strategy was the situation in the Indian Territory. Maintaining the loyalty of the civilized tribes remained McCulloch's mandate and his highest priority, since on their friendship depended the safety of northern Texas and western Arkansas.

Federal agents from Kansas were at work among them "with unlimited resources to promise," and disaffection was already spreading among the Cherokees and the Creeks. McCulloch therefore remained in northwestern Arkansas to keep a watchful eye toward the Arkansas River and to prepare his regiments for winter quarters.

He continued to maintain, as well, that "the sooner the Missouri forces are reorganized and mustered into the Confederate service the better, as they are at present not bound by any tie, and will remain in the field no longer than they think fit, no matter what may result from their withdrawal." Federal intelligence reports verified that Price's army had "no discipline, no roll-calls, no sentinels, nor picket to prevent passing in and out of Springfield. Rains drinking all the time. Price also drinking too much." Taking all of these factors into consideration, McCulloch advised Price to go into winter quarters on Spring River. The country was well supplied with grain and mills to grind it, and the Missourians, he surmised, would be able to take the field in the spring "in good condition, well supplied with everything that could be procured in the South during the winter." In the meantime, McCulloch would work to increase his own command to a respectable size. The two generals could reach no agreement, however, and the whole army was aware that Price and McCulloch were "not on good terms." Ross observed that "quarrels and jealousies exist between them that, I fear, prevent them from cooperating actively."[41]

With the campaign of 1861 at an end, Capt. John J. Good characterized the fall maneuvering in Missouri and Arkansas in rather bitter terms. "I had rather be in half a dozen fights than to do the marching and countermarching we have done since leaving home." But six months of marching and fighting had made veterans of McCulloch's recruits, and Sergeant Tunnard remarked how, when the Army of the West was reviewed on 25 November, the air of "light pageantry or holiday festival" that had attended the first months of soldiering had deserted the ranks. Now "the soiled and worn uniforms of the men, with their determined features, unshaven beards and unshorn locks, spoke of war in all its grim reality."[42]

With the threat from the Federals at least temporarily removed, McCulloch's army retired to an autumn idyll. The Army of the West pitched its tents in the open fields at Camp McCulloch in Cross Hollows, where the men began "wearing out the days in idleness or rambling in the woods or visiting the neighboring farms where an abundance of large red apples were to be had for the asking, and not unfrequently 'a little more cider, too.'" The army spent its evenings in groups around massive campfires, enlivened by stories of home or speculations upon the next campaign, which the men "vainly hoped might close the war." Cool nights, good tents, and an abundance of fat beef and fruit soon ended the epidemics of fevers that had ravaged the army, and the men considered the weeks at Camp McCulloch "altogether the most pleasant of our campaigning up to this time."[43]

FOURTEEN

Masterspirit of the Army

With the Federals now safely beyond the Osage River and most likely preparing for winter quarters, McCulloch turned his mind to the most pressing matter in his department, the unity of command between his army and that of Sterling Price. A great step toward solving this problem was at last taken on 31 October when Missouri's government in exile seceded from the Union. According to the articles of secession, Missouri was to petition to be admitted into the Confederacy with its whole "military force, material of war, and military operations" to be placed under the control of the president of the Confederate States. In order to allow a harmonious union of his own Confederate army and Price's Missouri State Guard, McCulloch proposed to Price and Governor Jackson the recommendation to Davis of Maj. Gen. Braxton Bragg, then commanding the Confederate army at Pensacola, Florida, to command the two divisions, since evidently neither present commander would serve under the other. Jackson, in his letter to Jefferson Davis announcing Missouri's secession, expressed his desire that Missouri forces be reorganized under the Confederate government and that a general be appointed to command all the forces that may be ordered to Missouri. The Missouri governor confessed to Davis that "there has not been that degree of harmony and concert of action between Generals Price and McCulloch that should exist between officers laboring in a common cause" and hoped that Davis would send a senior ranking officer to take charge of both. "Who the man shall be is of no consequence to me," he told Davis. Bragg, however, "would be very acceptable."[1]

Robert Ward Johnson, a Confederate senator from Arkansas, summed up the situation in a letter of appeal to Albert Sidney Johnston, commander of all Confederate forces west of the Allegheny Mountains. No officer above the rank of brigadier general was assigned to the trans-Mississippi Confederacy's northern frontier, he wrote, "a country as large as all Austria, Prussia, and Germany," and thus no unity of command could be expected. "Price and McCulloch have had some, and are liable to still more, serious disagreements," he pointed out, and "no one short of a major-general, and perhaps even a general, can conclusively give orders and command obedience." Senator Johnson refused to believe the news of Hunter's retreat and feared daily to hear of a battle in the West. A Confederate defeat, he predicted, would effectively nullify the treaties with the Cherokees and the Creeks and would render the situation on the frontier almost untenable. The Federals, he argued, were expending great energy and resources in securing Missouri, and their efforts should be matched by the Confederate government. Price's command, he realized, was but a fragile thing, and one defeat would disband "the disorderly and illy-united army." Only success could keep it together, and success could only be achieved by "an officer of the highest rank and experience and all other adequate war material for his operations." Johnson strongly urged Johnston to send such an officer and other resources west of the Mississippi right away. "If disaster befalls in your division it must lie at your door," he warned.[2]

The Federal authorities in Missouri took little heart from the disjointed condition of the Rebel command structure and remained deeply concerned about McCulloch's next move. On 26 November Brig. Gen. William T. Sherman advised Halleck to "look well to Jefferson City and the North Missouri Railroad" because he believed that Price aimed at both while McCulloch would menace Rolla. From St. Louis, Halleck informed McClellan that McCulloch and Price were said to be moving north, crossing the Osage near Osceola, intending to attack either Lexington or Jefferson

City. Halleck warned his commanders in the field that "insurrections are being organized on both sides of the Missouri River west of Sedalia, both to reenforce them and to destroy the Hannibal and St. Joseph Railroad." Even when the Federals became convinced that McCulloch was withdrawing into Arkansas, Halleck continued to believe it to be a ruse designed to draw him into a trap.[3]

Pvt. Sam Thompson of Douglas's battery recorded in his diary on 10 December that "much bitter talk has been heard by Missourians and many Arkansans, and some Texans against McCulloch, because he has refused to advance with Price into Missouri." This talk was indeed loud and bitter. Although it was, for the most part, based on ignorance of the situation in Missouri, on half-truths and lies from those who disagreed with McCulloch's assessment of the strategic balance in the region, and on an unfortunate discontinuity in the War Department's policy, it hurt McCulloch personally, demoralized his officers, and diminished the efficiency of his army. The principal instigator of this calumny was, of course, Sterling Price. "There are two main obstacles in the way of the successful prosecution of the war in this state," the Missouri general wrote to Jefferson Davis and Leonidas Polk on 23 December, "which is due mainly, if not altogether, to the conduct of General McCulloch."[4]

The most vocal of McCulloch's critics, however, was J. W. Tucker, former editor of the St. Louis *Daily State Journal* and present editor of a "portable paper which went with the Missouri forces." An outspoken partisan of Sterling Price, Tucker wrote a particularly irresponsible letter to the editor of the Fayetteville *Arkansian* on 24 December, roundly condemning McCulloch for failing to accompany Price into central Missouri or to supply him with weapons to arm recruits. In what John Henry Brown referred to as "the crowning act in a series of unjust and untrue allegations against one of the noble men of the Confederate states," Tucker declared that "with the exception of the battle of Springfield, not a sword has been drawn for the release of Missouri save by her own sons." Admitting that McCulloch's troops were "as brave men as ever went to battle," Tucker maintained that "they chafed like a caged lion to join the Missourians" but would not be allowed to do so by their commander.[5]

McCulloch's partisans, both in and out of the army, were swift to answer him. Edmund Ruffin, for example, considered McCulloch to be the most effective fighter in the Confederacy and to have performed "independently and almost without aid, as well as command from the Confederate government." McCulloch's troops remained intensely loyal, considering him "the most consummate department commander in the Confederate service." Remarking on the many complaints the president received from volunteers about various commanders' cruel treatment, McCulloch wrote to Brown, "Thank God, none of that kind are charged against me." Rose considered McCulloch's executive abilities to be of the highest order, a fact that became more apparent "by the sad contrast after his death." As the Texan's old antagonist Franz Sigel was to write years after the war, McCulloch's care for his men "was proverbial, and his ability in laying out encampments was extraordinary and challenged the admiration of our troops."[6]

Sergeant Tunnard wrote that McCulloch was "beloved, nay idolized, by the Louisianians and Texans, and the volunteers under him had undiminished confidence in his heroism, skill, and ability, having been with him and witnessed his indefatigable perseverance and labors in the face of a thousand difficulties." Sergeant Watson saw that McCulloch "was not sufficient of a red-tapeist or a politician to be much of a court favorite, and his influence at Richmond was not great." He was certain, however, that McCulloch's "known ability for command," coupled with "the confidence reposed in him by his army," would convince the War Department that interference with him in any way "would be bad policy."[7]

Stung by the criticism, coming from both Missouri and Richmond, of his beloved commander, John Henry Brown launched an emotional campaign of newspaper editorials in McCulloch's defense. Writing in the Dallas *Herald* on Christmas 1861, Brown reported that the general's "unremitting labors and sleepless devotion to the public have made a sensible impression upon his appearance," because while politicians and armchair generals had been plotting the advancement of their favorites and downplaying the role that "the masterspirit of the army" had played in the defense of their homes, McCulloch, "in plain citizens' clothes, without buttons, epaulettes, feathers, or stripes, has been in the woods with his men, setting them a noble example, and becoming acquainted with all the roads, paths, and passes in this country of underbrush and deep gorges." He had "toiled with unconquerable will" to build a respectable fighting force with material assistance from neither Richmond nor the states the army was to defend. Brown ventured that "no man in the Confederate States commands an army more attached to him." Even so, placing the cause of the South above his own, McCulloch had advised the government to send another general to command both Price and himself, "expressing perfect willingness to serve under such a man; and this, too, when his own army preferred him as a leader to any other person."

Nearly one thousand miles away in Richmond, however, Secretary Benjamin could not comprehend why, with the Federal army in Missouri separated into parts under different commanders, McCulloch had failed to pursue one of its elements. The administration was slow to unify the Confederate and Missouri commands, and with both Jefferson Davis and Judah P. Benjamin apparently failing to appreciate either his problems or his accomplishments, McCulloch determined to place his army in winter quarters, turn over the command to McIntosh, and visit Richmond in person in order to "give the administration correct information regarding affairs in the region before it acts on matters here." Benjamin wired his authorization, and McCulloch and his adjutant, Frank C. Armstrong, left Little Rock on 4 December en route to Richmond.[8]

Before leaving for Richmond, however, McCulloch arranged for the construction of winter quarters for his men. "The Government is having near a thousand houses built in northern Arkansas for our accommodation and as many stables are being built for our horses," Captain Douglas wrote to his wife. "Our quarters will be very much like a large town, with the very important difference that there will be no ladies there. Ours will be a lonely city." On 29 November Hébert's infantry brigade entered its winter quarters, Camp Benjamin in Benton County, Arkansas, two miles southeast of Cross Hollows. Situated in a narrow, level valley, the camp was bounded north and south by a high range of hills and was supplied with "an abundance of pure, sparkling water by a mountain stream." This stream also turned a mill that ground the corn and wheat the soldiers purchased from nearby farms. The cavalry was ordered into winter quarters at the mouth of Frog Bayou, "a beautiful stream of clear limpid water," on the northern bank of the Arkansas River, twelve miles below Van Buren.[9]

In McCulloch's absence, Price once again called upon the Army of the West to follow him to the Missouri. Lane, Montgomery, and Kansas jayhawker Charles R. Jennison and their "predatory bands" were ravaging the country and committing "the most barbarous outrages upon the people of that region," he informed McIntosh. At the same time they were effectually closing the roads to thousands of recruits who would join Price's army if they could get to it. Knowing that his own command was too small to force its way to the Missouri River and hold territory there for any length of time, Price assured McIntosh that his cooperation would enable the state guard to hold central Missouri "without risk or difficulty" and would threaten the railroads and river transport of the enemy. McIntosh demurred, reminding Price that "in a very short time it will be nearly impossible for wagons or artillery to move over the Missouri roads" and "the facility with which the enemy could concentrate a force on the Missouri River renders such a project at this season of the year almost madness." An additional cause, and perhaps the best, for McIntosh's refusal to go back into Missouri was a new threat to the Indian Territory.[10]

Just as the danger to McCulloch's front was, at least for the time, removed, a second hazard flared on his western flank. With McCulloch's attention and energies increasingly drawn to the defense of northwestern Arkansas, the War Department established the Indian Territory as a separate military department on 22 November 1861, promoted Albert Pike to brigadier general, and assigned him to command "the several Indian regiments raised or yet to be raised within the limits of the department." However, the Creeks and the Cherokees, especially, remained rent by the tension between Union and Confederate factions. John Ross's full-blooded Cherokee party had linked its fate with the southern cause under some duress and with no particular enthusiasm. Large numbers of Creeks, led by Opotheleyahola, had broken with the pro-southern majority and had defected into Kansas, where they were joined by similar groups of Unionist Indians from other tribes.

In November Opotheleyahola had returned to the Indian Territory, threatening to upset its treaty relations with the Confederacy. Col. Douglas H. Cooper, commander of the First Choctaw and Chickasaw Regiment, immediately moved to expel the disaffected chief, but on 9 December, having overtaken Opotheleyahola at Bird Creek in the Cherokee nation, he won only a marginal victory and allowed the "Tory" Indians to withdraw in good order.

On learning of Cooper's failure to destroy Opotheleyahola's renegades, McIntosh mounted twelve hundred troopers and set out in pursuit. Winter had arrived in grim earnest when the column mounted at dawn on 15 December, and the Third Texas's sixteen-year-old bugler remembered the eve of the showdown with Opotheleyahola's band as "the most disagreeable Christmas night that any of us had ever experienced." The next morning an Indian guide piloted the brigade to Salt Creek or, in the Cherokee tongue, Chustenahlah, where the Indians were massed upon a ridge, firing their guns and "cutting up all sorts of antics," indicating to the white men that "they considered their position impregnable, and all they wanted was for us to come on." McIntosh was happy to oblige them. When Walter P. Lane led a battalion of the Third Texas across Salt Creek and formed it into line of battle about one-quarter of a mile in front of the Indian position, Opotheleyahola's men "sat up a howl" and began to fire on the Texans, who promptly put spurs to horse and charged. In the face of a salvo of rifles and arrows the men of the Third Texas climbed over the breastworks, breaking Opotheleyahola's line. Riding among the fleeing Indians, the Texas cavalry shattered what little organization the warriors had retained. Elements of the Sixth and Ninth Texas, meanwhile, had swung wide around the flanks of Opotheleyahola's position, and as the Indians bolted for the rear, these two battalions closed on them in a perfect double envelopment. The fugitives were pursued for seven miles until no warriors remained in sight. Of the 2,000 Indians said to have been present, 200 were killed, and 160 women and children were captured. In addition, McIntosh counted "twenty Negroes, thirty wagons, seventy yoke of oxen, about five hundred Indian horses, several hundred head of cattle, one hundred sheep, and a great quantity of property of much value to the enemy" among the spoils. Only one warrior was captured, and he was wounded. McIntosh suffered fifty casualties, killed and wounded.

On 29 December McIntosh turned his column back toward Arkansas to winter quarters. As the column rode through Fort Gibson, John Ross held a council of his people and "in the most emphatic language expressed his determination to stand firm to the Government of the Confederate States," living or dying with his treaties. The battle of Chustenahlah had demonstrated to the Cherokees that southern forces were willing and able to act in their behalf and, in McIntosh's words, "intimidated many who probably meditated mischief." For the time being, all Federal resistance had been stamped out in the Cherokee nation, and the Indian Territory would firmly remain, for a time, part of the Confederacy.

The army's winter quarters were as sheltered and well constructed as McCulloch's limited resources could make them, and his men fared remarkably well through the brutal weather. On 1 February 1862 a cold sleet and rain began to fall on the cavalry camp, but George L. Griscom of the Ninth Texas Cavalry found the regiment's log cabins "well chinked" and, with their "good stove chimneys," quite comfortable. Surgeon Gammage agreed that "the winter winds whistled and the cold rains poured in vain, for securely sheltered in houses and warmed by ample fires," the men of his regiment "bid defiance to the elements." The heavy snows, in fact, proved a delight to "the pelicans from Louisiana," who had never seen snow remain on the ground for more than a day, and all enjoyed the massive snowball fights that flared between the companies.[11]

Homesickness and some grumbling naturally arose, and Captain Good often wished to be "in a good feather bed with [his] dark eyed wife"; but in general the soldiers remembered this as a happy time. Rations were "pretty plenty," said George Griscom, and the men felt "quite at home." The army's sportsmen "whipped the water of White River," while "another class of them indulged much in the national game." After each payday "the intoxicated and unhampered artist of the distillery" could easily be found, plying his trade and lending a helping hand "to the festivities of the season."[12]

But for the daily routine of drill, guard mount, and other mundane soldierly duties, "we would get lazy," Griscom declared. Best of all, "As there were no rumors of war here," wrote Arkansas private A. W. Sparks, "the boys commenced a life of pleasure and social dissipation in the fashionable circle of Frog Bayou." While purchasing apples, butter, and eggs from local farmers, the soldiers became acquainted with the farmers' daughters. On many evenings the men, with their girls riding behind them, would bring their fiddles to some farmer's house, and "then the fun would begin, and such dancing they would have!" "Dances—regular old-fashioned 'barn dances'—were the order of the night; and animated jig and reel followed the lively twanging of many an Arkansas Ole Bull's fiddle." Thus, Gammage recorded, "December and January passed away without any occurrence worthy of note."[13]

In Richmond, however, Price continued to agitate for an offensive thrust into Missouri, and delegates from the state guard in favor of such a maneuver lobbied the Confederate Congress and War Department. On 30 November Jefferson Davis settled on his choice for a new commander for the divided Confederate army in Missouri and Arkansas. Mindful of the difficulties between Price and McCulloch, Davis sought to bring their two armies "into harmonious cooperation" by selecting a single head to command both forces, and he called into his office Henry Heth, a West Point graduate and army veteran whose career Davis had been tracking with a more than cursory interest since before Heth's distinguished role in the battle of Blue Water in 1855. Although displaying fine potential for command in Virginia, Heth was only thirty-five years old and a colonel when Davis asked him, "Young man, how much rank can you stand?" When Heth modestly responded that Davis himself "must be the judge of that," the president informed the young colonel that he intended to make him a major general and send him to the trans-Mississippi, where "Price and McCulloch are fighting each other harder than they are fighting the enemy." Although Heth was prepared to depart for the West by 5 December, this announcement was "anything but pleasant" to him. Heth feared that the friends of both Price and McCulloch would object to his nomination on the grounds that the government should not "send a boy out west to supersede old veterans." Indeed, a delegation from Missouri informed him frankly that the Missouri army would follow no one but Price.[14]

Colonel Heth's youth and lack of experience drew considerable opposition to his nomination from the public, the press, and the House and Senate. Edmund Ruffin noted in his diary that Davis's plan to send Heth west as a major general "seems to be universally condemned," and he was sure that Congress would refuse to confirm the promotion. Ruffin agreed with Davis that because Price and McCulloch could not compromise, the appointment of a senior officer over them was proper. Such an officer, however, must be "previously of superior grade and also of established and high reputation." Either of the two Johnstons would have been suitable, he thought, but not this young colonel "whose only known ground for the designed great promotion and distinction is that he was educated at West Point."[15]

Davis continued to defend Heth vigorously, all the more, perhaps, because those who would block his appointment seemed also to be attacking the United States Military Academy, the institution Davis had so long championed. "If it is designed, by calling Heth a West Point cadet, merely to object of his education in the science of war," the president retorted, "it may pass for what it is worth; but if it is intended to assert that he is without experience, his years of active service on the frontier of Missouri and the territory to the west of it will, to those who examine before they censure, be a sufficient answer."[16]

By the time McCulloch arrived in Richmond, however, Heth's nomination seems to have been a dead letter. McCulloch met with him and found him to be "a very nice Gent" and thought that he "may be a first rate general." Because Heth had not been tested in battle, however, McCulloch was sure that Missouri would not rally to him. Consequently Heth's name had not been sent to Congress, and McCulloch informed Brown that it would not be sent because he had no chance of confirmation and Davis knew this to be true. Even Davis's determined defense could make no headway against popular opinion, and at last Heth called on Benjamin, telling the secretary that he did not believe he should be sent to command across the Mississippi. Heth was convinced and sought to convince Benjamin that once he reached Missouri, "they would both unite and fight me;

that I would find myself between the upper and nether mill stone; that these men would never second me in my efforts to beat the enemy, and I felt sure I would be compelled to relieve both and order them to Richmond." Benjamin agreed, and Heth remained in the East, ultimately to become a division commander in Robert E. Lee's Army of Northern Virginia.[17]

While McCulloch was in Richmond for an audience with Davis and Benjamin, a Missouri delegation was also in the Confederate capital to press Price's claim to the command of the Confederate army in the West. The Missourians assured Davis that by placing any other officer in command of the Missouri State Guard, the government would "paralyze our state and expose the entire Mississippi Valley to the enemy." Reminding the president of Price's service to the Confederate cause in Missouri and the great affection and loyalty felt for him by his men, the delegation predicted "the utter ruin which would follow us in the future if some stranger to our troops and people" were placed in Price's stead. Governor Jackson, however, did not necessarily share their assessment of Price's indispensability, and Davis "was firm and even impatient" in his opposition to the Missouri delegates' views. Although Price had done a good job and still had his kind personal regard, the president was determined not to appoint anyone from Missouri, Arkansas, or Texas to the command.[18]

McCulloch was no doubt correct in his assessment that the insistent urging of Price's admirers to have their favorite appointed a major general "only results in making Davis more determined not to do it." Price, he pointed out, was not a graduate of West Point, "which settles his claims to the command of any very larger force." Although he expected Price to be made a brigadier general in the Confederate States Army, he was sure that "a new order of things must take place before any civilians will be given any higher rank."[19]

McCulloch's trip to Richmond seems to have aided his own cause materially. From his interview with Davis he came away with the impression that the president agreed with him as to the foolhardiness of Price's Missouri invasion. McCulloch sought to convince Davis of the virtual impossibility of supplying an army at so great a distance from its base across the rugged, roadless tracks of the Ozark Mountains in the dead of winter. Perhaps mindful of Sam Houston's masterful San Jacinto campaign, in which a defense based upon a strategic withdrawal turned at the right moment into a decisive tactical offensive, he told the president that "an army in the field is like a spiral spring, the more it is pressed back toward its base, the stronger it becomes." Davis, he informed John Henry Brown, "is a military man by nature, and had he not been put through West Point would have done better as president than he is likely to do." In an observation reminiscent of Houston's and Crockett's speeches in the Senate and the House of Representatives, McCulloch described the president as making the mistake of thinking that "all men who have a knowledge of tactics can be generals or can command successfully in the field instead of thinking such men are only useful in the hands of those whom God has endowed with capacity to plan and execute movements calculated to insure success."[20]

Forwarding to Brown a list of officers recently promoted, he told his friend, "If you can see a major general who is not a West Pointer, you have better eyes than mine, and it will be so to the end of the chapter." Given his lack of a West Point commission and his history of cross-purposes with Davis, McCulloch "never expected promotion." If he was still at the head of his army in the spring, then his friends could expect something of him, "and they shall not be disappointed"; if not, he vowed not to thrust himself or his opinions upon the new commander of the Arkansas and Missouri theater. McCulloch thought it would be best to remain in Richmond until that man was appointed in order to brief him on the trans-Mississippi situation, "and then let him work out his own salvation."[21]

On 22 December McCulloch presented a report to Secretary of War Benjamin, detailing his activities since arriving at Fort Smith in May to create the Army of the West and explaining his decisions with regard to his dealings with Price. Although he vigorously protested that he had no wish to disparage the courage of either Price or the infantry and artillery "who fought heroically at the battle of Oak Hills," he wished to set straight the record concerning the extent of his cooperation with Price, the poor condition of Price's army in terms of both arms and discipline, and Price's ill-conceived strategy. As early as July 1861, he reminded Benjamin, he and Pearce had visited Price's headquarters and offered to aid him "in every possible way." The three commanders had agreed to march together on Springfield, although McCulloch's assignment to the Indian Territory had left him with no specific guidance as to whether or how to leave the Confederacy or cooperate with Missouri. The decision to march into Missouri with Price was his alone, and he asserted that he had made it at some risk, not knowing whether the government would approve his action or not. He described the incompetence of Rains's cavalry at Crane Creek and in allowing the Federal surprise at Oak Hills. Further, he reminded

Benjamin, following the battle of Oak Hills, his troops had an average of only twenty-five rounds of ammunition to the man. Heretofore, he told the secretary, he had kept many of these details a secret, eliding them even from his official reports in order to maintain "a feeling of friendship between the armies." As Brown later observed, however, the "magnanimous silence" was afterward "made an instrument to bruise and vilify him."[22]

With Heth's withdrawal from consideration for the trans-Mississippi command, and upon hearing the reports of McCulloch and Price's partisans, Davis and Benjamin, "after long and anxious consultation," wrote to McCulloch's first choice, Maj. Gen. Braxton Bragg, requesting that he accept the assignment. On 27 December the secretary of war informed Bragg that the "dissensions" between Price and McCulloch promised a "grievous disaster." Although he could not call McCulloch to command, Benjamin now seemed convinced of the rectitude of McCulloch's decision not to accompany Price to the Missouri River. While McCulloch's nine thousand "excellent troops" were in winter quarters, wrote Benjamin, "Price has advanced alone, and we fear with fatal rashness, into a district of country where he is likely to be surrounded and cut off by overwhelming forces." Furthermore, he informed Bragg, "the Army of Missouri is represented to be a mere gathering of brave but undisciplined partisan troops, coming and going at pleasure, and needing a master mind to control and reduce it to order and convert it to a real army." How potent McCulloch's recommendation might have been is only conjectural, but Davis and Benjamin could find no one but Bragg upon whom they felt they "could rely with confidence as commander-in-chief of the Trans-Mississippi Department."[23]

Bragg declined, however, accepting instead the command of the Second Corps of Albert Sidney Johnston's Army of Tennessee, and so the offer devolved upon Earl Van Dorn. Van Dorn was a personal friend of the president, had served in Texas with the Second Cavalry—"Jeff Davis's Own"—before the war, and had commanded the Department of Texas, a position McCulloch had greatly desired at the beginning of the war. Van Dorn, then serving in Virginia, accepted the offer and, on 10 January 1862, was assigned command of the Trans-Mississippi Department. R. S. Bevier of the Missouri State Guard described Van Dorn as "a dashing soldier, and a very handsome man, and his manners were graceful and fascinating. He was slight of stature, and his features were almost too delicately refined for a soldier, but this defect, if it was a defect, was converted into charm by the martial aspect of his mustache and imperial, and by an exuberant growth of brownish hair." Van Dorn was "known to be a fighting man," Bevier contended, "and we felt sure he would help us to regain our state."[24]

Bevier was almost alone, however, in his pleasure over the appointment, for both McCulloch's and Price's men idolized their present leaders. "Van Dorn sent here to rank both is inferior as a department commander to either Price or McCulloch," thought Pvt. Sam Thompson of the Texas battery. Lt. Col. Henry G. Bunn of the Fourth Arkansas considered Van Dorn "a fearless, dashing, and enterprising officer," but one who came to the trans-Mississippi "with a collar round his neck," namely, Davis's mandate to take the offensive immediately and to drive on St. Louis. Success "under such restraint was simply an impossibility. Such a burden has never been successfully borne by any military commander and never will be in the very nature of things." Pvt. Douglas J. Cater of the Third Texas Cavalry concurred. Although admitting that he was not privy to Van Dorn's plan of action, he vowed that "anybody could see that there was too great a hurry to bring on a battle without a better preparation."[25]

When Van Dorn telegraphed from Pocahantas, Arkansas, to "stop all retrograde movements, and that the tactics must now be to advance," McCulloch's troops scorned him with laughter. Although Van Dorn's manifesto, "accompanied by some very warlike expressions," appeared in local newspapers, no general order was read on parade, and the troops believed that their new commander's rhetoric was designed more for public consumption than for the army. "We considered it looked very well on paper, and though it had not been read off to us, it would no doubt be read in many a drawing room, where it would be better appreciated," wrote Watson.[26]

As the end of winter neared, Leonidas Polk became seriously concerned about the defense of southeastern Missouri. Col. Merriwether Jeff Thompson's Missouri "Swamp Rats" had disbanded at New Madrid, laying that vital river town open to Federal occupation and exposing the left flank of the Confederate defenses at Island Number Ten. Certain that the Federals would make no move in southwestern Missouri before spring, Polk begged Albert Sidney Johnston to transfer McCulloch's men to his command in the southeastern part of the state. There, he believed, they could be employed to "great, very great, advantage." Johnston did not wish to issue such an order himself but recommended to the War Department that half of McCulloch's command should be sent to Polk. Davis, with whom Polk was a great favorite, concurred, depriving the Army of the West of badly needed units on the eve of its spring campaign.

Earl Van Dorn
(Department of Archives and History, State of Mississippi)

Rumors ran rampant through the early part of January that Price had been appointed a major general and that McCulloch had been transferred to Virginia to command a cavalry division, leaving McIntosh to command McCulloch's army in Arkansas. McCulloch returned to his troops on 5 February, however, arriving at Fort Smith just in time to forward two infantry regiments, two cavalry regiments, and one artillery battery toward New Madrid and a cooperative effort with Polk's Army of Central Kentucky.

The march to New Madrid would take the detached regiments first to Pocahantas, Arkansas, where Van Dorn had established his headquarters, more than two hundred miles distant by way of roads that were "very bad, and in some places impassable." Many rivers ran across the line of march, unfordable in winter, and a spring rise on the Mississippi would overflow much of northeastern Arkansas. Despite such difficulties, McCulloch arranged for transport, surveyed the route, and sent parties of pioneers to repair the roads.[27]

Even with McCulloch's command diminished, Van Dorn remained confident that he could take St. Louis. With McCulloch's remaining troops, augmented by Price's column and the army he was attempting to raise at Pocahantas, Van Dorn planned to open the campaign by 20 March. Hoping to bring his combined command to a total of forty-five thousand men, Van Dorn planned to "push on by rapid marches to St. Louis, and attempt it at once by assault." Van Dorn boasted confidently, "The city once ours the state is ours."[28]

McCulloch questioned the wisdom of such a strategy, pointing out in a letter to Governor Francis Lubbock of Texas that by shifting his command so far east, Van Dorn would be leaving northwestern Arkansas and the Indian Territory unprotected, "and consequently this whole country will fall an easy prey to the Federal forces." Pike's Indians, he feared, would soon desert, and the enemy would then be able to "carry the war as far south as the frontier of Texas." He advised Lubbock, therefore, to send the new regiments, then forming in Texas, to Pike rather than to Van Dorn. McCulloch further recommended that Lubbock "have some experienced men from our state put in command of these regiments." President Davis, he believed, should yield to the governor's wishes in appointing regimental commanders, and McCulloch once again ventured that he "would feel more confident of these troops acquitting themselves well under an experienced officer rather than under the lead of a man who has nothing but a military education to recommend him."[29]

The question became moot, however, when once again Price's army appeared, entirely unexpected and in full retreat, in the midst of the Army of the West. As early as the first of February, according to Bevier, the Missouri troops had learned that Brig. Gen. Samuel R. Curtis, who now commanded the principal Federal army in Missouri, was advancing "in strong force" from Sedalia, Rolla, and Fort Scott and was making Price's position near Springfield untenable. Yet Price failed to inform McCulloch of his retreat.

On 16 February Price's army crossed the Missouri line. Once again the road south became "a scene that beggared description" as hundreds of citizens fled terror-stricken toward Arkansas, taking with them such of their property as they could. Army wagon trains and columns of retreating soldiers competed for right of way with carriages and buggies. Rose watched miles of "horsemen, footmen, delicate women, little children, all fleeing from the frightful demon of war." Price's division, more than one observer commented, was followed by "the most multitudinous and variegated wagon train ever concentrated on the continent." Rolling south along Telegraph Road was "every species of wheel vehicle, from jolting ox-cart to the most fantastically painted stage coach," and at the heads of the columns of infantry was a constellation of officers adequate to command an army of a hundred thousand. Its complement of generals was entirely disproportionate to the number of soldiers in the ranks, and the wags of McCulloch's command took up the cry as the Missourians crossed into Arkansas, "Here's your army of brigadier-generals and stage-coaches!"[30]

"Why was this sudden advance of the enemy by way of Springfield never suspected?" the men of McCulloch's army wondered. "Why had this large force come all the way from St. Louis and been concentrating in southern Missouri unknown to Price, who supposed himself kept constantly informed by his faithful adherents of all that was going on in Missouri?" They felt a bitter new grievance against the Missourians when informed of Price's retreat "only about ten miles in advance of his sluggish ox wagons." Nevertheless, once Van Dorn authorized McCulloch to march to Price's aid, the Army of the West was immediately en route, rushing up Telegraph Road toward a rendezvous with Price's men at Sugar Creek.[31]

On the morning of 17 February, Curtis made a dash upon Price's rear guard, and by 11:00 A.M. the men of the Third Louisiana, hearing cannonading and the rattle of small arms to the north, marched toward the sound of the guns. Union and Missouri artillery exchanged shot and shell, and Curtis ordered his cavalry to charge, overrunning a battery of Price's guns. The crisis of the battle was at hand when the Third Louisiana formed in line of battle, buttressing the teetering Missouri line. At that moment a resounding cheer went up the Rebel line when Ben McCulloch, who had been absent from the army surveying the route to Pocahantas, thundered to the front, having ridden more than seventy miles to lead his men in this fight. His sudden, unexpected appearance on the field was greeted by "such a storm of enthusiastic vivas as seldom greets anyone," and his horse was so startled it became decidedly unruly. "The Louisianians especially were wild with joy, throwing up their hats and elevating them on the points of their bayonets while giving deafening cheers." McCulloch raised his hat to his favorite regiment and said simply, "Men, I am glad to see you."[32]

Under McCulloch's sharp gray eye the Rebel line surged forward to retake Price's lost guns. "For a few moments," Rose recalled, the two lines "were intermingled in seemingly inextricable confusion," while "sabres and clubbed muskets were freely used." The double-barreled shotguns of Col. William Cocke Young's newly arrived Eleventh Texas Cavalry were especially effective in such melees, and the green Arkansas regiments of M. C. Mitchell and John B. Rector won their spurs charging the Federal line. By 4:00 P.M. the Federal advance was checked, and the Missourians proceeded unmolested. Watson dismissed this spirited rearguard action as "a trifling affair which never had a name."[33]

Leaving Price and McCulloch to fall back at their leisure, Curtis camped on the battlefield but sent his cavalry ahead to "annoy and explore" the road to Cross Hollows, twelve miles south of Sugar Creek. Cross Hollows, he explained to his superior, was McCulloch's "great boasted trap for the Federal Army," and he wanted all of his command present before he tested the Rebel lines there. With his infantry well placed and his artillery commanding the passes, McCulloch hoped that Curtis might be so rash as to attack him. On the night of 17 February McCulloch's men lay down to sleep in line of battle along the steep ridges of Cross Hollows. A steady fall of frozen rain soon commenced, and so sudden had been Curtis's appearance that most of the regiments had set fire to their winter quarters and marched to the front without tents or blankets; thus the night was miserable for the battle-weary Confederates. Gammage remembered sleeping—"if sleeping it could be called, where the entire night was pretty well divided between unavailing efforts to keep my feet from freezing and my body from floating in the thawing sleet"—on the ground near General McCulloch, who, like his men, was "exposed to the most inclement weather without shelter, and in fact almost without blankets."[34]

The next morning, strengthened by the arrival of the Fourth Arkansas Infantry and heartened by the great natural strength of the position at Cross Hollows, McCulloch set off with members of his staff to reconnoiter. He learned, to his great disappointment, that Curtis had not advanced from Sugar Creek. Instead, the Federal cavalry had moved to the Confederate left and occupied Bentonville, Arkansas, effectively flanking McCulloch and Price out of their strong position. The Confederates held their lines through the day, however, resting and trying vainly to keep warm.[35]

With Curtis's cavalry threatening their line of communications and with part of McIntosh's brigade still somewhere near Pocahantas, fifty miles distant, Price and McCulloch abandoned Cross Hollows at 4:00 P.M., 18 February, and Sergeant Watson recalled that the men "were glad to go anywhere," fearing they would have frozen to the ground had they stayed any longer at Cross Hollows. They were not so pleased, however, when they learned that the movement would be to the rear. The retreat was resumed at 10:00 A.M. through a bitterly cold rain. The road, recalled Rose, was "frozen hard as a rock and as slippery as glass." The soldiers' beards were frosted white, and the water in their canteens froze solid. Watson considered this retreat "a sad disaster," for had the whole army been on the Cross Hollows line, he believed, it could have held the place against much greater numbers and checked the advance of the enemy. To McCulloch, however, the withdrawal was an opportunity to demonstrate Sam Houston's observation on the eve of the battle of San Jacinto that "by falling back, Texas can rally and defeat any force that can come against her."[36]

Slowed by Price's trains and heavy snowfall, the Confederate army reached Fayetteville about midnight. That night the combined army bivouacked in the snow, although McCulloch's men had overtaken their wagons and were able at least to sleep under tents. They woke on the morning of 20 February to the smell of smoke and the crackling of flames. Unable to move his supplies due to a severe shortage of transportation and the surprising speed with which Price had abandoned Springfield, McCulloch had burned the large wooden storehouses filled with the army's bacon and flour. Although every wagon remaining in town was loaded with supplies and routed to Fort Smith, the soldiers were encouraged to take as much of anything as they wanted. To Surgeon Gammage, that morning in Fayetteville presented "one of the most disgraceful scenes that [he] ever saw." In addition to the opening of the government's warehouses to the soldiers and citizens, the outraged doctor observed, "the troops—our own troops—men who had come as everybody vainly thought, to protect the persons and property of the people," were sacking the town. Storehouses, smokehouses, and even, in some instances, private houses were broken into, and clothing, blankets, and other objects of value to the soldiers were carried away. To Watson, however, "this was an amusement." Price's and McCulloch's men supplied themselves with clothing, shoes, and rations. They roasted slices of bacon, which they pronounced "really excellent," and for bread they wound dough around sticks or ramrods and baked it over the flames of a campfire. Having eaten what they could, the soldiers filled their haversacks with bread and bacon streaming with grease. For the first time in days their clothes were dry and their bodies warm. This was "ever-lasting fun" to them, and they were in great good humor despite being described by their officers as "a set of greasy-looking cannibals."[37]

Long a student of military history, McCulloch was mindful of Napoleon's 1812 campaign in Russia. Remembering that the French offensive had broken down in the face of bad roads, the poverty of the country, and the Russians' "scorched earth" policy, McCulloch saw a similar theater of operations in Arkansas, and he placed his own army in the role of that of Marshal Mikhail Kutusov. As the last Confederate units marched out, the beautiful town of Fayetteville was, like Moscow, put to the torch. William Baxter, a Fayetteville resident of Union sympathies, reported how Rebel cavalry "dashed into town and began firing the buildings which had been used for military purposes." The stables of the Butterfield Overland Mail Company were destroyed, as were the steam mill and the Female College, "a large and beautiful structure, in the days of peace" but used by the Confederates as an arsenal and a cartridge factory. As the torch was applied, a volley of condemned shells burst as "loud as a park of artillery." Capt. David Pierson of the Third Louisiana watched as "the smoke and flame of its burning houses rose like a cloud in the heavens" as his company moved south. "It was the most horrible sight I ever witnessed," he wrote to his father.[38]

The Rebel army spent the night of 20 February at Hog Eye, Arkansas, eight miles south of Fayetteville, and resumed its retreat at dawn. During the night the weather had suddenly moderated, turning the roads to slush that was quickly cut up by the army's wagon trains. The exact location of the enemy was unknown, and the Third Louisiana was posted as a rear guard, "expecting an attack constantly night and day." To Pierson the retreat was "one of continued horror and suffering." The Federal vanguard occupied a smoldering Fayetteville at dawn on 21 February, farther south than it had ever been. As the Stars and Stripes was raised over the courthouse, the main buildings around the square were still burning. Curtis could boast that he was now "master of all the strongholds and larger cities of western Arkansas, and [held] a check on the rebels in the Indian country, being south of the Cherokees and east of the Choctaws."[39]

That night McCulloch's and Price's little armies arrived at Stricklers, a stage stop on the Butterfield Overland Mail before the war. The weather remained intensely cold, and the rain and mud were deemed "interminable." Private Sparks recalled that "the men, though warmly clothed, suffered no little" although their route took them through some of the most picturesque scenery on the North American continent. Many Texas and Louisiana soldiers, accustomed only to flat terrain, were awed by the sight. "On either side of the road the precipitous mountains rose hundreds of feet overhead, while gigantic icicles hung pendant from the overhanging rocks, like huge stalactites, and glittering in the brilliant rays of the cold winter sun, looked like the suspended spears of giants," wrote one man.[40]

At last, on 22 February 1862, the day the constitution of the Confederate States of America was ratified and Jefferson Davis was sworn in to a six-year term as president, Price and McCulloch arrived amid the Boston Mountains. "Almost famished and exhausted," McCulloch's division established Camp Defiance near Crawford, Arkansas. Price's division settled along Cove Creek, three miles west. The position was remarkably strong, dominating the approach from the north. Watson was convinced that the Confederates could hold it against double their numbers, and Rose deemed it "impregnable." Despite their rough treatment on the retreat from Little Sugar Creek, the men "were soon in good fighting trim" and eager for battle. Although McCulloch believed Curtis's army included 40,000 to 50,000 men, while he commanded 10,000 and Price about 8,000, those who had been on winter furlough were soon reporting for duty, and many fresh volunteers came with them to refill the ranks of McCulloch's veteran regiments. His command, now a division in the reorganized Army of the West, was divided into two brigades: the First, under McIntosh, newly promoted to brigadier general, was composed of five regiments and one independent troop of cavalry, and the Second, commanded by Hébert, was composed of six regiments of infantry, one regiment and a battalion of cavalry, and three batteries.

A new regulation in Arkansas allowed so-called emergency men to serve for a brief time when battle was expected and then to depart the service. Many men from Fayetteville, Bentonville, and other Arkansas communities joined McCulloch under this dubious law and were armed and drilled. Although far from an ideal solution to Confederate recruiting problems, according to Watson "the system did very well, and these men were of considerable assistance."[41]

More problematic were the regiments of Indians that Earl Van Dorn had ordered into Arkansas from the territory under Albert Pike. Always outspoken and often insubordinate, Pike was "relieved of the necessity of disobeying" Van Dorn's order only because he and his tribesmen were instructed to report to McCulloch. "I knew that he understood the Indian character and their mode of fighting and would not dream of using them as part of an army in the open field," Pike said of McCulloch. Nevertheless, when he arrived at Camp Defiance with his two thousand warriors "yelling forth a wild war whoop that startled the army out of all its propriety," Pike caused great consternation in the Rebel camp. The costume of their new allies elicited a great deal of comment, especially among the Louisiana, Arkansas, and Missouri troops who had never seen an Indian war party. In styles as varied as their highly individualistic cultures, the Cherokees, Creeks, and Choctaws were "dressed in a garb ranging from a common gent's suit to a breech clout and blanket." Most, however, wore "buckskin shirts, leggins and moccasins adorned with little bells and rattles." They had painted their faces for war and, according to Sparks, "were frightful to even look upon." The white soldiers could see no pattern to their garb or their face paint, "but each one seemed to have been painted according to the fancy of the artist." The brightly colored turkey feathers adorning their long black hair "completed unique uniforms not strictly cut according to army regulations." "Their arms were as varied as their apparel," Sparks remarked, and consisted mostly of old rifles, shotguns, and bows and arrows. Bevier observed that many were armed with only tomahawks and war clubs. The ensemble "presented an appearance somewhat savage."[42]

The army was of two distinct minds on the effectiveness of their new comrades. To Bevier, for example, although they were "awkward and unmanageable on the drill ground," the Cherokees were "cool and cautious in danger, catlike and sinewy in person, fine specimens of the 'noble red man,' and withal deft in the use of the rifle." They made good soldiers, "barrin' their mortal fear of the 'big kettles,'" as they called the cannon. However, to Col. John C. Moore, also of the Missouri division, the Indians "possessed the vices of their civilized conquerers and their uncivilized ancestors with the virtues of neither." He thought them worthless as soldiers and placed most of the blame on Pike, who, he said, "was not the kind of commander to develop a very high order of soldiership in any body of recruits, and least of all in a body of half-civilized Indians."[43]

McCulloch's tactics would now be those he had employed against Frémont's army during the previous autumn. He would hold his infantry and artillery in a naturally fortified position that could not be flanked and then send his cavalry to harass and weaken the enemy by defeating them in detail and bleeding them of supplies. At the same time he worked to recruit his own force until Curtis either felt compelled to attack him in his stronghold or retreat into Missouri. McCulloch lost no time in implementing his plan. As Curtis advanced beyond Fayetteville to within fifteen miles of Cove Creek, McCulloch ordered two large raiding parties to harass the Federal flanks and rear. On 24 February McCulloch dispatched Maj. Lawrence Sullivan Ross at the head of 250 men to circle to the enemy's rear from the east, and Maj. John Wilkins Whitfield with his independent battalion was to do the same from the west.[44]

Riding almost continually through the day and night, Ross's battalion passed the left end of Curtis's line and penetrated as far north as Keetsville, Missouri, seventy miles on his rear. The evening of 25 February was growing dark as the Rebel cavalry put spurs to their horses and galloped into town. Ordered to "shoot everything on the ground and stay on our horses," in a five-minute fight Ross's battalion scattered the three-hundred-man garrison and cut loose and stampeded some forty of its horses. Pvt. Newton Ashbury Keen remembered how he "charged up and down the street and fired my gun and hopped and yelled hardly having sense enough to know what I was doing, but it was sure war." After gathering horses, mules, wagons, and other valuables, the column returned to Camp Defiance.[45]

After a round trip raid of over four hundred miles, Ross returned without a single casualty, winning McCulloch's highest compliments for dash and gallantry. Major Whitfield, unfortunately, had not been so successful. His horses proved too jaded to perform the long and rapid march, and he never reached his objective. It was not long, however, before Ross's exploit had grown to mythic proportions. The usually reliable Watson reported his haul as "several army wagons with supplies of the enemy, and over a hundred prisoners." One of the prisoners, a Federal officer, delighted the army with his report that "he had seen considerable scouting in the bushes, but the Texans beat the Devil for reckless riding in the woods."[46]

With the success of the Keetsville raid, McCulloch's cavalry continued to harry Curtis's flanks and rear, "and almost every day," wrote Watson, "some prisoners or spoil was brought in." Two days after the Keetsville raid Col. B. W. Stone's Sixth Texas Cavalry left its mountain stronghold for

Bentonville, Arkansas, which it reached on 29 February. The Federal garrison made a stand on the eastern side of town, but the Sixth Texas brushed it aside and occupied Bentonville for the night before returning to Cove Creek. So successful were these raids that the men began to hope that when Van Dorn finally came, "he would just leave 'Ben' alone and he would soon have the whole of the enemy's army brought in by small lots at a time."[47]

Curtis apparently thought so too, because soon afterward he evacuated Fayetteville and retreated beyond Cross Hollows to a strong defensive position near Elkhorn Tavern, leaving only Sigel's division south of Little Sugar Creek to occupy Bentonville. Van Dorn resolved to defeat Curtis in detail, destroying Sigel's isolated command before it could rejoin the main Federal army, and then attack Curtis. Despite the dysentery, measles, smallpox, and malaria that remained prevalent among McCulloch's men, Van Dorn sent orders from Fort Smith for the army to prepare to march down from the Boston Mountains and into Fayetteville. The men were to carry ten days' rations and sixty rounds of ammunition. "The idea of ten days' cooked rations to be carried in their haversacks astonished the men, and they wondered if new haversacks were going to be issued," wrote Watson. "Most of the men could easily eat in one day all that could be crammed into [a haversack]. However, they were told to make themselves easy on that point, for it would be something new for the commissary if he could furnish more than three days' rations, and they might be assured that their haversacks would hold all the rations they would get."[48]

Nevertheless, McCulloch ordered his command to be ready to march as soon as Van Dorn arrived. On 15 February, the day before the disastrous fall of Fort Donelson in northern Tennessee, McCulloch had written to John Henry Brown expressing his reservations about the resolve of the southern people to pursue the war successfully. "We do not—as a people—seem to realize the magnitude of the revolution we are engaged in," he told his friend. "A few more losses will bring us to our senses and then we will come up to our work like men who intend to be free." The loss of Forts Donelson and Henry and the evacuation of Springfield and Fayetteville seem to have been the losses McCulloch believed would inspire his division to "go into battle determined to conquer or be left on the field," and now he was ready to advance. "We await your arrival anxiously," he wrote to his new commander.

With Hébert's brigade now reinforced to 4,637 men and 18 guns and McIntosh's cavalry brigade numbering 3,747, he was sure that "we now have force enough to whip the enemy," and with Curtis in retreat, the troops were sure a decisive battle was in the offing. “Our men are chafing for it and the universal sentiment is ‘let them come, no matter how many,’ ” wrote Pierson to his father. “The troops have confidence in McCulloch and shout like wild men when he passes along the line.” Keen noted that although “many a soldier boy expected his last night’s sleep” on the eve of the showdown they anticipated any day, they had “no fear as to the result.”[49]

FIFTEEN

My God! It's Old Ben!

At last, on 2 March, Van Dorn arrived on the Boston Mountains. Until now his only contribution to the Army of the West or the Missouri State Guard had been the battle flag that he had designed, sending it to his subordinates with instructions that they were to have one made for each regiment. Now, however, he was eager to take the offensive against Curtis's army and vowed to give battle. The enemy was lying only two days' march distant, not over eighteen thousand strong. Too, Curtis had failed to concentrate his forces, and Sigel's division at Bentonville might be cut off and destroyed. After disposing of Sigel, Van Dorn would throw his army against Curtis's main body on Little Sugar Creek. "I have no doubt of the result," Van Dorn wrote to Bragg. "If I succeed I shall push on."[1]

Van Dorn called on McCulloch and found him occupying a small farmhouse on the mountainside. "Comfortless and bare enough it was," Col. Dabney H. Maury, Van Dorn's chief of staff, noted. "In person, in manner and in character, McCulloch presented a strong contrast with Price." Maury found McCulloch to be at once calm and eager for the coming campaign. Despite earlier misgivings McCulloch "avowed his confidence" in Van Dorn's plan "and cooperated heartily for its success." In fact, recalled Maury, "His whole conduct during these operations impressed us very favorably as to his capacity for war."[2]

Later that morning McCulloch's division left Camp Defiance, abandoning its baggage train, tents, and such provisions as the men could not carry. Two days' rations were all that could be had rather than the ten that Van Dorn had prescribed. The army had marched but a short distance on the morning of 4 March when "the hardest kind of a snow storm," wet snow, melting as it came down, began to fall, making the road "very slippery and disagreeable." Maury admitted that he and Van Dorn "did not feel very bright" as they rode toward the head of the column until they passed and "were struck with the splendid appearance" of a large regiment, "the ever glorious Third Louisiana." As they came upon its flank, it halted, faced front, and presented arms. As Van Dorn reached the center of the line, the regiment gave him three cheers, and for the first time he and his chief of staff felt that they "were with soldiers."[3]

Addressing McCulloch's men for the first time, however, Van Dorn struck a Napoleonic note that rang hollow in the ears of the veterans of Oak Hills. "Soldiers," he boasted, "behold your leader! He comes to show you the way to glory and immortal renown." Promising to "hurl back the minions of the despots at Washington, whose ignorance, licentiousness, and brutality are equaled only by their craven natures," Van Dorn failed to impress an army that had fought well without him and preferred their own tested and proven leaders. Indeed, as Van Dorn's twentieth-century biographer, Robert G. Hartje, observes, "the contrast between the West Pointer and McCulloch was too obvious to many of the Westerners." The Mississippian was spit and polish mixed with a great deal of bombast—traits that the Arkansas, Louisiana, and Texas troops viewed with high disdain at best. Without McCulloch to see that his commands were obeyed, Van Dorn would have difficulty in controlling his frontier command, and even the loyal Maury admitted that McCulloch, "whose remarkable knowledge of the roads and country were much relied upon in the operations of that campaign," enabled Van Dorn to organize the two divisions into an army.[4]

In the saddle since dawn, Van Dorn struggled to take control of his army, but after riding hard all morning he suffered attacks of chills and fever, which sapped his strength. Unable to ride any farther, he continued the march in a horse-drawn ambulance. Hoping to cut Sigel's route of retreat before the Federal general realized that the Confederates were upon him, Van Dorn pressed his weary and half-frozen men until they began to fall out of the ranks, completely broken down. Some of the men remarked that "Van Dorn had forgotten he was riding and we were walking." In contrast, McCulloch rode with his own skirmishers, recognizable to troops all along the line. Cold, frostbitten infantrymen cheered him again and again and, as Hartje notes, "reserved their contempt for the little man in the ambulance."[5]

About midday the sun came out, drying the roads and allowing the column to make twenty-two miles that day. On the morning of 5 March the army passed through Fayetteville with McCulloch at the front, watching for signs of the enemy. "Some firing was heard that day," reported Watson, "but nothing of importance was done." The army camped for two hours on the night of the fifth a few miles south of Bentonville. Snow fell fast all night, and the cold remained bitter. There the Confederates learned from prisoners captured by McIntosh's scouting parties that Sigel still entertained no suspicion of their advance. The ever-optimistic Van Dorn was convinced that he could effect a complete surprise and could capture the Federals at Bentonville before they could fall back on Curtis. Two hours before day, therefore, McCulloch's cavalry moved out at the double-quick on Telegraph Road, hoping to reach Bentonville before Sigel heard of their coming. As the troopers reached the highlands two miles south of the town, however, Sigel's seven-thousand-man division was seen marching north. "Quick as thought," wrote Pvt. A. W. Sparks of the Ninth Texas Cavalry, the Third and Ninth Texas Cavalry regiments and Maj. William H. Brooks's First Arkansas Cavalry battalion "obliqued to the left and passed around the town" to the west while McCulloch sent the remainder of the Arkansas cavalry to skirt it on the right. If McIntosh's brigade could intercept Sigel's division above Bentonville and hold it in place, McCulloch could bring up his infantry to administer a death blow. But the Arkansas regiment lost its way, not reaching Telegraph Road until an hour or two after the left wing, while Sigel, enjoying his best day of the war, calculated exactly where the Rebel cavalry would reenter the road and placed his division in ambush.[6]

When the men of the Third Texas Cavalry rode into Sigel's trap, McIntosh attempted to retrieve the situation by ordering a charge, but fire from Sigel's masked batteries proved too much even for Greer's proud veterans. Confounded by surprise and shattered by the volume of Federal fire, the regiment could not be rallied for a second charge, despite McIntosh's best efforts. This skillful rearguard action bought Sigel the time to extricate his division, and when McCulloch reached the field with his infantry, rather than playing the hammer to McIntosh's anvil, he arrived only to see the Federal rear guard withdrawing in good order toward Little Sugar Creek. Setting out once again in pursuit along a road that led through a narrow canyon, the Confederate advance guard skirmished with the Union rear guard while Sigel used the terrain and his artillery to great advantage, keeping the Confederates at a respectful distance. The day's fighting ended when Sigel's division crossed Little Sugar Creek to rejoin Curtis's well-entrenched command. "Had we been one hour sooner we should have cut him off with his whole force, and certainly have beaten the enemy the next day," Van Dorn later lamented to Bragg.[7]

At the end of the day's frustrating chase the men of McCulloch's division rested on the southern bank of Little Sugar Creek, opposite Curtis's army. Dressed in a suit of dark, heavy velvet, McCulloch walked from campfire to campfire of the Third Louisiana. Seating himself at last on a rail near one of the fires, he chatted with the officers and men gathered thickly around him. That night, Tunnard later recalled, McCulloch was unusually reticent and spoke in a quiet, subdued voice, much unlike his customary "energetic, determined actions and speech." Only at the end of his fireside chat did he exclaim with some enthusiasm, "I tell you, men, the army that is defeated in this fight will get a h——l of a whipping!"[8]

Years later, a number of McCulloch's officers remembered how, that night, the twenty-sixth anniversary of the fall of the Alamo, the general lay on a blanket in front of a campfire, head in hands and seemingly lost in thought. At last he said to his staff, "Boys, we'll soon have bad news." In a quiet voice he recounted the recent fall of Forts Donelson and Henry and the retreat of Albert Sidney Johnston's army from Kentucky. He then predicted "a great battle" to be fought on the northern bank of the Tennessee River. Johnston would win, he told them, "if the South rallies to him; if not he will fail," and Memphis would fall to the enemy. Victories at Manassas and Oak Hills, he correctly observed, had "put the South asleep," making impossible the recruiting of units that ought to have been in the field. The North, on the other hand, had merely been stung from lethargy by its defeats. These battles were but skirmishes compared with what was to come, and McCulloch foresaw that the South's lost opportunities could be recovered only by great effort. Success was possible, he told his staff, only "if our people are resolved to make the sacrifice."[9]

The respite on Little Sugar Creek was brief; orders to advance came down soon after the men had eaten. Van Dorn had carefully questioned McCulloch, "who had an accurate knowledge of the locality," and learned that by making a flanking march of eight miles around Curtis's right wing on the Bentonville Detour he could not only avoid the formidable defenses on Little Sugar Creek but could place himself on Telegraph Road near Elkhorn Tavern, squarely on Curtis's rear. Van Dorn immediately adopted McCulloch's recommendation and halted his army on Curtis's front, threw out pickets, and bivouacked "as if for the night." Soon after dark, however, Price's division was in motion again, crossing Little Sugar Creek far to Curtis's right, marching north past old Camp McCulloch, and then turning east on the Bentonville Detour. Skirting the hamlet of Leetown, the leading division took this road eight miles around Pea Ridge, a 150-foot-high mountain extending two and one-half miles west from Elkhorn Tavern, and reentered Telegraph Road about three miles north of Curtis's headquarters. Once on Curtis's rear, Van Dorn would command the only road back to Missouri, placing the Federals in an inescapable trap.[10]

Unaccountably, however, Little Sugar Creek had not been bridged, and only two slim poles, laid side by side, spanned the icy creek to aid the soldiers' crossing. Fording was thus delayed for six or eight vital hours while the men struggled across, single file. The Bentonville Detour, in fact little more than a trail, had been obstructed by felled trees and other obstacles, and the head of Price's column did not gain Telegraph Road until nearly 10:00 A.M. on 7 March. Despite the unforeseen delay, Van Dorn achieved his primary objective, and, as one of Price's officers wrote, "The game seemed to be now in our own hands." Price's division advanced along Telegraph Road toward Elkhorn Tavern, finding only a few skirmishers and a single battery to oppose its progress. Without the loss of a man, Van Dorn and Price had turned Curtis out of a virtually impregnable position and placed the Missouri division squarely athwart the Federal line of communication. The Union army was still concentrated along Little Sugar Creek, facing the now-deserted Rebel camp. Soon discovering his peril, however, Curtis acted with speed and efficiency to meet the threat to his rear. With admirable presence of mind, the Federal commander began a masterful change of front under heavy pressure from Price's advance and by 11:30 was "pretty warmly engaged" along Telegraph Road. Nevertheless, the momentum remained with the Confederates, and the Missourians bore the enemy steadily back.[11]

McCulloch's division, meanwhile, was encountering maddening delays

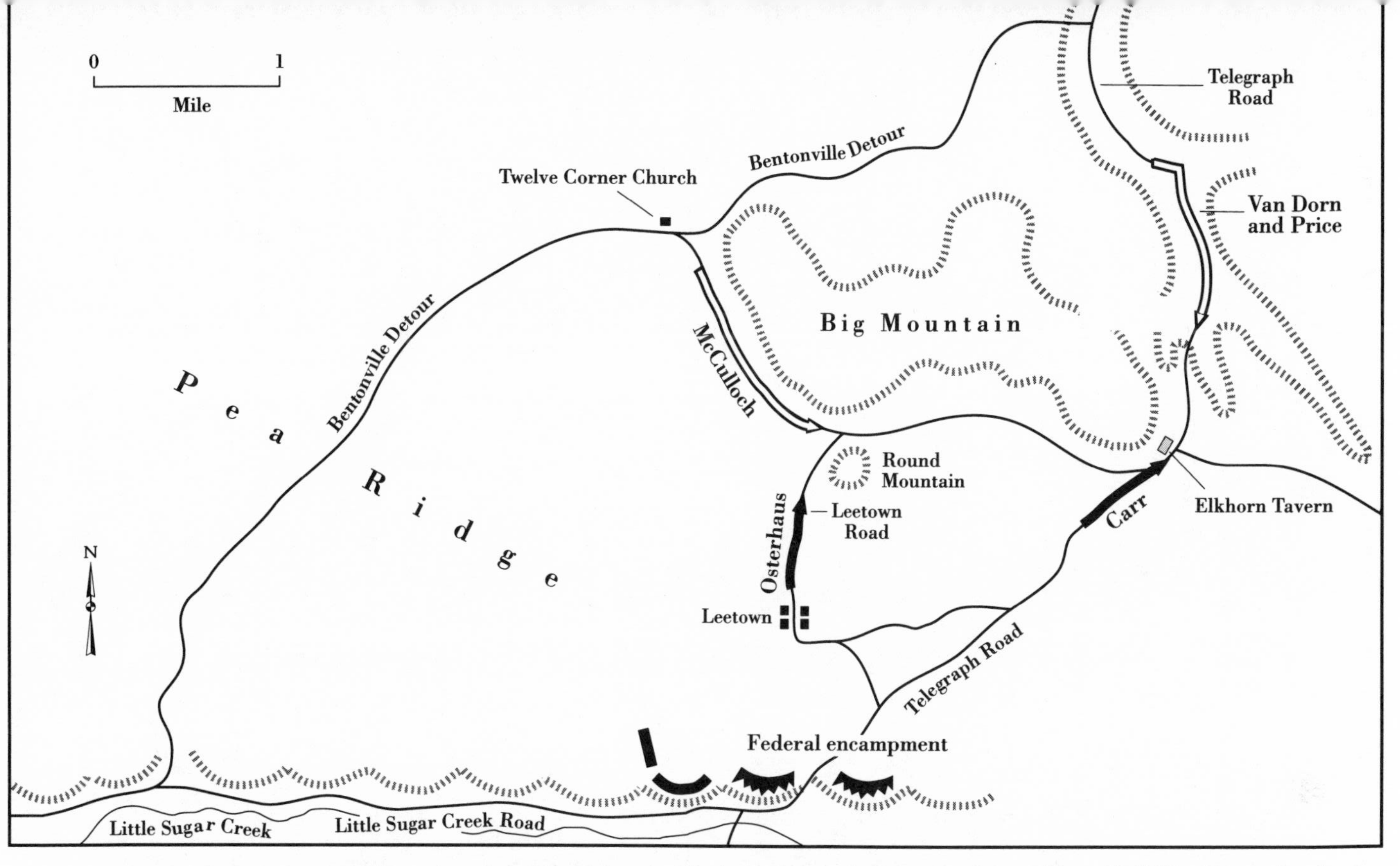

MAP 8. *Battle of Pea Ridge: Midday, 7 March (adapted from William L. Shea and Earl J. Hess,* Pea Ridge: Civil War Campaign in the West *[Chapel Hill: University of North Carolina Press, 1992])*

and misfortune. By 9:00 P.M. on 6 March his regiments were in marching order, ready to follow those of Price. The obstructions encountered by the Missouri division prevented McCulloch's men from moving out, however. The night was clear and bitterly cold, and Dr. Gammage recalled how "the men suffered immeasurably more while standing still than they possibly could had they been moving, however fast." Not until sunup did McIntosh's brigade follow the infantry and artillery on the narrow and obstructed road, but even then Pike's disorganized Choctaws, Cherokees, and Creeks choked the narrow roads, causing further delay.

The morning of 7 March 1862 dawned fair and clear, "as beautiful as any May morning," according to Gammage, and, over the creek at last, McCulloch placed McIntosh's cavalry brigade at the head of his column and set out to cover the six or seven miles between his position and the point on Telegraph Road where Price was fighting Curtis. Hébert's infantry brigade followed about 10:00 A.M. Under McCulloch's personal command it passed Leetown and marched up the valley toward the northern slope of Pea Ridge.[12]

With McCulloch's division at last on the Bentonville Detour and marching in good order toward the sound of Price's guns, the plan of battle was suddenly changed. With only some three miles separating the head of his column from Price's line of battle, McCulloch countermarched, retracing his steps to Round Mountain on the western flank of Pea Ridge, there to engage the enemy in a battle totally separated from that which Van Dorn and Price were fighting at Elkhorn Tavern. Although it was rumored in the army that Price and McCulloch wished to attack in separate columns in order that each might command his own men and "neither have priority or rank" over the other, the true reason for the change of plan in the midst of battle remains elusive. Col. Robert S. Bevier of the Fifth Missouri Infantry later wrote that "McCulloch sent to request that instead of closing up and joining us in our attack, he should strike the enemy from where he was" and received Van Dorn's consent. According to Maury's recollection, however, after the Missouri division closed with and was driving Curtis's front, Van Dorn sent McCulloch's ordnance officer, Lt. M. M. Kimmel, to order him to countermarch and attack Curtis's left flank at and below Elkhorn Tavern. Sul Ross later castigated Van Dorn for not "taking time to inform our generals—McCulloch and McIntosh—of the plans of the day by which the attack and the battle was to be conducted," sending only an order to attack the enemy on the western side of the mountain while he and Price would attack on the east. Gammage, who was standing near McCulloch when the courier from Van Dorn arrived, overheard only fragments of the conversation but understood Kimmel to say that Van Dorn "was mistaken" or that McCulloch "mistook the General." He was not sure which, but "something was said about a valley or 'hollow,'" and the courier pointed to a valley to the division's rear. McCulloch answered, "It is too late" since the valley was "a mile off." McCulloch then rode a little in front of the group that surrounded him and with a gesture of considerable impatience demanded, "Why don't they go on? What in the devil are they stopping for? Why don't they go on?" Col. Evander McNair then began to move his Fourth Arkansas Infantry back down the road it had just marched up.

Once the division changed front and was moving back toward Leetown, Sergeant Watson, marching at the head of the infantry brigade, was near McCulloch. "There was something in the general's countenance which betokened no good," he wrote. "I never saw such a change in a man's face. He seemed haggard and worn out with fatigue, but beyond this, there was in his countenance a mixed expression of melancholy, despair, and anger, which he seemed to try to hide, for, as he rode past he nodded to our captain, and said in an easy manner, 'We are going to take 'em on the other wing.' But it was easy to read through his countenance the expression—'Well, I will do it, but I know it is going to destruction.'"[13]

Retracing its line of march, the division debouched onto what Gammage described as "a level space covered by open but uncultivated fields and dense thickets of tangled vines and other undergrowth" reaching to the foot of Pea Ridge. Whatever opposition McCulloch's division might face was entirely hidden by the hills and woods and, as Watson wrote, "would have to be felt for." The division halted as it filed off the Bentonville Detour, and McCulloch drew up his three brigades in line of battle with the infantry and artillery on the left and the cavalry on the right. Pike and his Indians were to act as a dismounted reserve. Hearing the sound of Price's guns, only two miles to the east, without having time to reconnoiter the position or even locate the enemy, McCulloch plunged into the thick woods below the southwestern slopes of Pea Ridge toward Elkhorn Tavern.[14]

Perhaps Van Dorn had assumed that he and Price were facing Curtis's entire force at Elkhorn Tavern and that McCulloch would face no opposition as he marched to attack the enemy's left flank. Curtis, however, had dispatched Col. Peter J. Osterhaus with the Third Iowa Cavalry, eight troops of the First Missouri Cavalry, and three guns of Capt. Gustavus Elbert's Missouri Flying Artillery to hold McCulloch's division near Leetown. "It was patent," Osterhaus wrote after the battle, "that the enemy was preparing a most energetic attack on our right flank at the same time that they opened fire on our rear." Although the Federals were severely outnumbered, Osterhaus correctly judged that the safety of Curtis's defense of Elkhorn Tavern depended on checking McCulloch's advance. He therefore ordered Elbert's battery into line in the heavy underbrush and scrub oaks on a hill along McCulloch's line of march, and as the Confederate division skirted Round Mountain at about 11:00 A.M., the Federals opened fire from about five hundred yards on its right. "All at once," remembered Private Keen of the Sixth Texas, "away to the west end of the field, smoke arose and there came a rumbling noise like the heavens had split open, and a whistling noise like a square plantation tumbling through the air." A solid shot split an oak tree near where the young trooper sat.[15]

McCulloch, with Good's battery, was passing the Third Texas Cavalry just as the first shell went crashing through its ranks. Immediately he ordered Good to "wheel that battery into line." The gunners quickly unlimbered, and Good commanded Lt. James P. Douglas "to return them one." The Confederate riposte burst over a Federal gun, according to Good, killing all of their horses and most of the cannoneers.[16]

McCulloch then ordered the Third and Sixth Texas Cavalry regiments into reserve before sending McIntosh forward to carry the enemy battery. At McCulloch's command, McIntosh, "waving his saber overhead, led the furious and irresistible charge." Private Sparks, riding with the Ninth Texas Cavalry, compared the Rebel attack to "the impetuous rush of an avalanche." Pike's Indians were also ordered into the "helter-skelter charge, every Indian for himself, whooping and yelling at the top of his voice." When the battery opened on McCulloch's front, Osterhaus ordered Col. Cyrus Bussey's Third Iowa Cavalry forward against McCulloch's left. Meeting it in mid-career was "a wild, numerous, and irregular throng of cavalry, a great many Indians among them." Gammage, from his vantage point at the field hospital behind the Confederate line, saw the Federal cavalry dashing toward McIntosh's line and heard "the clash of swords" and "the shout of men" as the two lines of horsemen collided. The Rebel horse broke Bussey's charge and drove it from the field, forcing the enemy to abandon its three pieces of artillery. "This was our first view of a battlefield," wrote Pvt. William Harris of McNair's Fourth Arkansas Infantry, "and a fine sight it was!" The "war whoop" of the Indians mingled with the "Texas yell" as "the mad columns swept over the field," leaping an eight-rail fence and a ditch to take the battery, five hundred yards away, in less than ten minutes from the time that it opened fire. The supporting infantry and cavalry were routed "most completely," according to Lt. George L. Griscom of the Ninth Texas Cavalry.[17]

The Federal guns had a disastrously demoralizing effect upon the Creeks, Choctaws, and Cherokees, however, and as quickly as they could check their horses and turn, "back came every one of General Pike's Indians, faster than they had advanced, in a wild stampede to the rear." Private Harris met the retiring Indians as his regiment went into battle. "White man shoot wagon," they told him. Cater surmised that the Indian cavalry "was worth nothing to our army," coming onto the field only "to scalp and plunder" and fleeing at the first fire of Federal artillery.[18]

At 9:00 A.M. Osterhaus had ordered Col. Nicholas Greusel of the Thirty-sixth Illinois Infantry to pull his command out of its defensive position along Little Sugar Creek and to report to him at Leetown. Just as Osterhaus's line was in danger of disintegrating before McIntosh's wild assault, Greusel arrived with his own regiment plus the Twelfth Missouri Infantry, Company E of the Third Illinois, and the batteries of captains Louis Hoffman and Martin Welfley. While forming his line, Greusel was surprised by the "precipitate retreat" of Bussey's cavalry, but his own command stood firm and opened a brisk artillery fire on the pursuing Rebel cavalry, which, wrote Greusel, prevented its following up the retreat.

After observing McIntosh's triumph, McCulloch once more rode by the Texas battery, "with the glow of victory on his face, and asked only success." In reply to fire from Hoffman's and Welfley's guns, McCulloch led two of Good's sections forward through the woods and ordered them into battery, pointing out the location of the enemy artillery some five hundred yards to the front. Pvt. Robert H. Hughes remembered how McCulloch rode up to his gun and directed it to the edge of a wood lot, commanding a large open prairie to its left. He then indicated the two or three points of timber beyond the prairie at which he wished the gunners to direct their fire. The two batteries exchanged fire for nearly an hour, and according to Pvt. Sam Thompson, "The duel was a hot one." The men of Good's battery had arrived too late to participate in the battle of Oak Hills, so the "scream of the shell and the swoop of the solid shot was truly a baptism of fire for the boys. But with a coolness that veterans might envy," Thompson wrote, "every man stood to his guns and served the battery in splendid style."[19]

McCulloch then ordered Hébert's brigade to strip for battle and personally formed his regiments into line of battle. J. M. Bailey, color sergeant of the Sixteenth Arkansas, recalled McCulloch riding along his regiment's

Battle of Elkhorn Tavern. In the opening phase of the battle, Col. Peter J. Osterhaus reported, "a wild, numerous, and irregular throng of cavalry, a great many Indians among them, rushed towards us, breaking through our lines. A general discharge of fire-arms on both sides created a scene of wild confusion,

from which our cavalry, abandoning the three pieces of artillery, retreated."
Lithograph by Louis Kurz
(author's collection)

front, deploying skirmishers. At the same time McIntosh aligned three of his cavalry regiments and Whitfield's battalion somewhat to the right of the infantry. As the Federals were completely concealed by the undergrowth and broken terrain, none of the Confederates was certain of the location of the opposing line. McCulloch assured Hébert, however, that "as soon as you have drawn their fire, you shall have support speedily—and good support, too," from the cavalry and from such of Pike's Indians as could be rallied. At about 1:30 P.M. McCulloch personally led the infantry brigade as it advanced against Osterhaus's right wing, "with the object, no doubt, of observing the position of the enemy after the fire opened" and determining where the rest of the division could best be engaged.[20]

The brigade stepped out "with alacrity and cheerfulness," but due to the tangled and broken terrain, it was forced to halt after only two hundred yards to realign. While dressing its ranks, the infantry came under a severe fire of shell and grape but renewed the charge with great élan. The Confederate cavalrymen could hear volleys of musketry "crashing from the hills across the valley below, whilst the booming of cannon and the bursting of shells kept one continuous roar." Just as Hébert's men overran their objective, however, Col. Jefferson Columbus Davis's fresh brigade arrived on McCulloch's front and counterattacked Hébert's line, checking its advance and preventing its breakthrough to Elkhorn Tavern. Although the Federal division facing Price and Van Dorn was seriously challenged near the tavern, and its commander, Col. Eugene Asa Carr, had sustained three wounds, Curtis's transfer of Davis's brigade to the Leetown front proved one of the wisest moves of the day.[21]

The Missouri division, until this time, had slowly but relentlessly pushed back the Federal line, and by 2:00 P.M. Van Dorn was writing confidently to McCulloch that if his division would "continue to advance or even maintain its ground," Price could deliver the death blow to the enemy on Telegraph Road. Before the message was delivered, however, Maj. Edward Dillon of McCulloch's staff galloped up "with disaster on his face." Reining in beside Van Dorn, he whispered, "McCulloch is killed, McIntosh killed, Hébert is killed, and the attack on the front is ceased."[22]

With Davis's brigade stiffening resistance on the Leetown front, McCulloch, ever the ranger, rode to the front of the Confederate line, telling Lunsford L. Lomax and Frank C. Armstrong, "I will ride forward a little and reconnoiter the enemy's position." He instructed his staff to remain behind, however, saying, "Your gray horses will attract the fire of the sharpshooters." Mounted on his handsome sorrel, McCulloch passed

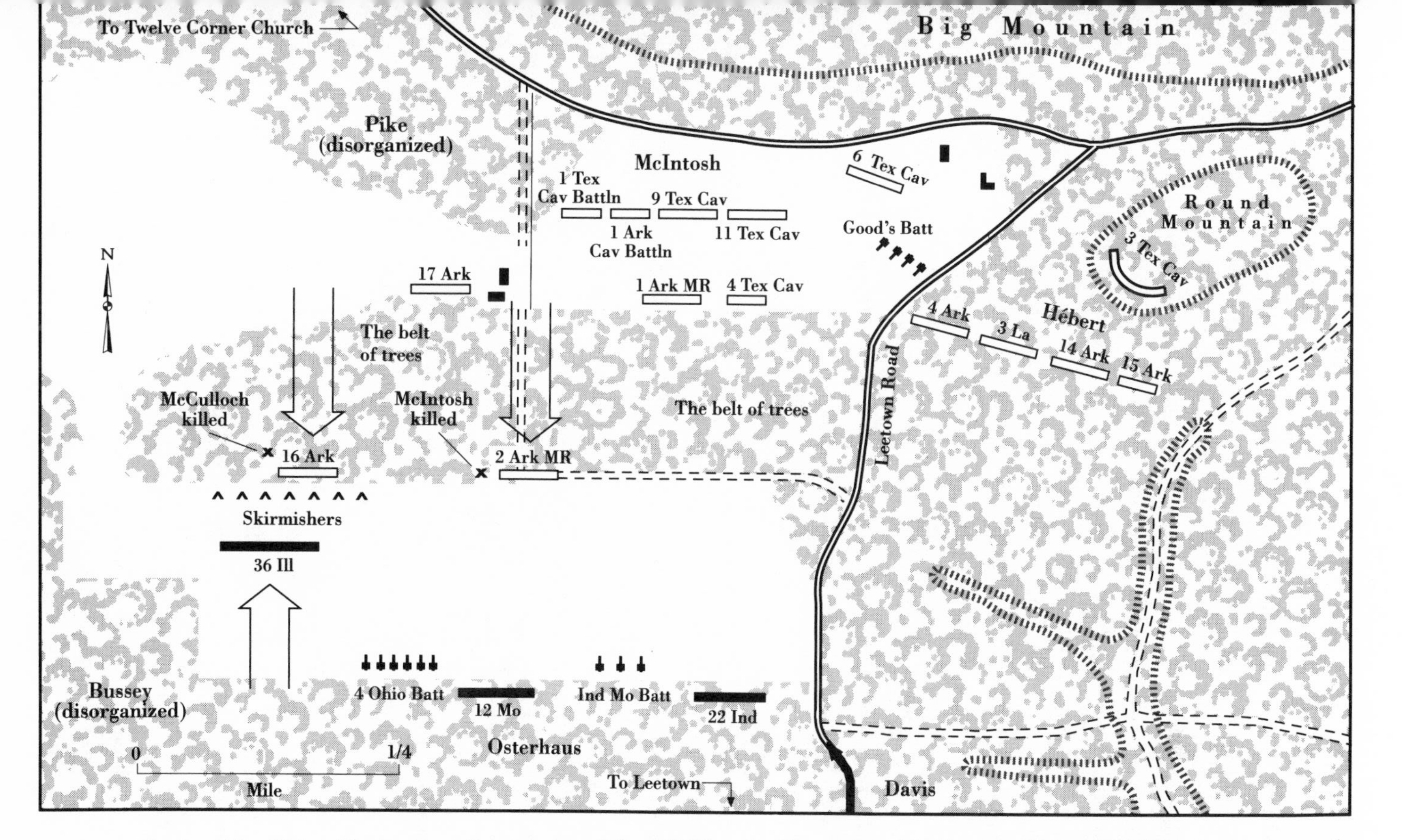

MAP 9. *Battle of Pea Ridge: The Leetown Front (adapted from William L. Shea and Earl J. Hess,* Pea Ridge: Civil War Campaign in the West *[Chapel Hill: University of North Carolina Press, 1992])*

quickly from sight, riding forward about three hundred yards to a line of brush on a slight elevation between the lines before stopping to view the enemy. "In a moment," reported Maj. John Henry Brown, "was heard a volley, fired from at least twenty-five rifles." The 1858 prophecy of the New York "witch, wizard, or imposter" that Ben McCulloch would die by a bullet on the battlefield was fulfilled. McIntosh and Lt. Samuel M. Hyams, Jr., adjutant of the Third Louisiana, had kept their commander in view as he rode forward and were perhaps the only Rebel witnesses to his death. Galloping furiously down the line, McIntosh met Captain Armstrong. "I fear the general is killed," he cried. "A whole company of skirmishers fired upon him; he clasped the pommel of his saddle and fell forward." Hyams later corroborated this account, adding that the general fell near a large tree, and his horse, wounded in four places, "ran furiously away," later to be appropriated by one of Pike's Indians.[23]

McIntosh, now in command of the division, at once ordered a charge to recover McCulloch's body and, "with that conspicuous gallantry which was part of his nature," wrote Private Rose, "led the foremost, sword in hand." Like Marshal Michael Ney, the impetuous McIntosh "was at home only amidst the raging of wild elements" and "courted the missions of danger with a fondness not surpassed by the affection of a lover for his mistress." Like Napoleon's "bravest of the brave" when confronted with the crisis of command at Waterloo, he reacted with the one weapon at his disposal, the charge. He achieved the death that Ney had sought, falling at the very muzzles of the enemy guns, sword in hand.

John F. Hill's Sixteenth and Frank A. Rector's Seventeenth Arkansas regiments succeeded in seizing the line of brush where McCulloch lay and recovering his body. Sergeant Bailey ascribed to Pvt. John Jones of Company D of Hill's regiment the distinction of discovering the body. By his account, Jones called to Bailey, "Here is Gen. McCulloch." Bailey found him lying full length on his back with a bullet hole in his right breast. The calm and placid expression on his face indicated that death was instantaneous and without a struggle. McCulloch's Morse rifle, which Bailey had seen him carrying not twenty minutes earlier, was gone, as were his field glasses and watch. Lt. Benjamin T. Pixley, adjutant of the Sixteenth Arkansas, was summoned, and either he or Colonel Rector covered McCulloch's body with his cloak, saying, "We must not let the men know that General McCulloch is killed." A nearby soldier caught a glimpse, however, and gasped, "My God, its poor old Ben!" A detail of four men from Company D carried the body a short distance to the rear where it was placed in Col.

W. B. Sims's ambulance and borne back through the Rebel ranks. The body of McIntosh, however, was not recovered until next day.[24]

Horror followed horror on the Confederate right. McIntosh's death occurred soon after that of McCulloch, and Louis Hébert, the ranking officer on the field, was captured along with Col. M. C. Mitchell of the Fourteenth Arkansas when the infantry, while pursuing Davis's retreating brigade, fell victim to a flanking attack by fresh Union troops. Pike, a skilled lawyer and a poet but not a soldier, spent the balance of the day in a vain attempt to rally his "little command of Indians" and did not learn until 3:00 P.M. that the authority had devolved upon him. He then gathered a handful of McCulloch's units and marched east to rejoin Van Dorn, leaving the largest part of the division again leaderless. Van Dorn apparently never thought of taking personal command of McCulloch's division, although he was only a short ride from the Leetown front and Price was perfectly capable of overseeing the operations of the Missouri division at Elkhorn Tavern.[25]

With no one to coordinate the movements of its units, McCulloch's division could only stand and receive the punishment of the enemy. Good's battery, stationed near the front, became the target of the concentrated fire of the Federal artillery, and no Confederate officer remained on the field to order it to retire or to support it with infantry or cavalry. "From this artillery fire we suffered severely," wrote Private Hughes, whose gun lost four of its seven men, ten of its twelve horses, and its caisson.[26]

Thomas J. Churchill of the First Arkansas Mounted Rifles was likewise stymied by a lack of orders and sought instruction for his idle regiment. Riding up to Good's battery he inquired of Pike as to the whereabouts of General McCulloch. "I think, Colonel, he must be dead upon the field," Pike replied, for "he cannot be found or heard from; and fearing the day is lost, I have ordered our troops to retire." Churchill's regiment therefore marched with Pike to Price's side of Pea Ridge.[27]

The Third and Sixth Texas Cavalry, serving as the division's mounted reserve, received no further orders and so stood subject to Federal artillery "playing full" upon them for the remainder of the day. "On account of the fall—the fated fall—of our illustrious Generals McCulloch and McIntosh," Col. B. Warren Stone wrote, the regiments were never engaged. Several hours elapsed before Stone learned certainly of McCulloch's fate; during that time he had dispatched officers and aides to every part of the field for orders. Because the Confederate line began to disintegrate before him and still he was not ordered to the front, Stone was left "in the most perplexed condition and mental anguish." Only when the infantry brigade gave way and the Federals attempted to turn his left flank late in the evening did he put the Sixth Texas Cavalry into motion.[28]

The Third Texas Cavalry, still one thousand strong, stood to horse near Round Mountain, likewise awaiting orders. "We did not know that McCulloch and McIntosh had been killed," wrote Private Cater, "but we knew that something was wrong" because the regiment was "idle too long." It "had not fired a gun and did not know why we were not ordered forward." During the day Greer had repeatedly sent messengers for orders from McCulloch and McIntosh, but none had arrived. Learning from Major Brown that the division's right wing was faring badly, and from Colonel McRae that the enemy "were advancing in overwhelming force," Greer at last ordered his regiment to the center of the field near where the division had first been fired upon that morning. Only then did he encounter officers from McCulloch's staff who informed him that he was the senior officer on the field. Greer at once assumed command of the remaining forces, but by this time the Rebel line was beginning to give way. After consulting with his officers, he ordered a general withdrawal.[29]

Throughout the afternoon, units of the infantry brigade continued fighting in isolation and without coordination. Although they repulsed all Federal attacks, the Confederate regiments began at last to drift from the field. As the Third Louisiana lost its momentum and ground to a halt for want of leadership, Sergeant Watson encountered the second lieutenant now commanding Company A who informed him of the deaths of McCulloch and McIntosh and the capture of Hébert. "Every field officer in the brigade is *hors de combat*," the lieutenant said, informing Watson that he did not know who commanded the brigade or even the regiment. "Well," responded Watson, "if McCulloch and McIntosh are gone, good-bye to the Army of the West."[30]

No sooner had the grievous news of McCulloch's and McIntosh's deaths reached Van Dorn than the tide of battle began to turn at Elkhorn Tavern as well. Alexander S. Asboth's fresh division arrived to sustain Carr's front, and while the exhausted Missourians held their ground, the Rebel offensive ground to a halt. After learning of McCulloch's death, Van Dorn ordered Greer to withdraw McCulloch's division and lead it to the aid of the Missouri division. Coincidentally, Greer had already issued the command. At 1:30 A.M. on 8 March, McCulloch's division started to Price's aid "in as good order as we ever went on dress parade."[31]

This residue of McCulloch's division marched around the northern slope of Pea Ridge to Telegraph Road and thence south to a junction with Price's men. Greer was ordered to Price's left, where for two hours he anchored the eastern flank of the Confederate line in idleness but under heavy cannonading. After a few piecemeal charges on the enemy and some desultory firing, apparently without spirit or object, Van Dorn ordered his army to disengage, leaving the Third Texas Cavalry to cover his retreat. Quitting the field at Elkhorn, Van Dorn moved entirely around Curtis's army and camped fourteen miles west of Fayetteville. "The Army of the West, which had never before turned its back to the foe, sullenly retired from the scene, leaving the defeated enemy in possession of the field," wrote Sparks.[32]

To the ordinary Confederate soldier, Van Dorn's retreat from Elkhorn Tavern was an inexcusable act of cowardice, especially considering his heavy reserve force and his cavalry's unbroken fighting spirit. "We whipped them! We butchered them!" wrote the sardonic Pvt. H. McBride Pridgen of Whitfield's cavalry battalion. "We exterminated them! and I don't believe there was but one man that escaped to tell the tale, and he stole my blankets!" McCulloch's cavalry brigade, "which consisted of about five thousand as fine men as ever rode astride a horse," was not committed to the fighting following the general's death. "We had lost McCulloch and McIntosh," wrote Cater, "but many of our troops had not fired a gun, and we were ready to make a forward move under command of Colonel Greer, with every hope of success." Van Dorn, to whom Sergeant Watson referred thereafter as "Damn Born," apparently lost his nerve and seems to have conducted his operation the day after McCulloch's death with a view only to quit the field with no further losses. He admitted to Albert Sidney Johnston that he had continued the battle on Price's front on 8 March "for the purpose only of getting off the field without the danger of panic." Van Dorn was pleased to report a successful disengagement but admitted "some losses."[33]

In his precipitate retreat the commanding general lost what little faith his men had invested in him. "General Van Dorn is very unpopular with the whole army," wrote David Pierson. "We all feel that our best friends and the champions of the west fell in the persons of McCulloch and McIntosh." Van Dorn defended his actions, however, with the excuse that his right wing was "somewhat disorganized" and his army was without provisions. These factors, coupled with what he saw as Curtis's strong position below Elkhorn Tavern, left him "no alternative," he explained to Judah P. Benjamin, "but to retire from the contest."[34]

To his sister Emily, Van Dorn wrote that he had "fought a great battle" and that although he "did not succeed in entirely routing the enemy," he had captured two batteries. With the loss of McCulloch and McIntosh, "prudence dictated me not to hazard another days [*sic*] fighting and I withdrew with tears in my eyes—the first battle in my life I was ever compelled to fall back from an enemy." Nevertheless, "a heavy blow was struck them," he boasted to Benjamin, "and they are somewhat paralyzed. I shall march to another field before they recover, and before their re-enforcements arrive."[35]

Pvt. Newton Keen, however, summed up the feelings of the soldiers: "General Van Dorn was perhaps the only man in the army that was whipped. He was a poor general and the men had no confidence in him." Keen was confident that he and his comrades "could have captured every wagon the Yankees had and could have crushed either wing of the army, but we had no general to lead us."[36]

Among the Confederates, from the lowest private to the commanding general, the untimely deaths of Ben McCulloch and his principal lieutenant were rendered accountable for the debacle at Elkhorn and the consequent collapse of southern control of Missouri. "We were whipping the Feds very nicely," wrote D. R. Garrett, "until McCulloch and McIntosh fell, & no sooner did they fall, & their whole command stampeded and scattered all over the mountains." Lieutenant Griscom lamented that when "that gallant patriot Ben McCulloch fell in front of his column near his favorite Third Louisiana Infantry," the division was so discouraged "that it done no more good, so to speak, during that battle." L. H. Graves, whose regiment was "exposed to the enemy's burnt-shells and minnie balls" with no chance to strike back, learned of McCulloch's death sometime between 10:00 and 11:00 P.M. "McCulloch and McIntosh falling accounts for us being so exposed to the Federal bullets without being ordered to return some of their fire," he maintained. "Had McCulloch and McIntosh lived, the victory would have been so complete on our side." Private Sparks agreed that "had McCulloch and McIntosh lived; had Hébert been spared us; or had Colonel Greer known that the carnival of death and misfortune had devolved the command upon himself," the Federal army would have been driven back upon Elkhorn Tavern, "where but the alternative of surrender or destruction" awaited it. In Sergeant Tunnard's mind as well, McCulloch's death "undoubtedly lost the battle. The enemy were completely beaten at every point, and had our reserve forces been ordered up at the proper moment, the victory would have been most signal," he wrote. But when the Louisianians learned of McCulloch's death, "many of these lion-hearted men threw themselves in wild grief upon the ground, weeping scalding tears in bitter sorrow. It is a fearful spectacle to see a strong-hearted man thus give way to his feelings. It demonstrates the devotion felt for General McCulloch, and shows how deeply he was enshrined in these brave souls." To Colonel Stone the crux of the battle came when "the gallant, chivalrous McCulloch fell, embalming his country's cause with his own blood, and depriving his admiring soldiery of their military chieftain and idol."[37]

Earl Van Dorn, no less than McCulloch's own men, lamented his loss. "I had found him," he wrote to Braxton Bragg, "in the frequent conferences I had with him, a sagacious, prudent counselor, and a bolder soldier never died for his country." In his general order to the army on 16 March 1862, the commanding general wrote that "the victorious advance of McCulloch's division upon the strong position of the enemy's front was inevitably checked by the misfortunes which now sadden the hearts of our countrymen throughout the Confederacy." McCulloch's fall, together with that of McIntosh, "in the full tide of success," completely undermined "the confidence and hope of their troops," Van Dorn maintained. "No success can repair the loss of such leaders. It is only left to us to mourn their untimely fall, emulate their heroic courage and avenge their death." Frank C. Armstrong later quoted Van Dorn as saying that he regretted "that he had not followed McCulloch's suggestions in regard to the anticipated battle and movements of the enemy" and that he "believed to the day of his death that had he given weight to them he would have been *successful* and *captured* Curtis' army." Van Dorn "learned too late," wrote Armstrong, "that he had not appreciated and had done McCulloch great injustice."[38]

AFTERWORD

I Leave My Soul to God Who Gave It, and My Body to the State of Texas

Although the loss of McCulloch was certainly the principal cause of the worst disaster to befall the Confederacy in the trans-Mississippi theater, the circumstances of his death remain the subject of much dispute, with some sources even attributing his demise to the marksmanship of the famous "Wild Bill" Hickok. Even the Confederate accounts of his death are contradictory, with Sul Ross reporting that "this noble and brave man" and one aide had ridden forward together and that he was found mortally wounded. "Well knowing the effect that knowledge would produce in the ranks," wrote Ross, McCulloch "had General McIntosh informed of the fact and laid down and quietly died with a frown on his face." Brown reported, however—and the nature of his wound would seem to verify—that his death was instantaneous.

Union colonels Osterhaus and Greusel were sure that McCulloch fell at the hand of a soldier of Company B of the Thirty-sixth Illinois, Peter

Pelican, who, in fact, stole McCulloch's gold watch and presented it to Colonel Greusel. Sgt. J. M. Bailey of the Sixteenth Arkansas, one of the first Confederates to reach McCulloch's body, confirms that the general's watch was missing and claims that after the war he was informed by Union veterans of Elkhorn that they learned of McCulloch's death by seeing his name engraved on the watch and were thus given hope to continue the struggle. The fact that Pelican was the first to reach McCulloch's body does not, however, prove that he killed the Confederate general or even that he was aware of his identity. Basing his opinion on the Federals' earliest reports of the battle, in which they claimed victory but did not mention the death of McCulloch, Brown assumes that the Federals did not know of his death for two days afterward. Confederate witnesses contend, moreover, that rather than by a single sharpshooter, McCulloch "was fired at by one entire company of skirmishers, and the pretense that he was killed by any . . . particular individual, is one of the things impossible ever to be determined by anyone."[1]

Brown's diary suggests that McCulloch's body was first buried on the field where he fell but was disinterred that night and was removed to Bentonville. Brown took possession of it there and drove it by ambulance first to Fayetteville on 8 March and then with the retreating army toward Fort Smith. At Van Buren, just north of Fort Smith, a detachment of the old Pulaski Battery received McCulloch's and McIntosh's bodies at the storerooms of Wallace & Ward, where they were prepared for burial. Two of the battery's caissons then bore the bodies to their graves in the government cemetery at Fort Smith.[2]

McCulloch's burial was perhaps the most lavish military funeral to that date in the Confederacy. The ceremony took place at noon on Monday, 10 March. McCulloch's body was borne to the cemetery with his aides, a detachment of cavalry, Capt. James G. Gaines's battery, Woodruff's battery, a detachment of infantry, and General Van Dorn and his staff leading the funeral caisson. The veterans of Oak Hills, under the command of N. B. Pearce, and then civilians, who were also invited to "perform this melancholy duty," followed.[3]

Minute guns sounded during the procession, and as the head of the column reached the grave, it halted and opened ranks. The general's coffin passed through, followed by the officers and soldiers of Oak Hills and the citizens who had followed his body. The funeral ritual was performed by the post chaplain, the Reverend Mr. Sanders, and a squad from the Ninth Texas Cavalry fired the parting salvo over their general's grave.[4]

On 11 March McCulloch's personal possessions were inventoried and mementos were distributed among the members of his staff and other longtime acquaintances. His "ivory pistol" went to Frank Armstrong and his spyglass to N. Bart Pearce. To Ben's mother, Brown brought a lock of his hair and a recent ambrotype photograph, and to Henry he gave the minié ball that felled his brother.[5]

On the twelfth McCulloch's body was again disinterred and prepared for transport to Texas. Not until 17 March, however, did the weather allow John Henry Brown, with only a driver and the general's black body-servant, John, as company, to depart Fort Smith in a mule-drawn wagon to deliver the general to his final resting place in Austin. McCulloch's funeral journey took thirty-three days. Memorial services were held at Sherman, Dallas, Waco, Belton, and half a dozen other Texas cities along the route, and Brown delivered eulogies ten times to the general whom he adored. "When Ben McCulloch fell," said Brown, "a star fell from its orbit. He was the most unselfish man I ever saw, and God made him a general of high order. I never estimated his character at a fourth of its exalted worth till I saw him in the service."[6]

From McKinney, Texas, on 26 March 1862, Brown wrote to inform Governor Francis Richard Lubbock that he was "thus far en route for Austin" with McCulloch's remains and expected to reach "the Asylum," the state school for the deaf near Austin, between 10:00 and 11:30 A.M. on 9 April. "I am thus precise," he wrote, "in that you, as the Chief Magistrate of our grief stricken State, may make all suitable and timely dispositions to receive and inter all that remains of the exalted patriot." Brown called on the governor to see that "the people know that true hearts may pay the last homage to the illustrious dead." Henry E. McCulloch, on learning that Ben's remains would not arrive in Austin until 9 April, determined to meet Brown en route. "This, as you know," he wrote to his old comrade Edward Burleson, Jr., "is a heavy blow upon me. I have come nearer sinking under it than any other that has ever fallen on me."[7]

On the morning of 9 April, Brown arrived in Austin with the general's body. They were met by Governor Lubbock, who "received it in the name of the State, feeling that she was honored in possessing the body of so true and grand a citizen," and escorted the remains to the state capitol, where they lay in state in the Representatives Hall from 4:00 P.M. on Wednesday until 2:00 P.M. on Thursday. At 11:00 A.M. Brown once more delivered his eulogy to the thousands of citizens assembled in the hall, narrating the course of the battle in which McCulloch died and rehearsing "the military accomplishments, patriotism, and noble single heartedness of our gallant Ranger General." Henry E. McCulloch, a colonel commanding the western district of Texas, then addressed the audience "in a voice tremulous with emotion." Ben, he told his fellow Texans, "had in his will commended his soul to his God, and bequeathed his body to his State." As executor of that will, Henry now commended that body to Governor Lubbock and with it pledged his own life. After Lubbock's response an "immense concourse," said to be a mile and a half long, the largest ever assembled in Texas, formed at the statehouse. The Reverend John W. Phillips of the Methodist Church read from the Scripture, and Bishop Alexander Gregg of the Episcopal Church offered a prayer. Brown once again delivered a eulogy. Governor Lubbock delivered an address, and Henry made closing remarks. McCulloch's coffin, draped in a Confederate flag and covered with bouquets and evergreens, was lowered into the ground in the state cemetery where, Lubbock later wrote, "it rests with the mortal remains of the great Albert Sidney Johnston."[8]

Ben McCulloch's will, read on 26 May 1862, left to Henry everything in his possession except "so much of my money as will purchase a Negro girl not to be less than twelve years of age" to serve as a maid to his niece Frances Rush McCulloch "in consideration of her kindness to me whilst sick" at her father's home in November and December 1857. He also requested that Henry see that their mother should "not need anything that money can purchase so long as there is one dollar left in my effects," and that his favorite nephew, Benjamin Eustace McCulloch, should be given "such portion of my effects as he may deem proper." Finally, as Henry had alluded on the day of Ben's funeral, the general had written, "I leave my soul to God who gave it, and my body to the State of Texas."[9]

Soon after McCulloch's death Sam Houston bitterly prophesied that Davis's "unhappy penchant for the West Point scrubs" would bring disaster to the Confederate cause, and Braxton Bragg wrote to Davis, "I do not see what can extricate us but God. The West Pointers have . . . generaled us to the verge of death itself." Indeed, like Van Dorn, many regular officers proved themselves poorly equipped to handle wartime commands. William T. Sherman's assessment, however, is closest to the truth. West Point, he wrote, had "in the past provided, and doubtless will in the future provide an ample supply of good officers." Should their numbers prove insufficient, Sherman was sure that America could "always safely rely on the great number of young men of education and force of character throughout the country, to supplement them." During the Civil War, he contended, "some of our best corps and division generals, as well as staff-officers, were from civil life." He further stated, however, that he did not know any of them "who did not express a regret that he had not received early in life instruction in the elementary principles of the art of war, instead of being forced to acquire this knowledge in the dangerous and expensive school of actual war."[10]

Although the difference between regular and volunteer officers on both sides was not always discernible, by the end of the Civil War the American military tradition had clearly experienced a sea change. Ironically, Jefferson Davis won his war, for thereafter the epaulet was increasingly the prerogative of the trained professional, and general's stars were to become more and more the exclusive province of leaders educated at West Point. The high ranking of men such as Ben McCulloch became increasingly anachronistic as education replaced experience as the sine qua non of leadership and advancement in the military as well as in most other aspects of American life.[11]

The true test of an officer, however, remained his ability to carry on large-scale operations and to fight successfully. His capacity to profit from experience was also a vital factor. Regulars alone were not privy to the principles of war. As one volunteer who rose to become a successful corps commander pointed out, those principles are so brief and simple that "they could be printed on the back of a visiting card." War, in the words of Britain's World War I prime minister, Lloyd George, "is not an exact science like chemistry or mathematics where it would be presumption on the part of anyone ignorant of its first rudiments to express an opinion contrary to those who had thoroughly mastered its principles. War is an art, proficiency in which depends more on experience than on study, and more on natural aptitude and judgment than on either."[12]

Judged by these criteria, Ben McCulloch was a successful officer and one deserving of greater rank, responsibility, and recognition than he received from the United States or the Confederate States War Department, both under the leadership or supervision of Jefferson Davis. McCulloch was not the American Cincinnatus. His ambition was to be a professional soldier, never to return to the plow. Although McCulloch was as well read on military history, tactics, and weapons development as almost any officer in the United States Army, the prizes that he most eagerly sought eluded him: a commission as colonel of a regiment of United States regulars and, during the Civil War, command of troops in Tennessee or Virginia. His aspirations came to naught in the face of Davis's inflexible vision of a United States and, later, a Confederate army based on the French and Prussian models, organized to perfection by Napoleon and Sharnhorst and led by officers trained at St. Cyr, the École Polytechnique, and the Kreigsakademie.

As commander of the Confederate trans-Mississippi district, burdened with Richmond's mandate to cooperate with the well-intentioned but strategically naive Sterling Price of Missouri, McCulloch received intense but undeserved criticism from both the press and the War Department, and he was superseded by a man of less capacity and judgment, Earl Van Dorn. His dramatic death at the battle of Elkhorn Tavern in March 1862 brought an abrupt close to a career defined by extremes of glory and frustration.

McCulloch, however, had proved himself resourceful and highly adaptive, and, given his outstanding organizational skills, his genius for reconnaissance, and, perhaps most important, the tremendously high regard of his troops, had he been spared to the South, he might well have gone on to higher command and greater glory. His failure to achieve higher command can be attributed solely to his lack of formal training and what William Watson characterized as his "utter abhorrence of all red-tape and bureau government." "Had the latter not been against him," the perceptive Sergeant Watson remarked, "he would have made his mark as a daring general and leader of a flying column."[13]

Notwithstanding his many setbacks at the hands of Jefferson Davis and despite his untimely death, Ben McCulloch did make his mark. Rising from private in the Tennessee militia to gunner in Sam Houston's army at San Jacinto to captain of Texas Rangers, McCulloch established a reputation as one of the finest young soldiers in a republic justly renowned for its military prowess. His vital service as chief of scouts on the staff of Zachary Taylor in Mexico broadened his reputation to national and even international proportions so that in the years between the war with Mexico and the Civil War he was elected or appointed major general of Texas militia, sheriff of Sacramento, United States marshal for eastern Texas, and peace commissioner to the Mormons. He was offered the post of governor of two Federal territories and was spoken of seriously as a candidate for governor of and senator from Texas. As the Confederate general responsible for the defense of the wing of the Confederacy west of the Mississippi River, McCulloch, virtually unassisted by Richmond, raised, organized, and led with remarkable skill and flawless courage a small but efficient army that, in August 1861, won a consequential victory at Oak Hills, ridding southern Missouri of Federal occupation.

However far-flung his fame, McCulloch remained very much a man of the people. A Jacksonian Democrat in an officer corps whose critics charged it with rampant Whiggish elitism, McCulloch never put on a uniform, never recoiled from sleeping on the bare ground or sharing a meager meal with his men, and delighted in swapping tales with them around the evening campfire. Even as a general he remained Old Ben to his soldiers and to the many civilians who knew him. From Arkansas, where in 1862 he commanded a brigade of Maj. Gen. John G. Walker's Texas Division, Henry E. McCulloch wrote to an old friend in Texas: "I find that my noble Brother made thousands of friends in this country, and I often meet those whom I have never seen before and see them shed tears when they speak of him. . . . Oh, that I could fill his place."[14]

Notes

PROLOGUE

1. *Register of Debates in Congress* (Washington, D.C.: Gales and Seaton, 1830), 25 February 1830, 583; *Congressional Globe*, 1856–58, pt. 1, 646, 672.

2. Richard Hofstader, *The American Political Tradition and the Men Who Made It* (New York: Knopf, 1955), 57–59; Samuel C. Reid, *The Scouting Expeditions of McCulloch's Texas Rangers* (Philadelphia: G. B. Zieber and Co., [1847]; reprint, Freeport, N.Y.: Books for Libraries, [1970]), 23; William H. Tunnard, *A Southern Record: The History of the Third Regiment Louisiana Infantry* (Baton Rouge: n.p., 1866; reprint, Dayton, Ohio: Morningside Bookshop, 1970), 107–8, 157–59.

CHAPTER ONE

1. W. H. Bailey, Sr., *The Genealogy of the Latham-Hill-Montfort-Littlejohn-McCulloch-Campbell and Brownrigg Families* (Houston: n.p., 1899), 39–44; Archibald Henderson, *North Carolina: The Old North State and the New* (Chicago: Lewis Pub. Co., 1941), 1:147, 209, 228, 276.

2. Bailey, *Genealogy*, 39–44; Victor M. Rose, *The Life and Services of Gen. Ben McCulloch* (Philadelphia: Pictorial Bureau of the Press, 1888; reprint, Austin: Steck Co., 1958), 26–27; unidentified newspaper clipping, Ben and Henry Eustace McCulloch Papers (hereafter referred to as McCulloch Papers), Barker Texas History Center, University of Texas at Austin (hereafter referred to as BTHC); *Scotsman*, 26 March 1892; Walter Clark, ed., *The State Records of North Carolina* (Goldsboro, N.C.: Nash Brothers, 1907), 9:1176, 22:896–99.

3. Samuel McCulloch to Alexander McCulloch, June 1803, McCulloch Papers, BTHC; G. W. D. Harris, Nashville *Christian Advocate*, 12 August 1846; unidentified newspaper clipping, McCulloch Papers, BTHC; Rose, *McCulloch*, 35; Alexander McCulloch to Frances L. McCulloch, 20 May 1801 and 9 September 1817, McCulloch Papers, BTHC.

4. Frances F. LeNoir McCulloch to Henry E. McCulloch, 23 January 1851, and Ben McCulloch to Frances F. LeNoir, 10 September 1861, McCulloch Papers, BTHC.

5. Dallas *Morning News*, 11 August 1937 (based on an interview with a neighbor—presumably Mrs. J. Y. McDaniel of Hillsboro, Texas, great-granddaughter of Alexander and Frances McCulloch—31 July 1937); see also Marquis James, *The Raven* (Indianapolis: Bobbs-Merrill, 1929), 26–27; Donald Day and Harry Herbert Ullon, eds., *The Autobiography of Sam Houston* (Norman: University of Oklahoma Press, 1954), 8; Llerena B. Friend, *Sam Houston: The Great Designer* (Austin: University of Texas Press, 1954), 6; Thomas W. Cutrer, ed., "'The Tallapoosa Might Truly Be Called the River of Blood': Maj. Alexander McCulloch and the Battle of Horseshoe Bend, March 27, 1814," *Alabama Review* 43, no. 1 (January 1990): 35–39; Alexander McCulloch to Frances L. McCulloch, 1 April 1813, McCulloch Papers, BTHC; Frank Lawrence Owsley, Jr., *Struggle for the Gulf Borderlands: The Creek War and the Battle of New Orleans, 1812–1815* (Gainesville: University Presses of Florida, 1981), 72–85.

6. Alexander McCulloch to Frances L. McCulloch, 3 September 1818, McCulloch Papers, BTHC.

7. Rose, *McCulloch*, 31–32, 39; B[en] M[cCulloch] Hord, "Gen. Ben McCulloch," *Confederate Veteran* 36 (July 1928): 261.

8. Tipton County, Tennessee, Court Records, 1:203; Austin *Southern Intelligencer*, 16 September 1857.

9. Rose, *McCulloch*, 37; Samuel C. Reid, *The Scouting Expeditions of McCulloch's Texas Rangers* (Philadelphia: G. B. Zieber and Co., [1847]; reprint, Freeport, N.Y.: Books for Libraries, [1970]), 85.

10. *Register of Debates in Congress* (Washington, D.C.: Gales and Seaton, 1830), 22 January 1830, 553–54.

11. Ibid., 25 February 1830, 583. The frontiersman's view of West Point as a school reserved exclusively for the education of the wealthy is especially ironic in that the academy was established by President Thomas Jefferson in hope of breaking the Federalist monopoly on the officer corps by giving a free military education to the sons of the poor. For a full discussion of Jefferson's plan, see Theodore J. Crackel, *Mr. Jefferson's Army: Political and Social Reform of the Military Establishment, 1801–1809* (New York: New York University Press, 1987), 54–73.

12. Reid, *McCulloch's Texas Rangers*, 24.

13. James Atkins Shackford, *David Crockett: The Man and the Legend* (Chapel Hill: University of North Carolina Press, 1956), 212–22.

14. H. E. McCulloch to Henry McArdle, 13 May 1889, "McArdle Companion: Battle Paintings," vol. 2, "The Battle of San Jacinto," Manuscript Division, Texas State Archives, Austin, Tex. (hereafter cited as TSA), 186; Ben McCulloch to Frances L. McCulloch, 23 October 1859, McCulloch Papers, BTHC.

15. Lewis E. Daniell, *Personnel of the Texas State Government, Embracing the Executive and Staff, Heads of the Departments, United States Senators and Representatives, Members of the XXth Legislature* (Austin: City Printing Co., 1887), 225; John Henry Brown, ed., *The Encyclopedia of the New West* (Marshall, Tex.: United States

Biographical Pub. Co., 1881), 295; J. W. Wilbarger, *Indian Depredations in Texas* (Austin: Hutchings Printing House, 1889; reprint, Austin: State House Books, 1985), 609; Rose, *McCulloch*, 40–41; Richard Boyd Hauck, *Crockett: A Bio-Bibliography* (Westport, Conn.: Greenwood Press, 1982), 47–50.

16. Eugene C. Barker, "The Texan Revolutionary Army," *Quarterly of the Texas State Historical Association* 9, no. 4 (April 1906): 258–59; H. M. Henderson, "A Critical Analysis of the San Jacinto Campaign," *Southwestern Historical Quarterly* 59, no. 3 (January 1956): 347–48; Eugene C. Barker, "The San Jacinto Campaign," *Quarterly of the Texas State Historical Association* 4, no. 4 (April 1901): 249–50, 302, 311, 320; Alexander Dienst, "The Navy of the Republic of Texas," *Quarterly of the Texas State Historical Association* 12, no. 3 (January 1909): 193–94; Ernest W. Winkler, "The 'Twin Sisters' Cannon," *Southwestern Historical Quarterly* 21, no. 1 (July 1917): 62–63; Henderson Yoakum, *History of Texas from Its First Settlement in 1685 to Its Annexation to the United States in 1846*, 2 vols. (New York: Redfield, 1856), 2:123; William Carey Crane, *Life and Literary Remains of Sam Houston of Texas* (Dallas: William G. Scarff and Co., [c. 1884]), 70; S. F. Sparks, "Recollections of S. F. Sparks," *Quarterly of the Texas State Historical Association* 12, no. 1 (July 1908): 66; H. M. Henderson, "San Jacinto," 346–58.

17. Noah Smithwick, *The Evolution of a State or Recollections of Old Texas Days* (Austin: Gammel, [1900]; reprint, Austin: University of Texas Press, 1983), 148–49.

18. Crane, *Houston*, 74–75; H. M. Henderson, "San Jacinto," 351–58; S. W. Cushing, *Adventures in the Texas Navy and the Battle of San Jacinto* (Austin: W. M. Morrison, 1985), 62–63; Robert Hancock Hunter, *The Narrative of Robert Hancock Hunter* (Austin: Cook Printing Co., 1936; Austin: Encino Press, 1966), 23.

19. Creed Taylor, *Tall Men with Long Rifles*, ed. James T. DeShields (San Antonio: Naylor Co., 1935, 1971), 244; "Recollections of James Monroe Hill of the Battle of San Jacinto," manuscript, James Monroe Hill Papers, BTHC, 9; W. C. Swearingen, "Documents," *Quarterly of the Texas State Historical Association* 15, no. 2 (October 1911): 158–59.

20. Amelia Williams and Eugene C. Barker, eds., *Writings of Sam Houston*, 8 vols. (Austin: University of Texas Press, 1938–43), 7:325.

21. H. P. N. Gammel, comp., *The Laws of Texas, 1822–1897*, 10 vols. (Austin: Gammel, 1898), 1:1112–13; *Memorial and Genealogical Record of Southwest Texas* (Chicago: Goodspeed Brothers, 1894), 579; Barker, "Texan Army," 259; Rose, *McCulloch*, 44–45; Daniell, *Personnel of the Texas State Government*, 225; H. E. McCulloch to Henry McArdle, 14 January 1891, 13 May 1889, "McArdle Companion," TSA, 2:188, 186; Yoakum, *History of Texas*, 2:300; Hord, "Gen. Ben McCulloch," 261.

22. Ferdinand Roemer, *Texas: With Particular Reference to German Immigration and the Physical Appearance of the Country* (San Antonio: Standard Printing Co., 1935; reprint, Waco: Texian Press for the German-Texan Heritage Society, 1983), 81–86; Daniell, *Personnel of the Texas State Government*, 226; Andrew Forest Muir,

ed., *Texas in 1837: An Anonymous Contemporary Narrative* (Austin: University of Texas Press, 1958), 91; W. Eugene Hollan, ed., *William Bollaert's Texas* (Norman: University of Oklahoma Press, 1956), 212–13.

23. H. E. McCulloch, quoted in Rose, *McCulloch*, 46; Gifford White, ed., *The 1840 Census of the Republic of Texas* (Austin: Pemberton Press, 1966), 57; Brown, *Encyclopedia of the New West*, 295; Thomas Lloyd Miller, ed., *Bounty and Donation Land Grants of Texas, 1835–1883* (Austin: University of Texas Press, 1967), 449.

CHAPTER TWO

1. Rupert N. Richardson, *The Comanche Barrier to South Plains Settlement: A Century and a Half of Savage Resistance to the Advancing White Frontier* (Glendale, Calif.: Arthur H. Clarke, 1933); T. R. Fehrenbach, *Comanches: The Destruction of a People* (New York: Knopf, 1979); Mildred P. Mayhall, *Indian Wars of Texas* (Waco, Tex.: Texian Press, 1965); Ernest Wallace and E. Adamson Hobel, *The Comanches: Lords of the South Plains* (Norman: University of Oklahoma Press, 1952).

2. Nathan Boone Burkett, "Early Days in Texas," manuscript, BTHC (hereafter cited as Burkett, "Reminiscences").

3. Andrew Jackson Sowell, *Rangers and Pioneers of Texas* (San Antonio: Shepard Bros. and Co., 1884; reprint, New York: Argosy Antiquarian, 1964; reprint, Austin: State House Press, 1991), 181.

4. John Henry Brown, *Indian Wars and Pioneers of Texas* (Austin: L. E. Daniell, 1880), 74; J. C. Duval, *Early Times in Texas* (Austin: Gammel, 1892; reprint, Austin: Steck and Co., 1935), 26; Francis S. Latham, *Travels in the Republic of Texas, 1842*, ed. Gerald S. Pierce (Austin: Encino Press, 1971), 16.

5. J. W. Wilbarger, *Indian Depredations in Texas* (Austin: Hutchings Printing House, 1889; reprint, Austin: State House Books, 1985), 288, 610; Lewis E. Daniell, *Personnel of the Texas State Government, Embracing the Executive and Staff, Heads of the Departments, United States Senators and Representatives, Members of the XXth Legislature* (Austin: City Printing Co., 1887), 226–27; Brown, *Indian Wars*, 73–74; J. C. Duval, *Early Times*, 26; James T. DeShields, *Border Wars of Texas* (Tioga, Tex.: Herald Co., 1912; reprint, Waco, Tex.: Texian Press, 1976), 287.

6. Daniell, *Personnel of the Texas State Government*, 227; Victor M. Rose, *The Life and Services of General Ben McCulloch* (Philadelphia: Pictorial Bureau of the Press, 1888; reprint, Austin: Steck Co., 1958), 48.

7. Daniell, *Personnel of the Texas State Government*, 226; Andrew Jackson Sowell, *Early Settlers and Indian Fighters of Southwest Texas* (Austin: Ben C. Jones and Co., 1900; reprint, New York: Argosy Antiquarian, [1964]; reprint, Austin: State House Press, 1986), 413, 416.

8. Sowell, *Early Settlers*, 415; Henry E. McCulloch to Frances L. McCulloch, 10 June 1840, BTHC; James Arthur Lyon Fremantle, *The Fremantle Diary: Being the*

Journal of Lt. Col. James Arthur Lyon Fremantle, Coldstream Guards, on His Three Months in the Southern States, ed. Walter Lord (Boston: Little, Brown, [c. 1954]), 46; Bertram Wyatt-Brown, *Southern Honor: Ethics and Behavior in the Old South* (New York: Oxford University Press, 1982), 21.

9. Sowell, *Early Settlers*, 418; Brown, *Indian Wars*, 64–65; John H. Jenkins and Kenneth Kesselus, *Edward Burleson: Texas Frontier Leader* (Austin: Jenkins Pub. Co., 1990), 187–97; Houston *Telegraph and Texas Register*, 15 May 1839.

10. Burkett, "Reminiscences," BTHC; John C. Duval, *The Adventures of Big-Foot Wallace* (Philadelphia: Claxton, Remsen, and Haffelfinger, 1871; reprint, Lincoln: University of Nebraska Press, [1966]), 22.

11. Rose, *McCulloch*, 50–55. The direct quotations attributed to Ben and Henry McCulloch, Alonzo Swietzer, and French Smith during this episode come from Victor Marion Rose, who, although a close friend of the McCulloch brothers, was not present during the exchange described, and so his comments must be taken at less than face value.

12. William Preston Johnston, *The Life of Gen. Albert Sidney Johnston* (New York: D. Appleton and Co., 1878), 69–80; John J. Linn, *Reminiscences of Fifty Years in Texas* (New York: D. & J. Sadler and Co., 1883), 346–47; Gerald S. Pierce, "A Minor Tragedy in the Texas Army: Lysander Wells and William D. Redd," *Texas Military History* 5 (Fall 1965): 121–29; William Ransom Hogan, *The Texas Republic: A Social and Economic History* (Norman: University of Oklahoma Press, 1946), 281–82; Austin *Texas Sentinel*, 16 May 1840.

13. John Lyde Wilson, *The Code of Honor or, Rules for the Government of Principals and Seconds in Dueling* (Charleston, 1838), reprinted in full in Jack K. Williams, *Dueling in the Old South: Vignettes of Social History* (College Station: Texas A&M University Press, 1980), 91; Rose, *McCulloch*, 50–51.

14. Williams, *Dueling*, 92; Rose, *McCulloch*, 51.

15. Rose, *McCulloch*, 51–55.

16. Williams, *Dueling*, 94; Record, Gonzales County District Court, April Term, A.D. 1840, Case 21st, 132–36.

17. *Journals of the Fourth Congress of the Republic of Texas, 1839–1840* (Austin: Von Boeckmann-Jones, [1929]), 13; John Henry Brown, ed., *The Encyclopedia of the New West* (Marshall, Tex.: United States Biographical Pub. Co., 1881), 295; Austin *Texas Sentinel*, 26 February 1840; Houston *Telegraph and Texas Register*, 28 October 1840; Record, Gonzales County District Court, April Term, A.D. 1840, Case 21st, 132–36; J. Milton Nance, *After San Jacinto: The Texas-Mexican Frontier, 1836–1841* (Austin: University of Texas Press, 1963), 236.

18. John Henry Brown, Dallas *Herald*, unidentified clipping in McCulloch Papers, BTHC.

19. "Opinions of the Supreme Court," January Term 1840, in *A Digest of the Laws of Texas: Containing a Full and Complete Compilation of the Land Laws; Together with the Opinions of the Supreme Court*, by James Wilmer Dallam (Baltimore: John

D. Toy, 1845), no. 1, n.p.; Jno. D. Morris, District Attorney, Gonzales County, 10 April 1840; George W. Davis, Clerk, District Court, Gonzales County, to Sheriff, Gonzales County, n.d.; W. W. T. Smith to John Hemphill, Fourth Judicial District, Spring Term 1840; Record, Gonzales County District Court, April Term, A.D. 1840, Special Term, May A.D. 1840, 151–54; A. Jones, Clerk, District Court, to Sheriff, Gonzales County, 7 November 1843; all in "The Republic of Texas vs. Henry E. McCulloch," Gonzales County Court House; Andrew Jackson Sowell, *Incidents Connected with the Early History of Guadalupe County, Texas* (Seguin, Tex.: C. L. Martin, n.d.), 39.

20. Henry E. McCulloch to Frances L. McCulloch, 10 June 1840, McCulloch Papers, BTHC.

21. Richardson, *Comanche Barrier*, 109–11; Mayhall, *Indian Wars of Texas*, 19–30.

22. Donlay E. Brice, *The Great Comanche Raid* (Austin: Eakin Press, 1987), 27–38; Wilbarger, *Indian Depredations in Texas*, 29; James N. Smith III, manuscript autobiography, BTHC, 209–12; Brown, *Indian Wars*, 79; DeShields, *Border Wars of Texas*, 324.

23. Houston *Telegraph and Texas Register*, 9 September 1840; Henderson Yoakum, *History of Texas from Its First Settlement in 1685 to Its Annexation to the United States in 1846*, 2 vols. (New York: Redfield, 1856), 1:300–302; Brown, *Encyclopedia of the New West*, 295; Linn, *Reminiscences*, 342.

24. Wilbarger, *Indian Depredations in Texas*, 29; Z. N. Morrell, *Flowers and Fruits from the Wilderness* (Boston: Gould and Lincoln, 1872; reprint, Waco, Tex.: Baylor University Press, 1976), 128; Brown, *Indian Wars*, 80.

25. Rose, *McCulloch*, 56; Sowell, *Incidents*, 29; "Brazos," *Life of Robert Hall* (Austin: Ben C. Jones and Co., 1898), 49; Catherine W. McDowell, ed., *Now You Hear My Horn: The Journal of James Wilson Nichols, 1820–1887* (Austin: University of Texas Press, 1967), 58, 59; Brown, *Indian Wars*, 80.

26. McDowell, *Now You Hear My Horn*, 62; Jenkins and Kesselus, *Edward Burleson*, 244–60; Sowell, *Rangers*, 207; Wilbarger, *Indian Depredations in Texas*, 32, 611; Brown, *Indian Wars*, 81; Sowell, *Early Settlers*, 418.

27. Brown, *Indian Wars*, 82; Wilbarger, *Indian Depredations in Texas*, 31; DeShields, *Border Wars of Texas*, 324; Smith manuscript, 214; John Henry Brown, quoted in Rose, *McCulloch*, 65.

28. McDowell, *Now You Hear My Horn*, 62; Wilbarger, *Indian Depredations in Texas*, 32; Sowell, *Rangers*, 209; Daniell, *Personnel of the Texas State Government*, 229; Brown, *Indian Wars*, 82; Brice, *Great Comanche Raid*, 45–46.

29. Austin *Texas Sentinel*, 28 November 1840; Henry McCulloch to Woodhouse, 26 September 1840, Matthew P. Woodhouse Papers, Manuscript Division, TSA; Austin *Texas Sentinel*, 31 November 1840.

30. Ben McCulloch et al., "Letter to Citizens of Victorian and Texana Respecting Indian Expedition," 9 September 1840, *Texas Indian Papers, 1825–1843, Edited from*

the Original Manuscript Copies in the Texas State Archives, ed. Dorman H. Winfrey et al., 4 vols. (Austin: Texas State Library, 1959), 1:115.

31. George T. Howard to Branch T. Archer, 12 November 1840, in Austin *Texas Sentinel*, 28 November 1840; Brice, *Great Comanche Raid*, 48; Henry McCulloch to Matthew Woodhouse, 16 August 1840, Woodhouse Papers, TSA.

CHAPTER THREE

1. Henry E. McCulloch to Matthew P. Woodhouse, 27 February 1841, Matthew P. Woodhouse Papers, Manuscript Division, TSA; H. P. N. Gammel, comp., *The Laws of Texas, 1822–1897*, 10 vols. (Austin: Gammel, 1898), 2:137–39.

2. McCulloch to Woodhouse, 27 February and 22 July 1841, Woodhouse Papers, TSA.

3. Allan Robert Purcell, "The History of the Texas Militia, 1835–1903" (Ph.D. diss., University of Texas, 1981), 78–79, 87–88; James K. Greer, *A Texas Ranger and Frontiersman: The Days of Buck Barry in Texas, 1845–1906* (Dallas: Southwest Press, 1932), 24–25; Gammel, *Laws*, 2:646–47; Ben McCulloch to Tom Green, 9 June 1844, Clarksville *Northern Standard*, 9 July 1844; Victor M. Rose, *The Life and Services of General Ben McCulloch* (Philadelphia: Pictorial Bureau of the Press, 1888; reprint, Austin: Steck Co., 1958), 67–68; J. W. Wilbarger, *Indian Depredations in Texas* (Austin: Hutchings Printing House, 1889; reprint, Austin: State House Books, 1985), 290; James Kimmins Greer, *Colonel Jack Hays: Texas Frontier Leader and California Builder* (New York: E. P. Dutton, 1952; reprint, College Station: Texas A&M University Press, 1987), 33–40, 108; Andrew Jackson Sowell, *Early Settlers and Indian Fighters of Southwest Texas* (Austin: Ben C. Jones and Co., 1900; reprint, New York: Argosy Antiquarian, [1964]; reprint, Austin: State House Press, 1986), 423; Andrew Jackson Sowell, *Rangers and Pioneers of Texas* (San Antonio: Shepard Bros. and Co., 1884; reprint, New York: Argosy Antiquarian, 1964; reprint, Austin: State House Press, 1991), 198; Walter Prescott Webb, *The Texas Rangers: A Century of Frontier Defense* (Boston: Houghton Mifflin, 1935; reprint, Austin: University of Texas Press, 1965), 67–77.

4. Joseph W. Hale, "Masonry in the Early Days of Texas," *Southwestern Historical Quarterly* 49, no. 3 (January 1946): 377; unidentified newspaper clipping, McCulloch Papers, BTHC; Frances Terry Ingmire, *Texas Ranger Service Records, 1830–1846* (St. Louis: Ingmire Publications, 1982), 92; James T. DeShields, *Border Wars of Texas* (Tioga, Tex.: Herald Co., 1912; reprint, Waco, Tex.: Texian Press, 1976), 349; Rose, *McCulloch*, 66; Wilbarger, *Indian Depredations in Texas*, 289; John Henry Brown, *Indian Wars and Pioneers of Texas* (Austin: L. E. Daniell, 1880), 84–85; Frances Terry Ingmire, comp., *Texas Frontiersmen, 1839–1860: Minutemen, Militia, Home Guard, Indian Fighters* (St. Louis: Ingmire Publications, 1982), 61; Henry E.

McCulloch to Matthew P. Woodhouse, 22 July and 27 February 1841, Woodhouse Papers, TSA; Henry E. McCulloch to Frances L. McCulloch, 29 August 1841, McCulloch Papers, BTHC.

5. McCulloch to Woodhouse, 5 December 1841, Woodhouse Papers, TSA; Henry E. McCulloch to Frances L. McCulloch, 29 August 1841, McCulloch Papers, BTHC; Sowell, *Early Settlers*, 20–23, 319; DeShields, *Border Wars of Texas*, 349; Harry McCorry Henderson, *Colonel Jack Hays, Texas Ranger* (San Antonio: Naylor Co., 1954), 20–21.

6. Clarksville *Northern Standard*, 24 October 1846; Houston *Telegraph and Texas Register*, 5 November 1845.

7. Rena Maverick Green, ed., *Memoirs of Mary A. Maverick, Arranged by Mary A. Maverick and Her Son Geo. Madison Maverick* (San Antonio: Alamo Printing Co., 1921; reprinted with introduction by Sandra L. Myres, Lincoln: University of Nebraska Press, 1989), 62.

8. James Kimmins Greer, *Hays*, 63; W. Eugene Hollan, ed., *William Bollaert's Texas* (Norman: University of Oklahoma Press, 1956), 33.

9. Miles S. Bennet, "Reminiscences of Western Texas," Miles S. Bennet Papers, BTHC; John Holland Jenkins III, *Recollections of Early Texas: The Memoirs of John Holland Jenkins* (Austin: University of Texas Press, 1958), 219–20.

10. 7 March 1842, John Winfield Scott Dancy Diary, BTHC, 113–14; James Kimmins Greer, *Hays*, 65; John Henry Brown, ed., *The Encyclopedia of the New West* (Marshall, Tex.: United States Biographical Pub. Co., 1881), 295.

11. 14 March 1842, Dancy Diary, BTHC, 115; Rose, *McCulloch*, 66; Francis S. Latham, *Travels in the Republic of Texas, 1842*, ed. Gerald S. Pierce (Austin: Encino Press, 1971), 25–38.

12. Amelia Williams and Eugene C. Barker, eds., *Writings of Sam Houston*, 8 vols. (Austin: University of Texas Press, 1938–43), 2:510; 16 March 1842, Dancy Diary, BTHC, 115.

13. J. Milton Nance, *Attack and Counterattack: The Texas-Mexican Frontier, 1842* (Austin: University of Texas Press, 1964), 88, 89, 98, 101.

14. Williams and Barker, *Writings of Sam Houston*, 2:83, 108–9.

15. Sam Houston to Ben McCulloch, 18 June 1842, *Writings of Sam Houston*, ed. Williams and Barker, 3:71–73.

16. George Washington Hockley to Ben McCulloch, 21 July 1842, Andrew Jackson Houston Collection, Archives Division, TSA.

17. *Civilian and Galveston Gazette*, 24 July 1842; Joseph Eve to Joseph Waples, 12 August 1842, *Diplomatic Correspondence of Texas*, 3 vols., ed. George Pierce Garrison (Washington, D.C.: Government Printing Office, 1908–11), 1:581; Hollan, *William Bollaert's Texas*, 130–31.

18. Rose, *McCulloch*, 67; Henry E. McCulloch, San Antonio *Express*, 14 September 1887; Lewis E. Daniell, *Personnel of the Texas State Government, Embracing the Executive and Staff, Heads of the Departments, United States Senators and Represen-*

tatives, Members of the XXth Legislature (Austin: City Printing Co., 1887), 231; Thomas Jefferson Green, *Journal of the Texian Expedition against Mier; Subsequent Imprisonment of the Author, His Sufferings, and Final Escape from the Castle of Perote, with Reflections upon the Present Political and Probable Future Relations of Texas, Mexico, and the United States* (New York: Harper and Brothers, 1845; reprint, Arno Press, 1973), 30–31; Z. N. Morrell, *Flowers and Fruits from the Wilderness* (Boston: Gould and Lincoln, 1872; reprint, Waco, Tex.: Baylor University Press, 1976), 168, 177; George R. Nielsen, "Mathew Caldwell," *Southwestern Historical Quarterly* 64, no. 4 (April 1961): 478–502; Sowell, *Rangers*, 213–14; Burkett, "Reminiscences," BTHC; Miles S. Bennet, Houston *Post*, unidentified clipping, Miles S. Bennet Papers, BTHC; Andrew Jackson Sowell, *Incidents Connected with the Early History of Guadalupe County, Texas* (Seguin, Tex.: C. L. Martin, n.d.), 34; [Doris] Shannon Garst, *Big Foot Wallace of the Texas Rangers* (New York: Julian Messner, 1951), 90; Sowell, *Early Settlers*, 420; John N. Seguin, *Personal Memoirs of John N. Seguin from the Year 1834 to the Retreat of General Wool from the City of San Antonio, 1842* (San Antonio: Ledger and Job Office, 1858; reprinted in *A Revolution Remembered: The Memoirs and Selected Correspondence of Juan N. Seguín*, ed. Jesús F. de la Teja [Austin: State House Press, 1991]), 119–20; Henry E. McCulloch, San Antonio *Express*, undated clipping, McCulloch Papers, BTHC.

19. Henderson, *Colonel Jack Hays*, 43; Nance, *Attack and Counterattack*, 388; John H. Jenkins, Sr., "Personal Reminiscences of Texas History Relating to Bastrop County, as Dictated to His Daughter-in-law, Mrs. Emma Himes Jenkins of Bastrop, Texas," typescript, BTHC, 110.

20. Thomas Jefferson Green, *Journal*, 34–35; Daniell, *Personnel of the Texas State Government*, 231; clipping from unidentified Gonzales newspaper, McCulloch Papers, BTHC; John Holland Jenkins III, *Recollections of Early Texas*, 100.

21. Miles S. Bennet, unidentified newspaper clipping, Miles S. Bennet Papers, BTHC; John Holland Jenkins III, *Recollections of Early Texas*, 112.

22. Daniell, *Personnel of the Texas State Government*, 231; Miles S. Bennet, "Journal of Early Life in Texas," Miles S. Bennet Papers, BTHC; Thomas Jefferson Green, *Journal*, 36–37.

23. John C. Duval, *The Adventures of Big-Foot Wallace* (Philadelphia: Claxton, Remsen, and Haffelfinger, 1871; reprint, Lincoln: University of Nebraska Press, [1966]), 159; Daniell, *Personnel of the Texas State Government*, 231.

24. Duval, *Big-Foot Wallace*, 159–60; Henderson, *Colonel Jack Hays*, 50.

25. Brown, *Indian Wars*, 65; Nance, *Attack and Counterattack*, 501.

26. James Kimmins Greer, *Hays*, 85; John Henry Brown, *History of Texas from 1685 to 1892*, 2 vols. (St. Louis: L. E. Daniell, [1892–93]), 2:237.

27. Harvey Alexander Adams, "[Journal of an] Expedition Against the Southwest," 7 December 1842, typescript, BTHC; Brown, *History of Texas*, 2:237–38; Daniell, *Personnel of the Texas State Government*, 231–32.

28. William Preston Stapp, *The Prisoners of Perote* (Austin: University of Texas Press, 1977), 24–28; Thomas W. Bell, *A Narrative of the Capture and Subsequent Sufferings of the Mier Prisoners in Mexico, Captured in the Cause of Texas, Dec. 26th, 1842, and Liberated September 16th, 1844* (DeSoto County, Miss.: R. Morris and Co., 1845), 16–17.

29. Nance, *Attack and Counterattack*, 566; Henderson, *Colonel Jack Hays*, 53; Samuel C. Reid, *The Scouting Expeditions of McCulloch's Texas Rangers* (Philadelphia: G. B. Zieber and Co., [1847]; reprint, Freeport, N.Y.: Books for Libraries, [1970]), 74; Bell, *Narrative*, 16, 17.

30. Daniell, *Personnel of the Texas State Government*, 231–32.

31. Thomas Jefferson Green, *Journal*, 74; Marilyn M. Sibley, ed., *Walker's Account of the Mier Expedition* (Austin: Texas State Historical Association, 1978), 34; Daniell, *Personnel of the Texas State Government*, 232–33.

32. Daniell, *Personnel of the Texas State Government*, 233.

33. Ibid., 234; Wilbarger, *Indian Depredations in Texas*, 612.

34. Daniell, *Personnel of the Texas State Government*, 233; Sibley, *Walker's Account*, 36–81; Henderson, *Colonel Jack Hays*, 87; Thomas Jefferson Green, *Journal*, 82–112; Duval, *Big-Foot Wallace*, 160; Sam W. Haynes, *Soldiers of Misfortune: The Somervell and Mier Expeditions* (Austin: University of Texas Press, 1990), 76.

35. Lucy A. Erath, ed., "Memoirs of Major George Bernard Erath," *Southwestern Historical Quarterly* 27, no. 1 (July 1923): 49–50.

CHAPTER FOUR

1. Houston *Telegraph and Texas Register*, 18 January, 15 March 1843.

2. Henry E. McCulloch to Frances L. McCulloch, 25 March 1844, and H[enry E. McCulloch], Gonzales *Inquirer*, undated clipping, McCulloch Papers, BTHC; J. W. Wilbarger, *Indian Depredations in Texas* (Austin: Hutchings Printing House, 1889; reprint, Austin: State House Books, 1985), 290; Frances Terry Ingmire, *Texas Ranger Service Records, 1830–1846* (St. Louis: Ingmire Publications, 1982), 92; W. Eugene Hollan, ed., *William Bollaert's Texas* (Norman: University of Oklahoma Press, 1956), 351; *Laws Passed by the Eighth Congress of the Republic of Texas* (Houston: Cruger and Moore, 1844), 1–26.

3. Henry E. McCulloch to M. P. Woodhouse, 5 December 1841, Matthew P. Woodhouse Papers, Manuscript Division, TSA; George W. Crockett, "Mustang Training," Centreville, Mich., *Western Chronicle*, 19 August 1858; Victor M. Rose, *The Life and Services of Gen. Ben McCulloch* (Philadelphia: Pictorial Bureau of the Press, 1888; reprint, Austin: Steck Co., 1958), 67; Harry McCorry Henderson, *Colonel Jack Hays, Texas Ranger* (San Antonio: Naylor Co., 1954), 28–31; *Journals of the Senate of the First Legislature of the State of Texas* (Clarksville, Tex.: Standard Office, 1848), 87.

4. Amelia Williams and Eugene C. Barker, eds., *Writings of Sam Houston,* 8 vols. (Austin: University of Texas Press, 1938–43), 4:269; Houston *Telegraph and Texas Register,* 18 October, 5 November 1845.

5. *Journals of the House of Representatives of the First Legislature of the State of Texas* (Clarksville: Standard Office, 1848), 4, 22, 25–26; Houston *Telegraph and Texas Register,* 31 December 1845; Clarksville *Northern Standard,* 11, 18 March 1846; Henry E. McCulloch to Frances L. McCulloch, 23 February 1846, McCulloch Papers, BTHC; John Henry Brown, ed., *The Encyclopedia of the New West* (Marshall, Tex.: United States Biographical Pub. Co., 1881), 295; Henry E. McCulloch to Frances L. McCulloch, 27 January and 16 August 1845, McCulloch Papers, BTHC; H. P. N. Gammel, comp., *The Laws of Texas, 1822–1897,* 10 vols. (Austin: Gammel, 1898), 3:1415; Allan Robert Purcell, "The History of the Texas Militia, 1835–1903" (Ph.D. diss., University of Texas, 1981), 9.

6. Justin H. Smith, *The War with Mexico,* 2 vols. (New York: Macmillan, 1919), 1:161, 464n; Dunbar Rowland, ed., *Jefferson Davis, Constitutionalist: His Letters, Papers, and Speeches,* 10 vols. (Jackson, Miss.: Mississippi Department of Archives and History, 1923), 1:442–44; Houston *Telegraph and Texas Register,* 6 May 1846.

7. Albert G. Brackett, *History of the United States Cavalry, From the Formation of the Federal Union to the 1st of June, 1863* (New York: Harper and Brothers, 1865; reprint, New York: Greenwood Press, 1968), 60; Houston *Telegraph and Texas Register,* 6 May 1846.

8. Samuel E. Chamberlain, *My Confession* (New York: Harper, [c. 1956]), 39.

9. A. Russell Buchanan, ed., "George Washington Trahern: A Texan Cowboy Soldier from Mier to Buena Vista," *Southwestern Historical Quarterly* 58, no. 1 (July 1954): 72–73; Brackett, *History of the U.S. Cavalry,* 62; Roswell S. Ripley, *The War with Mexico,* 2 vols. (New York: Harper and Brothers, 1849; reprint, New York: Burt Franklin, 1970), 1:98.

10. Ethan Allen Hitchcock, *Fifty Years in Camp and Field: Diary of Major-General Ethan Allen Hitchcock, U.S.A.,* ed. W[illiam] A[ugustus] Croffut (New York: G. P. Putnam's Sons, 1909), 310; Harry James Brown, ed., *Letters from a Texas Sheep Ranch: Written in the Years 1860 and 1867 by George Wilkins Kendall to Henry Stephens Randall* (Urbana: University of Illinois Press, 1959), 102.

All his life an avid collector of weapons, McCulloch began to collect arms patents and to endorse those new systems that he found most serviceable. On behalf of his friend Samuel Colt and Colt's new revolver, McCulloch wrote to Secretary of State James Buchanan on 26 March 1848, recommending "Mr. Colt's patent repeating pistols." Admitting "no small interest in the matter [him]self," as one who commanded rangers in the field and who hoped to command United States troops on the Texas frontier, McCulloch was convinced that the pistols were "the most effective fire arms to be found for mounted light troops in the kind of operations which that class of our soldiers are likely to be engaged in for the future, either in Mexico or among the numerous Indian tribes of the prairies." The new revolvers had by this time been in use among the Texas Rangers for about ten years, and McCulloch believed them "fairly tested, not only as to their destructive effects in hands of ordinary skill, but also as to their durability; having at this time in my possession one that has been used ten years without being repaired." A list of the battles in which the Colt revolver had "turned the tide of conflict in favor of the Texian rangers," McCulloch wrote, would "swell this letter into a volume of no ordinary size," but he concluded with the observation that "such is the estimation in which they are held by those that have used them" and that he had seen them purchased for as much as $150.

In honor of his national reputation as a ranger and scout, his love of weapons and arms technology, and his friendship with Samuel Colt, Ben McCulloch received Colt's second known presentation piece, serial number 1337 of the Whitneyville-Hartford Dragoon, the first having gone to President Polk. In keeping with the ranger motto, "Free as the breeze / Swift as a mustang / Tough as a cactus," Colt ordered the word "Free," with a wild horse and cactus, engraved near the base of the hammer, and the dedication "Presented by Sam Colt to Maj. Ben McCulloch, January 1, 1848." R. L. Wilson, *Colt Pistols, 1836–1976* (Dallas: Jackson Arms, 1976), 42–43; James E. Serven, *Colt Firearms: 1836–1958* (Santa Ana, Calif.: Serven Books, 1954), 47.

11. Walter Prescott Webb, *The Texas Rangers: A Century of Frontier Defense* (Boston: Houghton Mifflin, 1935; reprint, Austin: University of Texas Press, 1965), 94–95; Jonathan Duff Brown, "Reminiscences of Jno. Duff Brown," *Quarterly of the Texas State Historical Association* 12, no. 4 (April 1909): 305; Samuel C. Reid, *The Scouting Expeditions of McCulloch's Texas Rangers* (Philadelphia: G. B. Zieber and Co., [1847]; reprint, Freeport, N.Y.: Books for Libraries, [1970]), 26.

12. "Rough Notes," manuscript, George Wilkins Kendall Papers, BTHC, quoted in *Kendall of the Picayune*, by Fayette Copeland (Norman: University of Oklahoma Press, 1943), 169.

13. Rose, *McCulloch*, 69–70; Henderson, *Colonel Jack Hays*, 64; James K. Greer, *A Texas Ranger and Frontiersman: The Days of Buck Barry in Texas, 1845–1906* (Dallas: Southwest Press, 1932), 33.

14. Robert W. Johannsen, *To the Halls of the Montezumas: The Mexican War in the American Imagination* (New York: Oxford University Press, 1985), 16–18; George Wilkins Kendall, New Orleans *Daily Picayune*, 5 June 1846; Copeland, *Kendall of the Picayune*, 159–60.

15. "Samuel Chester Reid Family Papers," *Library of Congress Acquisitions, Manuscript Division, 1980*, 10–14; Reid, *McCulloch's Texas Rangers*, 20.

16. Jonathan Duff Brown, "Reminiscences," 304–5; "Samuel Chester Reid Family Papers," *Library of Congress Acquisitions, Manuscript Division, 1980*, 14.

17. Harry James Brown, *Letters from a Texas Sheep Ranch*, 102; Reid, *McCulloch's Texas Rangers*, 43–46; New Orleans *Daily Picayune*, 7 July 1846.

18. Reid, *McCulloch's Texas Rangers*, 43–46; Henry W. Barton, "Five Texas

Frontier Companies during the Mexican War," *Southwestern Historical Quarterly* 66, no. 1 (July 1962): 504.

19. Smith, *The War with Mexico*, 1:204, 2:479; Reid, *McCulloch's Texas Rangers*, 46–55; Ben McCulloch, "Forage Return," Fort Brown, 20 June 1846, collection of Floyd E. Risvold, Edina, Minn. (copy in author's collection); Houston *Telegraph and Texas Register*, 10 June 1846; Clarksville *Northern Standard*, 8 July 1846; Harry James Brown, *Letters from a Texas Sheep Ranch*, 102; Henderson, *Colonel Jack Hays*, 65; Barton, "Five Texas Frontier Companies," 504; Rose, *McCulloch*, 73–76.

20. Walter P. Lane, *Adventures and Recollections* (Marshall, Tex.: Tri-Weekly Herald Job Print, 1887; reprint, Marshall, Tex.: News Messenger Pub. Co., [c. 1928]; reprint, Austin: Pemberton Press, 1970), 94; Zachary Taylor to Roger Jones, 2 July 1846, House Executive Document 60, 30th Cong., 1st sess., 329–32; *Official Army Register, Corrected to August 31, 1847* (Washington, D.C.: Adjutant General's Office), 31 August 1847; Kendall, New Orleans *Daily Picayune*, 21 June 1846; Zachary Taylor to George T. Wood, Governors' Letters, TSA.

21. Kendall, New Orleans *Daily Picayune*, 19 July, 1 August 1846.

22. Reid, *McCulloch's Texas Rangers*, 32–33; [Benjamin F. Scribner], *A Campaign in Mexico, or a Glimpse of Life in Camp* (Philadelphia: Grigg, Elliot and Co., 1847; reprint, Austin: Jenkins Pub. Co., 1975), 45; Jonathan Duff Brown, "Reminiscences," 305.

23. Jesús F. de la Teja, ed., *A Revolution Remembered: The Memoirs and Selected Correspondence of Juan N. Seguín* (Austin: State House Press, 1991), 94–102; McCulloch to Zachary Taylor, 20 July 1846, McCulloch Papers, BTHC.

24. Ben McCulloch to William W. S. Bliss, 23 June 1846, McCulloch Papers, BTHC.

25. Reid, *McCulloch's Texas Rangers*, 53. For a thorough discussion of the bitter Anglo-Texan prejudice against Mexicans in the nineteenth century, see Arnoldo de Leon's *They Called Them Greasers: Anglo Attitudes toward Mexicans in Texas, 1821–1900* (Austin: University of Texas Press, 1983).

26. Grady McWhiney and Sue McWhiney, eds., *To Mexico with Taylor and Scott, 1845–1847* (Waltham, Mass.: Blaisdell Pub. Co., 1968), 123; Zachary Taylor, 10 June 1847, quoted in Williams and Barker, *Writings of Sam Houston*, 5:172–73.

27. McWhiney and McWhiney, *To Mexico with Taylor and Scott*, 123; Zachary Taylor, 10 June 1847, quoted in Williams and Barker, *Writings of Sam Houston*, 5:172–73; Kendall, New Orleans *Daily Picayune*, 2 August 1846.

28. Reid, *McCulloch's Texas Rangers*, 43–44; Kendall, New Orleans *Daily Picayune*, 2 August 1846; Jonathan Duff Brown, "Reminiscences," 305; Thomas Jefferson Green, *Journal of the Texian Expedition against Mier; Subsequent Imprisonment of the Author, His Sufferings, and Final Escape from the Castle of Perote, with Reflections upon the Present Political and Probable Future Relations of Texas, Mexico, and the United States* (New York: Harper and Brothers, 1845; reprint, Arno Press, 1973), 33.

29. Johannsen, *To the Halls of the Montezumas*, 24; Ben McCulloch to William W. S. Bliss, 23 June 1846, McCulloch Papers, BTHC.

30. Reid, *McCulloch's Texas Rangers*, 79–82; Kendall, New Orleans *Daily Picayune*, 25 August 1846; McCulloch to William Jenkins Worth, 9 August 1846, Manuscripts Section, Special Collections Division, Howard-Tilton Memorial Library, Tulane University, New Orleans, La.

31. Greer, *Buck Barry*, 38.

32. "O. P. O.," Clarksville *Northern Standard*, 19 September 1846, 27 March 1847; Houston *Telegraph and Texas Register*, 2 September 1846; Kendall, New Orleans *Daily Picayune*, 22 September, 28 August 1846; Reid, *McCulloch's Texas Rangers*, 91–103, 118; [Scribner], *Campaign in Mexico*, 50.

33. Reid, *McCulloch's Texas Rangers*, 127–29.

34. Kendall, New Orleans *Daily Picayune*, 6 October 1846.

35. Ibid.; Reid, *McCulloch's Texas Rangers*, 137–40.

36. [Luther Giddings], *Sketches of the Campaign in Northern Mexico in Eighteen Hundred Forty-Six and Seven by an Officer of the First Ohio Volunteers* (New York: J. P. Putnam, 1853), 143; John R. Kenley, *Memoirs of a Maryland Volunteer: War with Mexico in the Years 1846–7–8* (Philadelphia: J. B. Lippincott and Co., 1873), 99; Greer, *Buck Barry*, 40.

37. Reid, *McCulloch's Texas Rangers*, 141–54.

38. Greer, *Buck Barry*, 38.

39. William Jenkins Worth in Rowland, *Jefferson Davis*, 1:454; Reid, *McCulloch's Texas Rangers*, 156–59; Henderson, *Colonel Jack Hays*, 69; George Gordon Meade, *The Life and Letters of George Gordon Meade, Major General, United States Army*, 2 vols. (New York: C. Scribner's Sons, 1913), 1:133; George Wilkins Kendall Papers, BTHC.

40. Greer, *Buck Barry*, 34–35; Clarksville *Northern Standard*, 7 November 1846.

41. Greer, *Buck Barry*, 35–36; Meade, *George Gordon Meade*, 1:133–34; Reid, *McCulloch's Texas Rangers*, 158–67.

42. Reid, *McCulloch's Texas Rangers*, 167–86; Meade, *George Gordon Meade*, 1:134.

43. William Jenkins Worth in Rowland, *Jefferson Davis*, 1:455; Meade, *George Gordon Meade*, 1:135–36; *General Taylor and His Staff* (Philadelphia: Grigg, Elliot and Co., 1848), 203.

44. Reid, *McCulloch's Texas Rangers*, 190–94; Henderson, *Colonel Jack Hays*, 73; Meade, *George Gordon Meade*, 1:136–37; Greer, *Buck Barry*, 38–39; Buchanan, "George Washington Trahern," 72.

45. Rowland, *Jefferson Davis*, 1:452; Reid, *McCulloch's Texas Rangers*, 200–203; John C. Duval, *The Adventures of Big-Foot Wallace* (Philadelphia: Claxton, Remsen, and Haffelfinger, 1871; reprint, Lincoln: University of Nebraska Press, [1966]), 169; Chamberlain, *My Confession*, 56.

46. Reid, *McCulloch's Texas Rangers*, 224–25; Greer, *Buck Barry*, 41; [Giddings], *Sketches of the Campaign in Northern Mexico*, 221–22.

Returning to Texas with fourteen of his company, McCulloch camped one night on the northern bank of the Nueces. As some of the men were drifting off to sleep while others gathered firewood or were merely chatting around the fire, they were aroused by "that shrill peculiar cry familiar to most western Texans" of the Comanche raider. Two Indians dashed into camp, snapped the horses' picket ropes, and drove them back into the night. Only two of the rangers' mounts remained tethered, that of Ben McCulloch and one other. McCulloch and James Chesshire quickly mounted and made a dash after the fleeing Indians and the stolen horses. As the two Texans gained on the Comanches, the raiders dropped behind the horses, raised their shields, and began to loose their arrows at their pursuers. McCulloch's horse was struck and wounded, leaving McCulloch and one of the Indians on foot. Firing in the dark, none of the antagonists was able to hit an enemy, and McCulloch lost his revolver after firing only two or three shots. The Comanches broke off the engagement, leaving the plundered horses behind. Remarkably, some three months afterward, traveling over the same ground, he found the pistol and fired the remaining rounds "as though they had been loaded but the day before." Reid, *McCulloch's Texas Rangers*, 232; Clarksville *Northern Standard*, 14 November 1846; Serven, *Colt Firearms*, 50; Senate, 30th Cong., 2d sess., 1–18.

47. McCulloch Papers, BTHC; Reid, *McCulloch's Texas Rangers*, 3; Clarksville *Northern Standard*, 28 November 1846; *General Taylor and His Staff*; John Frost, *Pictorial History of Mexico and the Mexican War* (Philadelphia: Thomas, Cowperwait and Co., 1849); *The Mexican War and its Heroes; Being a Complete History of the Mexican War Embracing all the Operations under Generals Taylor and Scott, with a Biography of the Officers* (Philadelphia: J. B. Lippincott, 1857), 203.

CHAPTER FIVE

1. G. W. D. Harris, Nashville *Christian Advocate*, 12 August 1846; Ben McCulloch to Frances L. McCulloch, 30 November 1846, McCulloch Papers, BTHC.

2. Clarksville *Northern Standard*, 6 March 1847; Charles Spurlin, comp., *Texas Veterans in the Mexican War: Muster Rolls of Texas Military Units* (Victoria, Tex.: n.p., 1984), 198; Ben McCulloch to Major W. R. Scurry, appendix to *The History of Clarksville and Old Red River County*, by Pat B. Clark (Dallas: Mathis, Van Nort and Co., 1937), 246–47; Matamoras *Flag*, 30 June 1847, quoted in *Niles' National Register*, 17 July 1847, 308.

3. [Benjamin F. Scribner], *A Campaign in Mexico, or a Glimpse of Life in Camp* (Philadelphia: Grigg, Elliot and Co., 1847; reprint, Austin: Jenkins Pub. Co., 1975), 57–58.

4. George Durham, *Taming the Nueces Strip* (Austin: University of Texas Press, 1962), 38.

5. McCulloch to Scurry in Clark, *History of Clarksville*, 248–49.

6. Clarksville *Northern Standard*, 19 December 1846; McCulloch to Scurry in Clark, *History of Clarksville*, 250.

7. Antonio Lopéz de Santa Anna, *The Eagle: The Autobiography of Santa Anna*, ed. Ann Fears Crawford (Austin: Pemberton Press, 1967; Austin: State House Press, 1988), 89–92.

8. McCulloch to Scurry in Clark, *History of Clarksville*, 249–50.

9. Antonio Lopéz de Santa Anna to "All under His Command," San Luis Potosi, 26 January 1847, in *The Battle of Buena Vista with the Operations of the Army of Occupation for One Month*, by James Henry Carleton (New York: Harper and Brothers, 1848), 229–30; McCulloch to Scurry in Clark, *History of Clarksville*, 250.

10. Dunbar Rowland, ed., *Jefferson Davis, Constitutionalist: His Letters, Papers, and Speeches*, 10 vols. (Jackson, Miss.: Mississippi Department of Archives and History, 1923), 1:468, 469; McCulloch to Scurry in Clark, *History of Clarksville*, 250–56; Carleton, *Buena Vista*, 19.

11. K. Jack Bauer, ed., "General John E. Wool's Memoranda on the Battle of Buena Vista," *Southwestern Historical Quarterly* 77, no. 1 (July 1973): 115–16.

12. Carleton, *Buena Vista*, 64.

13. McCulloch to Scurry in Clark, *History of Clarksville*, 256–59.

14. [J. Marvin Hunter], "Jack Hays, the Texas Ranger," *Frontier Times* 4, no. 6 (March 1927): 19.

15. B[en] M[cCulloch] Hord, "Gen. Ben McCulloch," *Confederate Veteran* 36 (July 1928): 261. The sash is in the Ben and Henry Eustace McCulloch Papers of the Barker Texas History Center at the University of Texas at Austin. Rowland, *Jefferson Davis*, 1:467; [Scribner], *Campaign in Mexico*, 59.

16. Carleton, *Buena Vista*, 146–47; Samuel E. Chamberlain, *My Confession* (New York: Harper, [c. 1956]), 136–37; [Scribner], *Campaign in Mexico*, 70.

17. Zachary Taylor to Adjutant General, 3 August 1847, House Executive Document 60, 30th Cong., 1st sess., 1186.

18. McCulloch to Scurry in Clark, *History of Clarksville*, 259.

CHAPTER SIX

1. Victor M. Rose, *The Life and Services of Gen. Ben McCulloch* (Philadelphia: Pictorial Bureau of the Press, 1888; reprint, Austin: Steck Co., 1958), 121.

2. Ben McCulloch to Thomas Jefferson Rusk, 5 March 1848, Daughters of the Republic of Texas Library at the Alamo, San Antonio, Tex.

3. Ben McCulloch to Frances L. McCulloch, 9 May 1848, McCulloch Papers,

BTHC; McCulloch to Rusk, 5 March 1848, Daughters of the Republic of Texas Library at the Alamo.

4. D. E. Twiggs, Galveston, Tex., 30 November 1848, quoted in Gary Hendershott's "Texas and Indians" catalogue, sale 46, September 1987; *Register of Graduates and Former Cadets: United States Military Academy, 1948* (West Point, N.Y.: West Point Alumni Foundation, 1948), 386–88; Robert M. Utley, *Frontiersmen in Blue: The United States Army and the Indian, 1848–1865* (New York: Macmillan, 1967), 34.

5. Austin *Texas State Gazette*, 30 November 1850.

6. J. Frank Dobie, *Coronado's Children: Tales of Lost Mines and Buried Treasure of the Southwest* (Dallas: Southwest Press, 1930; reprint, Austin: University of Texas Press, 1978), 28–29.

7. John W. Rose to Preston Rose, 23 February 1849, Preston Rose Papers, BTHC; Benjamin Butler Harris, *Gila Trail: The Texas Argonauts and the California Gold Rush*, ed. Richard H. Dillon (Norman: University of Oklahoma Press, 1960), 30.

8. Ben McCulloch, power of attorney, Comptroller's Papers, TSA; McCulloch to Preston Rose, 28 August 1849, Rose Papers, BTHC; Austin *Texas State Gazette*, 1 September 1849.

9. Austin *Texas State Gazette*, 24 November 1849; Ben McCulloch to Frances L. McCulloch, 10 November 1849, McCulloch Papers, BTHC; Preston Rose to Polly Rose, 28 December 1849, Rose Papers, BTHC.

10. Ben McCulloch to Frances L. McCulloch, 10 November and 25 December 1849, and to Henry E. McCulloch, 24 December 1849, McCulloch Papers, BTHC; Preston Rose to Polly Rose, 28 December 1849, Rose Papers, BTHC.

11. Preston Rose to Polly Rose, 28 December 1849, Rose Papers, BTHC.

12. Ben McCulloch to Frances L. McCulloch, 10 November 1849, and to Henry E. McCulloch, 24 December 1849, McCulloch Papers, BTHC.

13. Ben McCulloch to Henry E. McCulloch, 24 December 1849, McCulloch Papers, BTHC.

14. Ben McCulloch to Henry E. McCulloch, 24 December 1849 and 28 June 1850, and to Frances L. McCulloch, 25 December 1849, McCulloch Papers, BTHC; Ben McCulloch to Sam Houston, 6 April 1851, Andrew Jackson Houston Collection, Archives Division, TSA.

15. McCulloch to Houston, 6 April 1850, Houston Collection, TSA; Ben McCulloch to Henry E. McCulloch, 24 December 1849 and 28 June 1850, and to Frances L. McCulloch, 5 May 1850, McCulloch Papers, BTHC.

16. McCulloch to Houston, 6 April 1851, Houston Collection, TSA.

17. Ibid.; Ben McCulloch to Henry E. McCulloch, 24 December 1849, McCulloch Papers, BTHC.

18. Ben McCulloch to Frances L. McCulloch, 10 September and 28 July 1851, McCulloch Papers, BTHC; McCulloch to Houston, 6 April 1851, Houston Collection, TSA.

19. Ben McCulloch to Henry E. McCulloch, 28 June 1850 and 10 September 1851, and to Frances L. McCulloch, 28 May 1851, McCulloch Papers, BTHC.

20. Ben McCulloch to Henry E. McCulloch, 24 December 1849, McCulloch Papers, BTHC.

21. Ben McCulloch to Frances L. McCulloch, 25 December 1849, McCulloch Papers, BTHC.

22. Preston Rose to Polly Rose, 12 February 1850, Rose Papers, BTHC.

23. Ben McCulloch to Frances L. McCulloch, 5 May 1850 and 28 July 1851, and to Henry E. McCulloch, 24 December 1849, McCulloch Papers, BTHC; McCulloch to Houston, 6 April 1851, Houston Collection, TSA.

24. Ben McCulloch to Frances L. McCulloch, 5 May 1850, McCulloch Papers, BTHC; McCulloch to Houston, 6 April 1851, Houston Collection, TSA.

25. Ben McCulloch to Henry E. McCulloch, 28 June 1850, and to Frances L. McCulloch, 20 August 1850, McCulloch Papers, BTHC; San Francisco *Herald*, quoted in Clarksville *Northern Standard*, 21 September 1850.

26. Ben McCulloch to Frances L. McCulloch, 20 August 1850, McCulloch Papers, BTHC.

27. McCulloch to Houston, 6 April 1851, Houston Collection, TSA.

28. McCulloch to Rusk, 16 April 1850, Thomas Jefferson Rusk Papers, BTHC; McCulloch to Houston, 6 April 1851, Houston Collection, TSA; Ben McCulloch to Henry E. McCulloch, 28 June 1850 and 10 September 1851, McCulloch Papers, BTHC.

29. Ben McCulloch to Frances L. McCulloch, 20 August 1850, BTHC; Sacramento *Placer Times*, 5 May 1849; Winfield J. Davis, *An Illustrated History of Sacramento County* (Chicago: Lewis Pub. Co., 1890), 23.

30. Davis, *Illustrated History of Sacramento County*, 25–28, 31; Sacramento *Daily Transcript*, 19 August 1850.

31. Sacramento *Placer Times Extra*, 15 August 1850; Sacramento *Daily Transcript*, 16 August 1850.

32. Sacramento *Daily Transcript*, 23 August, 2, 9 September 1850; Ben McCulloch to Frances L. McCulloch, 14 September 1850, McCulloch Papers, BTHC.

33. Ben McCulloch to Frances L. McCulloch, 14 September 1850, McCulloch Papers, BTHC.

34. Ibid.

35. Ben McCulloch to Frances L. McCulloch, 28 July 1851, McCulloch Papers, BTHC.

36. McCulloch to Houston, 6 April 1851, Houston Collection, TSA.

37. McCulloch to Rusk, 16 April 1851, Rusk Papers, BTHC.

38. Ibid.; Ben McCulloch to Frances L. McCulloch, 28 July 1851, McCulloch Papers, BTHC.

39. John Henry Brown, ed., *The Encyclopedia of the New West* (Marshall, Tex.:

United States Biographical Pub. Co., 1881), 296; Ben McCulloch to Frances L. McCulloch, 28 July 1851, McCulloch Papers, BTHC.

40. Ben McCulloch to Frances L. McCulloch, 10 September 1851, and to Henry E. McCulloch, 10 September 1851, McCulloch Papers, BTHC.

CHAPTER SEVEN

1. Ben McCulloch to Henry E. McCulloch, 18 March 1852, and Frances L. McCulloch to Henry E. McCulloch, 28 August 1851, McCulloch Papers, BTHC.

2. Ben McCulloch to Thomas Jefferson Rusk, 24 April 1852, Thomas Jefferson Rusk Papers, BTHC; S. D. C. Abbott to Henry E. McCulloch, 28 January 1852, and Ben McCulloch to Henry E. McCulloch, 3 January and 18 March 1852, McCulloch Papers, BTHC.

3. Ben McCulloch to Thomas Jefferson Rusk, 24 April 1852, Rusk Papers, BTHC.

4. Ben McCulloch to Henry E. McCulloch, 16 September and [?] October 1852, McCulloch Papers, BTHC.

5. Robert E. May, *Southern Dream of a Caribbean Empire, 1854–1861* (Baton Rouge: Louisiana State University Press, 1973), 9; Charles H. Brown, *Agents of Manifest Destiny: The Lives and Times of the Filibusters* (Chapel Hill: University of North Carolina Press, 1980), 105.

6. Ben McCulloch to Henry E. McCulloch, 9 June 1852 and 27 March 1853, McCulloch Papers, BTHC.

7. Ben McCulloch to Frances L. McCulloch, 12 August 1852, McCulloch Papers, BTHC.

8. Ibid.

9. Nat Benton to Frances L. McCulloch, 24 November 1852, and Ben McCulloch to Henry E. McCulloch, 16 September 1852 and 28 November 1853, McCulloch Papers, BTHC.

10. Ben McCulloch to Henry E. McCulloch, 28 November 1853, McCulloch Papers, BTHC.

11. Austin *Texas State Gazette*, 16 April 1853.

12. Galveston *Weekly News*, 30 August 1853; Henry E. McCulloch to Frances L. McCulloch, 4 December 1853, McCulloch Papers, BTHC; *Texas Almanac for 1857* (Galveston: Richardson and Co., 1856), 103.

13. Clarksville *Northern Standard*, 7 May 1853; Ben McCulloch to Thomas Jefferson Rusk, 10 May 1853, Rusk Papers, BTHC; Galveston *Weekly News*, 1 August 1854.

14. Robert Thomas Prichett, "Impeachment Proceedings in Congress against John Charles Watrous of Texas, 1851–1861" (M.A. thesis, University of Texas, 1937), 90–93, 191, 200; *Congressional Globe*, 1858–59, pt. 1, esp. 13; Galveston *News*, 10

March 1857; John Cleveland for Ben McCulloch to Robert McClelland, 16 July 1853, Federal Marshals' Papers, National Archives, Washington, D.C. (hereafter referred to as NA).

15. Cleveland to McClelland, Galveston, 16 July 1853, Federal Marshals' Papers, NA; Galveston *News*, 10 March 1857; LaGrange *Texas Monument*, 6 July 1853, quoted from the Nacogdoches *Chronicle*, 31 May 1853.

16. Ben McCulloch to Robert McClelland, 12 July 1853, Federal Marshals' Papers, NA.

17. John Henry Brown, *Indian Wars and Pioneers of Texas* (Austin: L. E. Daniell, 1880), 546–47; Austin *Texas State Gazette*, 25 June 1853; Cleveland to McClelland, 16 July 1853, Federal Marshals' Papers, NA; Galveston *Weekly News*, 30 August 1853.

18. Ernest C. Shearer, "The Carvajal Disturbances," *Southwestern Historical Quarterly* 55, no. 2 (October 1951): 226–27; Brownsville *Flag*, 2 August 1853, quoted in Austin *Texas State Gazette*, 13 August 1853.

19. Austin *Texas State Gazette*, 1 October 1853; McCulloch to McClelland, 21 December 1853, Federal Marshals' Papers, NA.

20. McCulloch to McClelland, 30 October and 17 November 1853, Federal Marshals' Papers, NA; Henry E. McCulloch to Frances L. McCulloch, 4 December 1853, McCulloch Papers, BTHC.

21. John Henry Brown, ed., *The Encyclopedia of the New West* (Marshall, Tex.: United States Biographical Pub. Co., 1881), 296; Ben McCulloch to Henry E. McCulloch, October 1853, McCulloch Papers, BTHC.

22. Amelia Williams and Eugene C. Barker, eds., *Writings of Sam Houston*, 8 vols. (Austin: University of Texas Press, 1938–43), 5:469, 486–87, 485, 488.

23. Dav. M. Cummin [?], Will. Trousdale, Benj. J. Hill to Jefferson Davis, 5 May 1854, Applications for Appointment, Civilian, Texas, no. 8, NA.

24. Ben McCulloch to Frances L. McCulloch, 6 August 1854, McCulloch Papers, BTHC.

25. Ben McCulloch to Frances L. McCulloch, 6 August 1854, and Franklin Pierce to Ben McCulloch, 22 August 1854, McCulloch Papers, BTHC.

26. Ben McCulloch to Frances L. McCulloch, 6 August 1854, McCulloch Papers, BTHC; McCulloch to John N. Gary, 22 October 1854, Letters Received by the Secretary of War, NA; Davis to McCulloch, 9 November 1854, Papers of Jefferson Davis and Family, Library of Congress, Washington, D.C.

27. Ben McCulloch to E. Whittlesy, 19 November 1854, Federal Marshals' Papers, NA.

28. Williams and Barker, *Writings of Sam Houston*, 7:364–65.

29. *Congressional Globe*, 1857–1858, pt. 1, 492–97, reprinted in Williams and Barker, *Writings of Sam Houston*, 6:466–86.

30. Ibid.; Theodore J. Crackel, *Mr. Jefferson's Army: Political and Social Reform of the Military Establishment, 1801–1809* (New York: New York University Press, 1987);

David Crockett to the United States House of Representatives, 25 February 1830, *Register of Debates in Congress* (Washington: Gales and Seaton, 1830), 6:583; Dunbar Rowland, ed., *Jefferson Davis, Constitutionalist: His Letters, Papers, and Speeches*, 10 vols. (Jackson, Miss.: Mississippi Department of Archives and History, 1923), 1:467. For a discussion of the early development of the regular army and its control by the wealthiest class, see Richard H. Kohn, *Eagle and Sword: The Federalists and the Creation of the Military Establishment in America, 1783–1802* (New York: Free Press, 1975).

31. Jefferson Davis's report to Franklin Pierce, 4 December 1854, quoted in *The Life of Gen. Albert Sidney Johnston*, by William Preston Johnston (New York: D. Appleton and Co., 1878), 183–88; Albert G. Brackett, *History of the United States Cavalry, From the Formation of the Federal Union to the 1st of June, 1863* (New York: Harper and Brothers, 1865; reprint, New York: Greenwood Press, 1968), 140.

32. John Henry Brown, *Encyclopedia of the New West*, 296.

33. Ben McCulloch to Henry E. McCulloch, 7 March 1855, McCulloch Papers, BTHC; William Preston to Eliza Johnston, 4 March 1855, Johnston Papers, Manuscripts Section, Special Collections Division, Howard-Tilton Memorial Library, Tulane University, New Orleans, La.

34. James L. Morrison, Jr., ed., *The Memoirs of Henry Heth* (Westport, Conn.: Greenwood Press, 1974), 124; Johnston, *Johnston*, 184–85; Rowland, *Jefferson Davis*, 464.

35. Ben McCulloch to Henry E. McCulloch, 7 March 1855, McCulloch Papers, BTHC.

36. Brackett, *History of the U.S. Cavalry*, 140; John Henry Brown, *Encyclopedia of the New West*, 296; Johnston, *Johnston*, 186.

37. Johnston, *Johnston*, 185, 228; Robert M. Utley, *Frontiersmen in Blue: The United States Army and the Indian, 1848–1865* (New York: Macmillan, 1967), 34.

38. For an admirable discussion of the controversy surrounding the United States Military Academy at West Point and the contrasting views of the partisans of regular and volunteer military organizations, see Marcus Cunliffe, *Soldiers and Civilians: The Martial Spirit in America, 1775–1865* (Boston: Little, Brown, 1968).

39. Ben McCulloch to Franklin Pierce, Washington *National Intelligencer*, 10 March 1855.

40. Henry E. McCulloch to Frances L. McCulloch, 21 March 1855, and Franklin Pierce to Ben McCulloch, 9 March 1855, McCulloch Papers, BTHC.

41. Ben McCulloch to Robert McClelland, 15 and 21 April 1855, Federal Marshals' Papers, NA.

42. Ben McCulloch to Robert McClelland, 16 June 1855, Federal Marshals' Papers, NA; Clarence C. Clendenen, *Blood on the Border: The United States Army and Mexican Irregulars* (New York: Macmillan, 1969), 18, 22; Shearer, "The Carvajal Disturbances," 228–30.

CHAPTER EIGHT

1. Ben McCulloch to Robert McClelland, 8 December 1855, Federal Marshals' Papers, NA.

2. George P. Rawick, ed., *The American Slave: A Composite Autobiography*, 12 vols., supplement, series 2, vol. 4, *Texas Narratives*, pt. 3 (Westport, Conn.: Greenwood Press, 1979), 1230–32; Randolph B. Campbell, *An Empire for Slavery: The Peculiar Institution in Texas* (Baton Rouge: Louisiana State University Press, 1989); Ben McCulloch to Henry E. McCulloch, 2 July 1856, McCulloch Papers, BTHC.

3. Ben McCulloch to Henry E. McCulloch, 2 July 1856, McCulloch Papers, BTHC.

4. Ben McCulloch to Henry E. McCulloch, 9 March and 2 July 1856, McCulloch Papers, BTHC.

5. Ben McCulloch to Henry E. McCulloch, 9 March 1856, McCulloch Papers, BTHC.

6. *Official Journal of Texas*, sixth legislature; H. P. N. Gammel, comp., *The Laws of Texas, 1822–1897*, 10 vols. (Austin: Gammel, 1898), 4:487–88; Ben McCulloch to Henry E. McCulloch, 2 July and 14 August 1856, and to Frances L. McCulloch, 24 July 1857, McCulloch Papers, BTHC. For an extended discussion of the southern concept of honor and its relationship to violence and slavery, see Bertram Wyatt-Brown, *Southern Honor: Ethics and Behavior in the Old South* (New York: Oxford University Press, 1982). Also useful are Edward L. Ayers's "Honor" and Thomas W. Cutrer's "Southwestern Violence," in *The Encyclopedia of Southern Culture*, ed. Charles Reagan Wilson and William Ferris (Chapel Hill: University of North Carolina Press, 1989).

7. Frances R. Lubbock, *Arkansas Democrat*, 6 September 1887. According to the *Philadelphia Press*, McCulloch was "one of Mr. Buchanan's most intimate friends." Frank Moore, ed., *The Rebellion Record: A Diary of American Events* (New York: G. P. Putnam, 1861), 1:24.

8. Ben McCulloch to Henry E. McCulloch, 20 December 1856 and 14 August 1854, McCulloch Papers, BTHC; Galveston *Weekly News*, 25 November 1856.

9. Ben McCulloch to Henry E. McCulloch, 20 December 1856, McCulloch Papers, BTHC.

10. Ben McCulloch to Black, 12 May 1857, and to J. Thompson, 2 July 1857; Peter H. Bell to James Buchanan, 22 February 1857; and Thomas J. Rusk and Sam Houston to James Buchanan, 30 March 1857, Federal Marshals' Papers, NA.

11. Ben McCulloch to Frances L. McCulloch, 24 July 1857, McCulloch Papers, BTHC.

12. Ben McCulloch to Henry E. McCulloch, 13 September 1857, McCulloch Papers, BTHC.

13. Ben McCulloch to Frances L. McCulloch, 24 July 1857, McCulloch Papers, BTHC; Austin *Southern Intelligencer*, quoted in the Clarksville *Northern Standard*,

17 October 1857; Ben McCulloch to Henry E. McCulloch, 13 September 1857, McCulloch Papers, BTHC.

14. Ben McCulloch to Jacob Thompson, 8 November 1857 and 19 January 1858, Federal Marshals' Papers, NA.

15. Ben McCulloch to Rush McCulloch, 31 January 1858, McCulloch Papers, BTHC.

16. Tuskegee, Ala., *Republican*, 24 September 1857.

17. George Wilkins Kendall, Austin *Texas State Gazette*, 1 September 1849; Ben McCulloch to Frances L. McCulloch, 7 February 1858, McCulloch Papers, BTHC; Sam Houston, *Congressional Globe*, 1857–58, pt. 1, 492–97, 646.

Even after the Civil War the notion of recruiting local units into temporary federal service to fight Indians did not become a dead letter. The French-born and -trained Col. Philippe Régis de Trobriand of the Thirteenth United States Infantry strongly urged that the Plains tribes could best be subdued "by forming auxiliary squadrons composed of frontiersmen who know the Indians and who are able to fight them in their own way." The recommendation, of course, came to nothing. Lucille M. Kane, ed. and trans., *Military Life in Dakota: The Journal of Philippe Régis de Trobriand* (St. Paul, Minn.: Alvord Memorial Commission, 1951), 65.

18. Dunbar Rowland, ed., *Jefferson Davis, Constitutionalist: His Letters, Papers, and Speeches*, 10 vols. (Jackson, Miss.: Mississippi Department of Archives and History, 1923), 1:467; Sam Houston, *Congressional Globe*, 1857–58, pt. 1, 492–97, 873–75. Houston here was alluding to George Washington's oft-quoted dictum that "to place any dependence upon militia is assuredly resting upon a broken staff."

19. Ben McCulloch to Frances L. McCulloch, 21 February 1858, McCulloch Papers, BTHC.

20. Ben McCulloch to Frances L. McCulloch, 7 February 1858, McCulloch Papers, BTHC.

21. *Congressional Globe*, 1856–58, pt. 1, 646, 672.

22. Rowland, *Jefferson Davis*, 1:449–50, 460; Ben McCulloch to Frances L. McCulloch, 21 February 1858, McCulloch Papers, BTHC.

23. Even during the period of the republic, Texans had harbored a deep suspicion of Mormons and their ways. In 1845 the people of the Red River counties were alarmed by a report that a number of Mormon families were emigrating from Missouri to found a colony in the Cross Timbers. Four years later a similar report caused great excitement in that section, causing settlers to threaten to turn out with their rifles and drive the immigrants from the country. Their ire subsided, however, when they found that the reputed Mormons were "peaceful, honest backwoodsmen from Kentucky and Tennessee." The editor of the Houston *Telegraph and Texas Register* suggested that should Mormons enter the Lone Star state, "the evil" could best be remedied by establishing a missionary station among them. "The Mormons," he thought, "doubtless could be converted with much less

difficulty than the heathen and they surely are objects more deserving of compassion than the Hindoos or Chinese." Houston *Telegraph and Texas Register*, 31 December 1845.

24. Letter to editor of *New York Times*, reprinted in Austin *Southern Intelligencer*, 16 September 1857; Norman F. Furniss, *The Mormon Conflict, 1850–1859* (New Haven: Yale University Press, 1960), 96; James Kimmins Greer, *Colonel Jack Hays: Texas Frontier Leader and California Builder* (New York: E. P. Dutton, 1952; reprint, College Station: Texas A&M University Press, 1987), 302.

25. LeRoy R. Hafen and Ann W. Hafen, eds., *The Utah Expedition, 1857–1858* (Glendale, Calif.: Arthur H. Clarke, 1958), 328.

26. Henry E. McCulloch to Frances L. McCulloch, 24 April 1858, McCulloch Papers, BTHC.

27. Houston *Telegraph and Texas Register*, 31 December 1845; Ben McCulloch, "Last Will and Testament," TSA; Hafen and Hafen, *Utah Expedition*, 329–32, 337–38; Samuel Cooper to Thomas S. Jesup, 10 April 1857, McCulloch Papers, BTHC.

28. Otis G. Hammond, ed., *The Utah Expedition, 1857–1858: Letters of Capt. Jesse A. Gove, 10th Infantry* (Concord, N.H.: New Hampshire Historical Society, 1928), 250, 255.

29. Hafen and Hafen, *Utah Expedition*, 338–39; Hammond, *Utah Expedition*, 277, 279.

30. John Van Deusen DuBois, *Campaigns in the West, 1856–1861 . . . Journal and Letters of John Van Deusen DuBois*, ed. George P. Hammond ([San Francisco: Grabhorn Press for] Arizona Pioneers Historical Society, 1949), 70.

31. Hammond, *Utah Expedition*, 280.

32. Ibid.; Hafen and Hafen, *Utah Expedition*, 347–48.

33. Edward Wheelock Tulledge, *The History of Salt Lake City and Its Founders* (Salt Lake City: E. W. Tulledge, [1886?]), 215–16.

34. Hafen and Hafen, *Utah Expedition*, 350–52; H. H. Bancroft, *History of Utah, 1540–1880* (San Francisco: History Co., 1889), 532.

35. Hafen and Hafen, *Utah Expedition*, 344–46; DuBois, *Campaigns in the West*, 69.

36. DuBois, *Campaigns in the West*, 70.

37. Hafen and Hafen, *Utah Expedition*, 346–54.

38. Hammond, *Utah Expedition*, 371.

39. Ibid., 377.

40. McCulloch to Young, n.d., McCulloch Papers, BTHC; James Buchanan, "Annual Message to Congress," in *The Works of James Buchanan*, ed. John Bassett Moore (Philadelphia: J. B. Lippincott Co., 1910), 10:217.

CHAPTER NINE

1. W. Woodward to James Buchanan, 9 August 1858, Federal Marshals' Papers, NA.

2. Ben McCulloch to Henry E. McCulloch, 8 September 1858, McCulloch Papers, BTHC.

3. Clement Eaton, "Frontier Life in Southern Arizona," *Southwestern Historical Quarterly* 36, no. 3 (January 1933): 173–92.

4. Galveston *Weekly News*, 7 December 1858; Dallas *Herald*, 2 February 1859.

5. Ben McCulloch to Jacob Thompson, 21 December 1857, Federal Marshals' Papers, NA; John Bassett Moore, ed., *The Works of James Buchanan* (Philadelphia: J. B. Lippincott Co., 1910), 10:257.

6. Moore, *Buchanan*, 10:257, 354–56; Diane M. T. North, ed., *Samuel Peter Heintzelman and the Sonora Exploring and Mining Company* (Tucson: University of Arizona Press, 1980), 149–56; John Henry Brown, ed., *The Encyclopedia of the New West* (Marshall, Tex.: United States Biographical Pub. Co., 1881), 296; Sidney Smith Johnson, *Texans Who Wore the Gray* ([Tyler, Tex.]: n.p., 1907), 36.

7. Amelia Williams and Eugene C. Barker, eds., *Writings of Sam Houston*, 8 vols. (Austin: University of Texas Press, 1938–43), 7:360–62; Ben McCulloch to Jacob Thompson, 3, 31 March, 19 April 1859, Federal Marshals' Papers, NA.

8. McCulloch to Thompson, 26 April 1859, Federal Marshals' Papers, NA; Galveston *News*, quoted in *The Life and Services of Gen. Ben McCulloch*, by Victor M. Rose (Philadelphia: Pictorial Bureau of the Press, 1888; reprint, Austin: Steck Co., 1958), 124.

9. Ben McCulloch to Frances L. McCulloch, 24 May 1859, McCulloch Papers, BTHC.

10. Ben McCulloch to Frances L. McCulloch, 20 March 1859, McCulloch Papers, BTHC.

11. Ben McCulloch to Frances L. McCulloch, 24 May 1859, McCulloch Papers, BTHC; C. A. Bridges, "The Knights of the Golden Circle: A Filibustering Fantasy," *Southwestern Historical Quarterly* 44, no. 3 (January 1941): 291.

12. William A. Albaugh and Edward N. Simmons, *Confederate Arms* (Harrisburg, Pa.: Stackpole Co., 1957), 248.

13. Albert G. Brackett, *History of the United States Cavalry, From the Formation of the Federal Union to the 1st of June, 1863* (New York: Harper and Brothers, 1865; reprint, New York: Greenwood Press, 1968), 142; Ben McCulloch to Frances L. McCulloch, 28 July 1859, McCulloch Papers, BTHC.

14. Ben McCulloch to Frances L. McCulloch, 23 October 1859, McCulloch Papers, BTHC.

15. Ben McCulloch to Frances L. McCulloch, 4 December 1859, McCulloch Papers, BTHC.

16. Ben McCulloch to Thomas H. Duggan, 22 December 1859, McCulloch Papers, BTHC.

17. Williams and Barker, *Writings of Sam Houston*, 7:397.

18. Ben McCulloch to Frances L. McCulloch, 1 January 1860, McCulloch Papers, BTHC.

19. Sam Houston to John B. Floyd, 13 February 1860, quoted in the Washington *National Intelligencer*, 20 March 1860.

20. Llerena B. Friend, *Sam Houston: The Great Designer* (Austin: University of Texas Press, 1954), 305; Williams and Barker, *Writings of Sam Houston*, 7:473–74.

21. Galveston *News*, quoted in Dallas *Herald*, 29 February 1860; Ben McCulloch to Frances L. McCulloch, 26 February 1860, McCulloch Papers, BTHC.

22. As Lee passed through Goliad on 18 February on his way from Indianola to San Antonio, where he was to take formal command of the department, he attracted the attention of Albert M. Lea, a West Point graduate and briefly acting secretary of war in the Fillmore administration, then chief engineer of the Aransas railroad. Lea promptly wrote to Houston, characterizing Lee as "well informed in matters of state, modest, brave, and thoughtful," a "Preux chevalier, sans peur and sans reproche." The new department commander, wrote Lea, "would not touch anything that he would consider vulgar filibustering, but he is not without ambition, and *under the sanction of the Good*, might be more than willing to aid you to pacificate Mexico." Should Houston, as a result of his planned Mexican operation, be called "from the Halls of the Montezumas" to the "White House at Washington," Lea advised, Lee would be "well fitted" to assume charge of Houston's "great idea of a Protectorate." Washington *National Intelligencer*, 20 March 1860; A. M. Lea to Sam Houston, 24 February 1860, Governors' Letters, TSA.

23. Ben McCulloch to Sam Houston, 6 April 1860, Amelia Williams Collection, BTHC.

24. Carl Coke Rister, *Robert E. Lee in Texas* (Norman: University of Oklahoma Press, 1946), 98–128; "Executive Record Book, 1861–1863," Archives Division, Texas State Library, Austin, Tex., 43, 44 (copy in Sam Houston letters, BTHC); Ben McCulloch to Frances L. McCulloch, 26 March 1860, McCulloch Papers, BTHC; Dallas *Herald*, 4 April 1860.

25. Ben McCulloch to Henry E. McCulloch, 22 January 1860, McCulloch Papers, BTHC.

26. C. R. P. in Dallas *Herald*, 18 April 1860; Walter L. Buenger, *Secession and the Union in Texas* (Austin: University of Texas Press, 1984), 48–49; Ben McCulloch to Frances L. McCulloch, 26 March 1860, McCulloch Papers, BTHC; *New York Herald*, 30 May 1860, quoted in Friend, *Houston*, 318; William Preston Johnston, *The Life of Gen. Albert Sidney Johnston* (New York: D. Appleton and Co., 1878), 228; William Kauffman Scarborough, ed., *The Diary of Edmund Ruffin* (Baton Rouge: Louisiana State University Press, 1972), 431; William C. Davis, *Breckinridge: Statesman, Soldier, Symbol* (Baton Rouge: Louisiana State University Press, 1974), 222–27.

27. Ben McCulloch to A. B. Moore, 25 July 1860, "The Collection of the Late Major General Samuel Wylie Crawford" (New York: American Art Association, 1915), lot number 292; Williams and Barker, *Writings of Sam Houston*, 8:110–11;

Friend, *Houston*, 36; Wigfall to Austin *Texas State Gazette*, Dallas *Herald*, 17 October 1860.

28. James Pike, *Scout and Ranger, Being the Personal Adventures of James Pike of the Texas Rangers in 1859–60* (Cincinnati: J. R. Hawley and Co., 1865; reprint, Princeton: Princeton University Press, 1932), 124–26; Sam Houston to Ben McCulloch, 28 August 1860, *Writings of Sam Houston*, ed. Williams and Barker, 8:127–28; Friend, *Houston*, 126–27, 308–9.

29. Henry E. McCulloch to Frances L. McCulloch, 12 September 1860, and Ben McCulloch to Frances L. McCulloch, 7 September and 21 October 1860, McCulloch Papers, BTHC; Dallas *Herald*, 5 December 1860; Scarborough, *Diary of Edmund Ruffin*, 500–501; Avery O. Craven, *Edmund Ruffin, Southerner: A Study in Secession* (Baton Rouge: Louisiana State University Press, 1966), 199.

30. Milledgeville *Herald*, 26 November 1860.

CHAPTER TEN

1. Victor M. Rose, *The Life and Services of Gen. Ben McCulloch* (Philadelphia: Pictorial Bureau of the Press, 1888; reprint, Austin: Steck Co., 1958), 128–29; Caroline B. Darrow, "Recollections of the Twiggs Surrender," in *Battles and Leaders of the Civil War*, ed. Robert V. Johnson and Clarence C. Buel (New York: Century Co., 1887–88; reprint, New York: T. Yoseloff, 1956), 1:34; U.S. War Department, *War of the Rebellion: A Compilation of the Official Records of the Union and Confederate Armies*, 70 vols. (Washington, D.C.: 1880–1901) (hereafter cited as *OR*; all references are to series 1 unless otherwise indicated), ser. 2, 1:1; Oran M. Roberts, *Texas*, vol. 11 of *Confederate Military History*, ed. Clement A. Evans (Atlanta: Confederate Pub. Co., 1899), 16–19.

2. Jeanne T. Heidler, " 'Embarrassing Situation': David E. Twiggs and the Surrender of the United States Forces in Texas, 1861," *Military History of the Southwest* 21, no. 2 (Fall 1991): 157–72; Roberts, *Texas*, 21; John C. Robertson to Henry E. McCulloch, 5 February 1861, McCulloch Papers, BTHC; Ernest William Winkler, ed., *Journal of the Secession Convention of Texas, 1861* (Austin: Texas Library and Historical Commission, 1912), 276, 366–67; Lewis E. Daniell, *Personnel of the Texas State Government, Embracing the Executive and Staff, Heads of the Departments, United States Senators and Representatives, Members of the XXth Legislature* (Austin: City Printing Co., 1887), 245.

3. Winkler, *Journal*, 269; Roberts, *Texas*, 24.

4. J. K. P. Blackburn, "Reminiscences of the Terry Rangers," *Southwestern Historical Quarterly* 22, no. 1 (July 1918): 38; Daniell, *Personnel of the Texas State Government*, 245.

5. Robert H. Williams, *With the Border Ruffians: Memoirs of the Far West, 1852–*

1868 (London: John Murray, 1908; reprint, Lincoln: University of Nebraska Press, 1982), 163.

6. *OR*, 1:581–82, 584, 590; Douglas Southall Freeman, *R. E. Lee: A Biography* (New York: Charles Scribner's Sons, 1949), 1:426–27; *OR*, ser. 2, 1:1; Winkler, *Journal*, 217.

7. San Antonio *Herald*, 16 February 1861, quoted in Dallas *Herald*, 27 February 1861.

8. Blackburn, "Reminiscences of the Terry Rangers," 38; Williams, *With the Border Ruffians*, 163; Darrow, "Recollections of the Twiggs Surrender," 34–35.

9. Morgan Wolfe Merrick, "Notes and Sketches of Campaigns in New Mexico, Arizona, Texas, Louisiana, and Arkansas by a Participant, Dr. M. W. Merrick, from Feb. 16, 1861, to May 26, 1865, Actual Service in the Field," manuscript, Daughters of the Republic of Texas Library at the Alamo, San Antonio, Tex.; Jerry D. Thompson, ed., *From Desert to Bayou: The Civil War Journal and Sketches of Morgan Wolfe Merrick* (El Paso: Texas Western Press, 1991), 3–8; Williams, *With the Border Ruffians*, 161–64.

10. Winkler, *Journal*, 274; Larkin Smith to William Hoffman, *OR*, ser. 2, 1:11–12.

11. McCulloch to Robertson, [18 February 1861?], Winkler, *Journal*, 276–77.

12. *Harper's Weekly*, 23 March 1861, 187; Winkler, *Journal*, 274–75; *OR*, 1:503, 517.

13. Blackburn, "Reminiscences of the Terry Rangers," 39.

14. San Antonio *Herald*, 16 February 1861; Winkler, *Journal*, 276.

15. *OR*, ser. 2, 1:1; Winkler, *Journal*, 277.

16. Freeman, *Lee*, 1:426–27; Carl Coke Rister, *Robert E. Lee in Texas* (Norman: University of Oklahoma Press, 1946), 158–61; Darrow, "Recollections of the Twiggs Surrender," 36.

17. *OR*, ser. 2, 1:1; Winkler, *Journal*, 277.

18. Freeman, *Lee*, 1:426–27; Rister, *Robert E. Lee in Texas*, 158–61.

19. *OR*, 1:1, 609; Ben McCulloch to Henry E. McCulloch, 14 April 1861, McCulloch Papers, BTHC.

20. Winkler, *Journal*, 372; *OR*, 1:609.

21. *OR*, 2:680; *Harper's Weekly*, 6 July 1861, 23; *OR*, 1:609–10; John Henry Brown, ed., *The Encyclopedia of the New West* (Marshall, Tex.: United States Biographical Pub. Co., 1881), 296–97; Henry E. McCulloch to Charles E. Jones, 22 January 1889, McCulloch Papers, BTHC.

22. Dallas *Herald*, 20 March 1861. For the most recent analysis of the continuing war against the Plains Indians, 1861–65, see David Paul Smith, *Frontier Defense in the Civil War: Texas' Rangers and Rebels* (College Station: Texas A&M University Press, 1992).

23. Dallas *Herald*, 13 March 1861.

24. John Bassett Moore, ed., *The Works of James Buchanan* (Philadelphia: J. B. Lippincott Co., 1910), 11:180; Winfield J. Davis, *An Illustrated History of Sacramento County* (Chicago: Lewis Pub. Co., 1890), 34; Jay Monaghan, *Civil War on the*

Western Border, 1854–1865 (Boston: Little, Brown, 1955), 157; Cincinnati *Commercial*, 18 March 1861; *Herald Extra*, 27 May 1861; Frank Moore, ed., *The Rebellion Record: A Diary of American Events* (New York: G. P. Putnam, 1861), 1:74; Sidney Smith Johnson, *Texans Who Wore the Gray* ([Tyler, Tex.]: n.p., 1907), 30.

25. Dallas *Herald*, 12 June 1861; Houston *Telegraph*, 27 May 1861, in Dallas *Herald*, 5 June 1861.

26. Winkler, *Journal*, 125, 132, 277; Edward Clark, Governor's Message to the Senators and Representatives of the Ninth Legislature of the State of Texas, November 1, 1861, *OR*, ser. 4, 1:713–22; *OR*, 53:646–47.

27. Richmond *Telegraphic News*, quoted in Dallas *Herald*, 17 April 1861; Roberts, *Texas*, 56; Stephen B. Oates, *Confederate Cavalry West of the River* (Austin: University of Texas Press, 1961), 63; Louis T. Wigfall to Colonel [?], 9 April 1861, Louis T. Wigfall Papers, BTHC.

28. Ben McCulloch to Henry E. McCulloch, 14 April 1861, McCulloch Papers, BTHC.

29. Ben McCulloch to Edward Clark, 9 April 1861, Frontier Protection Papers, BTHC; Ben McCulloch to Henry E. McCulloch, 9 April 1861, McCulloch Papers, BTHC; William A. Albaugh and Edward N. Simmons, *Confederate Arms* (Harrisburg, Pa.: Stackpole Co., 1957), 247–48.

30. Dallas *Herald*, 24 April, 22 May 1861; William F. Austin, *OR*, 1:634; Edward Clark to Texas Legislature, 1 November 1861, *OR*, ser. 4, 1:721.

31. Ben McCulloch to Henry E. McCulloch, 9 April 1861, McCulloch Papers, BTHC.

32. Dallas *Herald*, 15 May 1861.

33. Ben McCulloch to Henry E. McCulloch, 14 April 1861, McCulloch Papers, BTHC.

CHAPTER ELEVEN

1. Jefferson Davis to Victor Rose, 23 October 1883, Lawrence Sullivan Ross Papers, BTHC; John Henry Brown, ed., *The Encyclopedia of the New West* (Marshall, Tex.: United States Biographical Pub. Co., 1881), 296; Charles C. Jones to the Reverend and Mrs. C. C. Jones, 17 April 1861, *The Children of Pride*, ed. Robert Manson Myres (New Haven: Yale University Press, 1972), 665; Dallas *Herald*, 15 May 1861; C. Vann Woodward and Elisabeth Muhlenfeld, eds., *The Private Mary Chesnut: The Unpublished Civil War Diaries* (New York: Oxford University Press, 1984), 68; C. Vann Woodward, ed., *Mary Chesnut's Civil War* (New Haven: Yale University Press, 1981), 58.

2. Victor M. Rose, *Ross' Texas Brigade: Being a Narrative of Events Connected With Its Service in the Late War Between the States* (Louisville, Ky.: Courier-Journal Book and Job Rooms, 1881; reprint, Kennesaw, Ga.: Continental Book Co., 1960),

62; Jon L. Wakelyn, "'Civilian' Higher Education in the Making of Confederate Army Leaders," in *The Confederate High Command*, ed. Lawrence L. Hewitt and Roman J. Heleniak (Shippensburg, Pa.: White Mane Publishing Co., 1990), 74.

3. Rose, *Ross' Texas Brigade*, 62; B[en] M[cCulloch] Hord, "Gen. Ben McCulloch," *Confederate Veteran* 36 (July 1928): 261; Oran M. Roberts, *Texas*, vol. 11 of *Confederate Military History*, ed. Clement A. Evans (Atlanta: Confederate Pub. Co., 1899), 50; Ben McCulloch to Edward Clark, 14 April [*sic*] 1861, Frontier Protection Papers, BTHC; Cooper to McCulloch, 13 May 1861, *OR*, 3:575–76.

4. Leroy Pope Walker to Douglas H. Cooper, 13 May 1861, Samuel Cooper to Earl Van Dorn, 14 May 1861, and McIntosh to Cooper, 15 December 1861, *OR*, 8:713, 714, 3:574, 1:635; William Watson, *Life in the Confederate Army* (London: Chapman and Hall, 1887; reprint, New York: Scribner and Welford, 1888), 217–19.

5. McCulloch to Walker, 23 May 1861, *OR*, 3:583.

6. Des Arc *Citizen*, quoted in New Orleans *Delta*, 1 May 1861; Dallas *Herald*, 12 May, 24 July 1861; N. Bart Pearce, "Price's Campaign of 1861," *Publications of the Arkansas Historical Association* 4 (1917): 334–35; Brown, *Encyclopedia of the New West*, 296–97; Watson, *Life in the Confederate Army*, 182, 190.

7. Van Buren, Ark., *Press*, 5 June 1861; Watson, *Life in the Confederate Army*, 179; E. I. Stirman, "Career of Gen. Ben McCulloch," *Confederate Veteran* 21 (April 1913): 172.

8. Watson, *Life in the Confederate Army*, 179.

9. W. B. Parker, *Notes Taken During the Expedition Commanded by Capt. R. B. Marcy, U.S.A., Through Unexplored Texas, in the Summer and Fall of 1854* (Philadelphia: Hayes and Zell, 1856; reprint, Austin: Texas State Historical Association, 1984), 11; Watson, *Life in the Confederate Army*, 182, 190; Stephen B. Oates, "Recruiting Confederate Cavalry in Texas," *Southwestern Historical Quarterly* 64, no. 4 (April 1961): 469; Dallas *Herald*, 5 June 1861.

10. William Edward Woodruff, *With the Light Guns in '61–'65: Reminiscences of Eleven Arkansas, Missouri, and Texas Light Batteries in the Civil War* (Little Rock: Central Printing Co., 1903; reprint, Little Rock: Eagle Press, [1987]), 20–21, 34.

11. Ben McCulloch to Leroy Pope Walker, 20 and 21 May 1861, and Walker to McCulloch and McCulloch to Walker, 23 May 1861, *OR*, 3:581, 582, 583.

12. *OR*, 3:579–890; Ben McCulloch to Leroy P. Walker, 23 May 1861, *OR*, 3:583; Dabney H. Maury, quoted in R. S. Bevier, *History of the First and Second Missouri Confederate Brigades, 1861–1865, and From Wakarusa to Appomattox, A Military Anagraph* (St. Louis: Bryan, Brand & Co., 1879; reprint, Florissant, Mo.: Inland Printer, 1985), 95.

13. Van Buren, Ark., *Press*, 5 June 1861; Henry Rector to Jefferson Davis, 28 May 1861, and Thomas C. Hindman to Samuel Cooper, 5 June 1861, *OR*, 50:687, 691, 694.

14. John Tyler, Jr., to Thomas Overton Moore, 14 May 1861, *OR*, 53:682; William H. Tunnard, *A Southern Record: The History of the Third Regiment Louisiana*

Infantry (Baton Rouge: n.p., 1866; reprint, Dayton, Ohio: Morningside Bookshop, 1970), 32, 37; William D. Cater, ed., *"As It Was": The Story of Douglas John Cater's Life* ([San Antonio]: n.p., 1981; reprinted, with an introduction by T. Michael Parrish, as *"As It Was": Reminiscences of a Soldier of the Third Texas Cavalry and the Nineteenth Louisiana Infantry* [Austin: State House Press, 1990]), 117; Lester Newton Fitzhugh, ed., *Cannon Smoke: The Letters of Captain John J. Good, Good-Douglas Texas Battery, C.S.A.* (Hillsboro, Tex.: Hill Junior College Press, 1971), 102.

15. Woodruff, *With the Light Guns*, 34; Robert M. Utley, *The Indian Frontier of the American West, 1846–1890* (Albuquerque: University of New Mexico Press, 1984), 59–60; W. Craig Gaines, *The Confederate Cherokees: John Drew's Regiment of Mounted Rifles* (Baton Rouge: Louisiana State University Press, 1989).

16. McCulloch to Walker, 28 May 1861, *OR*, 3:587.

17. McCulloch to Walker, 12 June 1861, *OR*, 3:587; Woodward, *Mary Chesnut's Civil War*, 127; Francis Paul Prucha, *The Great Father: The United States Government and the American Indian* (Lincoln: University of Nebraska Press, 1984), 423–24; *OR*, ser. 4, 1:513–27, 542–54, 636–66, 669–87; McCulloch to Walker, 23 June 1861, *OR*, 3:596.

18. Gary E. Moulton, ed., *The Papers of Chief John Ross*, 2 vols. (Norman: University of Oklahoma Press, 1985), 2:474–75; Robert Lipscomb Duncan, *Reluctant General: The Life and Times of Albert Pike* (New York: E. P. Dutton, 1961), 172–79.

19. Ross to McCulloch, 17 June 1861, *OR*, 3:590–91; *OR*, 13:489–90.

20. McCulloch to Walker, 12 and 22 June 1861, *OR*, 3:590–91, 595–96, 600; McCulloch to Edward Clark, 30 June 1861, Frontier Protection Papers, BTHC; Richard B. McCaslin, "Conditional Confederates: The Eleventh Texas Cavalry West of the Mississippi River," *Military History of the Southwest* 21, no. 1 (Spring 1991): 92.

21. McCulloch to John Ross, 12 June 1861, *OR*, 3:591–92; Stephen B. Oates, *Confederate Cavalry West of the River* (Austin: University of Texas Press, 1961), 18–19; Prucha, *The Great Father*, 424; Gaines, *The Confederate Cherokees.*

22. McCulloch to Walker, 28 May 1861, *OR*, 3:588; Tunnard, *A Southern Record*, 106; William Harris and Ben Hardin to Dallas *Herald*, 21 August 1861; Pike to Earl Van Dorn, *OR*, 13:819; L. H. Graves, "L. H. Graves Diary, May 1, 1861–April 1, 1864," typescript, BTHC; Charles A. Buslé, "My Travels in the Indian Territory, etc., etc.," manuscript diary, Louisiana Collection, Louisiana State University Archives, Baton Rouge, La., 20–21.

23. Albert Castel, *General Sterling Price and the Civil War in the West* (Baton Rouge: Louisiana State University Press, 1968), 31; Walker to McCulloch, 4 July 1861, *OR*, 3:599, 603.

24. McCulloch to L. P. Walker, 29 June 1861, *OR*, 3:579–81, 582, 600, 602, 652; Oates, *Confederate Cavalry*, 64.

25. McCulloch to Edward Clark, 30 June 1861, Frontier Protection Papers,

BTHC; Samuel B. Barron, *The Lone Star Defenders: A Chronicle of the Third Texas Cavalry Regiment in the Civil War* (New York: Neale Pub. Co., 1908; reprint, Washington, D.C.: Zenger Pub. Co., 1983), 35; Max S. Lale, ed., "The Boy Bugler of the Third Texas Cavalry," pt. 1, *Military History of Texas and the Southwest* 14, no. 2 (1978): 76–77; Graves, "Graves Diary"; Rose, *Ross' Texas Brigade*, 17–18; McCaslin, "Conditional Confederates," 91; *OR*, 3:623.

26. Ben McCulloch to Edward Clark, 30 June 1861, Frontier Protection Papers, BTHC; Dallas *Herald*, 26 June 1861; *OR*, 3:590–91; Barron, *Lone Star Defenders*, 35, 39; Lale, "Boy Bugler," pt. 1, 73; Fitzhugh, *Cannon Smoke*, 105; James L. Nichols, *The Confederate Quartermaster in the Trans-Mississippi* (Austin: University of Texas Press, 1964), 17–27.

27. David Pierson to William H. Pierson, 30 May 1861, Pierson Family Papers, Manuscripts Section, Special Collections Division, Howard-Tilton Memorial Library, Tulane University, New Orleans, La.; G. B. Lipscomb to Jack Campbell, 8 July 1861, Jack Campbell Letters, 1860–61, BTHC; Nathaniel Lyon to George B. McClellan, 22 June 1861, *OR*, 3:11–12.

28. McCulloch to Walker, 14 June 1861, *OR*, 3:594–96.

29. Samuel Cooper to McCulloch, 26 June 1861, *OR*, 3:599; Arthur Carroll to McCulloch, 28 June 1861, quoted in Dallas *Herald*, 10 July 1861; McCulloch to L. P. Walker, 29 June 1861, *OR*, 3:599–600.

30. McCulloch to Albert Pike, 27 June 1861, "Ben McCulloch Letters," ed. Edward M. Coffman, *Southwestern Historical Quarterly* 60, no. 1 (July 1956): 120; *OR*, 3:606–8.

31. Dallas *Herald*, 10 July 1861.

32. McCulloch to L. P. Walker, 29 June 1861, *OR*, 3:600, 606; Ben McCulloch to John McCulloch, 30 June 1861, McCulloch Papers, BTHC; McCulloch to Judah P. Benjamin, 22 December 1861, *OR*, 3:743–44.

33. *OR*, ser. 2, 1:179–80; McCulloch to J. P. Benjamin, 22 December 1861, and McCulloch to Walker, *OR*, 3:743–44, 606–7; Pearce, "Price's Campaign of 1861," 336.

34. Ben McCulloch, "General McCulloch's Report," *Missouri Historical Review* 26, no. 4 (July 1932): 356.

35. Bevier, *First and Second Missouri*, 40, 317; Watson, *Life in the Confederate Army*, 191.

36. J. M. Schofield to Halleck, 13 February 1862, and McCulloch to Walker, 9 July 1861, *OR*, 3:94, 607.

37. Pearce, "Price's Campaign of 1861," 336; McCulloch to Walker, 9 July 1861, *OR*, 3:606; Victor M. Rose, *The Life and Services of Gen. Ben McCulloch* (Philadelphia: Pictorial Bureau of the Press, 1888; reprint, Austin: Steck Co., 1958), 188; Castel, *Sterling Price*, 27–28; McCulloch, "General McCulloch's Report," 365; McCulloch to J. P. Benjamin, 22 December 1861, *OR*, 3:744; Tunnard, *A Southern Record*, 38, 41; Pine Bluff *News*, quoted in Dallas *Herald*, 31 July 1861.

38. Tunnard, *A Southern Record*, 38; *OR*, 3:616.

39. Dallas *Herald*, 25 September 1861; Woodward, *Mary Chesnut's Civil War*, 191.

40. Rose, *McCulloch*, 134; Tunnard, *A Southern Record*, 41.

41. Walker to McCulloch, 4 July 1861, *OR*, 3:603.

42. *OR*, 3:610–11.

43. Thomas L. Snead, "The First Year of the War in Missouri," in *Battles and Leaders of the Civil War*, ed. Robert V. Johnson and Clarence C. Buel (New York: Century Co., 1887–88; reprint, New York: T. Yoseloff, 1956), 1:270–71; Bevier, *First and Second Missouri*, 31–32.

44. Snead, "The First Year of the War in Missouri," 270.

45. Franz Sigel, "The Pea Ridge Campaign," in *Battles and Leaders of the Civil War*, 1:318–19.

CHAPTER TWELVE

1. E. C. Cabell to Jefferson Davis, 6 July 1861, *OR*, 3:603.

2. William Watson, *Life in the Confederate Army* (London: Chapman and Hall, 1887; reprint, New York: Scribner and Welford, 1888), 210; N. Bart Pearce, "Price's Campaign of 1861," *Publications of the Arkansas Historical Association* 4 (1917): 337.

3. McCulloch to Walker and to Price, 15 July 1861, *OR*, 3:608, 610–12; Pearce, "Price's Campaign of 1861," 337.

4. McCulloch to Walker and C. F. Jackson to Sterling Price, 10 August 1861, *OR*, 3:612, 53:721–23.

5. W. E. Hughes, *The Journal of a Grandfather* (St. Louis: Nixon Jones Printing Co., 1912), 77–78; Polk to Walker, 28 July 1861, and Hardee to Price, 27 July 1861, *OR*, 3:617, 616; Nathaniel Cheairs Hughes, Jr., *General William J. Hardee: Old Reliable* (Baton Rouge: Louisiana State University Press, 1965), 78–79; Joseph Howard Parks, *General Edmund Kirby Smith, C.S.A.: The Fighting Bishop* (Baton Rouge: Louisiana State University Press, 1962), 174–78.

6. Pearce, "Price's Campaign of 1861," 338, 339; Thomas L. Snead, "The First Year of the War in Missouri," in *Battles and Leaders of the Civil War*, ed. Robert V. Johnson and Clarence C. Buel (New York: Century Co., 1887–88; reprint, New York: T. Yoseloff, 1956), 271.

7. A. W. Sparks, *The War Between the States as I Saw It: Reminiscences, Historical and Personal of Titus County Grays, Co. I, 9th Texas Cavalry, Ross's Texas Brigade* (Tyler, Tex.: Lee and Burnett, 1901; reprint, Longview, Tex.: D and D, 1987), 137, 147.

8. McCulloch to Price, 29 July 1861, *OR*, 3:102–3.

9. W[ashington] L[afayette] Gammage, *The Camp, the Bivouac, and the Battle Field* (Selma, Ala.: n.p., 1864; reprint, Little Rock: Arkansas Southern Press, 1958), 1; Pearce, "Price's Campaign of 1861," 337; McCulloch to Walker, 30 July 1861, *OR*, 3:622–23.

10. Max S. Lale, ed., "The Boy Bugler of the Third Texas Cavalry," pt. 1, *Military History of Texas and the Southwest* 14, no. 2 (1978): 79; William Edward Woodruff, *With the Light Guns in '61–'65: Reminiscences of Eleven Arkansas, Missouri, and Texas Light Batteries in the Civil War* (Little Rock: Central Printing Co., 1903; reprint, Little Rock: Eagle Press, [1987]), 34; *OR*, 3:744–45.

11. R. S. Bevier, *History of the First and Second Missouri Confederate Brigades, 1861–1865, and From Wakarusa to Appomattox, A Military Anagraph* (St. Louis: Bryan, Brand & Co., 1879; reprint, Florissant, Mo.: Inland Printer, 1985), 40–41; Watson, *Life in the Confederate Army*, 192; William H. Tunnard, *A Southern Record: The History of the Third Regiment Louisiana Infantry* (Baton Rouge: n.p., 1866; reprint, Dayton, Ohio: Morningside Bookshop, 1970), 157–59.

12. Pearce, "Price's Campaign of 1861," 340; Woodruff, *With the Light Guns*, 35–37. For first-person accounts of the skirmish at Dug Springs, see J. F. Smith, "The Battle of Oak Hill—A Fiery Baptism," and A. V. Reiff, "History of 'Spy' Company, Raised at Fayetteville, Ark.," in *The War of the 'Sixties*, comp. E[dward] R[idgeway] Hutchins (New York: Neale Pub. Co., 1912), 97, 165–69.

13. Tunnard, *A Southern Record*, 65.

14. *OR*, 3:745; Tunnard, *A Southern Record*, 157–59; Pearce, "Price's Campaign of 1861," 341.

15. Snead, "The First Year of the War in Missouri," 255–57; Bevier, *First and Second Missouri*, 41.

16. John M. Harrell, *Arkansas*, vol. 10 of *Confederate Military History*, ed. Clement A. Evans (Atlanta: Confederate Pub. Co., 1899), 23; Leonidas Polk to Leroy Pope Walker, 6 August 1861, *OR*, 4:381; Bevier, *First and Second Missouri*, 41; Watson, *Life in the Confederate Army*, 199; Thomas L. Snead, 4 August 1861, General Orders No. 16, *OR*, 53:720; Pearce, "Price's Campaign of 1861," 341; Snead, "The First Year of the War in Missouri," 270; Dallas *Herald*, 14 August 1861; Victor M. Rose, *The Life and Services of Gen. Ben McCulloch* (Philadelphia: Pictorial Bureau of the Press, 1888; reprint, Austin: Steck Co., 1958), 136; McCulloch to Walker, 30 July 1861, *OR*, 3:623; William Harris and Ben Hardin to the Dallas *Herald*, 21 August 1861; Sparks, *As I Saw It*, 135, 136.

17. Samuel B. Barron, *The Lone Star Defenders: A Chronicle of the Third Texas Cavalry Regiment in the Civil War* (New York: Neale Pub. Co., 1908; reprint, Washington, D.C.: Zenger Pub. Co., 1983), 35–36.

18. Watson, *Life in the Confederate Army*, 200; *OR*, 53:720–21; N. Bart Pearce, "Arkansas Troops in the Battle of Wilson's Creek," in *Battles and Leaders of the Civil War*, 1:298–99.

19. Watson, *Life in the Confederate Army*, 201–7; Bevier, *First and Second Missouri*, 42; Christopher Phillips, *Damned Yankee: The Life of General Nathaniel Lyon* (Columbia: University of Missouri Press, 1990), 240–43.

20. *OR*, 3:48; Lale, "Boy Bugler," pt. 1, 79.

21. Bevier, *First and Second Missouri*, 42–43.

22. Watson, *Life in the Confederate Army*, 208–10; Phillips, *Damned Yankee*, 242–43; McCulloch to Cooper, *OR*, 3:104, 745–46; Snead, "The First Year of the War in Missouri," 261–63.

23. McCulloch to Cooper, *OR*, 3:104, 745; Reiff, "History of 'Spy' Company," 170.

24. Pearce, "Arkansas Troops in the Battle of Wilson's Creek," 299; Bevier, *First and Second Missouri*, 42–43.

25. H. Clay Neville, "Wilson's Creek," *Southern Historical Society Papers* 38 (1910): 367; *OR*, 3:746.

26. Pearce, "Price's Campaign of 1861," 341–42; Bevier, *First and Second Missouri*, 42–43, 46; Rose, *McCulloch*, 138–39; *OR*, 3:746; Woodruff, *With the Light Guns*, 39.

27. Smith, "Battle of Oak Hill," 93–95; Reiff, "History of 'Spy' Company," 170–72; Watson, *Life in the Confederate Army*, 213.

28. Pearce, "Price's Campaign of 1861," 343; Snead, "The First Year of the War in Missouri," 271–72; Albert Castel, *General Sterling Price and the Civil War in the West* (Baton Rouge: Louisiana State University Press, 1968), 41.

29. J. M. Schofield, quoted in Harrell, *Arkansas*, 26; Snead, "The First Year of the War in Missouri," 268, 271, 298; *OR*, 3:127, 746; Pearce, "Price's Campaign of 1861," 339.

30. Barron, *Lone Star Defenders*, 44–45; Neville, "Wilson's Creek," 367–68.

31. *OR*, 3:96.

32. Castel, *Sterling Price*, 40; Bevier, *First and Second Missouri*, 50.

33. Woodruff, *With the Light Guns*, 47; Tunnard, *A Southern Record*, 50–51; Pearce, "Arkansas Troops in the Battle of Wilson's Creek," 299; *OR*, 3:104, 746; Rose, *McCulloch*, 139.

34. Snead, quoted in Harrell, *Arkansas*, 32–33; Watson, *Life in the Confederate Army*, 213–14, 217–19; McCulloch to Cooper, *OR*, 3:104; Pearce, "Arkansas Troops in the Battle of Wilson's Creek," 300.

35. Pearce, "Price's Campaign of 1861," 347; McCulloch to Cooper, *OR*, 3:73–74.

36. William D. Cater, ed., *"As It Was": The Story of Douglas John Cater's Life* ([San Antonio]: n.p., 1981; reprinted, with an introduction by T. Michael Parrish, as *"As It Was": Reminiscences of a Soldier of the Third Texas Cavalry and the Nineteenth Louisiana Infantry* [Austin: State House Press, 1990]), 99; Snead, quoted in Harrell, *Arkansas*, 34.

37. Cater, *"As It Was,"* 100, 101; Woodruff, *With the Light Guns*, 40, 41; McCulloch to Cooper, *OR*, 3:105.

38. Tunnard, *A Southern Record*, 52–53.

39. *OR*, 3:117; Pearce, "Arkansas Troops in the Battle of Wilson's Creek," 301; *OR*, 3:120; Tunnard, *A Southern Record*, 53; Watson, *Life in the Confederate Army*, 220.

40. Rose, *McCulloch*, 142; Neville, "Wilson's Creek," 368; Snead, quoted in Harrell, *Arkansas*, 35; McCulloch to Cooper, *OR*, 3:104–5.

41. Rose, *McCulloch*, 142; Woodruff, *With the Light Guns*, 49.

42. Neville, "Wilson's Creek," 368–69; Snead, "Arkansas Troops in the Battle of Wilson's Creek," 372–73; McCulloch to Cooper, *OR*, 3:105.

43. Rose, *McCulloch*, 139; *OR*, 3:119; Snead, quoted in Harrell, *Arkansas*, 35. From the Federal point of view, this action was much less glorious. Greer's charge, according to Capt. James Totten, "was the only demonstration made by [the Confederate] cavalry, and it was so *effete* and ineffectual in its force and character as to deserve only the appellation of child's play. Their cavalry is utterly worthless on the battle-field," he concluded. *OR*, 3:74.

44. McCulloch to Cooper, *OR*, 3:105.

45. Pearce, "Arkansas Troops in the Battle of Wilson's Creek," 30, 372–73; Pearce, "Price's Campaign of 1861," 348; McCulloch to Cooper, *OR*, 3:105.

46. Dallas *Herald*, 23 October 1861.

47. John C. Moore, *Missouri*, vol. 9 of *Confederate Military History*, ed. Clement A. Evans (Atlanta: Confederate Pub. Co., 1899), 62; J. B. Wymon and John D. Stevenson to John C. Frémont, 12 August 1861, *OR*, 53:500; *OR*, 3:54.

48. McCulloch to Cooper, *OR*, 3:105–6.

49. McCulloch to Walker, *OR*, 3:104, 746; Woodruff, *With the Light Guns*, 48.

50. McCulloch to Walker, *OR*, 3:104; Dallas *Herald*, 28 August 1861; Oran M. Roberts, *Texas*, vol. 11 of *Confederate Military History*, ed. Clement A. Evans (Atlanta: Confederate Pub. Co., 1899), 51.

51. Watson, *Life in the Confederate Army*, 230; Pearce, "Arkansas Troops in the Battle of Wilson's Creek," 299.

52. Reiff, "History of 'Spy' Company," 176; Cater, *"As It Was,"* 90; Pearce, "Price's Campaign of 1861," 348–49; Sparks, *As I Saw It*, 146; Rose, *McCulloch*, 135; Thomas R. R. Cobb, "Extracts From the Letters of Thomas R. R. Cobb to His Wife," *Southern Historical Society Papers* 28 (1900): 289; C. Vann Woodward, ed., *Mary Chesnut's Civil War* (New Haven: Yale University Press, 1981), 154; C. Vann Woodward and Elisabeth Muhlenfeld, eds., *The Private Mary Chesnut: The Unpublished Civil War Diaries* (New York: Oxford University Press, 1984), 135.

53. John Ross to McCulloch, 24 August 1861, *OR*, 3:673; *OR*, 3:691; Gary E. Moulton, ed., *The Papers of Chief John Ross*, 2 vols. (Norman: University of Oklahoma Press, 1985), 2:482–83.

54. Dallas *Herald*, 28 August 1861.

55. Dallas *Herald*, 18 September 1861; *OR*, 53:731; Walker to McCulloch, 28 August 1861, *OR*, 3:130.

CHAPTER THIRTEEN

1. Walter P. Lane, *Adventures and Recollections* (Marshall, Tex.: Tri-Weekly Herald Job Print, 1887; reprint, Marshall, Tex.: News Messenger Pub. Co., [c. 1928]; reprint, Austin: Pemberton Press, 1970), 84–85; Max S. Lale, ed., "The Boy Bugler of the Third Texas Cavalry," pt. 1, *Military History of Texas and the Southwest* 14, no. 2 (1978): 83.

2. H. Clay Neville, "Wilson's Creek," *Southern Historical Society Papers* 38 (1910): 369; Victor M. Rose, *Ross' Texas Brigade: Being a Narrative of Events Connected With Its Service in the Late War Between the States* (Louisville, Ky.: Courier-Journal Book and Job Rooms, 1881; reprint, Kennesaw, Ga.: Continental Book Co., 1960), 34–35; A. W. Sparks, *The War Between the States as I Saw It: Reminiscences, Historical and Personal of Titus County Grays, Co. I, 9th Texas Cavalry, Ross's Texas Brigade* (Tyler, Tex.: Lee and Burnett, 1901; reprint, Longview, Tex.: D and D, 1987), 149, 151.

3. William Edward Woodruff, *With the Light Guns in '61–'65: Reminiscences of Eleven Arkansas, Missouri, and Texas Light Batteries in the Civil War* (Little Rock: Central Printing Co., 1903; reprint, Little Rock: Eagle Press, [1987]), 51; Neville, "Wilson's Creek," 371; William H. Tunnard, *A Southern Record: The History of the Third Regiment Louisiana Infantry* (Baton Rouge: n.p., 1866; reprint, Dayton, Ohio: Morningside Bookshop, 1970), 77; *OR*, 53:728.

4. Woodruff, *With the Light Guns*, 52; W. R. Bradfute to Sterling Price, Camp Pond Springs, Missouri, 23 August 1861, quoted in John L. Heflin, Jr., "List 12-87," item no. 55, 8; *OR*, 3:362; *OR*, 53:727, 732.

5. *OR*, 3:747, 749; John Henry Brown, ed., *The Encyclopedia of the New West* (Marshall, Tex.: United States Biographical Pub. Co., 1881), 298–99; Hardee to Hindman, 15 and 20 August 1861, *OR*, 53:729–31; William Kauffman Scarborough, ed., *The Diary of Edmund Ruffin* (Baton Rouge: Louisiana State University Press, 1972), 2:108; Jefferson Davis to Victor Rose, 23 October 1883, Lawrence Sullivan Ross Papers, BTHC.

6. Victor M. Rose, *The Life and Services of Gen. Ben McCulloch* (Philadelphia: Pictorial Bureau of the Press, 1888; reprint, Austin: Steck Co., 1958), 188.

7. *OR*, 3:716, 747; Tunnard, *A Southern Record*, 78; Woodruff, *With the Light Guns*, 54–56; Brown, *Encyclopedia of the New West*, 298; William Watson, *Life in the Confederate Army* (London: Chapman and Hall, 1887; reprint, New York: Scribner and Welford, 1888), 232–33; McCulloch to Walker, 31 August and 2 September 1861, Walker to H. M. Rector, 4 and 5 September 1861, and Walker to McCulloch, *OR*, 3:689, 691, 692, 53:736, 3:688, 694.

8. W[ashington] L[afayette] Gammage, *The Camp, the Bivouac, and the Battle Field* (Selma, Ala.: n.p., 1864; reprint, Little Rock: Arkansas Southern Press, 1958), 11, 12, 13, 14.

9. Tunnard, *A Southern Record*, 78; *OR*, 53:727.

10. *OR*, 3:746; McCulloch to Hardee, 24 August 1861, *OR*, 3:672.

11. James Montgomery to J. H. Lane, 23 August 1861, *OR*, 3:453; *OR*, 3:454, 462, 488.

12. McCulloch to Hardee, 24 August 1861, *OR*, 3:672; Lale, "Boy Bugler," pt. 1, 84–87; Woodruff, *With the Light Guns*, 53–54; William D. Cater, ed., *"As It Was": The Story of Douglas John Cater's Life* ([San Antonio]: n.p., 1981; reprinted, with an introduction by T. Michael Parrish, as *"As It Was": Reminiscences of a Soldier of the*

Third Texas Cavalry and the Nineteenth Louisiana Infantry [Austin: State House Press, 1990]), 95; Gammage, *The Camp, the Bivouac and the Battle Field,* 14–19.

13. Good to Dallas friend, 6 September 1861, in Dallas *Herald,* 25 September 1861; Lester Newton Fitzhugh, ed., *Cannon Smoke: The Letters of Captain John J. Good, Good-Douglas Texas Battery, C.S.A.* (Hillsboro, Tex.: Hill Junior College Press, 1971), 58.

14. *OR,* 3:653.

15. Rose, *McCulloch,* 179; Dallas *Herald,* 31 July, 25 September 1861; Neville, "Wilson's Creek," 370–71.

16. *OR,* 3:109.

17. Woodruff, *With the Light Guns,* 53–54; Dallas *Herald,* 4 September 1861; Watson, *Life in the Confederate Army,* 242–45; Tunnard, *A Southern Record,* 79–82; Brown, *Encyclopedia of the New West,* 299; Amelia Williams and Eugene C. Barker, eds., *Writings of Sam Houston,* 8 vols. (Austin: University of Texas Press, 1938–43), 1:434–39; Cater, *"As It Was,"* 106; Gammage, *The Camp, the Bivouac and the Battle Field,* 17; Fitzhugh, *Cannon Smoke,* 56, 57.

18. McIntosh to Cooper, 7 December 1861, *OR,* 8:703; Watson, *Life in the Confederate Army,* 264; Polk to Jefferson Davis and J. J. Hooper to Jefferson Davis, 3 January 1862, and Cooper to McIntosh, 18 December 1861, *OR,* 8:729, 58:765, 8:703.

19. J. H. Robinson, quoted in Tunnard, *A Southern Record,* 157–59; Harris to Dallas *Herald,* 3 October 1861; Fitzhugh, *Cannon Smoke,* 133; Watson, *Life in the Confederate Army,* 239.

20. Sparks, *As I Saw It,* 152.

21. *OR,* 3:711; W. W. Mackall to McCulloch, 29 September 1861, *OR,* 3:708; Edward M. Coffman, ed., "Ben McCulloch Letters," *Southwestern Historical Quarterly* 60, no. 1 (July 1956): 118–22.

22. *OR,* 3:607–8; Edward Clark to L. P. Walker, 14 September 1861, *OR,* 4:104–5; Tunnard, *A Southern Record,* 85, 86.

23. Dallas *Herald,* 25 September 1861; Fitzhugh, *Cannon Smoke,* 66.

24. Samuel Cooper to McCulloch, 13 May 1861, and Judah P. Benjamin to Albert Sidney Johnston, 3 November 1861, *OR,* 3:575, 4:502–4; R. S. Bevier, *History of the First and Second Missouri Confederate Brigades, 1861–1865, and From Wakarusa to Appomattox, A Military Anagraph* (St. Louis: Bryan, Brand and Co., 1879), 59; Thomas L. Snead, "The First Year of the War in Missouri," *in Battles and Leaders of the Civil War,* ed. Robert V. Johnson and Clarence C. Buel (New York: Century Co., 1887–88; reprint, New York: T. Yoseloff, 1956), 150.

25. Fitzhugh, *Cannon Smoke,* 64–65, 74, 97; *OR,* 3:700–701; Cater, *"As It Was,"* 106; Hobart Key, Jr., and Max Lale, eds., *The Civil War Letters of David R. Garrett, Detailing the Adventures of the 6th Texas Cavalry, 1861–1865* (Marshall, Tex.: Port Caddo Press, [1963]), 27; McCulloch to J. P. Benjamin, 14 October 1861, *OR,* 3:719.

26. McCulloch to Pike, 27 September 1861, "Ben McCulloch Letters," ed. Coff-

man, 122; Dallas *Herald*, 9 October 1861; *OR*, 53:744; Fitzhugh, *Cannon Smoke*, 82; McCulloch to Frances L. McCulloch, 10 September 1861, McCulloch Papers, BTHC; Sul Ross to Lizzie Ross, 28 September, 5 October 1861, Lawrence Sullivan Ross Papers, Texas Collection, Baylor University, Waco, Tex.; Dallas *Herald*, 14 August, 25, 4 September, 23 October 1861; Gammage, *The Camp, the Bivouac and the Battle Field*, 18; James P. Douglas to Dear Sallie, 22 September 1861, "An Update: The Douglas Letters," ed. June P. Trop, *Chronicles of Smith County, Texas* 20, no. 1 (Summer 1983): 17.

27. Sul Ross to Lizzie Ross, 18 September, 14 October 1861, Ross Papers, Baylor University; Fitzhugh, *Cannon Smoke*, 93; David Pierson to William H. Pierson, 15 October 1861, Pierson Family Papers, Manuscripts Section, Special Collections Division, Howard-Tilton Memorial Library, Tulane University, New Orleans, La.

28. Lale, "Boy Bugler," pt. 1, 84–87; Gammage, *The Camp, the Bivouac and the Battle Field*, 17; Dallas *Herald*, 30 October 1861; Lawrence Sullivan Ross to Lizzie Ross, 14 October 1861, Ross Papers, Baylor University.

29. Fitzhugh, *Cannon Smoke*, 93; Lucia R. Douglas, ed., *Douglas's Texas Battery, C.S.A.* (Tyler, Tex.: Smith County Historical Society, 1966), 12; William Harris to Dallas *Herald*, 30 October 1861; Tunnard, *A Southern Record*, 94.

30. Fitzhugh, *Cannon Smoke*, 101; Price to Albert Sidney Johnston, 16 October 1861, *OR*, 3:720.

31. Watson, *Life in the Confederate Army*, 253, 259; Fitzhugh, *Cannon Smoke*, 94, 101; Gammage, *The Camp, the Bivouac and the Battle Field*, 19; Tunnard, *A Southern Record*, 95, 96; Sparks, *As I Saw It*, 154, 155.

32. McCulloch to Judah P. Benjamin, 8 November 1861, *OR*, 3:734; David Pierson to William H. Pierson, 8 November 1861, Pierson Family Papers; McCulloch to Price, 10 and 11 November 1861, *OR*, 3:736–38; Dallas *Herald*, 20 November, 30 October 1861; Gammage, *The Camp, the Bivouac and the Battle Field*, 19; Cater, *"As It Was,"* 107; Fitzhugh, *Cannon Smoke*, 101; Ross to wife, Camp Davis, Arkansas, 28 October 1861, Ross Papers, Baylor University; Watson, *Life in the Confederate Army*, 259, 263; Tunnard, *A Southern Record*, 95, 96; McCulloch to Price, 22 October 1861, *OR*, 3:721.

33. Douglas, *Douglas's Texas Battery*, 19–20; McCulloch to Price, 5 November 1861, *OR*, 3:731; *OR*, 3:736; Dallas *Herald*, 20 November 1861; Fitzhugh, *Cannon Smoke*, 114, 116; *OR*, 3:736; Tunnard, *A Southern Record*, 105; David Pierson to William H. Pierson, 8 November 1861, Pierson Family Papers.

34. McCulloch to Frances L. McCulloch, 8 November 1861, McCulloch Papers, BTHC; Fitzhugh, *Cannon Smoke*, 121.

35. *OR*, 3:747–48; Sparks, *As I Saw It*, 152; Watson, *Life in the Confederate Army*, 262.

36. Judith Ann Benner, *Sul Ross: Soldier, Statesman, Educator* (College Station: Texas A&M University Press, 1983), 70; Sul Ross to D. R. Tinsley, 10 October 1861, Ross Papers, Baylor University; Rose, *McCulloch*, 189; John Henry Brown to Dallas *Herald*, 20 November 1861; Douglas, *Douglas's Texas Battery*, 15–16; Tunnard, *A*

Southern Record, 95, 96; D. W. Davis to Judah P. Benjamin, Little Rock, 13 October 1861, and Benjamin to Davis, *OR*, 53:749, 3:718; Frank C. Armstrong to George W. Clark, 21 October 1861, quoted in Dallas *Herald*, 30 October 1861; Polk to A. S. Johnston, 24 October 1861, and William N. R. Beall to W. W. Mackall, 25 October 1861, *OR*, 3:724, 4:475.

37. Watson, *Life in the Confederate Army*, 262–63; Sparks, *As I Saw It*, 158; Ross to wife, 28 October 1861, Ross Papers, Baylor University; Gammage, *The Camp, the Bivouac and the Battle Field*, 20; Price to McCulloch, 26 October 1861, *OR*, 3:727; Douglas, *Douglas's Texas Battery*, 17; Fitzhugh, *Cannon Smoke*, 103.

38. Watson, *Life in the Confederate Army*, 267; McCulloch to Samuel Cooper, 19 November 1861, *OR*, 3:743; Stephen E. Ambrose, *Halleck: Lincoln's Chief of Staff* (Baton Rouge: Louisiana State University Press, 1962), 11–18.

39. Fitzhugh, *Cannon Smoke*, 123; Tunnard, *A Southern Record*, 106; McCulloch to W. W. Mackall, 21 November 1861, and to Samuel Cooper, 19 November 1861, and Frederick Steele to Halleck, 2 January 1862, *OR*, 52:216, 3:743, 8:479.

40. Price to McCulloch and McCulloch to Judah P. Benjamin, 23 October 1861, *OR*, 3:722, 748–49; Cater, *"As It Was,"* 95–97.

41. Brown, *Encyclopedia of the New West*, 298; Sparks, *As I Saw It*, 158; Frederick W. Steele to Halleck, 2 January 1862, and McCulloch to J. P. Benjamin, 14 October 1861, *OR*, 8:478–79, 3:719; Douglas, *Douglas's Texas Battery*, 17; Ross to wife, 28 October 1861, Ross Papers, Baylor University.

42. Watson, *Life in the Confederate Army*, 267; Fitzhugh, *Cannon Smoke*, 123; Tunnard, *A Southern Record*, 107.

43. Gammage, *The Camp, the Bivouac and the Battle Field*, 19.

CHAPTER FOURTEEN

1. *OR*, 53:754; Lucia R. Douglas, ed., *Douglas's Texas Battery, C.S.A.* (Tyler, Tex.: Smith County Historical Society, 1966), 19; C. F. Jackson to Jefferson Davis, 5 November 1861, *OR*, 53:755; McCulloch to Frances L. McCulloch, 8 November 1861, McCulloch Papers, BTHC; Dallas *Herald*, 27 November 1861; John Henry Brown, *War Bulletin*, 6 January 1862, quoted in *The Life and Services of Gen. Ben McCulloch*, by Victor M. Rose (Philadelphia: Pictorial Bureau of the Press, 1888; reprint, Austin: Steck Co., 1958), 190.

2. R. W. Johnson to Albert Sidney Johnston, 18 November 1861, *OR*, 4:563.

3. *OR*, 8:379, 382; Halleck to McClellan, 3 December 1861, and to Hunter, 29 November 1861, *OR*, 8:402, 392.

4. Jefferson Davis to Sterling Price, 20 December 1861, *Jefferson Davis, Constitutionalist: His Letters, Papers, and Speeches*, ed. Dunbar Rowland, 10 vols. (Jackson, Miss.: Mississippi Department of Archives and History, 1923), 5:182–83; [Price to Polk, 23 December 1861], *OR*, 8:729–30; Douglas, *Douglas's Texas Battery*, 176.

5. William H. Tunnard, *A Southern Record: The History of the Third Regiment Louisiana Infantry* (Baton Rouge: n.p., 1866; reprint, Dayton, Ohio: Morningside Bookshop, 1970), 120; Dallas *Herald*, 12 February 1862; Fayetteville *Arkansian*, 21 December 1861.

6. Brown, *War Bulletin*, quoted in Rose, *McCulloch*, 188; Tunnard, *A Southern Record*, 155–57; Dallas *Weekly Herald*, 25 December 1861, 12 February 1862; McCulloch to John Henry Brown, 2 December 1861, John Henry Brown Papers, BTHC; Rose, *McCulloch*, 182; Franz Sigel, "The Pea Ridge Campaign," in *Battles and Leaders of the Civil War*, ed. Robert V. Johnson and Clarence C. Buel (New York: Century Co., 1887–88; reprint, New York: T. Yoseloff, 1956), 1:318–19; Van Buren, Ark., *Press*, 18 September, 9, 31 October 1861; Bellville *Countryman*, 13 November 1861.

7. William Kauffman Scarborough, ed., *The Diary of Edmund Ruffin* (Baton Rouge: Louisiana State University Press, 1972), 2:238; Tunnard, *A Southern Record*, 119–20; William Watson, *Life in the Confederate Army* (London: Chapman and Hall, 1887; reprint, New York: Scribner and Welford, 1888), 244.

8. McCulloch to Judah P. Benjamin and to Samuel Cooper, 19 November 1861, Benjamin to McCulloch, 30 November 1861, and McCulloch to Benjamin, 4 December 1861, *OR*, 3:743, 8:699, 702; Dallas *Herald*, 18 December 1861; Benjamin to McCulloch, 5 December 1861, *OR*, 8:702; Benjamin Franklin Turner to Amasa Turner, 5 January 1862, *Batchelor-Turner Letters, 1861–1864*, ed. H. J. H. Rugley (Austin: Steck Co., 1961), 11.

9. Douglas, *Douglas's Texas Battery*, 21; W[ashington] L[afayette] Gammage, *The Camp, the Bivouac, and the Battle Field* (Selma, Ala.: n.p., 1864; reprint, Little Rock: Arkansas Southern Press, 1958), 21; Samuel B. Barron, *The Lone Star Defenders: A Chronicle of the Third Texas Cavalry Regiment in the Civil War* (New York: Neale Pub. Co., 1908; reprint, Washington, D.C.: Zenger Pub. Co., 1983), 62; Max S. Lale, ed., "The Boy Bugler of the Third Texas Cavalry," pt. 2, *Military History of Texas and the Southwest* 14, no. 3 (1978): 149–50.

10. *OR*, 8:702; McIntosh to Cooper and to Price, 14 December 1861, *OR*, 8:712; Stephen Z. Starr, *Jennison's Jayhawkers: A Civil War Cavalry Regiment and Its Commander* (Baton Rouge: Louisiana State University Press, 1974).

11. Homer L. Kerr, ed., *Fighting with Ross' Texas Cavalry Brigade, C.S.A.: Diary of Lieut. George L. Griscom, Adjutant, 9th Texas Cavalry Regiment* (Hillsboro, Tex.: Hill Junior College Press, 1976), 12; Gammage, *The Camp, the Bivouac and the Battle Field*, 21; A. P. Cartwright to Mrs. Amanda Cartwright, 1 February 1862, Americus Peyroux Cartwright Papers, BTHC.

12. Lester Newton Fitzhugh, ed., *Cannon Smoke: The Letters of Captain John J. Good, Good-Douglas Texas Battery, C.S.A.* (Hillsboro, Tex.: Hill Junior College Press, 1971), 133; Watson, *Life in the Confederate Army*, 239.

13. A. W. Sparks, *The War Between the States as I Saw It: Reminiscences, Historical and Personal of Titus County Grays, Co. I, 9th Texas Cavalry, Ross's Texas Brigade*

(Tyler, Tex.: Lee and Burnett, 1901; reprint, Longview, Tex.: D and D, 1987), 158; Kerr, *Fighting with Ross' Texas Brigade*, 12; Lale, "Boy Bugler," pt. 2, 155–56; Gammage, *The Camp, the Bivouac and the Battle Field*, 21.

14. *OR*, 8:88; John B. Clark et al. to Price, 13 December 1861, *OR*, 53:761–63; James L. Morrison, Jr., ed., *The Memoirs of Henry Heth* (Westport, Conn.: Greenwood Press, 1974), 124.

15. Scarborough, *Diary of Edmund Ruffin*, 2:182.

16. *OR*, 8:88.

17. McCulloch to John Henry Brown, 2 December 1861, John Henry Brown Papers, BTHC; Morrison, *Memoirs of Henry Heth*, 159–60.

18. Clark et al. to Price, 13 December 1861, *OR*, 53:761–63.

19. McCulloch to John Henry Brown, 2 December 1861, Brown Papers, BTHC. Price was to continue a thorn in the president's side throughout the war, and Davis regarded the Missouri general as the vainest man he ever met. Clement Eaton, *Jefferson Davis* (New York: Free Press, 1977), 188; Robert E. Shalhope, *Sterling Price: Portrait of a Southerner* (Columbia: University of Missouri Press, 1971), 214–16.

20. Scarborough, *Diary of Edmund Ruffin*, 2:191; McCulloch to John Henry Brown, 2 December 1861, Brown Papers, BTHC.

21. McCulloch to John Henry Brown, 2 December 1861, Brown Papers, BTHC.

22. *OR*, 3:744–49; John Henry Brown, ed., *The Encyclopedia of the New West* (Marshall, Tex.: United States Biographical Pub. Co., 1881), 298.

23. Tunnard, *A Southern Record*, 155–57; Dallas *Weekly Herald*, 12 February 1862.

24. Special Orders No. 8, 10 January 1862, and J. P. Benjamin to A. S. Johnston, 12 January 1862, *OR*, 8:734, 7:826; Thomas L. Snead, "The First Year of the War in Missouri," in *Battles and Leaders of the Civil War*, 1:275.

25. Diary of Private Sam Thompson, 5 March 1862, quoted in Douglas, *Douglas's Texas Battery*, 187; Charles Edward Nash, *Biographical Sketches of Gen. Pat Cleburne and Gen. T. C. Hindman Together with Humorous Anecdotes and Reminiscences of the Late Civil War* (Little Rock: Tunnah & Pittard, 1898), 135; William D. Cater, ed., *"As It Was": The Story of Douglas John Cater's Life* ([San Antonio]: n.p., 1981; reprinted, with an introduction by T. Michael Parrish, as *"As It Was": Reminiscences of a Soldier of the Third Texas Cavalry and the Nineteenth Louisiana Infantry* [Austin: State House Press, 1990]), 124.

26. Watson, *Life in the Confederate Army*, 282; Ross to wife, 1 March 1862, Lawrence Sullivan Ross Papers, Texas Collection, Baylor University, Waco, Tex.

27. Polk to Albert Sidney Johnston, 30 December 1861, and A. S. Johnston to J. P. Benjamin, 5 January 1861, *OR*, 7:808, 820; John Henry Brown, "Wartime Diary in Northwest Arkansas," ed. W. J. Lemke, *Flashback* 6, no. 6 (November 1956): 10; Van Buren, Ark., *Press*, 2 January 1862, in Dallas *Herald*, 22 January 1862; John Henry Brown, "'The Paths of Glory': The War-time Diary of Maj. John Henry Brown, C.S.A.," ed. W. J. Lemke, *Arkansas Historical Quarterly* 15, no. 4 (Winter 1956): 346; Van Dorn to McCulloch, 6 February 1862, *OR*, 8:748.

28. Van Dorn to Price, 7 and 14 February 1862, *OR*, 8:749, 751.

29. McCulloch to Francis Lubbock, 6 February 1862, Governors' Papers, Archives Division, Texas State Library, Austin, Tex.

30. Cater, *"As It Was,"* 123; Rose, *McCulloch*, 198; Sparks, *As I Saw It*, 170.

31. Watson, *Life in the Confederate Army*, 275; Cater, *"As It Was,"* 123; Lale, "Boy Bugler," pt. 2, 156; Rose, *McCulloch*, 198.

32. Watson, *Life in the Confederate Army*, 275–77; Rose, *McCulloch*, 198; Tunnard, *A Southern Record*, 124; Charles A. Bruslé to McCulloch, 16 February 1862, *OR*, 8:752–53.

33. Rose, *McCulloch*, 198; Watson, *Life in the Confederate Army*, 274.

34. Gammage, *The Camp, the Bivouac and the Battle Field*, 22, 23; *OR*, 8:61; Watson, *Life in the Confederate Army*, 277; Rose, *McCulloch*, 199; David Pierson to William H. Pierson, 22 February 1861 [*sic*], Pierson Family Papers, Manuscripts Section, Special Collections Division, Howard-Tilton Memorial Library, Tulane University, New Orleans, La.

35. Watson, *Life in the Confederate Army*, 277; Cater, *"As It Was,"* 123; Gammage, *The Camp, the Bivouac and the Battle Field*, 23.

36. Watson, *Life in the Confederate Army*, 276, 279; Rose, *McCulloch*, 199; Sam Houston to James Collingsworth, 15 March 1836, *The Papers of the Texas Revolution, 1835–1836*, ed. John Holland Jenkins III (Austin: Presidial Press, 1973), 5:82.

37. Gammage, *The Camp, the Bivouac and the Battle Field*, 23; R. S. Bevier, *History of the First and Second Missouri Confederate Brigades, 1861–1865, and From Wakarusa to Appomattox, A Military Anagraph* (St. Louis: Bryan, Brand and Co., 1879; reprint, Florissant, Mo.: Inland Printer, 1985), 92; Watson, *Life in the Confederate Army*, 279.

38. Watson, *Life in the Confederate Army*, 279; William Baxter, *Pea Ridge and Prairie Grove; or Scenes and Incidents of the War in Arkansas* (Cincinnati: Poe and Hitchcock, 1864; reprint, Van Buren, Ark.: Press-Argus, 1957), 59; David Pierson to William H. Pierson, 22 February 1862, Pierson Family Papers.

39. Gammage, *The Camp, the Bivouac and the Battle Field*, 23; Rose, *McCulloch*, 199; Watson, *Life in the Confederate Army*, 280; Pierson Family Papers; Baxter, *Pea Ridge*, 59; *OR*, 8:68.

40. Bevier, *First and Second Missouri*, 92; Sparks, *As I Saw It*, 169.

41. Gammage, *The Camp, the Bivouac and the Battle Field*, 23; Douglas, *Douglas's Texas Battery*, 27; Rose, *McCulloch*, 200; Sparks, *As I Saw It*, 164; David Pierson to [William H. Pierson], [March 1862], Pierson Family Papers; *OR*, 50:787; Watson, *Life in the Confederate Army*, 280.

42. *OR*, 13:819; Bevier, *First and Second Missouri*, 92–93; Sparks, *As I Saw It*, 28, 29.

43. Bevier, *First and Second Missouri*, 92–93; John C. Moore, *Missouri*, vol. 9 of *Confederate Military History*, ed. Clement A. Evans (Atlanta: Confederate Pub. Co., 1899), 76.

44. Watson, *Life in the Confederate Army*, 280, 282; Rose, *McCulloch*, 20.

45. Newton A. Keen, *Living and Fighting with the Sixth Texas Cavalry* (Gaithersburg, Md.: Butternut Press, 1986), 24; Clark Wright to Curtis, *OR*, 8:75.

46. Watson, *Life in the Confederate Army*, 282; Sparks, *As I Saw It*, 171; Tunnard, *A Southern Record*, 128.

47. Keen, *Sixth Texas Cavalry*, 25; Watson, *Life in the Confederate Army*, 282; Rose, *McCulloch*, 20.

48. Brown, " 'Paths of Glory,' " 347; McIntosh to Cooper, 15 December 1861, *OR*, 8:714; McCulloch to John Henry Brown, 2 December 1861, Brown Papers, BTHC; Robert G. Hartje, *Van Dorn: The Life and Times of a Confederate General* (Nashville: Vanderbilt University Press, 1967), 130; Dabney Herndon Maury, *Recollections of a Virginian* (New York: Charles Scribner's Sons, 1894), 186; Van Dorn to Bragg, 27 March 1862, *OR*, 8:283; Watson, *Life in the Confederate Army*, 282.

49. McCulloch to John Henry Brown, 15 January 1862, Brown Papers, BTHC; McCulloch to Van Dorn, 1 March 1862, *OR*, 8:763; Keen, *Sixth Texas Cavalry*, 27; David Pierson to William H. Pierson, 22 February 1861 [*sic*], Pierson Family Papers.

CHAPTER FIFTEEN

1. John Henry Brown, " 'The Paths of Glory': The War-time Diary of Maj. John Henry Brown, C.S.A.," ed. W. J. Lemke, *Arkansas Historical Quarterly* 15, no. 4 (Winter 1956): 347–48; Van Dorn to Price, 7 February 1862, to Bragg and to W. W. Mackall, 24 February 1862, *OR*, 8:749, 283, 755; Maury, quoted in *History of the First and Second Missouri Confederate Brigades, 1861–1865, and From Wakarusa to Appomattox, A Military Anagraph*, by R. S. Bevier (St. Louis: Bryan, Brand and Co., 1879; reprint, Florissant, Mo.: Inland Printer, 1985), 94; A. W. Sparks, *The War Between the States as I Saw It: Reminiscences, Historical and Personal of Titus County Grays, Co. I, 9th Texas Cavalry, Ross's Texas Brigade* (Tyler, Tex.: Lee and Burnett, 1901; reprint, Longview, Tex.: D and D, 1987), 171; Dabney H. Maury, "Van Dorn, The Hero of Mississippi," in *The Annals of the War, Written By Leading Participants, North and South* (Philadelphia: *Philadelphia Weekly Times*, 1878; reprint, Dayton, Ohio: Morningside House, 1988), 461–62.

2. Maury, in Bevier, *First and Second Missouri*, 95.

3. William Watson, *Life in the Confederate Army* (London: Chapman and Hall, 1887; reprint, New York: Scribner and Welford, 1888), 283; Dabney Herndon Maury, *Recollections of a Virginian* (New York: Charles Scribner's Sons, 1894), 186; Ephraim McD. Anderson, *Memoirs: Historical and Personal, Including Campaigns of the First Missouri Confederate Brigade* (St. Louis: Times Printing Co., 1868; reprint, Dayton, Ohio: Morningside Bookshop, 1972), 162.

4. Arkansas *Gazette*, 6 March 1862; Robert G. Hartje, *Van Dorn: The Life and*

Times of a Confederate General (Nashville: Vanderbilt University Press, 1967), 120; Maury, quoted in Bevier, *First and Second Missouri*, 95.

5. Homer L. Kerr, ed., *Fighting with Ross' Texas Cavalry Brigade, C.S.A.: Diary of Lieut. George L. Griscom, Adjutant, 9th Texas Cavalry Regiment* (Hillsboro, Tex.: Hill Junior College Press, 1976), 13; Anderson, *First Missouri Confederate Brigade*, 164; Hartje, *Van Dorn*, 124.

6. Anderson, *First Missouri Confederate Brigade*, 164; Watson, *Life in the Confederate Army*, 285; Victor M. Rose, *The Life and Services of Gen. Ben McCulloch* (Philadelphia: Pictorial Bureau of the Press, 1888; reprint, Austin: Steck Co., 1958), 201–2; Maury, *Recollections*, 186; Kerr, *Fighting with Ross' Texas Brigade*, 13–14; W[ashington] L[afayette] Gammage, *The Camp, the Bivouac, and the Battle Field* (Selma, Ala.: n.p., 1864; reprint, Little Rock: Arkansas Southern Press, 1958), 23–24; Sparks, *As I Saw It*, 173; Van Dorn to Bragg, *OR*, 8:283.

7. Sparks, *As I Saw It*, 172–73; Max S. Lale, ed., "The Boy Bugler of the Third Texas Cavalry," pt. 2, *Military History of Texas and the Southwest* 14, no. 3 (1978): 157–59; William D. Cater, ed., *"As It Was": The Story of Douglas John Cater's Life* ([San Antonio]: n.p., 1981; reprinted, with an introduction by T. Michael Parrish, as *"As It Was": Reminiscences of a Soldier of the Third Texas Cavalry and the Nineteenth Louisiana Infantry* [Austin: State House Press, 1990]), 125; Gammage, *The Camp, the Bivouac and the Battle Field*, 24; Maury, *Recollections*, 186; Kerr, *Fighting with Ross' Texas Brigade*, 14; Van Dorn to Bragg, *OR*, 8:283.

8. William H. Tunnard, *A Southern Record: The History of the Third Regiment Louisiana Infantry* (Baton Rouge: n.p., 1866; reprint, Dayton, Ohio: Morningside Bookshop, 1970), 130–31.

9. John Henry Brown to Victor Rose, quoted in Rose, *McCulloch*, 201–2.

10. Van Dorn to Bragg, *OR*, 8:283; Maury, quoted in Bevier, *First and Second Missouri*, 97.

11. Van Dorn to Bragg, *OR*, 8:283; Maury, quoted in Bevier, *First and Second Missouri*, 97; Sul Ross to D. R. Tinsley, 13 March 1862, Lawrence Sullivan Ross Papers, Texas Collection, Baylor University, Waco, Tex.

12. Gammage, *The Camp, the Bivouac, and the Battle Field*, 24–25; Cater, *"As It Was,"* 129; Newton A. Keen, *Living and Fighting with the Sixth Texas Cavalry* (Gaithersburg, Md.: Butternut Press, 1986), 28; Kerr, *Fighting with Ross' Texas Brigade*, 14; *OR*, 8:287; Sparks, *As I Saw It*, 173; John M. Harrell, *Arkansas*, vol. 10 of *Confederate Military History*, ed. Clement A. Evans (Atlanta: Confederate Pub. Co., 1899), 74–75.

13. Diary of Pvt. Sam Thompson, 5 March 1862, quoted in *Douglas's Texas Battery, C.S.A.*, ed. Lucia R. Douglas (Tyler, Tex.: Smith County Historical Society, 1966), 187; John Henry Brown, ed., *The Encyclopedia of the New West* (Marshall, Tex.: United States Biographical Pub. Co., 1881), 300; Ross to Tinsley, 13 March 1862, Ross Papers, Baylor University; Gammage, *The Camp, the Bivouac, and the Battle Field*, 25; Watson, *Life in the Confederate Army*, 289–90.

14. *OR*, 8:287; Sparks, *As I Saw It*, 174; Watson, *Life in the Confederate Army*, 292; Ross to Tinsley, 13 March 1862, Ross Papers, Baylor University. The definitive treatment of the battle of Pea Ridge or Elkhorn Tavern promises to be William L. Shea and Earl J. Hess's *Pea Ridge: Civil War Campaign in the West* (Chapel Hill: University of North Carolina Press, 1992). It is unfortunate for the present study that Shea and Hess's book was not available in time for me to profit from its contribution to the literature of the war.

15. Brown, *Encyclopedia of the New West*, 300; *OR*, 8:299; Keen, *Sixth Texas Cavalry*, 28.

16. Kerr, *Fighting with Ross' Texas Brigade*, 14; Sparks, *As I Saw It*, 174; *OR*, 8:299; Cater, "*As It Was*," 127, 129; Lester Newton Fitzhugh, ed., *Cannon Smoke: The Letters of Captain John J. Good, Good-Douglas Texas Battery, C.S.A.* (Hillsboro, Tex.: Hill Junior College Press, 1971), 162–63.

17. Kerr, *Fighting with Ross' Texas Brigade*, 14; P. J. Osterhaus in *OR*, 8:217; Sparks, *As I Saw It*, 174; Victor M. Rose, *Ross' Texas Brigade: Being a Narrative of Events Connected With Its Service in the Late War Between the States* (Louisville, Ky.: Courier-Journal Book and Job Rooms, 1881; reprint, Kennesaw, Ga.: Continental Book Co., 1960), 58; Keen, *Sixth Texas Cavalry*, 28; Douglas, *Douglas's Texas Battery*, 183–84.

18. Ebenezer Lafayette Dohoney, *An Average American* (Paris, Tex.: Privately printed, [1907]), 106; W. E. Hughes, *The Journal of a Grandfather* (St. Louis: Nixon Jones Printing Co., 1912), 80; Mamie Yeary, ed., *Reminiscences of the Boys in Gray, 1861–1865* (Dallas: Smith and Lamar, 1912; reprint, Dayton, Ohio: Morningside Bookshop, 1986), 355; Cater, "*As It Was*," 124, 129.

19. Hughes, *Grandfather*, 79; Douglas, *Douglas's Texas Battery*, 185; James P. Douglas to Tyler *Reporter*, 15 March 1862.

20. J. M. Bailey to *The News*, unidentified newspaper clipping in Daughters of the Republic of Texas Library at the Alamo, San Antonio, Tex.; Watson, *Life in the Confederate Army*, 293.

21. Gammage, *The Camp, the Bivouac and the Battle Field*, 25; Harrell, *Arkansas*, 74, 75; *OR*, 8:226; Watson, *Life in the Confederate Army*, 293–95.

22. *OR*, 8:284; Maury, *Recollections*, 187; Bevier, *First and Second Missouri*, 103.

23. Cater, "*As It Was*," 129; Rose, *McCulloch*, 203–4; Hartje, *Van Dorn*, 146; Albert G. Brackett, *History of the United States Cavalry, From the Formation of the Federal Union to the 1st of June, 1863* (New York: Harper and Brothers, 1865; reprint, New York: Greenwood Press, 1968), 142; Keen, *Sixth Texas Cavalry*, 28; Brown, quoted in Rose, *McCulloch*, 204–5; Brown, *Encyclopedia of the New West*, 300.

24. Rose, *McCulloch*, 204–5; Douglas, *Douglas's Texas Battery*, 184–85; Rose, *Ross' Texas Brigade*, 58; Cater, "*As It Was*," 129; Keen, *Sixth Texas Cavalry*, 28; Bevier, *First and Second Missouri*, 102; Bailey letter, Daughters of the Republic of Texas Library.

25. *OR*, ser. 2, 1:954; Jason W. James, *Memorable Events in the Life of Captain Jason W. James* ([Roswell, N.M.?: n.p., 1911?]), 27.

Of his capture, Hébert wrote that after his horse was wounded and his staff scattered by the Union attack, "suddenly a squadron of the enemy's cavalry cut off my retreat. I had with me thirty-one soldiers and subaltern officers. We had to go to the mountain—the road being in the possession of the enemy. At dusk we halted in a precipitous ravine for a moment. There we were surrounded by infantry, and we surrendered." Louis Hébert, "A Condensed Biography of Louis Hébert, Written by Himself," manuscript, Louis Hébert Papers, Louisiana Collection, Louisiana State University Archives, Baton Rouge, La.

26. Hughes, *Grandfather*, 80, 81; Douglas, *Douglas's Texas Battery*, 184–85.

27. Hughes, *Grandfather*, 83.

28. Sparks, *As I Saw It*, 16; Rose, *McCulloch*, 205; Kerr, *Fighting with Ross' Texas Brigade*, 14–15; *OR*, 8:301–3.

29. Cater, *"As It Was,"* 130; *OR*, 8:293, 299.

30. Watson, *Life in the Confederate Army*, 302–3.

31. E. I. Stirman, "Career of Gen. Ben McCulloch," *Confederate Veteran* 21 (April 1913): 173.

32. Douglas, *Douglas's Texas Battery*, 185; Elkhanah Greer to Col. D. H. Maury, 19 March 1862, *OR*, 8:293; Sparks, *As I Saw It*, 177.

33. Charles Edward Nash, *Biographical Sketches of Gen. Pat Cleburne and Gen. T. C. Hindman Together with Humorous Anecdotes and Reminiscences of the Late Civil War* (Little Rock: Tunnah & Pittard, 1898), 139; Hughes, *Grandfather*, 80, 81; B. P. Hollingsworth, "Battle of Elkhorn (Arkansas)," in *The New Texas School Reader, Designed for, and Dedicated to the Children of Texas* (Houston: E. H. Cushing, 1864), 137; Sparks, *As I Saw It*, 178.

34. Keen, *Sixth Texas Cavalry*, 28; Cater, *"As It Was,"* 132; Watson, *Life in the Confederate Army*, 290; Van Dorn to Albert Sidney Johnston, 9 March 1862, *OR*, 8:281; David Pierson to William H. Pierson, [March 1862], Pierson Family Papers, Manuscripts Section, Special Collections Division, Howard-Tilton Memorial Library, Tulane University, New Orleans, La.; Pike to Davis, *OR*, ser. 2, 1:869; Van Dorn to Judah P. Benjamin, 18 March 1862, *OR*, 8:282.

35. Van Dorn to Albert Sidney Johnston, 9 March 1862, *OR*, 8:281; Van Dorn to sister Emily Miller, 16 March 1862, manuscript collection of Foreman M. Lebold, Chicago, Ill., quoted in Hartje, *Van Dorn*, 159; Van Dorn to Judah P. Benjamin, 18 March 1862, *OR*, 8:282.

36. Keen, *Sixth Texas Cavalry*, 28.

37. Hobart Key, Jr., and Max Lale, eds., *The Civil War Letters of David R. Garrett, Detailing the Adventures of the 6th Texas Cavalry, 1861–1865* (Marshall, Tex.: Port Caddo Press, [1963]), 49; Kerr, *Fighting with Ross' Texas Brigade*, 15; L. H. Graves, "L. H. Graves Diary, May 1, 1861–April 1, 1864," typescript, BTHC, 68–69; Sparks, *As I Saw It*, 175; Tunnard, *A Southern Record*, 135; *OR*, 8:303.

38. Van Dorn to Bragg, *OR*, 8:285; *OR*, 8:330; Frank C. Armstrong to John Henry Brown, 13 March 1868, John Henry Brown Papers, BTHC.

AFTERWORD

1. McIntosh and Hyams observed McCulloch's fall, and McIntosh, although killed within fifteen to twenty minutes afterward, related to Armstrong what he had seen. Armstrong in turn told the story to Brown, and Hyams told Brown "the same facts in person." John Henry Brown, ed., *The Encyclopedia of the New West* (Marshall, Tex.: United States Biographical Pub. Co., 1881), 300; *Chicago Tribune*, 11 March 1862; John Henry Brown in Houston *Weekly Telegraph*, 13 August 1862; Nicholas Greusel, *OR*, 8:226; *OR*, 8:218; Joseph G. Rosa, *They Called Him Wild Bill: The Life and Adventures of James Butler Hickok* (Norman: University of Oklahoma Press, 1964), 56; Edgefield, S.C., *Advertiser*, 16 April 1862; copied from correspondent of the St. Louis *Democrat*; John Stiles Castle, ed., *Grandfather Was a Drummer Boy: A Civil War Diary and Letters of Charles B. Stiles* (Solon, Ohio: Evans Printing Co., 1986), 24; Bailey to *The News*, Daughters of the Republic of Texas Library at the Alamo, San Antonio, Tex.; Sul Ross to Dr. D. R. Tinsley, 13 March 1862, Lawrence Sullivan Ross Papers, Texas Collection, Baylor University, Waco, Tex.; Victor M. Rose, *The Life and Services of Gen. Ben McCulloch* (Philadelphia: Pictorial Bureau of the Press, 1888; reprint, Austin: Steck Co., 1958), 204.

A correspondent for the *New York Herald* wrote on the day after the battle that numerous prisoners reported McCulloch's death, "but the redoubtable ranger has been slaughtered on so many occasions, and afterward . . . turned up again, that we are skeptical. Perhaps Benjamin has been 'gathered to his fathers,' but nobody at present appears to see it."

According to another northern newspaper, McCulloch did not die of his wound until 11:00 P.M., "though he insisted he would recover, repeatedly saying with great oaths that he was not born to be killed by a Yankee." The correspondent, who claimed to have his facts from an unspecified prisoner, wrote that when McCulloch's physician assured him that he had but a brief time to live, he "looked up incredulously and saying, 'Oh, Hell!' turned away his head and never spoke after." The correspondent presumed that "if Ben really is dead," the southern papers would "put some very fine sentiment into his mouth in his closing moments," but he insisted on the truth of his story, observing that McCulloch's last words were "not very elegant or dramatic, but quite expressive, and in McCulloch's case decidedly appropriate." Quoted in *The Rebellion Record: A Diary of American Events*, ed. Frank Moore (New York: G. P. Putnam, 1861), 4:259; quoted in Sacramento *Union*, 24 April 1862.

2. William Edward Woodruff, *With the Light Guns in '61–'65: Reminiscences of Eleven Arkansas, Missouri, and Texas Light Batteries in the Civil War* (Little Rock:

Central Printing Co., 1903; reprint, Little Rock: Eagle Press, [1987]), 65; Wesley Thurman Leeper, *Rebels Valiant: Second Arkansas Mounted Rifles (Dismounted)* (Little Rock: Pioneer Press, 1964), 63.

3. Outlined in a general order dated 9 March 1862, McCulloch Papers, BTHC.

4. Broadside, BTHC; Ebenezer Lafayette Dohoney, *An Average American* (Paris, Tex.: Privately printed, [1907]), 107.

5. Most remarkable, however, was the disposition and subsequent story of McCulloch's side arms. At Elkhorn, Brown wrote, McCulloch "had belted around him a finely finished Colt's Navy revolver, presented to him long before by Mr. Colt, on which was engraved these words: 'BEN MCCULLOCH, PRESENTED BY THE INVENTOR.'" All six cylinders were loaded before the Army of the West crossed Little Sugar Creek on the morning of 7 March, and none were fired in the engagement. Brown removed this pistol from the general's body, together with his bowie knife, spyglass, and spectacles, in the ambulance that carried him from the battlefield. On his journey to Austin with McCulloch's body, Brown delivered the revolver, still loaded, to Alexander McCulloch, the son of Ben's elder brother John, then a private in Col. William H. Parsons's Twelfth Texas Cavalry, which had recently been ordered to Arkansas. Brown requested that he "retain the loads till he might be enabled to discharge them at the enemies of his country." Engaged for the first time at the battle of Searcy, Arkansas, on 27 May 1862, Alexander is said to have killed three of the enemy with his uncle's pistol, among them a major from whom he took a fine sword, which he sent to his Uncle Henry.

Another of McCulloch's revolvers experienced an even more remarkable career. Sergeant Bailey, the second Confederate to reach McCulloch's side at his death, stated that his side arms were then missing. Unseen for thirteen years, according to Colt historian and collector R. L. Wilson, McCulloch's Whitneyville-Hartford Dragoon revolver reemerged in 1875 when Charles Garvin, a guard for a survey party working on the Texas and Pacific railroad near Big Spring, Texas, fired at "what appeared to be a distant bush." The shot, however, felled an Indian in whose shoulder satchel Garvin discovered a Colt revolver numbered 1337—the McCulloch piece. Garvin returned to his home in Vermont in 1885, taking his prize with him. At Garvin's death in 1940 the revolver passed into the possession of his son, W. Burns Garvin, but only after the elder Garvin had expressed the wish that someday it would be returned to Texas. In 1945 the younger Garvin advertised "an old cap and ball Colt," which he wished to trade to a Texas collector for war bonds, in the Fort Worth *Star Telegram.* After much correspondence, Garvin sold the revolver to a pioneer Texas collector from whose estate it was purchased by its fifth owner after thirty years. For a time it was consigned to the collection of the Texas Ranger Hall of Fame at Fort Fisher in Waco, Texas. John Henry Brown, "'The Paths of Glory': The War-time Diary of Maj. John Henry Brown, C.S.A.," ed. W. J. Lemke, *Arkansas Historical Quarterly* 15, no. 4 (Winter 1956): 353; Houston *Daily Telegraph*, 13 August 1862; Anne J. Bailey, *Between the Enemy and Texas: Parsons's*

Texas Cavalry in the Civil War (Fort Worth: Texas Christian University Press, 1989), 58; R. L. Wilson, *Colt Pistols, 1836–1976* (Dallas: Jackson Arms, 1976), 44–45; Gaines de Graffenreid, *Guns of Fort Fisher* (Waco: Parks and Recreation Department, 1973), 13.

6. Brown, "'Paths of Glory,'" 352; Walter P. Lane, *Adventures and Recollections* (Marshall, Tex.: Tri-Weekly Herald Job Print, 1887; reprint, Marshall, Tex.: News Messenger Pub. Co., [c. 1928]; reprint, Austin: Pemberton Press, 1970), 94; Lester Newton Fitzhugh, ed., *Cannon Smoke: The Letters of Captain John J. Good, Good-Douglas Texas Battery, C.S.A.* (Hillsboro, Tex.: Hill Junior College Press, 1971), 167; Lawrence E. Honig, *John Henry Brown: Texian Journalist, 1820–1895* (El Paso: Texas Western Press, 1973), 28.

7. Henry E. McCulloch to Edward Burleson, Jr., 5 April 1862, Edward Burleson, Jr., Papers, BTHC.

8. Unidentified newspaper clipping, 7 April 1862, McCulloch Papers, BTHC; Brown, "'Paths of Glory,'" 358–59; Francis R. Lubbock, *Arkansas Democrat*, 6 September 1887.

9. Ben McCulloch, "Last Will and Testament," TSA.

10. Sam Houston to Nannie E. Houston, 14 April 1863, *Writings of Sam Houston*, ed. Amelia Williams and Eugene C. Barker, 8 vols. (Austin: University of Texas Press, 1938–43), 8:345; Braxton Bragg to Jefferson Davis, *OR*, ser. 2, 51:1005; William T. Sherman, *The Memoirs of General William T. Sherman by Himself* (n.p., 1875; Bloomington: Indiana University Press, 1957), 2:386. For an outspoken contemporary argument in favor of officers appointed from civil life over those trained at West Point, see John A. Logan's *The Volunteer Soldier of America* (Chicago: R. S. Peale, 1887). Logan was arguably the most successful Union combat officer among those who did not attend the academy. He briefly served as commander of the Army of the Tennessee, but when William T. Sherman relieved him from command of the army and of his corps as well, believing that a West Point graduate should command the premier Federal army in the west, Logan became a bitter and highly vocal enemy of the United States Military Academy.

11. For an overview of the move toward professionalization that pervaded American life after the Civil War, see Burton J. Bledstein, *The Culture of Professionalism: The Middle Class and the Development of Higher Education in America* (New York: Norton, 1976). For a discussion of the dual nature of the United States Army—at once professional and volunteer—see Russell F. Weigley, *History of the United States Army* (New York: Macmillan, 1967; reprint, Bloomington: University of Illinois Press, 1984). Weigley also treats the history of the professionalization of European armies in *The Age of Battles: The Quest for Decisive Warfare from Breitenfeld to Waterloo* (Bloomington: University of Indiana Press, 1991).

12. Jacob Dolson Cox, an Ohio attorney, was commissioned into the army with no military training and became a successful corps commander of the Army of the Tennessee. Jacob D. Cox, *Military Reminiscences of the Civil War* (New York:

Charles Scribner's Sons, 1900), 1:170–71; David Lloyd George, *War Memoirs of David Lloyd George* (Boston: Little, Brown, 1933), 3416.

13. William Watson, *Life in the Confederate Army* (London: Chapman and Hall, 1887; reprint, New York: Scribner and Welford, 1888), 179. McCulloch's ambition was a command in the East, and in consideration of his great reputation and his quarrel with Price, who knows but that, had he lived, he might not have been transferred to Virginia at the time that the Army of the West was moved to Mississippi in anticipation of the showdown at Shiloh. Such, at any rate, was the speculation of the rank and file of his army soon after Van Dorn took command. On 8 March 1861, one day after McCulloch's death at Elkhorn Tavern, John Bell Hood was promoted to brigadier general and on 12 March was appointed to the command of the Texas Brigade of the Army of Northern Virginia. Although a West Pointer and, like Van Dorn, a former officer of "Jeff Davis's Own" Second United States Cavalry, Hood was at the time an unknown. Edged out of his command by Price and Van Dorn, McCulloch was nevertheless too valuable for Davis to ignore. He would have been a natural choice for the command of the brigade that was soon to become "the Grenadier Guard" of Robert E. Lee's army. It seems altogether fitting that Texas's most famed military man and its finest fighting command should have been united. Perhaps equally apt, the ultimate irony of McCulloch's life occurred only after his death, and the command for which he had prepared and dreamed might have eluded him without even coming to his knowledge.

14. Henry E. McCulloch to Edward Burleson, Jr., 28 November 1862, Burleson Papers, BTHC.

Selected Bibliography

PRIMARY SOURCES

Manuscripts and Typescripts

Audited Military Claims and Public Debt Claims. Comptroller of Public Accounts Records. Archives Division, Texas State Library, Austin, Tex.

Bennet, Miles S. Papers, 1828–1900. 2 vols. Photocopy typescript. Barker Texas History Center, University of Texas at Austin.

Bennet, Valentine. Papers, 1838–43. Photocopy manuscript. Barker Texas History Center, University of Texas at Austin.

Bliss, Zenas R. "Reminiscences." Typescript. Barker Texas History Center, University of Texas at Austin.

Blocker, A. B. "Personal Experiences of a Sixteen Year Old Boy In the War Between the States." Typescript. Barker Texas History Center, University of Texas at Austin.

Brown, John Henry. Papers. Barker Texas History Center, University of Texas at Austin.

Buslé, Charles A. "My Travels in the Indian Territory, etc., etc." Manuscript diary. Louisiana Collection, Louisiana State University Archives, Baton Rouge, La.

Burkett, Nathan Boone. "Early Days in Texas." Manuscript. Barker Texas History Center, University of Texas at Austin.

Burleson, Edward, Jr. Papers. Barker Texas History Center, University of Texas at Austin.

Campbell, Jack. Letters, 1860–61. Barker Texas History Center, University of Texas at Austin.

Cartwright, Americus Peyroux. Papers. Barker Texas History Center, University of Texas at Austin.

Dancy, Jon Winfield Scott. Papers. Barker Texas History Center, University of Texas at Austin.

Dibrell, Garnett A. Collection. Archives Division, Texas State Library, Austin, Tex.

"Executive Record Book, 1861–1863." Archives Division, Texas State Library, Austin, Tex.

Ford, John S. "John C. Hays in Texas." Typescript. Barker Texas History Center, University of Texas at Austin.
———. "Memoirs." Typescript. Barker Texas History Center, University of Texas at Austin.
Graves, L. H. "L. H. Graves Diary, May 1, 1861–April 1, 1864." Typescript. Barker Texas History Center, University of Texas at Austin.
Griscom, George L. "Diary of George L. Griscom, Adjutant, Ninth Texas Cavalry." Manuscript. Barker Texas History Center, University of Texas at Austin.
Hébert, Louis. "A Condensed Biography of Louis Hébert, Written by Himself." Manuscript. Louis Hébert Papers, Louisiana Collection, Louisiana State University Archives, Baton Rouge, La.
Houston, Andrew Jackson. Collection. Archives Division, Texas State Library, Austin, Tex.
Huson, Hobart. "Iron Men: A History of the Republic of the Río Grande and the Federalist War in Northern Mexico." Typescript. Barker Texas History Center, University of Texas at Austin [1940].
Jefferson, John R. Papers. Barker Texas History Center, University of Texas at Austin.
Kendall, George Wilkins. Papers. Barker Texas History Center, University of Texas at Austin.
King, Valentine. Papers. Manuscript Division, Texas State Archives, Austin, Tex.
"McArdle Companion: Battle Paintings." Vol. 2, "The Battle of San Jacinto." Manuscript Division, Texas State Archives, Austin, Tex.
McCulloch, Ben and Henry Eustace. Papers. Barker Texas History Center, University of Texas at Austin.
Morgan, Wolfe Merrick. "Notes and Sketches of Campaigns in New Mexico, Arizona, Texas, Louisiana, and Arkansas by a Participant, Dr. M. W. Merrick, from Feb. 16, 1861, to May 26, 1865, Actual Service in the Field." Manuscript. Daughters of the Republic of Texas Library at the Alamo, San Antonio, Tex.
Pierson Family Papers. Manuscripts Section, Special Collections Division, Howard-Tilton Memorial Library, Tulane University, New Orleans, La.
Pilgrim, Thomas J. Papers. Barker Texas History Center, University of Texas at Austin.
Rose, Preston. Papers. Barker Texas History Center, University of Texas at Austin.
Ross, Lawrence Sullivan. Papers. Barker Texas History Center, University of Texas at Austin.
———. Papers. Texas Collection, Baylor University, Waco, Tex.
Ross, Ruben. Papers. Barker Texas History Center, University of Texas at Austin.
Rusk, Thomas Jefferson. Papers. Barker Texas History Center, University of Texas at Austin.
Smith, James N, III. Manuscript autobiography. Barker Texas History Center, University of Texas at Austin.

Stuart. Ben C. Papers and Scrapbooks, 1872–1926. Rosenberg Library, Galveston, Tex.

———. "Texas Indian Fighters and Frontier Rangers." Manuscript Division, Texas State Archives, Austin, Tex.

Texas Veterans' Association Papers. Barker Texas History Center, University of Texas at Austin.

Woodhouse, Matthew P. Papers. Manuscript Division, Texas State Archives, Austin, Tex.

Books

Acheson, Sam, and Julie Hudson O'Connell, eds. *George Washington Diamond's Account of the Great Hanging at Gainesville, 1862*. Austin: Texas State Historical Association, 1963.

Anderson, Ephraim McD. *Memoirs: Historical and Personal, Including Campaigns of the First Missouri Confederate Brigade*. St. Louis: Times Printing Co., 1868. Reprint. Dayton, Ohio: Morningside Bookshop, 1972.

Anderson, John Q., ed. *Brokenburn: The Journal of Kate Stone, 1861–1868*. Baton Rouge: Louisiana State University Press, 1955, 1972.

Barrett, Thomas. *The Great Hanging at Gainesville, Cooke County, Texas, October, A. D. 1862*. Gainesville, Tex.: n.p., 1885. Reprint. Austin: Texas State Historical Association, 1961.

Barron, Samuel B. *The Lone Star Defenders: A Chronicle of the Third Texas Cavalry Regiment in the Civil War*. New York: Neale Pub. Co., 1908. Reprint. Washington, D.C.: Zenger Pub. Co., 1983.

Baxter, William. *Pea Ridge and Prairie Grove; or Scenes and Incidents of the War in Arkansas*. Cincinnati: Poe and Hitchcock, 1864. Reprint. Van Buren, Ark.: Press-Argus, 1957.

Bevier, R. S. *History of the First and Second Missouri Confederate Brigades, 1861–1865, and From Wakarusa to Appomattox, A Military Anagraph*. St. Louis: Bryan, Brand and Co., 1879. Reprint. Florissant, Mo.: Inland Printer, 1985.

A Private Soldier. [Blessington, J. P.] *The Campaigns of Walker's Texas Division*. New York: Lange, Little and Co., 1875.

Brackett, Albert G. *History of the United States Cavalry, From the Formation of the Federal Union to the 1st of June, 1863*. New York: Harper and Brothers, 1865. Reprint. New York: Greenwood Press, 1968.

"Brazos." *Life of Robert Hall*. Austin: Ben C. Jones and Co., 1898.

Brown, Harry James, ed. *Letters from a Texas Sheep Ranch: Written in the Years 1860 and 1867 by George Wilkins Kendall to Henry Stephens Randall*. Urbana: University of Illinois Press, 1959.

Brown, Norman D., ed. *Journey to Pleasant Hill: The Civil War Letters of Cap-*

tain Elija P. Petty, Walker's Texas Division. San Antonio: University of Texas Institute of Texan Cultures, 1982.

Carleton, James Henry. *The Battle of Buena Vista with the Operations of the Army of Occupation for One Month.* New York: Harper and Brothers, 1848.

Castle, John Stiles, ed. *Grandfather Was a Drummer Boy: A Civil War Diary and Letters of Charles B. Stiles.* Solon, Ohio: Evans Printing Co., 1986.

Cater, William D., ed. *"As It Was": The Story of Douglas John Cater's Life.* [San Antonio]: n.p., 1981. Reprinted as *"As It Was": Reminiscences of a Soldier of the Third Texas Cavalry and the Nineteenth Louisiana Infantry,* with introduction by T. Michael Parrish. Austin: State House Press, 1990.

Chabot, Frederick. *The Perote Prisoners: Being the Diary of James L. Truehart.* San Antonio: Naylor Co., 1924.

Chamberlain, Samuel E. *My Confession.* New York: Harper, [c. 1956].

Clark, James Lemuel. *Civil War Recollections of James Lemuel Clark.* College Station, Tex.: Texas A&M University Press, 1984.

Clark, Walter, ed. *The State Records of North Carolina,* vol. 22. Goldsboro, N.C.: Nash Brothers, 1907.

Cox, Jacob D. *Military Reminiscences of the Civil War.* New York: Charles Scribner's Sons, 1900.

Cushing, S. W. *Adventures in the Texas Navy and the Battle of San Jacinto.* Austin: W. M. Morrison, 1985.

Dacus, Robert H. *Reminiscences of Company "H," First Arkansas Mounted Rifles.* Dardanelle, Ark.: Post Dispatch Print, 1897.

Davis, Jefferson. *Rise and Fall of the Confederate Government.* New York: Appleton and Co., 1881.

Day, Donald, and Harry Herbert Ullon, eds. *The Autobiography of Sam Houston.* Norman: University of Oklahoma Press, 1954.

de la Teja, Jesús F., ed. *A Revolution Remembered: The Memoirs and Selected Correspondence of Juan N. Seguín.* Austin: State House Press, 1991.

Dohoney, Ebenezer Lafayette. *An Average American.* Paris, Tex.: Privately printed, [1907].

Douglas, Lucia R., ed. *Douglas's Texas Battery, C.S.A.* Tyler, Tex.: Smith County Historical Society, 1966.

DuBois, John Van Deusen. *Campaigns in the West, 1856–1861 . . . Journal and Letters of John Van Deusen DuBois.* Edited by George P. Hammond. [San Francisco: Grabhorn Press for] Arizona Pioneers Historical Society, 1949.

Duval, J. C. *Early Times in Texas.* Austin: Gammel, 1892. Reprint. Austin: Steck and Co., 1935.

Fitzhugh, Lester Newton, ed. *Cannon Smoke: The Letters of Captain John J. Good, Good-Douglas Texas Battery, C.S.A.* Hillsboro, Tex.: Hill Junior College Press, 1971.

Fremantle, Arthur James Lyon. *The Fremantle Diary: Being the Journal of Lt.*

Col. Arthur James Lyon Fremantle, Coldstream Guards, on His Three Months in the Southern States. Edited by Walter Lord. Boston: Little, Brown, [c. 1954].

Gammage, W[ashington] L[afayette]. *The Camp, the Bivouac, and the Battle Field.* Selma, Ala.: n.p., 1864. Reprint. Little Rock: Arkansas Southern Press, 1958.

Gammel, H. P. N., comp. *The Laws of Texas, 1822–1897.* 10 vols. Austin: Gammel, 1898.

General Regulations for the Government of the Army of the Republic of Texas, Printed in Accordance with a Joint Act of Congress, Approved January 23rd, 1839. Houston: Intelligencer Office, 1839.

[Giddings, Luther]. *Sketches of the Campaign in Northern Mexico in Eighteen Hundred and Forty-Six and Seven by an Officer of the First Ohio Volunteers.* New York: J. P. Putnam, 1853.

Green, Rena Maverick, ed. *Memoirs of Mary A. Maverick, Arranged by Mary A. Maverick and Her Son Geo. Madison Maverick.* San Antonio: Alamo Printing Co., 1921. Reprinted with introduction by Sandra L. Myres. Lincoln: University of Nebraska Press, 1989.

Green, Thomas Jefferson. *Journal of the Texian Expedition against Mier; Subsequent Imprisonment of the Author, His Sufferings, and Final Escape from the Castle of Perote, with Reflections upon the Present Political and Probable Future Relations of Texas, Mexico, and the United States.* New York: Harper and Brothers, 1845. Reprint. Arno Press, 1973.

Greer, James K. *A Texas Ranger and Frontiersman: The Days of Buck Barry in Texas, 1845–1906.* Dallas: Southwest Press, 1932.

Gulick, Charles Adams, ed. *The Papers of Mirabeau Buonaparte Lamar.* 6 vols. Austin: A. C. Baldwin and Sons, 1921–28.

Hafen, Ann W., ed. *Documentary Account of the Utah Expedition.* New York: Arthur Clark, 1982.

Hafen, LeRoy R., and Ann W. Hafen, eds. *The Utah Expedition, 1857–1858.* Glendale, Calif.: Arthur H. Clarke, 1958.

Hammond, Otis G., ed. *The Utah Expedition, 1857–1858: Letters of Capt. Jesse A. Gove, 10th Infantry.* Concord, N.H.: New Hampshire Historical Society, 1928.

Harris, Benjamin Butler. *The Gila Trail: The Texas Argonauts and the California Gold Rush.* Edited by Richard H. Dillon. Norman: University of Oklahoma Press, 1960.

Heitman, Francis B. *Historical Register and Dictionary of the United States Army.* 2 vols. Washington, D.C.: Government Printing Office, 1903. Reprint. Urbana: University of Illinois Press, 1965.

Henry, William S. *Campaign Sketches of the War With Mexico.* New York: Harper and Brothers, 1847.

Hitchcock, Ethan Allen. *Fifty Years in Camp and Field: Diary of Major-General Ethan Allen Hitchcock, U.S.A.* Edited by W[illiam] A[ugustus] Croffut. New York: G. P. Putnam's Sons, 1909.

Hollan, W. Eugene, ed. *William Bollaert's Texas.* Norman: University of Oklahoma Press, 1956.
Hughes, W. E. *The Journal of a Grandfather.* St. Louis: Nixon Jones Printing Co., 1912.
Hunter, Robert Hancock. *The Narrative of Robert Hancock Hunter.* Austin: Cook Printing Co., 1936. Reprint. Austin: Encino Press, 1966.
Hutchins, E[dward] R[idgeway], comp. *The War of the 'Sixties.* New York: Neale Pub. Co., 1912.
Ingmire, Frances Terry, comp. *Texas Frontiersmen, 1839–1860: Minutemen, Militia, Home Guard, Indian Fighters.* St. Louis: Ingmire Publications, 1982.
———. *Texas Ranger Service Records, 1830–1846.* St. Louis: Ingmire Publications, 1982.
Jackson, Ronald Vern, Gary Ronald Teeples, and David Schaefermeyer, eds. *Texas 1850 Census Index.* Bountiful, Utah: Accelerated Indexing Systems, 1976.
James, Jason W. *Memorable Events in the Life of Captain Jason W. James.* [Roswell, N.M.?]: n.p., [1911?].
Jenkins, John Holland, III, ed. *The Papers of the Texas Revolution, 1835–1836.* Austin: Presidial Press, 1973.
———. *Recollections of Early Texas: The Memoirs of John Holland Jenkins.* Austin: University of Texas Press, 1958.
———. *Robert E. Lee on the Rio Grande: The Correspondence of Robert E. Lee on the Texas Border, 1860.* Austin: Jenkins Pub. Co., 1988.
Jones, John B. *A Rebel War Clerk's Diary.* New York: Sagamore Press, 1958.
Journals of the Fourth Congress of the Republic of Texas, 1839–1840. Austin: Von Boeckmann-Jones, [1929].
Journals of the House of Representatives of the First Legislature of the State of Texas. Clarksville, Tex.: Standard Office, 1848.
Journals of the Senate of the First Legislature of the State of Texas. Clarksville, Tex.: Standard Office, 1848.
Kane, Lucille M., ed. and trans. *Military Life in Dakota: The Journal of Philippe Régis de Trobriand.* St. Paul, Minn.: Alvord Memorial Commission, 1951.
Keen, Newton A. *Living and Fighting with the Sixth Texas Cavalry.* Gaithersburg, Md.: Butternut Press, 1986.
Kenley, John R. *Memoirs of a Maryland Volunteer: War with Mexico in the Years 1846–7–8.* Philadelphia: J. B. Lippincott and Co., 1873.
Kerr, Homer L., ed. *Fighting with Ross' Texas Cavalry Brigade, C.S.A.: Diary of Lieut. George L. Griscom, Adjutant, 9th Texas Cavalry Regiment.* Hillsboro, Tex.: Hill Junior College Press, 1976.
Key, Hobart, Jr., and Max S. Lale, eds. *The Civil War Letters of David R. Garrett, Detailing the Adventures of the 6th Texas Cavalry, 1861–1865.* Marshall, Tex.: Port Caddo, [1963].

Lane, Walter P. *Adventures and Recollections.* Marshall, Tex.: Tri-Weekly Herald Job Print, 1887. Reprint. Marshall, Tex.: News Messenger Pub. Co., [c. 1928]. Reprint. Austin: Pemberton Press, 1970.

Latham, Francis S. *Travels in the Republic of Texas, 1842.* Edited by Gerald S. Pierce. Austin: Encino Press, 1971.

Lee, Nelson. *Three Years Among the Comanches.* Albany: n.p., 1859. Reprint. Norman: University of Oklahoma Press, 1957.

Linn, John J. *Reminiscences of Fifty Years in Texas.* New York: D. & J. Sadler and Co., 1883. Reprint. Austin: State House Press, 1986.

Logan, John A. *The Volunteer Soldier of America.* Chicago: R. S. Peale, 1887.

McCulloch, Henry E. *General Henry McCulloch's Defense of Himself and His Administration of the Affairs of the Institution for the Deaf and Dumb of the State of Texas Against the Charge Contained in the Report of the Sub-committee of the Joint Committee on Asylums of the Sixteenth Legislature.* Austin: E. W. Swindell, 1879.

McDowell, Catherine W., ed. *Now You Hear My Horn: The Journal of James Wilson Nichols, 1820–1887.* Austin: University of Texas Press, 1967.

Maury, Dabney Herndon. *Recollections of a Virginian.* New York: Charles Scribner's Sons, 1894.

Maverick, Mary A. *Memoirs of Mary A. Maverick.* San Antonio: Alamo Printing Co., 1921.

Meade, George Gordon. *The Life and Letters of George Gordon Meade, Major General, United States Army.* New York: Charles Scribner's Sons, 1913.

Miller, Thomas Lloyd, ed. *Bounty and Donation Land Grants of Texas, 1835–1883.* Austin: University of Texas Press, 1967.

Moore, Frank, ed. *The Rebellion Record: A Diary of American Events,* vols. 1, 4. New York: G. P. Putnam, 1861, 1862.

Moore, John Bassett, ed. *The Works of James Buchanan.* Philadelphia: J. B. Lippincott Co., 1910.

Morrell, Z. N. *Flowers and Fruits from the Wilderness.* Boston: Gould and Lincoln, 1872. Reprint. Waco, Tex.: Baylor University Press, 1976.

Morrison, James L., Jr., ed. *The Memoirs of Henry Heth.* Westport, Conn.: Greenwood Press, 1974.

Moulton, Gary E., ed. *The Papers of Chief John Ross.* 2 vols. Norman: University of Oklahoma Press, 1985.

Muir, Andrew Forest, ed. *Texas in 1837: An Anonymous Contemporary Narrative.* Austin: University of Texas Press, 1958.

Muster Rolls of the Texas Revolution. Lufkin, Tex.: Daughters of the Republic of Texas, 1986.

Myres, Robert Mason, ed. *The Children of Pride: A True Story of Georgia and the Civil War.* New Haven: Yale University Press, 1972.

Nash, Charles Edward. *Biographical Sketches of Gen. Pat Cleburne and Gen. T. C. Hindman Together with Humorous Anecdotes and Reminiscences of the Late Civil War*. Little Rock: Tunnah and Pittard, 1898.

Newcomb, James Pearson. *Sketch of Secession Times in Texas and Journal of Travel from Texas through Mexico to California*. San Francisco: n.p., 1863.

North, Diane M. T., ed. *Samuel Peter Heintzelman and the Sonora Exploring and Mining Company*. Tucson: University of Arizona Press, 1980.

Olmstead, Frederick Law. *A Journey through Texas, Or, a Saddle-Trip on the Southwestern Frontier*. New York: Dix, Edwards, and Co., 1857. Reprint. Austin: University of Texas Press, 1978.

Parker, W. B. *Notes Taken During the Expedition Commanded by Capt. R. B. Marcy, U.S.A., Through Unexplored Texas, in the Summer and Fall of 1854*. Philadelphia: Hayes and Zell, 1856. Reprint. Austin: Texas State Historical Association, 1984.

Pike, James. *Scout and Ranger, Being the Personal Adventures of James Pike of the Texas Rangers in 1859–60*. Cincinnati: J. R. Hawley and Co., 1865. Reprint. Princeton: Princeton University Press, 1932.

Pomfrey, J. W. *A True Disclosure and Exposition of the Knights of the Golden Circle, Including the Secret Signs, Grips, and Charges of the Three Degrees As Practiced by the Order*. Cincinnati: n.p., 1861.

Raines, C. W., ed. *Six Decades in Texas; Or Memoirs of Francis Richard Lubbock, Governor of Texas in War-Times, 1861–63; A Personal Experience in Business, War, and Politics*. Austin: Ben C. Jones and Co., 1900.

Reid, Samuel C. *The Scouting Expeditions of McCulloch's Texas Rangers*. Philadelphia: G. B. Zieber and Co., [1847]. Reprint. Freeport, N.Y.: Books for Libraries, [1970].

Rodríguez, José María. *Rodriguez Memoirs of Early Texas*. San Antonio: Passing Show Printing Co., 1913.

Roemer, Ferdinand. *Texas: With Particular Reference to German Immigration and the Physical Appearance of the Country*. San Antonio: Standard Printing Co., 1935. Reprint. Waco: Texian Press for the German-Texan Heritage Society, 1983.

Rose, Victor M. *Ross' Texas Brigade: Being a Narrative of Events Connected With Its Service in the Late War Between the States*. Louisville, Ky.: Courier-Journal Book and Job Rooms, 1881. Reprint. Kennesaw, Ga.: Continental Book Co., 1960.

Rowland, Dunbar, ed. *Jefferson Davis, Constitutionalist: His Letters, Papers, and Speeches*. 10 vols. Jackson, Miss.: Mississippi Department of Archives and History, 1923.

Rugley, H. J. H., ed. *Batchelor-Turner Letters, 1861–1864*. Austin: Steck Co., 1961.

Santa Anna, Antonio Lopéz de. *The Eagle: The Autobiography of Santa Anna*.

Edited by Ann Fears Crawford. Austin: Pemberton Press, 1967. Reprint. Austin: State House Press, 1988.

Scarborough, William Kauffman, ed. *The Diary of Edmund Ruffin.* 2 vols. Vol. 1, *Toward Independence: October 1856–April 1861.* Vol. 2, *The Years of Hope: April 1861–June 1863.* Baton Rouge: Louisiana State University Press, 1972.

[Scribner, Benjamin F.] *A Campaign in Mexico, or a Glimpse of Life in Camp.* Philadelphia: Grigg, Elliot and Co., 1847. Reprint. Austin: Jenkins Pub. Co., 1975.

Seguin, John N. *Personal Memoirs of John N. Seguin from the Year 1834 to the Retreat of General Wool from the City of San Antonio, 1842.* San Antonio: Ledger and Job Office, 1858. Reprinted as *A Revolution Remembered: The Memoirs and Selected Correspondence of Juan N. Seguín,* edited by Jesús F. de la Teja. Austin: State House Press, 1991.

Sherman, William T. *The Memoirs of General William T. Sherman by Himself.* N.p., 1875. Reprint. Bloomington: Indiana University Press, 1957.

Sibley, Marilyn M., ed. *Walker's Account of the Mier Expedition.* Austin: Texas State Historical Association, 1978.

Smith, S. Compton. *Chile con Carne; or the Camp and Field.* New York: Miller and Curtis, 1857.

Smithwick, Noah. *The Evolution of a State or Recollections of Old Texas Days.* Austin: Gammel, [1900]. Reprint. Austin: University of Texas Press, 1983.

Snead, Thomas L. *The Fight for Missouri from the Election of Lincoln to the Death of Lyon.* New York: Charles Scribner's Sons, 1888.

Sparks, A. W. *The War Between the States as I Saw It: Reminiscences, Historical and Personal of Titus County Grays, Co. I, 9th Texas Cavalry, Ross's Texas Brigade.* Tyler, Tex.: Lee and Burnett, 1901. Reprint. Longview, Tex.: D and D, 1987.

Spurlin, Charles, comp. *Texas Veterans in the Mexican War: Muster Rolls of Texas Military Units.* Victoria, Tex.: n.p., 1984.

Stanley, David Sloane. *Personal Memoirs of Major-General D. S. Stanley, U.S.A.* Cambridge: Harvard University Press, 1917. Reprint. Gaithersburg, Md.: Olde Soldier Books, 1987.

Stanton, Donald J., Goodwin F. Berquist, and Paul C. Bowers, eds. *The Civil War Reminiscences of General M. Jeff Thompson.* Dayton, Ohio: Morningside Bookshop, 1988.

Stapp, William Preston. *The Prisoners of Perote.* Austin: University of Texas Press, 1977.

Sterne, Louis. *Seventy Years of Active Life.* London: n.p., 1912.

Taylor, Creed. *Tall Men with Long Rifles.* Edited by James T. DeShields. San Antonio: Naylor Co., 1935, 1971.

Taylor, Richard. *Destruction and Reconstruction: Personal Experiences of the Late War.* New York: Appleton and Co., 1879.

Terrell, Alexander Watkins. *From Texas to Mexico and the Court of Maximillan in 1865*. Dallas: Book Club of Texas, 1933.

Thompson, Jerry D., ed. *From Desert to Bayou: The Civil War Journal and Sketches of Morgan Wolfe Merrick*. El Paso: Texas Western Press, 1991.

Tunnard, William H. *A Southern Record: The History of the Third Regiment Louisiana Infantry*. Baton Rouge: n.p., 1866. Reprint. Dayton, Ohio: Morningside Bookshop, 1970.

U.S. War Department. *War of the Rebellion: A Compilation of the Official Records of the Union and Confederate Armies*. 70 vols. Washington, D.C.: 1880–1901.

Wallis, Jonnie Lockhart. *Sixty Years on the Brazos: The Life and Letters of Dr. John Washington Lockhart, 1824–1900*. Los Angeles: n.p., 1930. Reprint. New York: Argonaut, 1966.

Watson, William. *Life in the Confederate Army*. London: Chapman and Hall, 1887. Reprint. New York: Scribner and Welford, 1888.

White, Gifford, ed. *The 1840 Census of the Republic of Texas*. Austin: Pemberton Press, 1966.

Williams, Amelia, and Eugene C. Barker, eds. *Writings of Sam Houston*. 8 vols. Austin: University of Texas Press, 1938–43.

Williams, Robert H. *With the Border Ruffians: Memoirs of the Far West, 1852–1868*. London: John Murray, 1907. Reprint. Lincoln: University of Nebraska Press, 1982.

Winfrey, Dorman H., et al., eds. *Texas Indian Papers, 1825–1843, Edited from the Original Manuscript Copies in the Texas State Archives*. 4 vols. Austin: Texas State Library, 1959. Reprinted as *The Indian Papers of Texas and the Southwest, 1825–1916*. 5 vols. Austin: Pemberton Press, 1966.

Winkler, Ernest William, ed. *Journal of the Secession Convention of Texas, 1861*. Austin: Texas Library and Historical Commission, 1912.

Woodruff, William Edward. *With the Light Guns in '61–'65: Reminiscences of Eleven Arkansas, Missouri, and Texas Light Batteries in the Civil War*. Little Rock: Central Printing Co., 1903. Reprint. Little Rock: Eagle Press, [1987].

Woodward, C. Vann, ed. *Mary Chesnut's Civil War*. New Haven: Yale University Press, 1981.

Woodward, C. Vann, and Elisabeth Muhlenfeld, eds. *The Private Mary Chesnut: The Unpublished Civil War Diaries*. New York: Oxford University Press, 1984.

Worley, Ted R., ed. *They Never Came Back: The Story of Co. F. Fourth Arks. Infantry C. S. A. As Told By Their Commanding Officer Capt. John W. Lavender*. Pine Bluff, Ark.: Southern Press, 1956.

[Wright, Marcus J., ed.] *List of the Field Officers, Regiments and Battalions in the Confederate States Army, 1861–1865*. Washington, D.C.: Government Printing Office, [1891?]. Reprint. Bryan, Tex.: J. M. Carroll and Co., 1983.

———. *List of the Staff Officers of the Confederate States Army, 1861–1865*. Wash-

ington, D.C.: Government Printing Office, 1891. Reprint. Bryan, Tex.: J. M. Carroll and Co., 1983.
Yeary, Mamie, ed. *Reminiscences of the Boys in Gray, 1861–1865.* Dallas: Smith and Lamar, 1912. Reprint. Dayton, Ohio: Morningside Bookshop, 1986.

Newspaper and Journal Articles and Brief Memoirs

Anderson, Charles. "A Paper Read before the Cincinnati Society of Ex-Army and Navy Officers, January, 3d, 1884." Cincinnati: Peter G. Thompson, 1884.
Barr, Alwyn, ed. "Records of the Confederate Military Commission in San Antonio, October 10, 1862." *Southwestern Historical Quarterly* 70, no. 1 (July 1966): 93–109.
Bauer, K. Jack, ed. "General John E. Wool's Memoranda on the Battle of Buena Vista." *Southwestern Historical Quarterly* 77, no. 1 (July 1973): 111–23.
Billingsley, William Clyde, ed. " 'Such Is War': The Confederate Memoirs of Newton Asbury Keen," pt. 1. *Texas Military History* 6, no. 4 (Winter 1967): 239–53.
Blackburn, J. K. P. "Reminiscences of the Terry Rangers." *Southwestern Historical Quarterly* 22, no. 1 (July 1918): 38–77.
Brown, John Henry. " 'The Paths of Glory': The War-time Diary of Maj. John Henry Brown, C.S.A." Edited by W. J. Lemke. *Arkansas Historical Quarterly* 15, no. 4 (Winter 1956): 344–59.
———. "Wartime Diary in Northwest Arkansas." Edited by W. J. Lemke. *Flashback* 6, no. 6 (November 1956): 3–11.
Brown, Jonathan Duff. "Reminiscences of Jno. Duff Brown." *Quarterly of the Texas State Historical Association* 12, no. 4 (April 1909): 296–311.
Buchanan, A. Russell, ed. "George Washington Trahern: A Texan Cowboy Soldier from Mier to Buena Vista." *Southwestern Historical Quarterly* 58, no. 1 (July 1954): 60–90.
Cobb, Thomas R. R. "Extracts From the Letters of Thomas R. R. Cobb to His Wife." *Southern Historical Society Papers* 28 (1900): 280–301.
Coffman, Edward M., ed. "Ben McCulloch Letters." *Southwestern Historical Quarterly* 60, no. 1 (July 1956): 118–22.
Crockett, George W. "Mustang Training; or, A Lesson Not Taught by Prof. Rarey: A Sketch of Prairie Life in the Southwest." *Western Chronicle* (Centreville, Mich.), 19 August 1858, 1.
Cutrer, Thomas W., ed. " 'The Tallapoosa Might Truly Be Called the River of Blood': Maj. Alexander McCulloch and the Battle of Horseshoe Bend, March 27, 1814." *Alabama Review* 43, no. 1 (January 1990): 35–39.
Darrow, Caroline B. "Recollections of the Twiggs Surrender." In *Battles and Leaders of the Civil War,* edited by Robert V. Johnson and Clarence C. Buel. Vol. 1. New York: Century Co., 1887–88. Reprint. New York: T. Yoseloff, [1956].

Erath, Lucy A., ed. "Memoirs of Major George Bernard Erath." *Southwestern Historical Quarterly* 27, no. 1 (July 1923): 27–51.

Greer, James K., ed. "The Diary of James Buckner Barry, 1860–1862." *Southwestern Historical Quarterly* 36, no. 2 (October 1932): 144–62.

H. "General H. E. McCulloch." Gonzales *Inquirer*, 27 August 1873.

Harris, G. W. D. "Alexander McCulloch." Nashville *Christian Advocate*, 12 August 1846.

Hollingsworth, B. P. "Battle of Elkhorn (Arkansas)." In *The New Texas School Reader, Designed for, and Dedicated to the Children of Texas*, 132–40. Houston: E. H. Cushing, 1864.

Kendall, George Wilkins. "Bill Dean, the Texan Ranger." *Spirit of the Times*, 11 July 1846.

Lale, Max S., ed. "The Boy Bugler of the Third Texas Cavalry," pts. 1 and 2. *Military History of Texas and the Southwest* 14, nos. 2 and 3 (1978): 71–92, 147–67.

Lemley, Harry J., ed. "Historic Letters of General Ben McCulloch and Chief John Ross in the Civil War." *Chronicles of Oklahoma* 40, no. 3 (Autumn 1962): 286–94.

Lubbock, Francis R. "Confederate Reunion." Arkansas *Democrat*, 6 September 1887.

McCulloch, Ben. "General McCulloch's Report." *Missouri Historical Review* 26, no. 4 (July 1932): 355–66.

McCulloch, Ben, to Major W. R. Scurry. Appendix to *The History of Clarksville and Old Red River County* by Pat B. Clark. Dallas: Mathis, Van Nort and Co., 1937.

McCulloch, Henry E. "About Old Fort Croghan." *The News*, 28 March 1887. Clipping in McCulloch Family Papers, Barker Texas History Center, University of Texas at Austin.

———. "Mexican War Soldiers." Galveston *News*, 11 April 1881.

———. "Report of the Superintendent of the Texas Institution for the Deaf and Dumb to the Governor of Texas." Austin, 1876.

Maury, Dabney H. "Recollections of the Elkhorn Campaign." *Southern Historical Society Papers* 2 (1876): 180–92.

———. "Van Dorn, The Hero of Mississippi." In *The Annals of the War, Written By Leading Participants, North and South*, 460-66. Philadelphia: *Philadelphia Weekly Times*, 1878. Reprint. Dayton, Ohio: Morningside House, 1988.

Nance, J. Milton, ed. "Brigadier General Adrian Woll's Report of His Expedition into Texas in 1842." *Southwestern Historical Quarterly* 58, no. 4 (April 1955): 523–52.

Neville, H. Clay. "Wilson's Creek." *Southern Historical Society Papers* 38 (1910): 363–72.

Noble, John Willock. "Battle of Pea Ridge or Elk Horn Tavern." In *Commandry of Missouri, War Papers, and Personal Reminiscences, 1861–1865*, 1:211–43. St. Louis: Military Order of the Loyal Legion of the United States, 1892.

Pearce, N. Bart. "Arkansas Troops in the Battle of Wilson's Creek." In *Battles and Leaders of the Civil War*, edited by Robert V. Johnson and Clarence C. Buel, 1:298–303. New York: Century Co., 1887–88. Reprint. New York: T. Yoseloff, [1956].

———. "Price's Campaign of 1861." *Publications of the Arkansas Historical Association* 4 (1917): 332–51.

Regan, John H. "A Conversation with Governor Houston." *Quarterly of the Texas State Historical Association* 3, no. 4 (April 1900): 279–81.

Roland, Charles P., and Richard C. Robbins, eds. "The Diary of Eliza (Mrs. Albert Sidney) Johnston: The Second Cavalry Comes to Texas." *Southwestern Historical Quarterly* 60, no. 4 (April 1957): 463–500.

Sigel, Franz, ed. "The Military Operations in Missouri in the Summer and Autumn of 1861." *Missouri Historical Review* 26, no. 1 (July 1932): 354–67.

———. "The Pea Ridge Campaign." In *Battles and Leaders of the Civil War*, edited by Robert V. Johnson and Clarence C. Buel, 1:314–34. New York: Century Co., 1887–88. Reprint. New York: T. Yoseloff, [1956].

Snead, Thomas L. "The First Year of the War in Missouri." In *Battles and Leaders of the Civil War*, edited by Robert V. Johnson and Clarence C. Buel, 1:262–77. New York: Century Co., 1887–88. Reprint. New York: T. Yoseloff, [1956].

Sparks, S. F. "Recollections of S. F. Sparks." *Quarterly of the Texas State Historical Association* 12, no. 1 (July 1908): 61–79.

Stirman, E. I. "Career of Gen. Ben McCulloch." *Confederate Veteran* 21 (April 1913): 172–73.

Swearingen, W. C. "Documents." *Quarterly of the Texas State Historical Association* 15, no. 2 (October 1911): 156–60.

Trop, June P., ed. "An Update: The Douglas Letters." *Chronicles of Smith County, Texas* 20, no. 1 (Summer 1983): 13–27.

Wheeler, T. B. "Reminiscences of Reconstruction in Texas." *Quarterly of the Texas State Historical Association* 11, no. 1 (July 1907): 56–65.

SECONDARY SOURCES

Books

Adamson, Hans Christian. *Rebellion in Missouri, 1861: Nathaniel Lyon and His Army of the West.* Philadelphia: Chilton Co., 1961.

Albaugh, William A. *Tyler, Texas, C.S.A.: The Story of the Confederate States Ordnance Works at Tyler, Texas, 1861–1865.* Harrisburg, Pa.: Stackpole Co., 1958.

Albaugh, William A., and Edward N. Simmons. *Confederate Arms.* Harrisburg, Pa.: Stackpole Co., 1957.

Alsopp, Fred W. *Albert Pike: A Biography.* Little Rock: Parke-Harper Co., 1928.

Ambrose, Stephen E. *Halleck: Lincoln's Chief of Staff.* Baton Rouge: Louisiana State University Press, 1962.

Anderson, Mabel Washborne. *The Life of General Stand Watie: The Only Indian Brigadier General in the Confederate Army and the Last General to Surrender.* Pryor, Okla.: n.p., 1931.

Bailey, Anne J. *Between the Enemy and Texas: Parsons's Texas Cavalry in the Civil War.* Fort Worth: Texas Christian University Press, 1989.

Bailey, W. H., Sr. *The Genealogy of the Latham-Hill-Montfort-Littlejohn-McCulloch-Campbell and Brownrigg Families.* Houston: n.p., 1899.

Baker, D. W. C. *A Texas Scrapbook Made Up of History, Biography, and Miscellany of Texas and Its People.* New York: A. S. Barnes and Co., 1875.

Ball, Lary D. *The United States Marshals of New Mexico and Arizona Territories, 1846–1912.* Albuquerque: University of New Mexico Press, 1978.

Bancroft, H. H. *History of Utah, 1540–1880.* San Francisco: History Co., 1889.

Bauer, K. Jack. *The Mexican War, 1846–1848.* New York: Macmillan, 1974.

———. *Zachary Taylor: Soldier, Planter, Statesman of the Old Southwest.* Baton Rouge: Louisiana State University Press, 1985.

Bearss, Edwin C. *The Battle of Wilson's Creek.* N.p.: George Washington Carver Birthplace District Association, 1975.

Bearss, Edwin C., and A. M. Gibson. *Fort Smith: Little Gibraltar on the Arkansas.* Norman: University of Oklahoma Press, 1969.

Benner, Judith Ann. *Sul Ross: Soldier, Statesman, Educator.* College Station: Texas A&M University Press, 1983.

Brown, Charles H. *Agents of Manifest Destiny: The Lives and Times of the Filibusters.* Chapel Hill: University of North Carolina Press, 1980.

Brown, John Henry. *Indian Wars and Pioneers of Texas.* Austin: L. E. Daniell, 1880.

Brown, John Henry, ed. *The Encyclopedia of the New West.* Marshall, Tex.: United States Biographical Pub. Co., 1881.

Buenger, Walter L. *Secession and the Union in Texas.* Austin: University of Texas Press, 1984.

Carreno, Alberto. *Jefes del Ejército Mexicano en 1847: Biografías de Generales de Divisíon y de Brigada ye de Coroneles.* Mexico, D.F.: Imprenta y Fotopia de la Secretaría de Fomento, 1914.

Castel, Albert. *General Sterling Price and the Civil War in the West.* Baton Rouge: Louisiana State University Press, 1968.

Clairborne, John Francis Hamtramck. *Life and Correspondence of John A. Quitman, Major-General, U.S.A., and Governor of the State of Mississippi.* 2 vols. New York: Harper and Brothers, 1860.

Clendenen, Clarence C. *Blood on the Border: The United States Army and Mexican Irregulars.* New York: Macmillan, 1969.

Collier, Calvin L. *The War Child's Children: The Story of the Third Regiment, Arkansas Cavalry, C.S.A.* Little Rock: Pioneer, 1965.

Copeland, Fayette. *Kendall of the Picayune.* Norman: University of Oklahoma Press, 1943.

Crane, William Carey. *Life and Literary Remains of Sam Houston of Texas.* Dallas: William G. Scarff and Co., [c. 1884].

Craven, Avery O. *Edmund Ruffin, Southerner: A Study in Secession.* Baton Rouge: Louisiana State University Press, 1966.

Cunliffe, Marcus. *Soldiers and Civilians: The Martial Spirit in America, 1775–1865.* Boston: Little, Brown, 1968.

Daniell, Lewis E. *Personnel of the Texas State Government, Embracing the Executive and Staff, Heads of the Departments, United States Senators and Representatives, Members of the XXth Legislature.* Austin: City Printing Co., 1887.

Davis, William C. *Breckinridge: Statesman, Soldier, Symbol.* Baton Rouge: Louisiana State University Press, 1974.

Davis, Winfield J. *An Illustrated History of Sacramento County.* Chicago: Lewis Pub. Co., 1890.

Deaton, E. L. *Indian Fights on the Texas Frontier: A True Account of Exciting Encounters in Hamilton, Comanche, Brown, Erath, and Adjoining Counties.* Hamilton, Tex.: C. M. Boynton, 1894. Reprint. Fort Worth: Pioneer Pub. Co., 1927.

de Leon, Arnoldo. *They Called Them Greasers: Anglo Attitudes toward Mexicans in Texas, 1821–1900.* Austin: University of Texas Press, 1983.

DeShields, James T. *Border Wars of Texas.* Tioga, Tex.: Herald Co., 1912. Reprint. Waco, Tex.: Texian Press, 1976.

Dixon, Sam Houston, and Louis Wiltz Kemp. *The Heroes of San Jacinto.* Houston: Anson Jones Press, 1932.

Dobie, J. Frank. *Coronado's Children: Tales of Lost Mines and Buried Treasure of the Southwest.* Dallas: Southwest Press, 1930. Reprint. Austin: University of Texas Press, 1978.

Dougan, M. B. *Confederate Arkansas: The People and Politics of a Frontier State in Wartime.* Tuscaloosa: University of Alabama Press, 1976.

Duncan, Robert Lipscomb. *Reluctant General: The Life and Times of Albert Pike.* New York: E. P. Dutton, 1961.

Duval, John C. *The Adventures of Big-Foot Wallace.* Philadelphia: Claxton, Remsen, and Haffelfinger, 1871. Reprint. Lincoln: University of Nebraska Press, [1966].

Dyer, Brainerd. *Zachary Taylor.* Baton Rouge: Louisiana State University Press, 1946.

Eaton, Clement. *Jefferson Davis.* New York: Free Press, 1977.

Egan, Ferol. *The El Dorado Trail: The Story of the Gold Rush Routes across Mexico.* Lincoln: University of Nebraska Press, [1970].

Freeman, Douglas Southall. *R. E. Lee: A Biography*, vol. 1. New York: Charles Scribner's Sons, 1949.

Friend, Llerena B. *Sam Houston: The Great Designer.* Austin: University of Texas Press, 1954.

Frost, John. *The Mexican War and Its Warriors.* New Haven: H. Mansfield, 1849.

Furniss, Norman F. *The Mormon Conflict, 1850–1859.* New Haven: Yale University Press, 1960.

Gaines, W. Craig. *The Confederate Cherokees: John Drew's Regiment of Mounted Rifles.* Baton Rouge: Louisiana State University Press, 1989.

Gardner, Charles K. *A Dictionary of the Army of the United States.* New York: G. P. Putnam, 1853.

General Taylor and His Staff. Philadelphia: Grigg, Elliot and Co., 1848.

Greer, James Kimmins. *Colonel Jack Hays: Texas Frontier Leader and California Builder.* New York: E. P. Dutton, 1952. Reprint. College Station: Texas A&M University Press, 1987.

Hale, Douglas. *The Third Texas Cavalry in the Civil War.* Norman: University of Oklahoma Press, 1992.

Hamilton, Holman. *Zachary Taylor: Soldier of the Republic.* New York: Bobbs Merrill, 1941.

———. *Zachary Taylor: Soldier in the White House.* New York: Bobbs Merrill, 1951.

Harrell, John M. *Arkansas.* Vol. 10 of *Confederate Military History*, edited by Clement A. Evans. Atlanta: Confederate Pub. Co., 1899.

Hartje, Robert G. *Van Dorn: The Life and Times of a Confederate General.* Nashville: Vanderbilt University Press, 1967.

Harwell, Thomas Fletcher. *Eighty Years Under the Stars and Bars, Including Biographical Sketches of "100 Confederate Soldiers I Have Known," Information Concerning the Organization of The United Confederate Veterans, Organization of Camp Ben McCulloch, United Confederate Veterans Near Driftwood, Hays County, Texas.* N.p., n.d.

Hauck, Richard Boyd. *Crockett: A Bio-Bibliography.* Westport, Conn.: Greenwood Press, 1982.

Hawkins, Wallace. *The Case of John C. Watrous: United States Judge for Texas.* Dallas: University Press in Dallas, 1950.

Haynes, Sam W. *Soldiers of Misfortune: The Somervell and Mier Expeditions.* Austin: University of Texas Press, 1990.

Henderson, Archibald. *North Carolina: The Old North State and the New.* Chicago: Lewis Pub. Co., 1941.

Henderson, Harry McCorry. *Colonel Jack Hays, Texas Ranger.* San Antonio: Naylor Co., 1954.

Hogan, William Ransom. *The Texas Republic: A Social and Economic History.* Norman: University of Oklahoma Press, 1946.

Holcombe, [Return Ira], and Adams. *An Account of the Battle of Wilson's Creek or Oak Hills—On Saturday, August 10 1861, in Green County, Missouri.* Springfield, Mo.: Dow and Adams, 1883. Reprint. Springfield, Mo.: Springfield Public Library, 1961.
Honig, Lawrence E. *John Henry Brown: Texian Journalist, 1820–1895.* El Paso: Texas Western Press, 1973.
Horton, Louise. *Samuel Bell Maxey: A Biography.* Austin: University of Texas Press, 1974.
Hughes, Nathaniel Cheairs, Jr. *General William J. Hardee: Old Reliable.* Baton Rouge: Louisiana State University Press, 1965.
Hughes, W. J. *Rebellious Ranger: Rip Ford and the Old Southwest.* Norman: University of Oklahoma Press, 1964.
Huntington, Samuel P. *The Soldier and the State: The Theory and Politics of Civil-Military Relations.* Cambridge, Mass.: Harvard University Press, Belknap Press, 1957.
Irby, James A. *Backdoor at Bagdad: The Civil War on the Rio Grande.* El Paso: Texas Western Press, 1977.
James, Marquis. *The Raven.* Indianapolis: Bobbs-Merrill, 1929.
Jenkins, John H., and Kenneth Kesselus. *Edward Burleson: Texas Frontier Leader.* Austin: Jenkins Pub. Co., 1990.
Johannsen, Robert W. *To the Halls of the Montezumas: The Mexican War in the American Imagination.* New York: Oxford University Press, 1985.
Johnson, Francis White. *A History of Texas and Texans.* Chicago: American Historical Society, 1914.
Johnson, Sidney Smith. *Texans Who Wore the Gray.* [Tyler, Tex.]: n.p., 1907.
Johnston, William Preston. *The Life of Gen. Albert Sidney Johnston.* New York: D. Appleton and Co., 1878.
Kerby, Robert Lee. *The Confederate Invasion of New Mexico and Arizona, 1861–1862.* Los Angeles: Westlore Press, 1958.
King, Alvy L. *Louis T. Wigfall: Southern Fire-eater.* Baton Rouge: Louisiana State University Press, 1970.
Kirkland, Frazar. *The Pictoral Book of Anecdotes and Incidents of the War of the Rebellion.* Hartford: Hartford Pub. Co., 1867.
Kohn, Richard H. *Eagle and Sword: The Federalists and the Creation of the Military Establishment in America, 1783–1802.* New York: Free Press, 1975.
Ladd, Horatio O. *History of the War with Mexico.* Boston: D. Lothrop, [c. 1891]. Reprint. New York: Dodd, Meade, and Co., [c. 1911].
Lavender, David. *Climax at Buena Vista: The American Campaigns in Northern Mexico, 1846–1847.* New York: Lippincott, 1966.
Leeper, Wesley Thurman. *Rebels Valiant: Second Arkansas Mounted Rifles (Dismounted).* Little Rock: Pioneer Press, 1964.
Livermore, Thomas L. *Numbers and Losses in the Civil War.* Boston: Houghton Mifflin, 1901. Reprint. Bloomington: University of Illinois Press, 1957.

Long, E. B. *The Civil War Day by Day: An Almanac, 1861–1865.* New York: Doubleday and Co., 1971.

Lonn, Ella. *Desertion in the Civil War.* New York: Century Co., 1928.

Lord, Francis A. *Civil War Collector's Encyclopedia.* Secaucus, N.J.: Castle, 1982.

McElroy, John. *The Struggle for Missouri.* Washington, D.C.: National Tribune Co., 1909.

McMullen, Thomas A., and David Walker. *Biographical Directory of American Territorial Governors.* Westport, Conn.: Meckler, 1984.

McWhiney, Grady. *Braxton Bragg and Confederate Defeat.* New York: Columbia University Press, 1969.

Mansfield, Edward D. *The Mexican War.* New York: A. S. Barnes and Co., 1849.

May, Robert E. *Southern Dream of a Caribbean Empire, 1854–1861.* Baton Rouge: Louisiana State University Press, 1973.

Mayhall, Mildred P. *Indian Wars of Texas.* Waco, Tex.: Texian Press, 1965.

Millett, Allan R., and Peter Maslowski. *For the Common Defense: A Military History of the United States.* New York: Free Press, 1984.

Moody, Claire N. *Battle of Pea Ridge or Elkhorn Tavern.* Little Rock: Arkansas Valley Printing, 1956.

Moore, John C. *Missouri.* Vol. 9 of *Confederate Military History,* edited by Clement A. Evans. Atlanta: Confederate Pub. Co., 1899.

Nance, J. Milton. *After San Jacinto: The Texas-Mexican Frontier, 1836–1841.* Austin: University of Texas Press, 1963.

———. *Attack and Counterattack: The Texas-Mexican Frontier, 1842.* Austin: University of Texas Press, 1964.

Nichols, James L. *The Confederate Quartermaster in the Trans-Mississippi.* Austin: University of Texas Press, 1964.

Oates, Stephen B. *Confederate Cavalry West of the River.* Austin: University of Texas Press, 1961.

———. *Visions of Glory.* Norman: University of Oklahoma Press, 1970.

Owsley, Frank Lawrence, Jr. *Struggle for the Gulf Borderlands: The Creek War and the Battle of New Orleans, 1812–1815.* Gainesville: University Presses of Florida, 1981.

Parks, Joseph Howard. *General Edmund Kirby Smith, C.S.A.: The Fighting Bishop.* Baton Rouge: Louisiana State University Press, 1962.

———. *General Leonidas Polk, C.S.A.: The Fighting Bishop.* Baton Rouge: Louisiana State University Press, 1954.

Phillips, Christopher. *Damned Yankee: The Life of General Nathaniel Lyon.* Columbia: University of Missouri Press, 1990.

Prucha, Francis Paul. *The Great Father: The United States Government and the American Indian.* Lincoln: University of Nebraska Press, 1984.

———. *The Sword of the Republic: The United States Army on the Frontier, 1783–1846.* New York: Macmillan Co., 1969.

Rampp, Larry C., and Donald L. Rampp. *The Civil War in the Indian Territory.* Austin: Presidial Press, 1975.

Rea, Ralph R. *Sterling Price: The Lee of the West.* Little Rock: Pioneer Press, 1959.

Richardson, Rupert N. *The Comanche Barrier to South Plains Settlement: A Century and a Half of Savage Resistance to the Advancing White Frontier.* Glendale, Calif.: Arthur H. Clarke, 1933.

Ripley, Roswell S. *The War With Mexico.* 2 vols. New York: Harper and Brothers, 1849. Reprint. New York: Burt Franklin, 1970.

Rister, Carl Coke. *Robert E. Lee in Texas.* Norman: University of Oklahoma Press, 1946.

Roberts, Oran M. *Texas.* Vol. 11 of *Confederate Military History*, edited by Clement A. Evans. Atlanta: Confederate Pub. Co., 1899.

Roland, Charles P. *Albert Sidney Johnston: Soldier of Three Republics.* Austin: University of Texas Press, 1964.

Rosa, Joseph G. *They Called Him Wild Bill: The Life and Adventures of James Butler Hickok.* Norman: University of Oklahoma Press, 1964.

Rose, Victor M. *The Life and Services of Gen. Ben McCulloch.* Philadelphia: Pictorial Bureau of the Press, 1888. Reprint. Austin: Steck Co., 1958.

Ryan, Gary D., and Timothy K. Nenninger, eds. *Soldiers and Civilians: The U.S. Army and the American People.* Washington, D.C.: National Archives and Records Administration, 1987.

Serven, James E. *Colt Firearms: 1836–1958.* Santa Ana, Calif.: Serven Books, 1954.

Shackford, James Atkins. *David Crockett: The Man and the Legend.* Chapel Hill: University of North Carolina Press, 1956.

Shalhope, Robert E. *Sterling Price: Portrait of a Southerner.* Columbia: University of Missouri Press, 1971.

Shea, William L., and Earl J. Hess. *Pea Ridge: Civil War Campaign in the West.* Chapel Hill: University of North Carolina Press, 1992.

Sigel, Stanley. *A Political History of the Texas Republic, 1836–1845.* Austin: University of Texas Press, 1956.

Smith, David Paul. *Frontier Defense in the Civil War: Texas' Rangers and Rebels.* College Station: Texas A&M University Press, 1992.

Smith, Justin H. *The War with Mexico.* 2 vols. New York: Macmillan, 1919.

Sowell, Andrew Jackson. *Early Settlers and Indian Fighters of Southwest Texas.* Austin: Ben C. Jones and Co., 1900. Reprint. New York: Argosy Antiquarian, [1964]. Reprint. Austin: State House Press, 1986.

———. *Incidents Connected with the Early History of Guadalupe County, Texas.* Seguin, Tex.: C. L. Martin, n.d.

———. *Life of "Big Foot" Wallace.* [Devine, Tex.?]: n.p., 1899.

———. *Rangers and Pioneers of Texas.* San Antonio: Shepard Bros. and Co., 1884. Reprint. New York: Argosy Antiquarian, 1964. Reprint. Austin: State House Press, 1991.

Starr, Stephen Z. *Jennison's Jayhawkers: A Civil War Cavalry Regiment and Its Commander*. Baton Rouge: Louisiana State University Press, 1974.

Thomas, Lately [Robert V. P. Steele]. *Between Two Empires: The Life Story of California's First Senator, William McKendree Gwin*. Boston: Houghton Mifflin, 1969.

Thorpe, T[homas] B[angs]. *Our Army on the Rio Grande*. Philadelphia: Carey and Hart, 1846.

Thrall, Homer S. *A Pictorial History of Texas*. St. Louis: N. D. Thompson and Co., 1879.

Tulledge, Edward Wheelock. *The History of Salt Lake City and Its Founders*. Salt Lake City: E. W. Tulledge, [1886?].

Utley, Robert M. *Frontiersmen in Blue: The United States Army and the Indian, 1848–1865*. New York: Macmillan, 1967.

Warner, Ezra J. *Generals in Gray: Lives of the Confederate Commanders*. Baton Rouge: Louisiana State University Press, 1959.

Webb, Walter Prescott. *The Great Frontier*. Boston: Houghton Mifflin, 1952. Reprint. Austin: University of Texas Press, 1964.

———. *The Texas Rangers: A Century of Frontier Defense*. Boston: Houghton Mifflin, 1935. Reprint. Austin: University of Texas Press, 1965.

———. *The Texas Rangers in the Mexican War*. Austin: Jenkins Garrett Press, 1975.

Weber, David J. *The Mexican Frontier, 1821–1846*. Albuquerque: University of New Mexico Press, 1982.

———. *Northern Mexico on the Eve of the United States Invasion*. New York: Arno Press, 1976.

Weigley, Russell F. *The Age of Battles: The Quest for Decisive Warfare from Breitenfeld to Waterloo*. Bloomington: University of Indiana Press, 1991.

———. *History of the United States Army*. New York: Macmillan, 1967. Reprint. Bloomington: University of Illinois Press, 1984.

Wilbarger, J. W. *Indian Depredations in Texas*. Austin: Hutchings Printing House, 1889. Reprint. Austin: State House Books, 1985.

Williams, Clayton. *Never Again: Texas, 1848–1861*. San Antonio: Naylor Co., 1969.

Williams, Jack K. *Dueling in the Old South: Vignettes of Social History*. College Station: Texas A&M University Press, 1980.

Wilson, R. L. *Colt Pistols, 1836–1976*. Dallas: Jackson Arms, 1976.

Wilstack, Frank J. *Wild Bill Hickok: The Prince of Pistoleers*. New York: Garden City Pub. Co., 1926.

Woodworth, Steven E. *Jefferson Davis and His Generals: The Failure of Confederate Command in the West*. Lawrence: University of Kansas Press, 1990.

Wooten, Dudley G., ed. *A Comprehensive History of Texas*. 2 vols. Dallas: William G. Scarff and Co., 1898. Reprint. Austin: Texas State Historical Association, 1986.

Wyatt-Brown, Bertram. *Southern Honor: Ethics and Behavior in the Old South.* New York: Oxford University Press, 1982.
Yoakum, Henderson. *History of Texas from Its First Settlement in 1685 to Its Annexation to the United States in 1846.* 2 vols. New York: Redfield, 1856.

Articles

Barker, Eugene C. "The San Jacinto Campaign." *Quarterly of the Texas State Historical Association* 4, no. 4 (April 1901): 237–343.
———. "The Texan Revolutionary Army." *Quarterly of the Texas State Historical Association* 9, no. 4 (April 1906): 227–61.
Barr, Alwyn. "Texas Coastal Defense, 1861–1865." *Southwestern Historical Quarterly* 45, no. 1 (July 1961): 1–31.
Barton, Henry W. "Five Texas Frontier Companies during the Mexican War." *Southwestern Historical Quarterly* 66, no. 1 (July 1962): 17–30.
———. "The Problem of Command in the Army of the Republic of Texas." *Southwestern Historical Quarterly* 62, no. 3 (January 1959): 299–311.
———. "The United States Cavalry and the Texas Rangers." *Southwestern Historical Quarterly* 63, no. 4 (April 1960): 496–510.
Binkley, William C. "Activities of the Texan Revolutionary Army after San Jacinto." *Journal of Southern History* 6, no. 3 (August 1904): 331–46.
Bridges, C. A. "The Knights of the Golden Circle: A Filibustering Fantasy." *Southwestern Historical Quarterly* 44, no. 3 (January 1941): 287–302.
"Captain Ben McCulloch." *Frontier Times* 23, no. 4 (December 1945): 47–49.
Cooley, Rita W. "The Office of the United States Marshal." *Western Political Quarterly* 12, no. 1 (March 1959): 123–41.
Dienst, Alexander. "The Navy of the Republic of Texas." *Quarterly of the Texas State Historical Association* 12, no. 3 (January 1909): 165–203.
Dunn, Roy Sylvan. "The KGC in Texas, 1860–1861." *Southwestern Historical Quarterly* 70, no. 4 (April 1967): 543–73.
Eaton, Clement. "Frontier Life in Southern Arizona." *Southwestern Historical Quarterly* 36, no. 3 (January 1933): 173–92.
Elliott, Claude. "Union Sentiment in Texas, 1861–1865." *Southwestern Historical Quarterly* 50, no. 4 (April 1947): 449–77.
Ewing, Floyd F., Jr. "Origins of Unionist Sentiment on the West Texas Frontier." *West Texas Historical Association Year Book* 32 (1956): 21–29.
———. "Unionist Sentiment on the Northwest Texas Frontier." *West Texas Historical Association Year Book* 33 (1957): 58–70.
Fitzhugh, Lester N. "Saluria, Fort Esperanza, and Military Operations on the Texas Gulf Coast, 1861–1864." *Southwestern Historical Quarterly* 61, no. 1 (July 1957): 66–100.

Franks, Kenny A. "Operations against Opotheleyahola." *Military History of Texas and the Southwest* 10, no. 3 (1973): 187–96.

Friend, Llerena. "Additional Items for the Winkler Check List of Texas Imprints, 1846–1860." *Southwestern Historical Quarterly* 65, no. 1 (July 1961): 101–7.

———. "The Texan of 1860." *Southwestern Historical Quarterly* 62, no. 1 (July 1958): 1–17.

Gage, Larry Jay. "The Texas Road to Secession and War: John Marshall and the Texas State Gazette, 1860–1861." *Southwestern Historical Quarterly* 62, no. 2 (October 1958): 191–226.

Gunn, Jack W. "Ben McCulloch: A Big Captain." *Southwestern Historical Quarterly* 58, no. 1 (July 1954): 1–21.

Hale, Douglas. "The Third Texas Cavalry: A Socioeconomic Profile of a Confederate Regiment." *Military History of the Southwest* 19, no. 1 (Spring 1989): 1–26.

Hale, Joseph W. "Masonry in the Early Days of Texas." *Southwestern Historical Quarterly* 49, no. 3 (January 1946): 374–83.

Heidler, Jeanne T. "'Embarrassing Situation': David E. Twiggs and the Surrender of the United States Forces in Texas, 1861." *Military History of the Southwest* 21, no. 2 (Fall 1991): 157–72.

Henderson, H. M. "A Critical Analysis of the San Jacinto Campaign." *Southwestern Historical Quarterly* 59, no. 3 (January 1956): 344–62.

Hendricks, Sterling Brown. "The Somerville Expedition to the Rio Grande, 1842." *Southwestern Historical Quarterly* 23, no. 2 (October 1919): 112–40.

Hord, B[en] M[cCulloch]. "Gen. Ben McCulloch." *Confederate Veteran* 36 (July 1928): 261–62.

Horton, Louise W. "General Sam Bell Maxey: His Defense of North Texas and the Indian Territory." *Southwestern Historical Quarterly* 74, no. 4 (April 1971): 507–24.

Hunter, J. Marvin. "General Ben McCulloch." *Frontier Times* 5 (June 1928): 353–54.

[Hunter, J. Marvin]. "Jack Hays, the Texas Ranger." *Frontier Times* 4, no. 6 (March 1927): 17–32.

Koch, Lerna Clara. "The Federal Indian Policy in Texas, 1845–1860." *Southwestern Historical Quarterly* 29, no. 1 (July 1925): 19–35.

McCaslin, Richard B. "Conditional Confederates: The Eleventh Texas Cavalry West of the Mississippi River." *Military History of the Southwest* 21, no. 1 (Spring 1991): 87–99.

Meserve, John Bartlett. "Chief Opotheleyahola." *Chronicles of Oklahoma* 9, no. 4 (December 1931): 439–53.

Neighbours, Kenneth F. "The Taylor-Neighbors Struggle over the Upper Rio

Grande Region of Texas in 1850." *Southwestern Historical Quarterly* 61, no. 4 (April 1958): 431–63.

Nielsen, George R. "Mathew Caldwell." *Southwestern Historical Quarterly* 64, no. 4 (April 1961): 478–502.

Oates, Stephen B. "John S. 'Rip' Ford: Prudent Cavalryman, C.S.A." *Southwestern Historical Quarterly* 64, no. 3 (January 1961): 289–314.

———. "Recruiting Confederate Cavalry in Texas." *Southwestern Historical Quarterly* 64, no. 4 (April 1961): 463–77.

———. "Texas under the Secessionists." *Southwestern Historical Quarterly* 67, no. 2 (October 1963): 167–212.

Padgitt, James T. "Colonel William H. Day: Texas Ranchman." *Southwestern Historical Quarterly* 53, no. 4 (April 1950): 346–66.

Pierce, Gerald S. "A Minor Tragedy in the Texas Army: Lysander Wells and William D. Redd." *Texas Military History* 5 (Fall 1965): 121–29.

Ramsdell, Charles W. "The Texas State Military Board, 1862–1865." *Southwestern Historical Quarterly* 27, no. 4 (April 1924): 253–75.

Rippy, J. Fred. "Border Troubles along the Rio Grande, 1848–1860." *Southwestern Historical Quarterly* 23, no. 2 (October 1919): 91–111.

Shearer, Ernest C. "The Carvajal Disturbances." *Southwestern Historical Quarterly* 55, no. 2 (October 1951): 201–30.

Spurlin, Charles. "Camp Life of Texas Volunteers in the Mexican War." *Military History of Texas and the Southwest* 15, no. 4 (n.d.): 37–44.

———. "Mobilization of the Texas Militia for the Mexican War." *Military History of Texas and the Southwest* 15, no. 3 (n.d.): 21–40.

———. "Texas Volunteers in the Monterrey Campaign," pts. 1 and 2. *Military History of Texas and the Southwest* 16, nos. 1 and 2 (n.d.): 5–22, 137–42.

———. "With Taylor and McCulloch through the Battle of Monterrey." *Military History of Texas and the Southwest* 6, no. 3 (Fall 1967): 203–21.

Tyler, Ronnie C. "The Callahan Expedition of 1855: Indians or Negroes?" *Southwestern Historical Quarterly* 70, no. 4 (April 1967): 574–85.

Wakelyn, Jon L. " 'Civilian' Higher Education in the Making of Confederate Army Leaders." In *The Confederate High Command*, edited by Lawrence L. Hewitt and Roman J. Heleniak. Shippensburg, Pa.: White Mane Pub. Co., 1990.

Walker, Olive Todd. "Ester Amanda Sherrill Cullins: A Pioneer Woman of the Texas Frontier." *Southwestern Historical Quarterly* 47, no. 3 (January 1944): 234–49.

———. "Major Whitfield Chalk, Hero of the Republic of Texas." *Southwestern Historical Quarterly* 60, no. 3 (January 1957): 358–68.

Winkler, Ernest W. "The 'Twin Sisters' Cannon." *Southwestern Historical Quarterly* 21, no. 1 (July 1917): 61–68.

UNPUBLISHED DISSERTATIONS, THESES, AND MANUSCRIPTS

Barr, Alwyn Chester, Jr. "Confederate Artillery in the Trans-Mississippi." M.A. thesis, University of Texas, 1961.

Bullock, Neal Terry. "The Confederate Services of General Ben McCulloch." M.A. thesis, University of Arkansas, 1957.

Caperton, John. "Sketch of Colonel John C. Hays, Texas Ranger." Barker Texas History Center, University of Texas at Austin.

Gunn, Jack Winton. "Life of Ben McCulloch." M.A. thesis, University of Texas, 1947.

Pierce, Gerald S. "The Army of the Texas Republic, 1836–1845." Ph.D. diss., University of Mississippi, 1963.

Pritchett, Robert Thomas. "Impeachment Proceedings in Congress against John Charles Watrous of Texas, 1851–1861." M.A. thesis, University of Texas, 1937.

Purcell, Allan Robert. "The History of the Texas Militia, 1835–1903." Ph.D. diss., University of Texas, 1981.

Ruckman, Caroline Silsby. "The Frontier of Texas during the Civil War." M.A. thesis, University of Texas, 1926.

Walker, Sarah Elizabeth. "San Antonio during the Civil War." M.A. thesis, Sam Houston State Teachers College, 1942.

Wallace, James Oldham. "San Antonio during the Civil War." M.A. thesis, St. Mary's University, 1940.

Index